GOOD LIFE

The Insider's Guide to the Bay Area

PENINSULA & SAN JOSE

Good Life Peninsula & San Jose Insider's Guide
Copyright © 1995 Good Life Publications.

Printed in the United States of America on recycled paper.

First edition published September, 1992 as *Guide to the Good Life on the Peninsula*. Second edition.

ISBN 1-886776-00-8 Softcover $12.95.

Interior design: Good Life Publications
Maps: Suzanne Joyal and Good Life Publications
Cover Design: Dale Horstman, threenine Design

Please send all comments, corrections, and additions for future editions to:

Good Life Publications
760 Market St., #759
San Francisco, California 94102
(415) 989-1844
(415) 989-3122 fax
GLIFE@AOL.COM

Special Sales
Good Life guides are available at bulk discounts for conventions, corporate gifts, fundraising sales premiums, and sales promotions. Special editions, including custom covers, excerpts of existing guides, and corporate imprints, can be created for large orders. For more information, contact Good Life Publications.

TABLE OF CONTENTS

Introduction

Welcome to the *Good Life Peninsula & San Jose Insider's Guide*. This book is an expanded version of *Guide to the Good Life on the Peninsula*, which was itself an outgrowth of *Guide to the Good Life at Stanford*, first published in 1991 to provide new arrivals with a resource to help them enjoy the Bay Area. This latest edition provides more expanded covereage of the San Francisco Peninsula and San Jose, including profiles of cities from Brisbane and Daly City to San Jose and Campbell.

This book still maintains the original purpose: providing information about the Bay Area to help new residents enjoy it easily without having to struggle with learning the ins and outs of a new home. We understand that there is life beyond San Francisco. That's why we created the only Northern California guidebook written specifically for the millions of people who live in and visit the Peninsula and San Jose. In addition to city profiles, we have gathered extensive information about over 300 Peninsula restaurants, entertainment, shopping, sports, and day-trips. We also understand that the people who made Silicon Valley the famous entrepreneurial hotbed that it is today are too busy to spend weeks planning a weekend getaway, which is why we included chapters on popular weekend travel destinations: Big Sur, Monterey, Marin, the Wine Country, Mendocino, Tahoe, and Yosemite. In each of these sections we gathered the kind of information that will enable you to plan a trip quickly, get there easily, and spend your money wisely while there. We didn't forget about San Francisco either, with detailed desciptions of neighborhoods and reviews of over 60 great restaurants.

Even seasoned, longtime residents should appreciate the convenience of a single source of information about enjoying the Good Life instead of a collection of ragged newpaper clippings. Plus, they might even discover new Bay Area treasures: a hole-in-the-wall restaurant with great food, a beach in the redwoods, or new ski area.

In the following pages, you will find both humorous and practical information. In the never-ending search for comprehensiveness, we included and expanded as much as we could. If we overlooked some gem or gave you a bum steer, let us know! One cautionary note: prices are subject to change without notice (ditto hours of operation), so if you're watching your wallet or watch, play it safe and call ahead.

We hope that you have as much fun using the book as we did putting it together.

Acknowledgments

When we first created *Guide to the Good Life in Stanford* in the summer of 1991, we wanted to create a unique local's guide to the Bay Area, one providing a combination of practical advice for newcomers and tips on enjoying the Good Life. In the process, we set totally unreasonable goals and deadlines for ourselves. Thanks to the innumerable people who joined our enthusiastic frenzy, we created the first Good Life guide. With the creation of each new edition and each new guide, our indebtedness grows. Once again, I would like to offer thanks to all of the generous, hard-working writers and researchers who helped create this wealth of information. In particular, I would like to thank them for sharing their advice, insight, and secrets with a world of strangers. We hope our readers share our enthusiasm for these special places.

Special thanks to those who helped create this latest work. Andrea Agarwal and Jeremy Chipman for their patience while checking the 1,000s of facts, figures, and numbers in this book, proofing countless pages of text, and researching and writing whatever was needed. Tracey Broderick has once again added that something extra through her editing, all under the burden of the Good Life Style Guide. Dale Horstman did a terrific job on the cover, and I sincerely appreciate his willingness to work with us. Eric Weaver and Elizabeth and Peter Dumanian once again provided expert advice as our South Bay Lifestyle Consultants, as well as invaluable general support and assistance. Ken Bosley did a great job as a general consultant and sounding board. Finally, a special thank you to Suzanne Joyal for her patience and support.

—Peter Massik

BASIC INFORMATION

The San Francisco Peninsula is many things—a cultural Mecca, a political anomaly, a real-estate nightmare—but it is also a beautiful 42-mile stretch of land dividing San Francisco Bay from the Pacific Ocean. San Francisco fills the narrow tip; from there the Peninsula widens on its way south and joins the mainland below the southern edge of the Bay in San Jose. The land along the Bay is flat and low. To the west these lowlands rise steeply into the Santa Cruz Mountains, which run down the Peninsula's spine. West of the mountains, the land drops more gradually towards the Pacific.

Most of the Peninsula's urban development has occurred in the flatter areas on the eastern half of the Peninsula. The open corridor running south along Hwy 101 is densely settled, as is the corridor along El Camino Real (Hwy 82), which runs from Daly City to Santa Clara, seemingly displaying a Taco Bell every few miles. Before World War II, all the towns in the area between San Francisco and San Jose had their own unique identity. The rapid population growth after the war sent the towns sprawling into each other, maintaining little of their individuality in the mass of suburbia. More recently, I-280 was constructed along the Santa Cruz Mountain foothills, and development is now also creeping west, especially around San Jose. The Santa Cruz mountains have been logged extensively over the last 150 years, but remain otherwise relatively undisturbed. The coast has been developing rapidly around Half Moon Bay, but the area still remains blessedly primarily agricultural, especially south of Half Moon Bay.

Climate

California owes much of its dramatic population growth over the past 50 years to its attractive, Mediterranean climate. Many say the Peninsula's weather is the best in the state, neither too warm nor too cool. In fact, Redwood City adopted the slogan "Climate Best by Government Test" after a local office for the National Climatic Data Center declared that the surrounding area won some sort of climatic beauty contest.

Generally, residents and visitors can look forward to warm days and cool nights all year round. However, there is substantial variation from region to region, month to month, and year to year. The coastal areas along the Pacific Coast bear the brunt of winter storms sweeping off the ocean, and are cooled—chilled—by ocean breezes and fog the rest of the year. The Santa Cruz Mountains wring moisture from winter storms, getting significantly more rainfall than low-lying areas and even some occasional snow. Because the mountains shelter the bayside flatlands from the ocean, most Peninsula residents enjoy warm days and moderate rainfall. The weather gets hotter and drier further south and east, meaning further from the ocean. The average year-round daily Peninsula temperature is 70 degrees Fahrenheit, the nighttime low is 45. Daytime highs near 100 are common during the summer, especially in the South Bay, while freezes happen occasionally during winter evenings in the low valleys. Almost all rainfall comes between October and April. San Francisco and the northern Peninsula average over 20 inches of rain per year; San Jose, under 14 inches; and Saratoga, almost 30 inches. Anyone familiar with the recent drought knows how little these averages can mean for any specific year: between 1988 and 1990 San Jose received less than 10 inches each year; while in 1983 it received over 30.

Background and Economy

For thousands of years the Peninsula was inhabited by the Ohlone Indians, who lived peacefully in small tribal settlements. The Ohlone way of life was decimated by European settlement, which began after Spanish explorer Don Gaspar de Portola's discovery of San Francisco Bay in October 1769 initiated mission development along the Peninsula. A community based on farming grew as Mexican land-grant settlement followed Mexican Independence. This way of life expanded as American occupation replaced Mexican with the Gold Rush in 1849 and statehood in 1850, and continued until World War II. The land was cleared for grazing and farming, the Santa Cruz Mountain redwoods were cut to build San Francisco, and small towns grew along the railway between San Francisco and San Jose.

Until WWII the Santa Clara Valley was an agricultural community filled with orchards, while the northern Peninsula was a country playground for wealthy San Franciscans. Much of the Peninsula was used as a staging area for troops on their way to the Pacific. After the war, many who had worked in or passed through the area decided to stay, and the population exploded. The enormous growth spurt established much of the area's housing and determined its largely suburban character. The military-industrial economy fed this growth with companies like Lockheed and FMC. Stanford's influence gave this development a technological bent, and sowed the seeds for the creation of Silicon Valley. The success of companies like Hewlett-Packard, Varian, Intel, and Apple computer has fueled the Peninsula's continuing growth, and now San Mateo and Santa Clara counties have some of the highest per capita incomes and housing prices in the nation. Recent cutbacks in military spending and consolidation in the computer business have put a damper on growth and led some to flee north and east, but the region remains an economic powerhouse, and those per capita rankings remain high.

Tourist Information and Maps

The following tourist information offices can give you small maps and additional information about the region. American Automobile Association (AAA) members can get information and maps free at any of their offices—see the *Automobile* section for more information.

San Francisco Visitor Information Center: 900 Market St., San Francisco, (415) 391-2000; events hotline (415) 391-2001. • M-F 9am-5:30pm; Sa 9am-3pm; Su 10am-2pm.

San Francisco Convention and Visitor's Bureau: 201 Third St., # 900, San Francisco, (415) 974-6900. • M-F 8:30am-5pm.

San Mateo County Convention and Visitors Bureau: 111 Anza Blvd., #410, Burlingame, (415) 348-7600. • M-F 8:30am-5pm.

San Jose Convention and Visitors Bureau: 333 W. San Carlos St., #1000, San Jose, (408) 295-9600, (800) SAN-JOSE/726-5673. • M-F 8am-5pm.

Emergencies

If you are faced with an emergency that threatens life or property and demands immediate attention, dial 911 on any telephone. You will be connected with an emergency operator who can immediately direct your call to the appropriate place. Do not use this number if you do not have an emergency. To reach the police or other agencies for non-emergency questions, look up their number in your local phone book.

Dress, Smoking, Tipping

Dress in California is generally quite casual. Business types wear their suits, but many high-tech companies allow employees to wear "Gap-casual" clothes, especially on Friday, often an official "dress-down" day. Very few restaurants require a coat and tie, although some may object to a full-blown grunge look. The only restaurants where you might feel out of place without formal dress are old-style continental restaurants. Many people do dress up for the performing arts (especially the opera), and especially for those all-important opening nights.

Smoking generates a considerable amount of controversy in California, but most local governments have now passed regulations banning smoking in some way in public buildings, work areas, and restaurants. Look for huddled crowds of embarrassed people smoking outside doorways, and expect clouds of smoke in those bars and cafés that do allow smoking.

Unless otherwise noted on the menu or the check, restaurants do not include a gratuity on the bill. The standard tip is 15 percent of the tab, more for excellent service, less if the service was somehow offensive. It is also customary to tip taxi drivers, airport baggage handlers, parking valets, and most hotel service staff.

Phones

Pacific Bell (800-974-2355) is the local phone company throughout Northern California. Contact them to establish any new service, but be prepared to pay an exorbitant setup fee of approximately $40 per line plus wiring charges for installation of jacks (you are free to do the wiring yourself or hire a third-party contractor). The California Public Utilities Commission (CPUC) recently changed the way it regulates local toll calls, allowing competition among phone companies for toll calls regulated by the CPUC (intraLATA calls over 16 miles).

In addition to Pacific Bell, you can now use AT&T, MCI, Sprint, or any other phone company for these calls, although you will have to dial an access code to use these other services. Competition has lowered the charges and promotional offers abound, but the fees for basic phone service were actually increased. Similarly, public telephones have been deregulated. Many are owned and operated by Pacific Bell; many others are owned by private companies. While these phones may outwardly look similar to Pacific Bell phones, service can be erratic. Most important, for long-distance calls, many of these other phones connect you to obscure carriers that charge obscene rates. Any local calls cost 20¢ and more for calls over 16 miles. The number for local directory information is 411, and for another area code the number is 1-(area code)-555-1212. Dial 0 to reach the operator if you get confused (understandably) at any point.

Utilities

Pacific Gas and Electric (PG&E) provides local gas and electric service to most homes in the area. Consult your phone book for the local office nearest you. While the climate is moderate, many homes and apartments are poorly insulated and you can expect to use heat intermittently from October to April, especially in the hills. Air conditioning is helpful on many summer days, especially in the southern and eastern parts of the Peninsula. Most cities are responsible for their own water and garbage services; curbside recycling is common in most communities as landfill space becomes scarce.

Media

Newspapers

There's no shortage of media in the area, although coverage is generally provincial and heavily focused on local issues. Generally, each town has its own free weekly which is delivered to all residents. The advent of desktop publishing has created a staggering number of other free publications—covering many specific geographic areas and special interests (children, biking, children who bike, etc.). There are four major daily papers in the area. In San Francisco, the *Chronicle* is the morning paper and the *Examiner* the afternoon paper. They combine to produce one Sunday edition, which includes the "Datebook" section (better known as the "Pink Pages"), one of the best overall guides to events, arts, and entertainment in the Bay Area. San Mateo county is served by *The Times*. San Jose is served by the *Mercury News,* which plays heavily to the local high-tech audience and has a reputation for good writing. The best known free weeklies in San Francisco are the *Bay Guardian* and the *SF Weekly.* The best known free weekly in the South Bay is *The Metro.* All three provide extensive arts and entertainment listings, as well as in-depth political reporting with an alternative—leftist—edge.

TV

2	KTVU	FOX	Oakland
4	KRON	NBC	San Francisco
5	KPIX	CBS	San Francisco
7	KGO	ABC	San Francisco
9	KQED	PBS	San Francisco
11	KNTV	ABC	San Jose
14	KDTV	UNI (Spanish)	San Francisco
20	KOFY	IND	San Francisco
36	KICU	IND	San Jose
44	KBHK	IND	San Francisco

AM Radio

560	KSFO	Talk.
610	KFRC	Pop music.
680	KNBR	Talk, sports. (NBC)
740	KCBS	News, traffic. (CBS)
810	KGO	News, talk. (ABC)
910	KNEW	Country and western music.

FM Radio

88.5	KQED	S.F. public radio, news, talk.
89.5	KPOO	S.F. community radio, diverse multi-ethnic music.
89.7	KFJC	Foothill College radio. Diverse progressive.
90.1	KZSU	Stanford College radio. Rock, rap, etc.
90.3	KUSF	USF college radio. Diverse progressive.
91.1	KCSM	San Mateo public radio, jazz.
92.3	KSJO	Classic rock.
93.3	KYCY	Country.
94.1	KPFA	Berkeley public radio, diverse music, talk.
94.5	KFOX	Classic rock.
94.9	KSAN	Modern country.
96.5	KOIT	Light rock.
97.3	KRQR	Classic rock.
98.5	KOME	Modern rock, Howard Stern.
98.9	KSOL	Soul, from 70s disco to contemporary.
100.9	KKHI	Classical music.
102.1	KDFC	Classical music.
102.9	KBLX	"Quiet Storm": adult contemporary.
103.7	KKSF	Adult contemporary, easy listening.
104.5	KFOG	Album-oriented rock, old and new.
104.9	KBRG	Spanish.
105.3	KITS	"Live 105": modern rock.
106.1	KMEL	Contemporary hits, dance.
107.7	KYLD	Contemporary hits, dance.

TRANSPORTATION

DRIVING & AUTOMOBILES

Because California is the land of the automobile, it is also the land of automobile regulations. Bringing a car to California from another state has its hassles, not the least of which is the cost. Under state law, if you don't obtain California registration at the Department of Motor Vehicles (DMV) within 20 days of establishing California residency, you face a stiff fine. Residency can be established by: voting; your dependents attending public schools; filing for a home owner's property tax exemption; obtaining any other privilege or benefit not ordinarily extended to nonresidents. When you make your home here, you must also get a California driver's license within 10 days (see below).

Auto Registration

Perhaps you've already heard the horror stories about the DMV—long lines, endless forms, bored and condescending staff. Well, it's all true. Going to the DMV is a long, complicated, and exceedingly frustrating exercise in bureaucracy. But don't lose hope—you can save yourself some of the agony by calling ahead to make an appointment.

To register your car, you must fill out an application, present a California smog certificate, and show your out-of-state registration and title. The DMV will mail an application if you call ahead. Fill this form out carefully, since it could cost you. For example, if you go to the DMV more than 20 days after you the day you claim to have moved here, the DMV will charge a penalty fee. You should also know that your registration cost depends on your car's value; think twice before you brag that your '71 bug is a priceless classic. In general, find out how the DMV will treat any information before you volunteer it. (But remember that making false statements to the DMV is a crime.)

You must also have your car smog-checked before you go to the DMV, but not more than 90 days before. Many gas stations and repair shops perform this service. The fees vary from $20 to $50, but all shops must abide by certain rules regarding repairs and re-testing on cars which fail the tests. Unfortunately, because California has the strictest auto emissions standards in the nation, most out-of-state cars don't comply with California smog regulations. Even after you get your smog certificate you'll most likely be required to pay a $300 smog impact fee. The certificate indicates that your car is as clean as it can be; the fee is because your car's best isn't good enough.

And as if all this weren't enough, if you bought your car less than 90 days before you entered California, you'll also owe any difference between California's fairly hefty sales tax and the sales tax you paid in the state of purchase.

Driver's Licenses

First off, driving tests are normally waived for license renewals and holders of valid out-of-state licenses, so relax if you fit that bill. If you don't but you're at least 18 years old, you may be given a license after you've passed a written test on road regulations, a vision test (bring your contacts or glasses), and a driving test. You must also prove you are a legal resident. Driving tests are given by appointment only, so call ahead. You supply the car for the test—in full working condition—as well as a licensed driver to accompany you to the test. The $12 application fee is good for three tries within 12 months. Once you've completed this obstacle course, you're photographed and thumbprinted (or fingerprinted, if you have no thumbs), and let loose on the road.

5

DMV Offices

Most DMV offices are open M-F 8am-5pm, Th till 6:30pm.

Daly City: 1500 Sullivan Ave., (415) 994-5700.

El Cerrito: 6400 Manila Ave., (510) 235-9171.

Gilroy: 8200 Church St., (408) 842-6488.

Los Gatos: 600 N. Santa Cruz Ave., (408) 354-6541.

Mountain View: 595 Showers Dr., (415) 968-0610.

Redwood City: 300 Brewster Ave., (415) 368-2837.

San Francisco: 1377 Fell St., (415) 557-1179.

San Jose: 111 W. Alma Way, (408) 277-1301.

San Jose/Santa Theresa: 180 Martinvale Ln., (408) 244-4511.

San Mateo: 425 N. Amphlett Blvd., (415) 342-5332.

Santa Clara: 3665 Flora Vista Ave., (408) 277-1640.

AAA

You can probably save yourself quite a bit of grief by joining the American Auto Association, better known nationwide as Triple A and in our fair state as the California State Automobile Association (CSAA). CSAA helps you register your car and complete many DMV-procedures. They also provide emergency road service—they tow your car, change your tire, deliver fuel if you run out, and get you into your car if you lock yourself out, usually without asking embarrassing questions. Other benefits include an information service providing answers to technical questions, diagnostic clinics for low prices, auto-maintenance classes, free maps, and traveler's checks. (All Offices Open M-F 8:30am-5pm)

Cupertino: 1601 S. Saratoga-Sunnyvale Rd., (408) 996-3553.

Daly City: 455 Hickey Blvd., (415) 994-8400.

Palo Alto: 430 Forest Ave., (415) 321-0470.

Los Gatos: 101 Blossom Hill Rd., (408) 395-6411.

Mountain View: 900 Miramonte Ave., (415) 965-7000.

Redwood City: 20 El Camino Real, (415) 364-0620.

San Francisco: 150 Van Ness Ave., (415) 565-2012.

San Jose: 5340 Thornwood Dr., (408) 629-1911.

San Mateo: 1650 S. Delaware St., (415) 572-1160.

Santa Clara: 80 Saratoga Ave., (408) 985-9300.

Sunnyvale: 755 S. Bernardo Ave., (408) 739-4422.

Automobile Rental

A quick glimpse in your phone book will reveal that there's no shortage of rental car agencies in the Bay Area. All of the major national organizations are well represented, as are many smaller agencies. You'll find the most agencies at the airports, but many maintain smaller operations throughout the area, especially in large hotels. When comparison shopping, remember that rental rates are as volatile as air fares; you can expect to pay more during summer vacation than any other random weekend. Always ask about weekend, frequent flyer, student, and AAA discounts. Your rate is usually set when you make the reservation, not when you actually pick up the car, so plan ahead and book during a slow time. Always get your confirmation number, in case the rental agency loses track of your reservation. Keep in mind that many companies require a major credit card. You should also know that if you're under 25, you're a special insurance liability—which may be reflected in an extra surcharge. And if you're under 21, most companies won't even talk to you.

Alamo Rent A Car: (800) 327-9633.

Avis Rent A Car: (800) 831-2847.

Budget Rent-A-Car: (800) 527-0700.

Dollar Rent A Car: (800) 800-4000.

Enterprise Rent-A-Car: (800) 325-8007.

Hertz: (800) 654-3131.

National: (800) 227-7368.

PUBLIC TRANSPORTATION

The Bay Area has an extensive public transportation network, with many interconnecting systems linking us all together. This makes traveling around without a car relatively easy, albeit slow. There's often more than one way to get someplace, so it's definitely worth taking a little time to find the fastest or most appropriate way.

In terms of buses, Santa Clara Transit Agency (TA) and San Mateo County (SamTrans) each operate municipal bus lines that together cover destinations from San Francisco to Gilroy, meeting in between at the Stanford Shopping Center. Alameda County (AC) Transit serves the East Bay, while Golden Gate Transit serves the North Bay, each with links to San Francisco. MUNI serves San Francisco. Finally, the Dumbarton Express connects Palo Alto to the East Bay. As for trains, BART connects San Francisco with the East Bay, CalTrain runs down the Peninsula between San Francisco and San Jose (and even Gilroy), Santa Clara TA operates light rail trains in San Jose and Santa Clara, and MUNI operates some trains in San Francisco. Golden Gate Transit and the Red and White Fleet operate ferries that can get you from San Francisco to the North Bay, while the Alameda/Oakland Ferry Service operates ferries between San Francisco and Oakland.

If you need to know more, call the numbers given below. Once you get through the frequently busy phone lines, the operators are usually helpful; most will also send free timetables and maps within a couple of days. If you're stuck as to how to get from one place to another, try calling a Visitor Information Center (see Basic Information section).

AC Transit: (510) 839-2882. Alameda County Transit (AC Transit) covers the East Bay from Richmond to Fremont, with stops at every East Bay BART station. Transbay buses run across the Bay Bridge from Oakland to San Francisco's Transbay Terminal, mostly during rush hour. Express routes, which operate only during rush hour, go from downtown Oakland south to the suburbs as far as San Leandro and Hayward.

The fare for Local or Intercity Express buses is $1.10 (youth, seniors and disabled 55¢), Transbay routes cost $2.20 (youth, seniors and disabled $1.10). Monthly passes are $40 for adults ($21 discount), or $75 for a Transbay pass. Local passes can be upgraded to get across the Bay by paying $1.10 (55¢) per journey. Books of 10 Local bus tickets cost $9 (discount $4.50) and are available at local stores; call (800) 559-INFO for store locations. Transfers are available for an extra 25¢, and bus-BART transfers can be bought in BART stations, valid only for the bus stop outside that particular BART station. Generally, buses run every 30 minutes during the day, every 15 minutes during commute hours, and every 30 or 60 minutes evenings and weekends.

Alameda/Oakland Ferry Service: (510) 522-3300. These ferries run from Alameda and Oakland to San Francisco, either the Ferry Building at the Embarcadero or Pier 39 at Fisherman's Wharf. In Oakland they leave from Jack London Square and in Alameda from the Main Street Terminal; both locations have free parking. On weekdays, ferries leave about every 90 minutes. They run between the East Bay and the Ferry Building from 6am to 8pm and run to Fisherman's Wharf from 9am to 7pm. On weekends, ferries travel only twice daily, leaving Pier 39 at 8:55am and 4:30pm and the Ferry Building at 9:10am and 4:45pm. They return from Alameda at 10:10am and 5:15pm and leave Oakland at 10am and 5:30pm. The journey takes about 30 minutes. Tickets cost $3.75 each way ($2.50 for disabled and seniors and $1.50 for children 5-12 years old).

BART: (415) 992-2278. Bay Area Rapid Transit (BART) is a quick, clean way to get from San Francisco to the East Bay, from Fremont out to Concord and up to Richmond. Unfortunately, the only Peninsula station is in Daly City, although service to Colma is scheduled to begin in mid- to late-1995. SamTrans buses serve the Daly City station directly and come quite close to downtown San Francisco BART stations. Trains run every 15 to 20 minutes and more often during peak hours. Rail service runs daily until about midnight starting at 4am on weekdays, 6am on Saturdays, and 8am on Sundays. Fares currently range from 90¢ to $3.45 for a one-way ticket, but are scheduled to increase over the next few years.

BART connects to MUNI, SamTrans, and Golden Gate Transit in San Francisco, as well as to AC Transit and Santa Clara TA buses in the East Bay. You can connect from CalTrain to BART via MUNI in San Francisco by taking the 15, 30 or 45 bus from the CalTrain station at Fourth and Townsend to the Montgomery Street BART station on Market, or if going the other way, by taking the 30 or 45 from the Powell Street BART station along Fourth Street to the CalTrain station. To connect from BART in the East Bay to the mid-Peninsula, take the Dumbarton Express bus (see below) or, during commute hours, the SamTrans 90E bus from Hayward BART to San Mateo. Three Santa Clara TA buses go to the Fremont BART station: the #140 from Mountain View, the #141 from Great America in Santa Clara, and the #180 from downtown San Jose.

CalTrain: (800) 660-4BUS/4287. CalTrain runs from San Francisco south to San Jose and Gilroy, stopping at stations every two to five miles. Trains run approximately every hour from 5am to 10pm on weekdays, and more often during rush hour. Weekend and holiday trains run 6am to 10pm every two hours. On Friday and Saturday nights, the last train south from San Francisco leaves at midnight. The trip from San Francisco to San Jose takes 90 minutes, and from San Francisco to Palo Alto it takes an hour. Rush hour express trains cut these times significantly.

Fares depend on the distance traveled. Examples of one-way fares include: San Francisco to Palo Alto for $3.25, San Francisco to San Jose for $4.50, and Palo Alto to San Jose for $2.75. Regular riders can save with a variety of passes, including ten-ride (valid for 90 days), monthly, weekly, and weekend passes. San Francisco to Palo Alto ten-ride passes cost $28, monthly passes run $87.50, weekly passes cost $31.20, and weekend passes are $8. During the week, if you travel further than your pass normally allows, you can pay to upgrade. On weekends, all passes are valid for travel as far as you like. Seniors, the disabled, and youths under 18 get discounts on tickets and monthly passes. If you have a MUNI Fastpass, you may ride CalTrain free on all journeys that begin and end within San Francisco. An important little tip: buy your ticket at the station window if it is open, because CalTrain adds a surcharge if you pay your fare on board when the station is open.

If you have a monthly CalTrain pass you may *transfer* free to connecting TA buses and get $1.00 off *transfers* to SamTrans buses. CalTrain monthly ticket holders can also purchase a Peninsula Pass for $25, which provides free local MUNI, TA, Light Rail, and SamTrans service (not limited to transfers), as well as partial credit for the Dumbarton Express and SamTrans express lines.

The CalTrain terminus in San Francisco is at Fourth and Townsend Streets; but be warned, the station is south of Market far from downtown. You'll probably want to take a MUNI bus to your final destination. Several buses stop at the station: the 15, 30, 42 and 45, as well as the 80X, 81X and 82X shuttle buses which operate between the station and downtown only during commute hours. Bus shuttles connect many Peninsula CalTrain stations with local workplaces, and there is also bus service between the San Jose station and Santa Cruz. A shuttle bus runs between San Francisco International Airport and the Millbrae station; it runs *weekdays only*, but it does meet most of these trains.

Parking is available at most stations for a minimal fee. To bring non-collapsible bikes on the trains, a permit must be obtained by mail in advance. Please note that some rush-hour trains prohibit bicycles and a maximum of 12 bicycles is permitted per train (if you're unlucky number 13, you must wait for the next train).

Dumbarton Express: (408) 321-2300, (800) 894-9908. The Dumbarton Bridge Express bus runs across its namesake, and is probably the most convenient way to get from the mid-Peninsula to the southern part of the East Bay on weekdays. There is only one route, between Palo Alto and the Union City BART station in the East Bay. It runs weekdays only, hourly during the day and every 15 minutes during rush hour. The fare is $1.75 for adults or $1.00 for youth; a monthly pass will set you back $60.

Golden Gate Transit: (415) 332-6600. Golden Gate Transit provides bus service in the North Bay and ferry service between Marin and San Francisco. Buses run through Marin, Contra Costa, Sonoma, and San Francisco counties, with weekend routes to Stinson Beach and Point Reyes. Bus routes in San Francisco begin at the Transbay Terminal located at First and Mission. Basic service operates every 15 to 90 minutes, while commute routes from West Marin to San Francisco operate every 2 to 20 minutes. Bus fares vary from $1.10 to $4.50 depending on how far you travel; exact change is required.

Golden Gate Transit also operates two ferry routes across the bay, from San Francisco to Larkspur and San Francisco to Sausalito. Ferries depart from the Ferry Building at Embarcadero and Market in San Francisco. During commuter hours only, free shuttles are available to and from the ferry terminals and the surrounding areas in Marin or downtown San Francisco. On weekdays, ferries run every 30 to 60 minutes from 5:30am to 8:25pm. On weekends and holidays, there are five ferries each way, spread between 9:45am and 6pm. The Sausalito ferry departs every 90 minutes, on weekdays from 7am to 7pm; on Saturday, Sunday, and holidays it runs from 11am to 8pm. From Larkspur, the fare is $2.50 on weekdays and $4.25 on weekends and holidays. The ferry from Sausalito costs $4.25 daily.

MUNI: (415) 673-MUNI/6864. The much maligned MUNI often gets a bad rap for its erratic service and surly drivers, yet San Francisco's Municipal Railway is one of the most comprehensive transit systems in the country in terms of geographic coverage: Wherever you are in the city, at least one bus stop is within a two-minute walk. MUNI's system consists mostly of electric buses, with a few motor buses, five light rail train routes, and the famous cable cars thrown in. Many bus shelters have a map of the bus lines (although not every bus stop has a shelter); a map of all routes is available at many convenience and drug stores for $2.50.

Most buses run from 6am to midnight, although there are a few that stop at 6pm. The OWL routes run all night; the commuter (X) lines are fast routes straight downtown during rush hour. Limited (L) buses are faster than regular lines as they only stop at every third or fourth regular stop. Buses run from every two minutes to every 30 during the day; OWL routes usually run about every hour. Timetables are available on the buses, but they are so approximate that most people just go to the bus stop and wait. Be warned, you may be in for the odd and infuriating 45 minute wait, especially in the evening.

TRANSPORTATION

The train routes (MUNI Metro) run from downtown west along Market Street, branching south and west to various parts of the city; trains are typically faster than buses along equivalent routes.

Bus and light rail fare is $1 (35¢ for youth/senior/disabled) and includes a transfer, valid for two more rides over the next one-and-a-half hours. Exact change is required. A monthly Fast Pass costs $35 for adults and $8 for youth, seniors and the disabled. The pass is also valid for BART and CalTrain within San Francisco.

Red and White Fleet: (800) 229-2784. The Red and White Fleet offers ferry service from pier 43 1/2 on Fisherman's Wharf in San Francisco to Sausalito, Tiburon, and Angel Island, and from the Ferry Building at Embarcadero and Market in San Francisco to Tiburon. The trip to Tiburon from the Ferry Building is for commuters, running only Monday through Friday during commute hours. Ferries from Fisherman's Wharf are tourist oriented: the Sausalito and Tiburon boats operate from about 11am to 5pm on weekdays and 10:40am to 6pm on weekends and holidays (later during the summer). The Angel Island ferry makes only one trip during the week, but makes three on weekends and holidays. Adult tickets to Sausalito and Tiburon cost $5.50 each way; children ages 5-11 pay $2.75 each way. Angel Island tickets cost $9 round-trip.

SamTrans: (800) 660-4BUS/4287. SamTrans runs throughout San Mateo County, as well as to and from downtown San Francisco, San Francisco International Airport, and games at Candlestick Park. Four bus routes go to San Francisco International Airport: the 7B, the 7F, the 3B and the 3X.

Buses generally run every 30 or 60 minutes beginning at 6am. Many of them stop around 6pm, although several continue until midnight; some run during commute hours only. On Saturdays, the service is a lot sparser; on Sundays, even more so. Bikes are allowed on buses and there are Park and Ride lots along some routes.

The fare is $1 for regular adult service, 50¢ for youths, 35¢ for disabled, and 25¢ for seniors. Express service is $1.50, $1.75, or $2.00 for adults, depending on the route taken, with limited discounts available. Monthly passes can be bought for each different fare, any of which may be upgraded for a single journey by paying the cash difference.

SamTrans connects in various places with BART, CalTrain, AC Transit, Golden Gate Transit, the Dumbarton Express, and the Santa Clara County Transportation Agency. Passes and transfers from some of these companies are valid on certain SamTrans buses.

Santa Clara County TA: (408) 321-2300, (800) 894-9908. The Santa Clara County Transportation Agency (TA) operates both the buses and the Light Rail system within Santa Clara County. The regular adult fare is $1.10, or $1.75 to $2.25 for express commuter services. The youth fare is 55¢, and seniors and disabled pay 35¢. Day passes are also available for twice these amounts. Monthly passes cost $33 for a regular pass, $16.50 for youths, $6 for seniors and the disabled, and $50 or $55 for the two types of express passes. Bus service begins at around 6am. Many buses continue until midnight and some till 2am, but a few stop after commute hours. They run every 15 to 30 minutes, less frequently in the evening. On weekends and holidays, buses start between 7am and 9am; some run until around 6pm and others as late as midnight. Weekend buses run every 30 to 60 minutes.

Light Rail Transit (LRT) currently has just one rail route, from the southern part of San Jose to the Great America Theme Park in Santa Clara. The Light Rail has connections to many bus lines which also connect to CalTrain, SamTrans, AC Transit, BART, Amtrak, and the Dumbarton Bridge Express. Tickets or passes from some of these companies may be accepted as part or full payment towards your TA ticket, and SamTrans accepts TA monthly and day passes as full fare at mutual stops.

GETTING AWAY

Air Travel

San Jose Airport (SJO) is one of the best-kept secrets around. It's close to Silicon Valley and smaller and easier to negotiate than **San Francisco International Airport** (SFO), but most people still insist on flying into SFO, probably because there are many more flights. **Oakland Airport** (OAK) is less convenient, but serves bargain airlines like Southwest.

Oakland Airport: (510) 577-4000.

San Francisco Airport: (415) 876-7809, (415) 761-0800.

San Jose Airport: (408) 277-4759.

Airport Transportation

Driving

San Francisco International Airport (SFO) is located 14 miles south of San Francisco. Choose your route to SFO depending on your starting point and traffic; bad congestion, especially on Hwy 101 when there is a game at Candlestick Park, can cause severe delays. Take Hwy 101 to San Bruno; the airport exit is between Millbrae Avenue and I-380. Or take I-280 to I-380 to Hwy 101 south and follow the signs into the airport (you never actually get on Hwy 101).

For San Jose International Airport, take Hwy 101 to just north of San Jose; you'll see the airport at Guadalupe Parkway. Turn right off Guadalupe onto Brokaw—Brokaw becomes Airport Boulevard and takes you to the airport.

To drive to the Oakland Airport, take either the Dumbarton or San Mateo Bridge to I-880 north. Exit at Hegenberger Road, which takes you straight to the airport. From San Francisco or the north Peninsula, take the Bay Bridge (I-80) east to I-580 east to I-980 south to I-880 south. Exit at Hegenberger Road.

Public Transportation

See *Public Transportation* section above for additional information on the companies and routes mentioned here.

Four SamTrans buses routes go to **San Francisco International Airport**: the 7B, the 7F, the 3B. and the 3X. The 7F express route stops at SFO on its trip between Palo Alto and San Francisco. Allow yourself a good hour for the ride from Stanford to SFO, or 40 minutes from Redwood City. The 7B local route stops at SFO on its trip between Redwood City and San Francisco. Allow yourself a little over an hour from Redwood City to SFO, 45 minutes from San Mateo. The adult fare for both buses is $1 from the Peninsula to the airport.

From San Francisco, both buses start at the Transbay Terminal at First and Mission Streets. The 7B follows surface streets, takes an hour from San Francisco, and costs $1, while the 7F follows Hwy 101, takes 40 minutes, and costs $1.75. The problem with the 7F is that only hand luggage is allowed between San Francisco and the airport. (Baggage can be taken between the airport and Palo Alto, or on the 7B.) The buses run from 6am until midnight.

The other two buses, the 3B and the 3X, run from the Daly City BART station to the airport. The 3B follows surface streets to the airport. The 3X follows I-280 and I-380 for most of its route. The adult fare for both buses is $1.

CalTrain also serves SFO. Hop a train to the Millbrae Station, then take the free CalTrain shuttle to the terminal building; the shuttle operates on *weekdays only*.

San Jose Airport is served by TA Light Rail Transit (LRT) and buses. From the Light Rail Metro/Airport Station in San Jose, catch the free Metro Airport Shuttle on the southbound side of First Street. The shuttle runs every 10 minutes from 6am to 8am, then every 15 minutes until 6:48pm. After 6:48pm, you can catch the #65 bus on the northbound side of First Street. The #65 bus runs from the Santa Clara CalTrain station to downtown San Jose to the Almaden LRT station, stopping at the airport and the Metro/Airport LRT station on its route. It runs every 30 minutes during rush hour and every hour at other times, but usually takes only 15 minutes to get from Santa Clara to the airport terminal. Peninsula residents can reach Santa Clara via either CalTrain or the #22 TA bus, which travels down El Camino from Palo Alto.

BART serves **Oakland Airport** via the Oakland Coliseum Station on the Fremont line. From the station, the AirBART shuttle costs $2 each way and runs about every 10 minutes, less frequently during evenings and weekends. See *Public Transportation* section above for information on how to reach BART.

Private Shuttles

Airport shuttles are usually faster and simpler, but more expensive. Do some research on all the different companies—the best deal depends on your situation. Many shuttles offer discounts when they pick up more than one person at a location; some charge extra if you exceed a baggage limit. Always make reservations well in advance for rides to the airport, and when you do, let the shuttle service know if you have any special luggage requirements, such as a bike or ten bags.

Airport Connection: (415) 872-2552.

BayPorter Express: (415) 467-1800.

Express Airport Shuttle: (408) 378-6270.

SFO Airporter: (415)) 495-8404.

South and East Bay Airport Shuttle: (800) 548-4664.

Super Shuttle: (415) 558-8500.

VIP Airport Shuttle: (408) 378-8VIP, 800-235-8847.

Land Travel

Amtrak: (800) USA-RAIL (872-7245). Amtrak connects the Bay Area to the rest of the world via depots in San Jose, Oakland, and Berkeley. The San Jose station is conveniently next to the CalTrain station. Amtrak buses take passengers from San Francisco to Oakland, and stop at the San Francisco CalTrain station. Those familiar with Amtrak train service between Boston and Washington D.C. will be mystified by Amtrak's dizzying schedules and amazed at how few actual trains run on the West Coast routes; the majority of service is provided by buses. There are several trains a day from San Jose and Oakland to Sacramento, and several others to the Central Valley. One train goes all the way up the Pacific Coast, from San Diego and Los Angeles through San Jose to Seattle and Vancouver, Canada. Another train runs east from Oakland through Truckee and Reno—passing through spectacular Sierra scenery—on the way to Salt Lake City, Denver, and Chicago. Most long-distance trains require reservations.

Greyhound: (800) 231-2222, (415) 495-1575. Greyhound Bus is an inexpensive alternative. You won't get anywhere in a hurry, but you won't pay through the nose either. Greyhound has three main Bay Area depots: in San Francisco's Transbay Terminal at First and Mission, in downtown San Jose at 70 Almaden Avenue, and in downtown Oakland at 2103 San Pablo Avenue. There is also a minor Peninsula stop at 252 Mayfield Avenue in Mountain View near San Antonio Road and Alma Street. Greyhound's best deals are with the Ameripass, which gives you unlimited rides and an unrestricted schedule for a fixed fee. Make reservations more than two weeks in advance for discounts.

NEIGHBORHOODS AND HOUSING

Keep in mind that many comments about Peninsula and South Bay communities are relative. It's hard to understand how housing in a community with a median home price of $350,000 can be called plentiful and affordable, but remember that median income and median housing prices for these counties are among the nation's highest. What may seem affordable by local standards will probably seem incredibly expensive compared to other markets. Similarly, the relative maturity of various communities can't be compared to the East Coast or the Old Country. Although European settlement actually began in the late 18th century, most development here has occurred since World War II. Palo Alto and Redwood City really are old and established communities compared to cities like Sunnyvale and Milpitas, which have boomed in the last 20 years.

Describing school districts becomes even more relative. Generally, schools in San Mateo and Santa Clara Counties are better than average for California. (There was a time when California's public schools were considered some of the best in the country, although that is not the case anymore.) Even within any city, there are typically large variations from school to school in the learning environment and rankings. Most students can get a good education in most schools with enough focus and enough hard work. But for parents that went to Stanford and want to make sure their children will go there too, an above average school isn't good enough—which is why they pay to live in a town like Palo Alto, where the schools actually are among the best in the country.

Yet there are a few general rules about the cities and towns of the Peninsula and the South Bay. As you climb from the Bay up the Santa Cruz Mountain foothills, house size and housing prices go up with the elevation. And as price increases, so does the average age of the community. This altitudinal gradation is certainly not unique to California; after all, it takes time to save enough for a down payment and most people earn more as they get older. But since Proposition 13 passed in California, the assessed value of a house for tax purposes has been kept below market value until it is sold. Now many long-time homeowners don't want to move because buying a new house would dramatically increase their property taxes.

The following towns are listed in roughly geographic order from north to south; estimated 1990 population is in parenthesis.

Brisbane (3,000)

This tiny, blue-collar town is best known for its office complexes east of Hwy 101 and for San Bruno Mountain, the huge bald knob that straddles this part of the Peninsula. After years of debate and litigation, it looks as though a large residential development will be built on the northeast side of San Bruno Mountain, adding a lot of residential units to a town filled primarily with commercial and industrial development. The moderately priced residential area—mostly pre-WWII single-family homes—is squeezed into an isolated valley on the steep slopes of San Bruno Mountain and further cut off from neighboring towns by a lagoon. Brisbane refers to itself as "The City of the Stars," in honor of a holiday season tradition of decorating houses with large star-shaped Christmas lights. Schools are above average for the northern Peninsula.

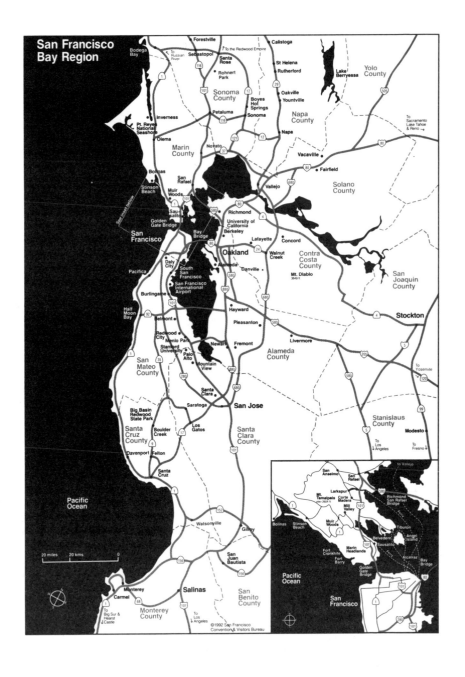

Daly City (94,076)

Although Daly City is San Mateo County's largest city, it is really more a part of San Francisco than the Peninsula. Located just south of the City, it exhibits an urban diversity rare on the Peninsula and even has a BART station, giving it excellent access to San Francisco. A recent influx of immigrants has given Daly City a large growth spurt; it now boasts a young and very diverse population—including northern California's largest Filipino community. Daly City has a long history as a refuge: in 1906, many San Francisco residents fleeing the destruction of the Great Quake and fire found safety on John Daly's ranch.

The city itself is located near a gap in the coastal mountains. Pacific-bound airplanes taking off from San Francisco airport cross this gap going west, while ocean winds and fog cross the gap going east. Housing prices are reasonable for the broad mix of homes and apartments, as is typical for the northern Peninsula. The ridges above I-280 are lined with rows and rows of identical houses, looking like so many Monopoly game pieces. Now, even newer construction follows this careful pattern. The schools fall into many districts and are quite variable but generally solid, especially considering the pressure the town's rapid growth and large immigrant population have put on the system.

Colma (1,100)

Very few people actually live in Colma, a town best known for its cemeteries: when San Francisco ran out of space, it banned cemeteries and moved all its dead to Colma. It has been burying them there ever since. Other than cemeteries, Colma is primarily home to commercial developments such as Auto Row on Serramonte Boulevard and the 280 Metro Center.

South San Francisco (56,000)

Few people driving into San Francisco from the south have missed the huge white letters on San Bruno Mountain grandly proclaiming "South San Francisco—The Industrial City." (The name originated with a large meat-packing operation at the turn of the century.) Today you'll find more office parks, electronics firms, and airport hotels than industry, but there are still many printing firms and warehouses that moved from San Francisco in search of cheaper real estate. Some people might be disturbed by the ocean winds that blow through the gap near Daly City and shoot through town, but South San Francisco's location near the airport and the intersection of Hwy 101 and I-380 makes transportation convenient, enhancing its commercial appeal.

Despite its early industrial development—which left a beautiful, historic downtown along Grand Avenue between Airport Boulevard and Chestnut Avenue—most of the housing came along after WWII. The neat, closely spaced, boxy houses and moderate prices resemble those in neighboring towns. Schools are typical of the northern Peninsula, which is highly variable. South San Francisco has grown recently with an influx of immigrants from Latin America and the Pacific, and, as with California as a whole, whites are no longer a majority.

San Bruno (39,000)

San Bruno is located on the narrowest point on the Peninsula, where I-380 connects Hwy 101 to I-280. The eastern edge of town borders San Francisco Airport. As you might expect from a town at the center of the region's transportation system, commercial development dominates the area. San Bruno is home to three shopping centers within a mile of each other: Tanforan Park, Towne Center, and Bayhill Shopping Center. As its name implies, Towne Center serves as a *de facto* downtown, although there is an historic downtown along San Mateo Avenue, which is lined with small-town-America storefronts and international grocery stores. Office parks and industrial areas, including a huge Gap corporate campus, are also well represented. Things may get even more commercial if a BART line extension to the airport puts a station in San Bruno.

San Bruno marks the dividing line between the northern Peninsula and the rest of it. The town resembles its northern neighbors in that housing is generally smaller, denser, and less expensive than in Millbrae and other towns heading south. Yet reflecting its status as a border town, housing prices and average income in San Bruno are slightly higher than those found to the north. As usual, the most developed areas lie along El Camino, and the more residential areas sit in the hills towards I-280. San Bruno fits into three school districts, with the best schools associated with San Mateo and Millbrae to the south. Because it is less expensive than its southern neighbors and has grown faster, San Bruno and its neighbors generally have more young adults and young families.

Millbrae (21,100)

Millbrae lies in the shadow, if not the very flight path, of San Francisco Airport. Industrial development associated with the airport in the eastern half of Millbrae exacerbates the normal Peninsula pattern of industrial and commercial development along Hwy 101, a mix of apartments and houses along El Camino, and larger single-family homes in the hills towards I-280. The future may bring other changes related to the airport: a BART station for the airport may be located in Millbrae. In the meantime, other planned upgrades to the town include a Millbrae Avenue overpass to make it easier for traffic to get across the CalTrain tracks. El Camino is a busy commercial strip with numerous Asian restaurants, including the Hong Kong Flower Lounge, a celebrated ostentatious temple of Hong Kong Cantonese seafood. A small downtown shopping area on Broadway parallel to El Camino has made a major step in establishing its credibility: it got a Starbucks coffee bar.

Millbrae resembles neighboring bedroom communities like Burlingame in most respects, including housing, income, schools, and so forth: much of the housing was built in the post-war boom, and it is expensive. One difference is that nearly one third of the population is over 55, something more typical in exclusive enclaves like Hillsborough and Atherton. The schools are variable, but generally good.

Burlingame (27,000)

While most Peninsula cities struggle to maintain one downtown, Burlingame has two: one on Broadway, and the other on Burlingame Avenue. Credit CalTrain for giving Burlingame two train stations, one for each area. Admittedly, the retail strip on Broadway is pretty small, with just a few restaurants, Asian markets, and carpet stores. The real action is on Burlingame Avenue between El Camino and the CalTrain station. There you'll find a host of restaurants, cafés, and retail shops—including the requisite Starbucks, Noah's, Peet's, and Gap—amidst a bustle of small-town energy. Around the two downtowns you'll find quiet, suburban streets with a mix of houses and high-rise apartments. The eastern side of Burlingame along Hwy 101 is filled with commercial development, much of it serving nearby San Francisco International Airport. Hotels, restaurants, and car rental lots keep springing up, especially along Bayshore Highway. Hillsborough borders the western edge of Burlingame; north of Hillside Drive Burlingame curves around Hillsborough up to I-280.

Perhaps it's Hillsborough's influence, but Burlingame houses are anomalously big and expensive. Compared to Millbrae or San Mateo, real estate costs are significantly higher, while rents and average incomes are lower. These housing prices limit new families, although the schools are generally very good. Burlingame's proximity to the airport makes it convenient for sales and consulting types, as well as other frequent flyers, although noise could be a problem.

Hillsborough (10,700)

As the northern Peninsula's stereotypically exclusive, hillside residential community, Hillsborough offers the typical mix of large homes, quiet streets, low crime, and excellent schools. It is typically neck and neck with Atherton for highest average income and home prices on the Peninsula. Don't expect to see anybody strolling around town: sidewalks and street lights are prohibited. Don't look for many young adults either—established wealthy families come here for the schools and stay for a safe old age.

San Mateo (85,500)

San Mateo, the city that made the county what it is today. Although Redwood City is older and the actual county seat, San Mateo plays a more central role: it's larger, located in the center of the county, has housing prices and incomes right at the county median, and even boasts the region's main shopping center in Hillsdale Mall. San Mateo sets the tone; it even has its own Central Park. The bustling downtown along Third and Fourth Streets between El Camino and the CalTrain station has a diverse mix of restaurants, cafés, and shops, although competition from superstores and the mall has hurt some downtown businesses.

San Mateo's neighborhoods are predictably typical of the mid-Peninsula, with lots of quiet, tree-lined streets, a mix of houses and apartments from the last 100 years (with an abundance of units reflecting the post-WWII boom years), and commercial and industrial development along Hwy 101. Neighborhoods in the hills west of El Camino are generally more expensive. The neighborhoods along the train tracks near downtown have been attracting a diverse mix of recent immigrants, especially Hispanics. Schools are variable, but generally pretty good, with the high school especially well regarded.

Foster City (28,200)

The word earthquake carries a lot of weight in Foster City: this lagoon community was created 30 years ago on landfill, the same stuff that turned to Jell-O under San Francisco's Marina district during the 1989 Loma Prieta quake. Residents, mostly highly educated professionals, insist that Foster City's construction is designed to withstand earthquakes; in fact, Foster City did survive the '89 quake quite well. The city was built by one developer, T. Jack Foster, at the base of the San Mateo bridge on what was known as Brewer's Island. He created a clean, modern planned community with a centrally-planned mix of houses, town homes, condominiums, offices, shopping centers, and parks. Because it's built on a reclaimed portion of the Bay, canals and sloughs wind through town; Leo Ryan Park is an excellent place to learn to sail or windsurf.

Since Foster City was built only 30 years ago, it has a decidedly youthful—some would say yuppie—character, with relatively few older residents. Plenty of high-income professionals create high real estate prices, especially high rents. The schools are part of the San Mateo School District, and are variable but pretty good. Foster City's location at the intersection of Hwy 101 and Hwy 92 makes it convenient to many points, but this central spot does mean a lot of other traffic passing through.

Belmont (24,100)

Sister city to neighboring San Carlos, Belmont sits at the very geographic center of the Peninsula, halfway between San Francisco and San Jose. Belmont's wooded hillsides also consist almost entirely of quiet upper–middle-class suburban neighborhoods. In fact, Belmont has even less commercial and industrial activity than San Carlos, although the city scored a recent coup when it convinced Oral-B to move its headquarters in. Housing is slightly less expensive in Belmont than in San Carlos, and apartments are more plentiful, although single-family homes still predominate the market. Perhaps it's the apartments, but Belmont has more young adults and fewer elderly residents than San Carlos. Schools are generally very good, as is access to Hwy 101.

San Carlos (25,700)

San Carlos epitomizes the quiet upper–middle-class suburban bedroom community. Together with Belmont—even phone bills lump the two together as SNCRSBLMNT—it provides a comfortable small-town haven in the heart of the mid-Peninsula. Need we say it? The residential areas lie primarily west of El Camino; industrial and retail development dominates the land east of El Camino. The historic CalTrain station, built in 1888 in the style of architect H. H. Richardson, is now a state historic landmark. Nearby on Laurel Street, a tiny downtown is slowly taking shape, with restaurants, bars, and cafés attracting pedestrian traffic.

Although San Carlos got an early start as a Peninsula community, the population boom and much of the town's housing came after WWII, just as it did in most neighboring communities. Housing is predominantly expensive suburban homes, and the population is predominantly established families. Schools, especially the elementary systems, are good. While San Carlos is centrally located in the mid-Peninsula, traffic can be a problem: access to I-280 is slow, and Hwy 101 tends to clog up in the vicinity.

Redwood City (68,700)

Redwood City's hard-working history goes back to the 1800s, when the city earned its name as a lumber town: redwood trees cut in the hills above what is now Woodside were processed in Redwood City and shipped through its port to construction sites in San Francisco. When the city placed a billboard along Hwy 101 proclaiming itself "Palo Alto without the attitude," few people took the comparison seriously: while Redwood City has redeveloped its historic downtown around Broadway and Main Streets, sprucing up the brick sidewalks and adding gas-lamp streetlights, nobody will mistake this blue-collar city for tony Palo Alto. The city's latest project, Sequoia Station—a yuppie village-like shopping center with a Safeway, Starbucks, Noah's, Barnes & Noble, and more—was planned right at the CalTrain station, a boon for public transit. Redwood City is the San Mateo County seat, and many government offices, from the DMV to the courthouse, are also near downtown. One of the Peninsula's more ethnically diverse communities, Redwood City has an especially large Hispanic community; the retail strip along Middlefield Road between Hwy 84 and Fifth Avenue is lined with Mexican restaurants and markets.

The area near Hwy 101 is predominantly industrial, loaded with corporate offices, shopping centers, and warehouses; as you go southwest across El Camino into the hills it becomes increasingly suburban residential. As the oldest city in the area, Redwood City has the most diverse housing and well established neighborhoods. Apartments are more plentiful to the northeast, houses to the southwest. Housing is plentiful and generally less expensive than in surrounding communities, making Redwood City popular with young singles and families. The schools are as diverse as the community.

Atherton (7,200)

One of the Bay Area's most exclusive towns, Atherton consists almost exclusively of large homes, many large enough to rightfully earn the sobriquet "mansion." Minimum lot sizes are strictly enforced, and absolutely no retail businesses are allowed. In fact, about the only notable landmark in the place is Menlo College. Atherton sits quite unobtrusively on the flats between Menlo Park and Redwood City. Its elementary schools are very highly rated; older students that stay in the public school system attend Menlo Atherton High, which is not as good. Prominent resident celebrities include Gap founder Don Fisher, investment tycoon Charles Schwab, and sports stars Barry Bonds and Joe Montana. Access to Hwy 101 and I-280 is pretty good, and Atherton's CalTrain station has a residents-only parking policy.

Woodside (5,000)

Nestled in the wooded valleys of the Santa Cruz Mountains, Woodside is best known as home of the horsey set—don't be surprised by the sight of country gentry trotting down the streets on their steeds. More of a village than a town, Woodside life centers around its historic downtown. Robert's Market sits at the heart of things along Woodside Road (Hwy 84) between I-280 and Kings Mountain Road, along with the town hall and the library. There's not much else to the actual town, but the large areas of open space that surround it—Huddart, Wunderlich, and Edgewood County Parks—provide excellent trails for hiking, riding horses, and biking.

The houses are hidden in the woods and hills. Many are full-blown mansions, replete with pools and pool houses, tennis courts and tennis pavilions, and stables and even some stableboys. Despite the town's high price tag, Woodside is much quieter and less ostentatious than nearby Atherton; Woodside residents prefer the seclusion of their trees. There is a good elementary school, but older students attend Woodside High in Redwood City.

Menlo Park (28,000)

Downtown Menlo Park has a remarkable number of clock repair shops. Their customers must all come from other towns, because Menlo Park seems wholly committed to ignoring time, pinning its identity on a post-WWII vision of small-town America. The modest downtown centered around Santa Cruz Avenue still boasts old-time coffee shops serving grilled cheese sandwiches and independent pharmacies where treatments still outnumber cosmetics. Resisting the onslaught of the automobile, the town has narrowed the main thoroughfare, El Camino Real, from three lanes to two, causing an unfortunately modern inconvenience, the continuous traffic jam.

The central part of town between Middlefield Road and Alameda de las Pulgas consists primarily of quiet tree-lined streets, modest ranch homes, and small apartment complexes left from the 1950s. The area is popular with senior citizens, but many young families are attracted by the housing prices, which are somewhat below those of neighboring Palo Alto. Stanford University's influence is almost as strong here as in Palo Alto—you'll find many faculty families and quite good schools. Heading east toward Hwy 101, apartments start to outnumber houses and the character becomes more blue-collar. The area east of Hwy 101 resembles East Palo Alto, with new industrial parks growing all over. Sun Microsystems is building an enormous new corporate headquarters at the base of the Dumbarton Bridge. The western side of town has been developed into a modern townhouse community, Sharon Heights, complete with landscaped lawns and golf courses. Sand Hill Road leads to I-280 and the famous office complexes housing America's largest concentration of venture capital firms.

Portola Valley (4,300)

This tiny enclave in the Santa Cruz Mountains above Stanford provides a retreat for wealthy inhabitants to tend their gardens and horses. Surrounded by remote portions of the Stanford campus and acres of open space and parks, the seclusion is disturbed only by the packs of bicyclists who whir along the twisting mountain byways. As you might expect, housing consists primarily of large, expensive, modern homes set into the hillsides. When these houses are put up for rent, they are very popular with groups of Stanford students, especially if they have a hot tub. Schools are good, although the town is so small kids must go off to Woodside High in Redwood City.

Palo Alto (55,900)

Ever since the *San Francisco Chronicle* named Palo Alto the best place to live in the Bay Area, residents have been referring to their community as "Perfect Palo Alto." While it's supposed to be a joke, the phrase does embody a scarcely concealed smugness characteristic of Palo Alto. And why not? With its long-standing ties to neighboring Stanford University, Palo Alto has become a regional center, drawing visitors from all over the Peninsula to its many attractions. The vibrant downtown area along University Avenue between Middlefield and Alma has a remarkable number of restaurants, cafés, bookstores, and movie theaters, including the beautifully restored Stanford Theatre. (Historic teetotaler Leland Stanford would be appalled to watch young singles flock to nighttime hot spots.) Visitors are also drawn to the glittering Stanford Shopping Center, home to department stores like Neiman Marcus, omnipresent chains like the Gap, and tony boutiques like Polo and Shreve. Not many towns can offer their residents large parks like Arastradero Preserve, Foothills Park, and Palo Alto Baylands—each an oasis of solitude—but only Palo Alto would have the exclusive residents-only policy it enforces at Foothills.

As you would expect, apparent perfection has a price, and the price tags per square foot for Palo Alto houses are among the highest anywhere. Palo Alto has mature neighborhoods with diverse housing, ranging from the stately old shingled homes along the tree-lined streets south and east of downtown to bungalow cottages south of campus to boxy ranch homes and apartment complexes on both sides of El Camino Real. The high real estate prices provide a tax base that supports some of the best city services found anywhere. The school system is consistently top-rated (also reflecting Stanford's influence), and at a time when most cities are paring back essential services, Palo Alto can afford to repave cracked sidewalks. Residents are predominantly tied to either Stanford or local high-tech employers such as Hewlett-Packard, Varian, Digital, and Syntex. Residents range from Stanford students to yuppies to longtime natives, although housing costs exclude many young families from the area.

East Palo Alto (23,500)

Located on the edge of the Bay at the base of the Dumbarton Bridge, East Palo Alto was primarily ranchland until World War II. Things look different today as this small city, recently made infamous for having the nation's highest per capita murder rate, struggles with urban problems such as crack and gangs. However, marketing efforts to promote the relatively low real estate prices and ready access to the bridge have lured fast growing high-tech firms to the office parks and warehouses on the border with east Menlo Park. Discussions continue with various developers to keep this trend going, with all kinds of plans in the works for corporate headquarters, malls, and more.

One of the Peninsula's most diverse communities, the residential section of town is a mix of the people who migrated to the area in the last fifty years, especially Hispanics, Pacific Islanders, and African Americans from the southern states. Some parts of East Palo Alto are still dangerous and depressing, but the city does provide affordable housing in a region which has almost none. East Palo Alto also proves that neighbors can pull together in the face of adversity: residents have the strongest sense of community on the Peninsula. And the phenomenally wealthy neighbors have actually been a benefit of late: neighboring communities have been helping East Palo Alto by lending police support, starting innumerable community programs like school tutoring and entrepreneurship incubators, and just generally getting involved.

Mountain View (67,500)

Mountain View has recently remodeled its downtown along Castro Street between Central Expressway and El Camino Real. The makeover has included brick sidewalks, gas-lamp streetlights, and newly street-side planted trees (which bedevil would-be parallel parkers). The crowning centerpiece is the pink city hall and neighboring Center for the Performing Arts. This remodel has resulted in a restaurant boom along Castro and surrounding streets. Most of the restaurants serve some sort of Asian cuisine—Chinese, Indian, Japanese, Thai—but you can certainly find other types if you have the craving. The new downtown, combined with Mountain View's Shoreline Park—a reclaimed landfill with a large outdoor amphitheater, sailing lake, and miles of trails through marshland—is turning Mountain View into something of a regional attraction.

Mountain View's first boom occurred after WWII and was fed by employment at nearby Moffett Field Naval Air Station and NASA Ames Research Center. The Navy recently left Moffett and handed it over to NASA, but the war economy's legacy is an abundance of modest ranch homes and boxy apartment buildings. This plentiful housing stock (affordable compared to nearby Palo Alto and Los Altos) attracts a diverse mix of singles to its apartments and young families to its homes. Mountain View has been especially popular with many Hispanic immigrants. The more established neighborhoods west of El Camino and south of Castro Street resemble those in Palo Alto and Los Altos. Adding to the family-friendly character, Mountain View has pretty good elementary schools and all the necessary modern conveniences in the plentiful new strip malls. The completion of Hwy 85 provides a key link from Mountain View to other parts of Silicon Valley, making the connection from Hwy 101 to I-280 in Cupertino a breeze.

Los Altos (26,300)

Los Altos is the archetypical upper–middle-class suburb, the kind of place you might see in a Driver's Ed film. Nice family homes with well-landscaped yards dot tree-lined streets. The quaint downtown village runs along Main Street across First, Second, and Third Streets. The schools, especially the elementary ones, are excellent. Even the street signs are rustic carved wood.

However, modern times have invaded Los Altos. The coffee shops downtown are Starbucks and Peet's, the bakery is Le Boulanger, and the real retail activity occurs in the strip malls along El Camino and San Antonio Road. Most importantly, modern-day real estate values in Los Altos are exorbitant, freezing out most young families and singles. As a result, the 1990 census reported that nearly one-third of the population was 55 or older. In fact, we've heard that even families who arrived before it became unaffordable have decided to sell their homes and move someplace less expensive.

Los Altos Hills (7,500)

The rolling hills above Los Altos provide exquisite views for those fortunate enough to live here. These lucky few—average household income is triple the county average—enjoy large homes on large lots surrounded by a ring of open space preserves. If you like the outdoors, you can choose from Arastradero to the north, Foothill and Los Trancos to the west, or Monte Bello and Rancho San Antonio to the south. Some residents keep their own horses for exploring the hills. This exclusively residential community has no town center or commercial activity. In fact, the only non-residential spot in the area is Foothill College, which brings some nice performances to its auditorium. The K-12 school system also has a very good reputation. Remember that as with the other extremely exclusive communities, there are very few young adults to be found in Los Altos Hills.

Sunnyvale (117,300)

Along with Cupertino and Santa Clara, Sunnyvale lies at the heart of Silicon Valley; the city even maintains a patent library to keep the high-tech community pulsing. Vice President Al Gore singled out Sunnyvale as one of the most well-run cities in America, which is particularly impressive given that Sunnyvale is the second-largest city in the county with over 100,000 residents. The heart of this neat, well-kept city is a pair of shopping malls, TownCenter and Town & Country. For those who prefer the Main Street model, Sunnyvale's original downtown along Murphy Street (next to the CalTrain station) is experiencing a resurgence with quite a few new restaurants, cafés, and bars opening up.

As with most fast-growing American cities, the dominant housing form is the multistory condominium/town home, which is usually surrounded by enough strip malls to meet all the basic needs for food and clothing. These are mixed indiscriminately with the ubiquitous red-tile–roofed office complexes housing all those high-tech companies. While the city has a wide mix of residents, it's the young singles and young families who are most visible, especially on the tennis courts and in the pools of those condominium complexes. Housing prices are moderate by area standards (between Cupertino and Santa Clara) and there is enough of a mix to allow most people to find something in their price range. Schools are a mixed bag.

Cupertino (40,000)

The influence of Apple Computer and the high-tech economy permeates Cupertino. There aren't any futuristic monorails; rather, much of Cupertino has the look of a functional suburban boomtown, with large blocks of "townhominiums" and wide boulevards lined with an endless string of strip malls. Apple's sprawling, ever-growing complex of buildings dominates a large area of town around De Anza Boulevard south of I-280. Perhaps because it includes the foothills at the base of the Santa Cruz Mountains, Cupertino is more upscale than Sunnyvale and Santa Clara: homeowners outnumber apartment dwellers, housing is more expensive, schools better, and families older and more established. Some of the more established neighborhoods even have a "traditional suburban" feel: older trees, diverse one-story homes, and neighborhood shopping centers.

In addition to Apple and the high-tech economy, Cupertino boasts De Anza College and its Flint Center for Performing Arts, an auditorium that hosts many of the region's performing arts companies, along with the occasional national act. Just west on Stevens Creek Boulevard you'll find Vallco Fashion Park, Cupertino's main mall. The newly completed Hwy 85 has eased some of the terrible congestion on Cupertino's streets and made an easy link north to Hwy 101 and south to San Jose.

Santa Clara (92,200)

Santa Clara got a jump on the rest of Silicon Valley when the Spaniards founded Mission Santa Clara in 1777 near what was to become San Jose. Today, the mission site is home to the Jesuit-run Santa Clara University, located in a setting as close to downtown as suburbia allows, albeit quite sparse. Nearby you'll find the city hall, the Triton Museum of Art, and a CalTrain station. Currently the city is involved in a contentious effort to develop a downtown plan; it will probably be a while before any significant downtown takes shape in Santa Clara. After WWII, Santa Clara readily embraced industrial development, as exemplified by local industrial giant FMC, once Farm Machinery Corporation and now a military contractor. Santa Clara even has its own convention center to compete with San Jose. The result of all this early activity is that the residential neighborhoods are older than those in Sunnyvale and Cupertino, and the area along Hwy 101 is heavily industrialized. The numerous ethnic restaurants and shops on El Camino reflect the residents' diverse backgrounds, including large Italian and Indian populations.

Perhaps related to its older neighborhoods, or maybe related to the high level of industrial development and nearby San Jose Airport, housing in Santa Clara is more affordable than in Sunnyvale or Mountain View. The relatively affordable prices attract a wide range of residents, including young singles and families scarce in pricier towns. Families will find Santa Clara convenient to its most well-known attraction—Great America, a giant amusement park north of Hwy 101. Schools generally lag behind those of neighbors in Sunnyvale, Mountain View, and Cupertino.

San Jose (749,800)

Both within the Bay Area and beyond, San Jose suffers in the shadow of San Francisco. While it lacks San Francisco's cosmopolitan air and attitude, San Jose actually outdoes San Francisco in many ways. San Jose was California's first city and first capital; it is now the Bay Area's biggest city, sprawling far and wide across the Santa Clara Valley where nothing but orchards once flourished. Because there has been so much room to spread out, San Jose has maintained a rather suburban style and structure. Nevertheless, the ethnic diversity created by residents from all over the world, especially Latin America and Southeast Asia, makes San Jose rich in its own culture and history. Using wealth created by Silicon Valley's high-tech economy, San Jose created a glittering new downtown by redeveloping the area around Market and San Carlos Streets: in addition to many good restaurants and a lively club scene, there's the new arena that makes a home for the NHL Sharks and draws big names like Streisand and Pavarotti (neither of whom played in San Francisco). San Jose also has its own airport, museums, and performing arts companies. But along with size comes typical urban problems, and San Jose has, like most big American cities, struggled with crime, drugs, gangs, and deteriorating public schools.

As with any large city, housing is diverse. San Jose reflects its rapid post-WWII growth; its subdivisions show representatives from each decade, the 50s ranch homes to the modern "townhominiums." Prices are extremely variable from neighborhood to neighborhood, but generally lower than other Peninsula and South Bay cities. Perhaps reflecting its rapid growth, San Jose has far more children and far fewer older residents than its neighbors. All these children put a lot of pressure on the school system, which does a pretty good job by city standards. But, as you would expect in such a diverse area, schools are quite variable. Also typical of such a sprawling city, San Jose has terrible traffic problems and attendant smog. Recent improvements include a new light rail system and Hwy 85, connecting southern San Jose with Cupertino and Sunnyvale.

Campbell (36,000)

Campbell's ragged border with San Jose—which almost surrounds it—makes it look like it was captured by a giant amoeba. Nevertheless, Campbell has carved out its own niche as an archetypically quiet, middle-class suburban community. It offers plenty of housing at lower prices than in most other Silicon Valley towns, giving Campbell a younger population than more established South Bay communities. Schools are variable but adequate. To keep its fresh face and increase its retail base, Campbell is planning to redevelop the downtown area. The name of the PruneYard shopping center is one of Campbell's few ties to its pre-war life as a fruit farming community.

Monte Sereno (3,100)

Both the smallest city and southernmost prestige community in Santa Clara County, Monte Sereno occupies a protected enclave between Saratoga and Los Gatos. Most of the details on housing, demographics, and so forth from Saratoga and Los Altos Hills apply to Monte Sereno as well. Its character is closer to those of Saratoga and Los Altos Hills, although its commercial needs are met by nearby Los Gatos.

Saratoga (28,000)

This former logging and resort town has become one of the South Bay's most exclusive residential communities. Saratoga's location on the edge of the Santa Cruz Mountains, on the way to Saratoga Gap and Big Basin, once made it convenient for loggers and vacationers and now gives residents a nearby escape to the many parks along Skyline Drive. Two estates located in the hills above town, The Mountain Winery and Villa Montalvo, feature popular summer programs in their outdoor amphitheaters (see the *Arts & Entertainment* section for more information). In addition to the performances, Villa Montalvo actually has a large villa surrounded by nature trails and redwood groves. The villa is now used as an artists' sanctuary; a gallery displays many of the artists' works to the public. Another nearby park, Hakone Gardens, houses a replica of a 17th-century Zen garden. Downtown you'll find a quaint retail strip along Big Basin Way with lots of pricey Continental restaurants, boutiques, and antique shops. In Saratoga, even the strip malls have wooden buildings instead of concrete slabs.

It's hard to tell what houses in Saratoga look like because they all seem to be hidden behind fences, especially in the flatter parts of town. While most seem to be expensive single-family homes, they are modest compared to the mansions common in other exclusive hillside communities. As you would expect in a community with few rental properties and high housing prices, there are more older residents and fewer young singles and families than down in the Valley. For those that can afford it, the schools are excellent. While Saratoga is a bit secluded at the edge of the Santa Clara Valley, the recent completion of Hwy 85 provides a quick route north to Cupertino and east to San Jose.

Los Gatos (27,400)

Los Gatos has quieted down since the days when it was a rowdy logging town and stagecoach stop at the edge of the mountains. Fortunately, on its way to becoming a pricey bedroom community, it maintained many of its historic buildings, including those in the downtown area. Nature did try its own urban renewal when the Loma Prieta quake in 1989 damaged many of the town's historic structures, but most of the damage has been repaired. In keeping with the theme, Los Gatos puts its shopping malls in historic buildings: Old Town Shopping Plaza is housed in an old grammar school.

Most schools in Los Gatos have fared better, and today they are considered excellent. While housing is generally expensive, there is enough variety in the size and types of units available for rent and sale to allow access to newcomers. Consequently, you'll find more young adults in Los Gatos than in Saratoga or Los Altos. Improved access to the rest of the Valley via newly completed Hwy 85 should make commuting easier, but could threaten the town's funky individuality.

Milpitas (48,100)

Milpitas marks the border between Santa Clara Country and Alameda County. As such, it represents a mix of high-tech (Santa Clara) and suburbia (Alameda). Historically a blue-collar community, Milpitas has attracted numerous high-tech production facilities to its ever-growing industrial parks, and median income is relatively high. Perhaps by selling residents' discretionary income Milpitas has also promoted unparalleled retail development: In addition to drawing Wal-Mart and just about every other large American retailer, Milpitas managed to have an old Ford plant converted into the Great Mall of America, the country's biggest shopping mall.

Milpitas remains a rapidly growing, relatively new community, with plenty of housing at the lowest prices around. This combination has resulted in a community with very few elderly residents, but what Milpitas lacks in age diversity, it makes up for in ethnic diversity. Unfortunately, Milpitas's transportation system has not kept up with its growth, and traffic on Hwy 880 and Hwy 237 is some of the worst in the entire Bay Area. As an unfortunate consequence of being on the border of Santa Clara and Alameda counties, BART stops just north in Fremont, and Santa Clara Light Rail Transit only travels to the south, in San Jose. The schools are variable, but generally lag behind county averages.

ATTRACTIONS

In general, the Peninsula and San Jose are places where real people live and work, rather than famous tourist destinations like San Francisco. But what happens when you, the Peninsula resident, get the dreaded Visitors From Out of Town? They come into your house, take over your living room, and suddenly assume that you're the final word on everything worth seeing or doing in the area. Well, the end is not at hand—you're in control. With the *Good Life* on your side, you can impress any parent or grade-school rival. Most of the *Good Life* is filled with interesting and exciting activities, from highbrow arts to lowbrow amusements, from museums to sports, from day trips to weekend—or even week-long—getaways. But for those hard-to-please guests who want real tourist attractions, the kind that come with colorful brochures and their own postcards, we've compiled the following list of attractions. Even hardened locals might be surprised to discover something new here.

Filoli House and Gardens: Cañada Rd., Woodside, (415) 364-2880. Built as a country retreat by San Francisco silver magnate William B. Bourn, Filoli (as in "To **FI**ght, to **LO**ve, to **LI**ve") became famous as the mansion in the opening shot of the 80s television series *Dynasty*. Designed by the famous San Francisco architect Willis Polk and completed in 1917, the clematis-draped brick building was deeded to the National Trust for Historic Preservation in 1975. Unsupervised tours of the 43-room mansion on its 654-acre estate give you the opportunity to roam through the house at your own pace and linger in the various grand salons. The gardens, now reaching maturity, are laid out as a succession of "rooms," each having its own design and personality. Throughout the seasons, the plantings provide an ever-changing palette of brilliant color nestled against the Santa Cruz Mountains. • Guided tours by reservation Feb. to Nov. Tu-Th, Sa; call for current hours. Self-guided tours F 10am-2pm. $8.

Lick Observatory: Mount Hamilton Rd. (off Alum Rock Rd.), San Jose, (408) 274-5061. The Observatory was created over 100 years ago by James Lick, a millionaire obsessed with the idea of life on the moon and gathering his own proof. After San Francisco rejected his plans, he built it on Mount Hamilton. It takes about an hour to climb the windy road to the observatory by car, but the guided tours of the telescopes and their views are quite interesting. • M-F 12:30pm-5pm; Sa-Su 10am-5pm. Free.

NASA/Ames Research Center: Moffett Field (off Hwy 101), Mountain View, (415) 604-6497. Tour NASA's field laboratory and see a wind tunnel, gigantic flight hangar, and flight simulator laboratory. The two-hour tour covers about two miles. • Tours by reservation only. Free.

Ralston Hall: College of Notre Dame, 1500 Ralston Ave., Belmont, (415) 508-3501. Take an historic tour of this 80-room Victorian mansion, now part of the College of Notre Dame. The first floor is filled with authentic 19th-century antiques. • Tours for groups of 4 to 40 by appointment, Tu-F 9am-3pm. $5.

Stanford Linear Accelerator (SLAC): 2575 Sand Hill Rd., Menlo Park, (415) 926-2204. Tour the two-mile electron accelerator and receive a crash course in particle physics. Tours take two hours. • Tours by reservation. Free.

Stanford University Campus Tours: Visitor Information Center, Stanford Quadrangle, Palm Dr., Stanford Campus, (415) 723-2560. Let friendly student guides familiarize you with the campus. Bubbling over with information and anecdotes about campus history, guides lead an hour-long stroll by such campus landmarks as Memorial Church (restored following damage in the '89 quake) and the Rodin Sculpture Garden, featuring numerous works by the namesake sculptor (including the haunting *Gates of Hell*). • Tours daily 11am and 3:15pm, except during finals week, between sessions, and on some holidays. Free.

Sunset Magazine: 80 S. Willow Rd., Menlo Park, (415) 321-3600. Follow a self-guided tour of the magazine's test kitchens and gardens. • M-F 10:30am, 2:30pm. Free.

Villa Montalvo: 15400 Montalvo Rd. (off Hwy 9), Saratoga, (408) 741-3421. An Italian Renaissance-style villa built in the redwoods for Senator James Phelan, who bequeathed it for use as an artists' sanctuary. The gallery displays some of the artists' works to the public. Outside, nature trails wind through redwood groves where the villa hosts a performance series in its outdoor amphitheater. • M-F 8am-5pm; Sa-Su, holidays 9am-5pm. Free.

Wineries: While they lack the notoriety of wineries in Napa and Sonoma, South Bay wineries offer a closer opportunity to taste a variety of excellent wines in a more intimate setting. And don't underestimate the quality of these wines—Ridge in particular is known for its world-class reds. For additional information, contact the **Santa Clara Valley Wine Growers Association** at (408) 778-1555 or the **Santa Cruz Mountain Winegrowers Association** at (408) 479-9463.

David Bruce: 21439 Bear Creek Rd. (off Hwy 17), Los Gatos, (408) 354-4214. Picnic facilities. • Tasting W-Su noon-5pm. Free.

J. Lohr: 1000 Lenzen Ave., San Jose, (408) 288-5057. Tasting daily 10am-5pm; free. Tours Sa-Su 11am, 2pm.

Mirassou Champagne Cellars: 300 College Ave., Los Gatos, (408) 395-3790. • Tasting W-Su noon-5pm. Tours daily 1:30pm, 3:30pm. Free.

Mirassou Vineyards: 3000 Aborn Rd., San Jose, (408) 274-4000. • Tasting M-Sa noon-5pm, Su noon-4pm. Free.

Ridge Vineyards: 17100 Monte Bello Rd., Cupertino, (408) 867-3233. Picnic facilities. • Tasting Sa, Su 11am-3pm. Free.

Sunrise Winery: 13100 Monte Bello Rd., Cupertino, (408) 741-1310. Picnic facilities. • Tasting F-Su 11am-3pm. Free.

HOTELS AND INNS

Tariffs listed below are for the standard corporate rate during the week. Many hotels have a variety of rates, offering much more luxurious and expensive suites as well as discounts for weekends, big corporations, frequent flyers, AAA members, and more.

Brisbane to San Mateo

Best Western El Rancho Inn: 1100 El Camino Real, Millbrae, (415) 588-8500. This large motor inn has the pink-flamingos look to go with the pools, but the rooms are modern enough and it's cheaper than the airport hotels on the Bay. $75.

Crown Sterling Suites Hotel: 150 Anza Blvd., Burlingame, (415) 342-4600. A huge airport hotel on the Bay. As the name implies, all rooms are suites with separate living room area including refrigerator, coffee-maker, microwave, and sink. $123-$159.

Doubletree Hotel San Francisco Airport: 835 Airport Blvd., Burlingame, (415) 344-5500. A standard no-frills airport hotel. $109-$119.

Holiday Inn Express: 350 N. Bayshore Blvd., San Mateo, (415) 344-6376. Your basic motel, convenient to Hwy 101 and downtown San Mateo. $60-$70.

Hyatt Regency San Francisco Airport: 1333 Old Bayshore Hwy., Burlingame, (415) 347-1234 or (800) 233-1234. Classic Hyatt, with a large atrium lobby. Standard business-luxe rooms. $159-$184.

Marriott San Francisco Airport: 1800 Old Bayshore Hwy., Burlingame, (415) 692-9100 or (800) 228-9290. This comfortable upscale business hotel has a surprise—you can rent mountain bikes for local explorations along the Bay. $135.

Westin San Francisco Airport: 1 Old Bayshore Hwy., Millbrae, (415) 692-3500. A big airport conference hotel with a pool, spa, business services, and the like. $145-$165.

Belmont to Mountain View

Best Western Executive Suites: 25 Fifth Ave., Redwood City, (415) 366-5794, (800) 785-0005. Comfortable, affordable rooms. Amenities include an exercise and steam room, a sauna, and an outdoor hot tub. Other niceties include complimentary continental breakfast, coffee makers in each room, and cable TV. $75-$90.

Best Western Mountain View Inn: 2300 El Camino Real, Mountain View, (415) 962-9912, (800) 785-0005. All the newly redecorated rooms and suites are tastefully furnished and include a refrigerator, microwave, coffee maker, and sitting areas. Enjoy your complimentary continental breakfast and then sweat it off in the pool and fitness center. $79.

The Cardinal Hotel: 235 Hamilton Ave., Palo Alto, (415) 323-5101. This hotel features a famous, high-ceilinged Spanish-style great hall of a lobby with its buffed tile floor and baronial light fixtures. The hotel has been remodeled and the rooms sport a bright and cheerful new look, not to mention that they're clean and well kept. $45-$175.

Cowper Inn: 705 Cowper Ave., Palo Alto, (415) 327-4475. Want sublime, leafy, antiquey, New England ambiance? They provide porches for smokers and sherry in the parlor for everyone. $55-$105.

Glass Slipper Motel: 3941 El Camino Real, Palo Alto, (415) 493–6611. Unquestionably the cheapest (and some might say cheesiest) rooms around, all decorated Disneyland-style. This kind of kitsch you should experience at least once. $40.

Garden Court Hotel: 520 Cowper St., Palo Alto, (415) 322–9000. This is undoubtedly the executive choice in downtown Palo Alto. All those handsome young men in livery parking cars and hauling luggage will make any guest feel like a visiting dignitary. The rooms are pleasant and overscale, outfitted with expensive (if somewhat standard) designer touches. Best of all, the room service is catered by Il Fornaio, one of Palo Alto's finest restaurants. $175-$195.

Holiday Inn Palo Alto: 625 El Camino Real, Palo Alto, (415) 328–2800. The hotel recently underwent a major renovation, and rooms are still in pristine condition. There's a splendid pool in the courtyard, as well as Japanese water gardens on the grounds. The inn is just across El Camino from Stanford and thus often booked up, so plan ahead. $119–$144.

Hotel California: 2431 Ash St., Palo Alto, (415) 322–7666. Each room is a bit different from the other, and each is attractively furnished with brass beds and the like. Breakfast is purchased at Harlan's Bakery downstairs using vouchers given out by the hotel. There's a center patio, a communal kitchen complete with microwave, a coin-operated washer and dryer, and a place to iron. $48–$60.

Hotel Sofitel San Francisco Bay: 223 Twin Dolphin Dr., Redwood City, (415) 598-9000, (800) 221-4542. A big, corporate hotel close to all the new industrial development along the Bay, especially Oracle (which gets special rates). $150.

Hyatt Rickeys: 4219 El Camino Real, Palo Alto, (415) 493–8000. A luxury hotel with all of the expected frills, Hyatt Rickeys is sprawled over 22 acres of landscaped grounds in buildings from three to six stories high. $109–$190.

Menlo Park Inn: 1315 El Camino Real, Menlo Park, (415) 326-7530. Centrally located and newly renovated, Menlo Park Inn has refrigerators, VCRs, and microwaves in the rooms and a complimentary continental breakfast. $80.

Residence Inn Mountain View: 1854 W. El Camino Real, Mountain View, (415) 940-1300. A Marriott property, this hotel is all suites and penthouses with working fireplaces. Guests are coddled with complimentary cocktails, valet laundry service, a "sport court," and a health club. 1–6 nights $139, 7–29 nights $129, 30 nights $104.

Stanford Park Hotel: 100 El Camino Real, Menlo Park, (415) 322–1234. A shingled brick and oak building that conjures up images of ye olde English inn. Somehow this luxury hotel feels as quiet as a country inn, despite that fact that it's smack dab on El Camino Real. The Stanford Park is very convenient to the Stanford Shopping Center and campus. $180.

San Jose & South Bay

Best Western Downtown: 455 S. Second St., San Jose, (408) 298-3500. A basic downtown motel—more economical than the historic landmarks. $70.

Cupertino Inn: 10889 N. De Anza Blvd., Cupertino, (408) 996-7700. The Cupertino is very convenient for those trips to Apple Computer. Rates include breakfast and afternoon hors d'oeuvres. $118-$133.

The Fairmont: 170 S. Market St., San Jose, (408) 998-1900. The centerpiece to San Jose's downtown redevelopment boasts over 500 luxury rooms, a rooftop pool, fitness center, and a variety of restaurants. $190-$200.

The Hensley House: 456 N. Third St., San Jose, (408) 298-3537. This Victorian B&B in downtown San Jose can offer you private bathrooms, gourmet breakfasts, and afternoon hors d'oeuvres. $75-$125.

Hotel De Anza: 233 W. Santa Clara St., San Jose, (408) 286-1000. A national historic landmark, this art deco hotel was recently restored as part of the renovation of downtown San Jose. $145.

Hotel Sainte Claire: 302 S. Market St., San Jose, (408) 295-2000 or (800) 824-6835. This recently remodeled historic hotel is smaller than the Fairmont and quite luxurious. The Spanish-tiled interior courtyard offers a distinctive touch, and the hotel houses a branch of the Il Fornaio restaurant chain. $120-$155.

The Inn at Saratoga: 20645 Fourth St., Saratoga, (408) 867-5020, (800) 543-5020 (within CA), or (800) 338-5020 (outside CA). Both business travelers and vacationers looking for a spa retreat will enjoy this tasteful, romantic inn overlooking Saratoga Creek. $145.

Madison Street Inn: 1390 Madison St., Santa Clara, (408) 249-5541. Period furnishings give this small Victorian B&B its charm, while modern touches such as a pool, hot tub, and excellent breakfasts add to the appeal. $60-$85.

Motel 6: 2560 Fontaine Rd., San Jose, (408) 270-3131. Your basic motel—it's cheap and south of downtown near Hwy 101 and Tully Road. $40.

San Jose Hilton and Towers: 300 Almaden Blvd., San Jose, (408) 287-2100 or (800) HILTONS. One of the newest big hotels, the San Jose Hilton was built to serve the new convention center. $110-$160.

Santa Clara Marriott: 2700 Mission College Blvd., Santa Clara, (408) 988-1500. If you're heading to a convention in Santa Clara, this big corporate hotel can easily take care of you. $139-$154.

Wyndham Garden: 1300 Chesapeake Ter., Sunnyvale, (408) 747-0999. Have a craving for a nice business hotel with pool, spa, etc.? Try the Wyndham, located near the Lawrence Expressway and Hwy 237, not far from Santa Clara Convention Center (or Great America if you have children). $99.

GETTING SETTLED

The Peninsula and South Bay is a largely suburban, residential area; the locals shop primarily in large, regional malls and ubiquitous neighborhood strip malls. Nevertheless, many downtown areas near CalTrain stations have been revived into viable shopping districts reminiscent of the 1800s. You won't find huge stores like Macy's or J.C. Penny in any of these downtowns, but you will find many unique shops and boutiques, as well as plenty of cafés and restaurants.

Serramonte Shopping Center: 3 Serramonte Ctr., Serramonte and Callan Blvds., Daly City, (415) 992-8686. This large mall even packs them in from San Francisco for tenants like Macy's, Mervyn's, and Montgomery Ward.

Downtown Burlingame: Burlingame Ave. (between El Camino Real and California Dr.), Burlingame. The hottest downtown in the area attracts a bustle of strollers and shoppers to its ever-growing list of cafés and shops. Even San Francisco celebrity chefs are moving in, with Reed Herron opening a bright blue Café Marimba.

Hillsdale Shopping Center: El Camino Real and Hillsdale Blvd., San Mateo, (415) 345-8222. Hillsdale offers Macy's, Sears, Nordstrom, Emporium, and Mervyn's as anchor stores. This enclosed mall was recently renovated, and is a major draw in the northern Peninsula.

Stanford Shopping Center: El Camino Real and Quarry Rd., Palo Alto, (415) 617-8585. The Stanford Shopping Center is to compulsive shoppers what a casino is to gamblers—a Mecca of temptation. You'll find a staggering assortment of upscale stores such as Ralph Lauren, Neiman Marcus, and Saks Fifth Avenue, as well as more modest department stores like Macy's, Nordstrom, and Emporium. There are also many smaller specialty boutiques like The Gap, The Limited, and The Nature Company, plus a few that aren't even part of a chain. When you're tired of running up the credit card, stop off for a cappuccino at an outdoor café on the Street Market, one corner of the outdoor mall that boasts a trompe l'oeil wall painted like a quaint French street.

Downtown Palo Alto: University Ave. (between Alma St. and Middlefield Rd.), Palo Alto. New restaurants and cafés seem to open up daily amidst the wide variety of bookstores, specialty shops, eateries, and movie theaters. Day or night, downtown is full of people. Downtown bookstores include Stacey's (which has one of the most up-to-date stocks of books by local authors), and Bell's Books, with its fascinating collection of rare books and old manuscripts. While you can find just about everything downtown, from hand lotion to contemporary art, you will be hard-pressed to shop for clothes there.

Town and Country Village: El Camino Real and Embarcadero Rd., Palo Alto, (415) 325-3266. • Stevens Creek Blvd. and Winchester Blvd., San Jose, (408) 345-4670. • Washington and Mathilda Aves., Sunnyvale, (408) 736-6654. These open-air shopping centers share a folksy, 1950s-style wood exterior. A mix of small retail establishments, ranging from women's and men's specialty shops, to jewelry stores and delicatessens, can be found along the corridors. There are also a number of travel agencies and ticketing offices for most major airlines.

Castro Street Mountain View: Castro St. (between Central Expwy. and El Camino Real), Mountain View. Several years ago, Mountain View completely restored Castro Street. At first, it looked a little new, a little forced, but it has now developed its own identity as Gourmet Gulch (because of the abundance and variety of restaurants that line the street). You'll also find a number of specialty shops on Castro Street, including several interesting Chinese markets. Good news—the Castro Street branch of Printers Inc. bookstore has expanded and added an outdoor café.

Sunnyvale TownCenter: 2502 Town Center Ln., Sunnyvale, (408) 245-6585. The major anchors are Macy's, Montgomery Ward, and J.C. Penny at this smaller regional mall with a tiny, redwood-filled courtyard so shoppers can find tranquility during breaks.

Vallco Fashion Park: I-280 and Wolfe Rd., Cupertino, (408) 255-5660. Vallco doesn't have the ambiance of the Stanford Shopping Center, but it does have an ice-skating rink! Here, you'll find more than 175 stores on parquet wood floors, set amid lavish landscaping. Three stores—Emporium, Sears, and J.C. Penney—provide the mooring for a wide variety of shops and restaurants.

Valley Fair Shopping Center: Stevens Creek Blvd. and I-880, San Jose, (408) 248-4451. Valley Fair makes a close relative to Vallco Fashion with its similar stores and similar eats. Valley Fair is one of the largest indoor malls around, complete with a handy "food terrace." Macy's was the first store built on the site, and in its early days the department store used to run a small carnival on its roof—hence the name.

Oakridge Mall: Santa Teresa Blvd. and Blossom Hill Rd., San Jose, (408) 578-2910. This smaller mall's major tenants include Macy's, Nordstrom, and Montgomery Ward.

The PruneYard: Bascom Ave. and Campbell Ave., Campbell, (408) 371-4700. This picturesque shopping center's name recalls the era when Campbell was filled with orchards. Now mostly smaller and specialty shops fill the Pruneyard.

Downtown Saratoga: Big Basin Way, Saratoga. An assortment of upscale specialty shops, clothing and antique stores await Saratoga shoppers.

BANKS

Deciding on a bank account is one of the most confusing decisions of modern life. We all need one, but there are so many choices and so many options. Unfortunately, consumer groups claim that California has the least consumer-friendly banking in the nation. While most people choose their bank based on its location, you can call several to see which offers the best deal; most banks offer an ever-changing variety of accounts, one of which is bound to meet your needs. Keep these generalities in mind while you make your decision.

Most banks charge a fee when you use their ATM card at a different bank's machine, so consider which ATMs are most convenient to you. Bank of America has the most ATMs in California; Wells Fargo is second in the state. The Peninsula has a host of slightly smaller chains, such as Citibank and First Interstate, as well as many local banks. These smaller banks offer policies which—whether catering to wealthier customers or students—are likely to be different than those of the big banks and should be thoroughly considered.

BOOKSTORES

Although it's San Francisco that is reputed to be the most literary city in the country, bookworms needn't venture beyond our own Peninsula. Although the national chains— Barnes & Noble, B. Dalton, Waldenbooks, and Crown Books—dominate the local mall scene, independent bookstores and used-book dealers can be found in Palo Alto, Menlo Park, and beyond.

A Clean Well Lighted Place For Books: Oaks Shopping Center, 21269 Stevens Creek Blvd., Cupertino, (408) 255-7600. This large, modern store is the South Bay outpost of a well-regarded Bay Area trio of stores. As the name implies, it's well organized and packed with books; just don't look for any dusty corners to sit in while browsing poetry.

B. Dalton Bookseller: 20510 Stevens Creek Blvd., Cupertino, (408) 257-5530. • Eastridge Shopping Center, Tully Rd. and Capitol Expwy., San Jose, (408) 270-1070. • Oakridge Mall, Santa Teresa Blvd. and Blossom Hill Rd., San Jose, (408) 226-0387. • Valley Fair Shopping Center, Stevens Creek Blvd. and I-880, San Jose, (408) 246-6760. National chain.

Barnes and Noble: 1940 S. El Camino Real, San Mateo, (415) 312-9066. • Sequoia Station, 1091 El Camino Real, Redwood City, (415) 299-0117. • Hamilton Plaza, 1650 Bascom Ave., Campbell, (408) 369-9808. • 3600 Stevens Creek Blvd., San Jose, (408) 984-3495. National chain.

Books Inc.: Stanford Shopping Center, El Camino Real and Quarry Rd., Palo Alto, (415) 321-0600. • Town & Country Village, Stevens Creek Blvd. and Winchester Blvd., San Jose, (408) 243-6262. This local chain is one of the oldest booksellers in California, and no wonder: One-quarter of their stock is always 50 to 90 percent off. Chefs should investigate the substantial cookbook selection.

Crown Books: 332 Gellert Blvd., Daly City, (415) 994-7990. • Super Crown, 765 Broadway, Millbrae, (415) 697-3224. • 121 E. Fourth Ave., San Mateo, (415) 579-1184. • 57 El Camino Real, San Carlos, (415) 595-2811. • 4500 El Camino Real, Los Altos, (415) 949-1044. • Super Crown, 789 E. El Camino Real, Sunnyvale, (408) 732-7057. • 1234 W. El Camino Real, Sunnyvale, (408) 732-8007. • Super Crown, 19640 Stevens Creek Blvd., Cupertino, (408) 973-8100. • Super Crown, Main St. Shopping Ctr., Santa Teresa Blvd. and Blossom Hill Rd., San Jose, (408) 629-1033. • Westgate Shopping Ctr., 1600 Saratoga Ave., San Jose, (408) 374-9283. • 37 N. Santa Cruz Ave, Los Gatos, (408) 395-9449. National chain specializing in discounted bestsellers.

Heintzelman's Bookstore: 205 State St., Los Altos, (415) 941-1842. An attentive staff and a friendly cat tend to customers at this small general bookstore.

Kepler's Books: 1010 El Camino Real, Menlo Park, (415) 324-4321. Kepler's boasts an enormous and literary fiction selection that attracts readers from all over the South Bay and doubles as a hangout for literary types. Tables and chairs accommodate hard-core browsers, while the more decisive can devour their purchases at the popular Café Borrone next door. Kepler's also sponsors frequent readings and book signings by visiting authors, all free. Kepler's Annex, on the other side of the café, sells remaindered books at bargain prices.

Linden Tree Children's Records and Books: 170 State St., Los Altos, (415) 949-3390. Features a large collection of children's books, records, and tapes.

Phileas Fogg's Books, Maps & More for the Traveler: Stanford Shopping Ctr., El Camino Real and Quarry Rd., Palo Alto, (415) 327-1754. If you're going on a journey, make this your first stop. It's worth it for the extensive map and guidebook selection.

Printers Inc.: 310 California Ave., Palo Alto, (415) 327-6500. • 301 Castro St., Mountain View, (415) 961-8500. This revered pair of stores boasts a large literature collection offering titles from both mainstream and small presses, a separate room for poetry and literary theory, and a large travel section. The Palo Alto shop has added a large café next door, and the Mountain View shop has a new outdoor patio. Printers Inc. also sponsors frequent readings and book signings by visiting authors, all free and open to one and all.

Stacey's Bookstore: 219 University Ave., Palo Alto, (415) 326-0681. • 19625 Stevens Creek Blvd., Cupertino, (408) 253-7521. The business reference book selection is what gives this small local chain its reputation.

Tower Books: 2727 S. El Camino Real, San Mateo, (415) 570-7444. • 630 San Antonio Rd., Mountain View, (415) 941-7300. Like neighboring Tower Records, Tower Books is open every day of the year, and all best-sellers are always discounted 30 percent. As you might expect, Tower also has a good selection of books on tape.

Waldenbooks: Serramonte Shopping Ctr., Serramonte and Callan Blvds., Daly City, (415) 755-3373. • Tanforan Park, 1150 El Camino Real, San Bruno, (415) 583-7717. • 1354 Burlingame Ave., Burlingame, (415) 343-4231. • TownCenter, 2754 TownCenter Ln., Sunnyvale, (408) 739-9000. • Vallco Shopping Ctr., 10123 N. Wolfe Rd., Cupertino, (408) 255-0602. • Pavilion Mall, 150 S. First St., San Jose, (408) 292-6416. • Eastridge Shopping Ctr., Tully Rd. and Capitol Expwy., San Jose, (408) 274-1301. National chain with smaller stores.

Used and Specialty

Ananda Book Buyers: 317 Castro St., Mountain View, (415) 968-READ. Ananda has an ample fiction section that emphasizes mystery and sci-fi, as well as an eclectic mix of just about everything else.

Bell's Books: 536 Emerson St., Palo Alto, (415) 323-7822. Search through several rooms of tightly packed floor-to-ceiling bookshelves for specialties like literary biographies and books on horticulture, history, and Christianity. Bell's, the oldest bookstore in Palo Alto (established in 1935), is a refined store—quality used and rare books live here; grungy paperbacks do not. Call first to sell.

Recycle Book Store: 138 E. Santa Clara St., San Jose, (408) 286-6275. This large store with an especially strong sci-fi selection also features a good collection of used hardcovers.

Wessex Books: 558 Santa Cruz Ave., Menlo Park, (415) 321-1333. Wessex has an outstanding fiction selection, and the philosophy and history sections are also good.

FOOD

Grocery Stores

The local grocery scene is dominated by two giants, Safeway and Lucky. They each have stores in virtually every city on the Peninsula. The stores vary quite a bit in size and selection, with newer stores typically much larger than older ones. Generally, Safeway stores tend to be a little more upscale, while Lucky stores tend to be a little less expensive. Most branches of both chains are open 24 hours a day. In addition to the giants, Bell Market and Petrini's are local chains with an area presence; Bell is mainstream, while Petrini's is upscale. Many neighborhoods have preserved small, independent grocers, as well as a range of specialty, ethnic, and health food stores. Many cities also hold weekend farmers' markets from spring through the fall. Finally, virtually any store in California can sell alcoholic beverages, so don't be surprised to see a beer cooler in your drug store or rare, expensive wines in your neighborhood supermarket.

Specialty Markets

Beltramo's: 1540 El Camino Real, Menlo Park, (415) 325-2806. Beltramo's claims to have "one of the world's largest and finest selections of wines and spirits," stocks over 3,500 wines, and has one of the broadest selections of beer around.

Cosentino's Vegetable Haven: South Bascom and Union Aves., San Jose, (408) 377-6661. • 3521 Homestead Rd., Santa Clara, (408) 243-9005. For South Bay denizens, Cosentino's is *the* food emporium. In addition to the high-quality vegetables, Cosentino's has a great selection of bulk items, gourmet goods, and ethnic goodies—look for quinoa, couscous, gourmet mustards, and a good selection of olive oils.

Cost Plus: 785 Serramonte Blvd., Colma, (415) 994-7090. • Hillsdale Mall, El Camino Real and Hillsdale Blvd., San Mateo, (415) 341-7474. • 1910 El Camino Real, Mountain View, (415) 961-6066. • 4050 Stevens Creek Blvd., San Jose, (408) 247-3333. • Blossom Hill Rd. and Almaden Expwy., San Jose, (408) 267-6666. A bargain Mecca for fine wines, coffees, teas, and imported foods.

Draeger's Supermarket: 1010 University Dr., Menlo Park, (415) 688-0677. • 342 First Street, Los Altos, (415) 948-4425. This upscale food emporium has a full-service butcher, an above-average produce department, and an extensive wine section. Draeger's carries a nice selection of domestic and imported cheeses. Draeger's also has a wonderful selection of European goods, including a score of olive oils, gourmet mustard, fine vinegars, and a stupendous deli. The Menlo Park location is larger.

Fiesta Latina: 1424 Cary Ave., San Mateo, (415) 343-0193. A very complete Latin American produce and dry goods market with many hard-to-find items. Fresh produce includes plantains, yucca, taro roots, and various fruits. Fiesta Latina also stocks frozen fruit concentrates, including tamarind and guanabana. Their selection of dried chilies is also good. Among the Filipino products you'll find pancit and coconut vinegar.

Halal Meats Deli & Grocery: 1538 Saratoga-Sunnyvale Rd., San Jose, (408) 865-1222. The highlight here is the halal butcher with good chicken, lamb, goat, and beef. The produce section is small. They also carry lawash, sumac, pomegranate molasses, sour cherry syrup, couscous, and basmati rice.

La Costeña: 2078 Old Middlefield Way, Mountain View, (415) 967-0507. La Costeña carries many hard-to-find Latin American products, especially Mexican and Salvadoran ones. They also carry Colombian papa criolla and Peruvian ullucos. La Costeña has an excellent selection of dried chilies and Mexican herbs, including epazote. They even have a small produce section with fresh yucca and plantains.

Monterey Market: Stanford Shopping Ctr., El Camino Real and Quarry Rd., Palo Alto, (415) 329-1340. People who seek out good produce and value prices swear by this festive market. The fresh, colorful offerings include Latin American staples like plantains and guava, and Asian essentials like bok choy and Chinese green beans (not to mention a good variety of exotic mushrooms). The prices are hard to beat for such top-of-the-line produce.

New Castro Market: 340 Castro St., Mountain View, (415) 962-8899. One of the best markets anywhere in the Bay Area for Asian groceries. The highlight of the store is probably the fish and meat department, which is as complete as any in the Bay Area. There is fresh fish and seafood especially for sushi. The noodle section fills an entire aisle with noodles from Taiwan, Japan, Viet-nam, Thailand, and Korea. Other highlights include various chili sauces, numerous fish sauces, and many varieties of soy sauces.

Nishioka Brothers Fish Market: 665 N. Sixth St., San Jose, (408) 295-2985. A complete Japanese food store with a wonderful selection of fresh and frozen fish for sushi.

Noah's Bagels: 1152 Burlingame Ave., Burlingame, (415) 342-8423. • 1067 El Camino Real, Redwood City, (415) 299-9050. • 278 University Ave., Palo Alto, (415) 473-0751. • 15996 Los Gatos Blvd., Los Gatos, (408) 358-5895. Noah's has attracted almost fanatical devotion from fans of its almost-but-not-quite New York bagels. Noah's has an extensive offering of bagel fixings. Look for a new store opening on Santa Cruz Avenue in Menlo Park.

Oakville Grocery: Stanford Shopping Center, El Camino Real and Quarry Rd., Palo Alto, (415) 328-9000. Another upscale food emporium with a particularly nice wine selection (the proprietor owns the Joseph Phelps vineyard). The Oakville Grocery carries a fine selection of domestic and imported cheeses at high prices, along with excellent breads and crackers. Well over a dozen olive oils, other gourmet oils such walnut and avocado, numerous vinegars, and dried exotic mushrooms can be found on these tempting shelves.

Peet's Coffee and Tea: 1309 Burlingame Ave., Burlingame, (415) 548-0494. • 899 Santa Cruz Ave., Menlo Park, (415) 325-8989. • 153 Homer Ave., Palo Alto, (415) 325-2091. • 367 State St., Los Altos, (415) 941-6722. • 798-1 Blossom Hill Rd., Los Gatos, (408) 358-6311. Alfred Peet introduced Bay Area residents to premium coffee and tea blends from all over the world long before Starbucks took over the West Coast. They also stock a good selection of espresso makers, mugs, and tea kettles.

Race Street Fish & Poultry: 1935 W. El Camino Real, Mountain View, (415) 964-5811. Like the truly excellent fish and poultry market that it is, Race Street carries a great selection of seafood including crab, crawfish, shrimp, squid, octopus, oysters, mussels, and live lobsters. If you want chicken, rabbit, or duck, you got it, and Race Street can also handle special orders for game meats such as pheasant and quail.

San Bruno Supermarket: 2480 San Bruno Ave., San Francisco, (415) 468-5788. A true gem—a supermarket with an excellent assortment of Asian goods and products. The produce section is complete and carries fresh galangal, Thai eggplant, Japanese squash, bitter melon, and various Chinese cabbages. The meat department has a good selection of beef, pork, lamb, and chicken as well as some fresh fish.

Schaub's Meat, Fish & Poultry: Stanford Shopping Ctr., El Camino Real and Quarry Rd., Palo Alto, (415) 325-6328. One of the best premium butcher shops on the Peninsula, offering a wide variety of fresh meats, including fish and seafood, as well as prepared rotisserie chicken and fajitas. They also carry a variety of terrific homemade sausages. Schaub's is a good bet for duck and rabbit, and the butchers can special order exotic game meats like pheasant and alligator.

Takahashi Market: 221 S. Claremont St., San Mateo, (415) 343-0394. This complete Japanese market sells fresh fish and all the necessary items for sushi. Check out the complete section of popular Chinese items including hoisin sauce, fermented black beans, and chili oils. Among the Southeast Asian goods on the shelves are fish sauce, dried lemongrass, laos powder, coconut milk and dried galangal roots. There's even a selection of prepared Hawaiian foods, including poi and lau-lau.

Trader Joe's: Various locations throughout Northern California. Call (800) 746-7857 for the location and phone number of the store nearest you. What else would you find at Trader Joe's but reasonable prices and gourmet specialties—their wine prices rival the large discount stores. They carry natural foods, frozen seafood, a huge variety of wine, and an unbelievably low-priced offering of imported and micro-brewed beer.

Whole Foods: 774 Emerson St., Palo Alto, (415) 326-8666. • 15980 Los Gatos Blvd., Los Gatos, (408) 358-4434. Whole Foods provides an abundant variety of organic foods in a soothing shopping experience. Among the goodies are a good fresh seafood section, organic and conventionally grown produce, a variety of bulk rices, whole grains and granolas, a bakery and deli, a meat market featuring organic meat and homemade sausages, and a great selection of wine and beer. To top it all off, an on-site masseur at the Palo Alto store will relax you after you shop. (Really—no joke.)

HOME FURNISHINGS

General Purpose Stores

If you're looking to buy everything for your home at one stop and don't mind how much it costs, a department store is the place to go. Macy's and the Emporium are two of the best around. But if you want to do the one-stop-shop thing, you're not looking to make the feature pages of *Architectural Digest*, and you don't want to pay department store prices, you can also check out the many good discount stores in the area.

Bed and Bath Superstore: 555 Ninth St., San Francisco, (415) 252-0490. The name is pretty self explanatory—shop for bargains on bedding, towels, and bathroom accessories, as well as nightstands, shelves, and the like. You can also find a wide selection of cookware, plates, and glassware, plus that incredible San Francisco commodity—great parking.

Cost Plus Imports: 2552 Taylor St., San Francisco, (415) 928-6200. • 785 Serramonte Blvd., Colma, (415) 994-7090. • 1910 W. El Camino Real, Mountain View, (415) 961-6066. • 4050 Stevens Creek Blvd., San Jose, (408) 247-3333. Cost Plus Imports is a discount import store with reasonably priced furniture and kitchenware. Several types of kitchen tables are available, as well as rattan sofas and chairs. The collection of odd knickknacks, including huge paper fans and ethnic figurines, is a must-see.

Crate and Barrel: 125 Grant Ave., San Francisco, (415) 986-4000. • 180 El Camino Real, Palo Alto, (415) 321-7800. • 2855 Stevens Creek Blvd., Santa Clara, (408) 243-7500. Crate and Barrel is your best bet for a broad array of reasonably priced kitchenware. The store is packed to the gills with tableware, cooking utensils, table linens, and other kitchen items. They also have a limited selection of kitchen appliances and furniture. Service is excellent.

Emporium: 835 Market St., San Francisco, (415) 764-2222. • Stonestown Galleria, 19th Ave. and Winston Dr., San Francisco, (415) 753-4000. • Tanforan Park Shopping Center, 1150 El Camino Real, San Bruno, (415) 877-7700. • Hillsdale Mall, El Camino Real and Hillsdale Blvd., San Mateo, (415) 572-5555. • Stanford Shopping Center, El Camino Real and Quarry Rd., Palo Alto, (415) 326-1111. • 701 El Camino Real, Mountain View, (415) 969-1111. • Valley Fair Mall, 3051 Stevens Creek Blvd., Santa Clara, (408) 296-1111. • Eastridge Mall, 2190 Tully Rd., San Jose, (408) 238-5555. • 5353 Almaden Expwy., San Jose, (408) 265-1111. The Emporium is a very similar store to Macy's, though it doesn't have quite as large a selection in many categories.

Macy's: Union Square, Stockton and O'Farrell Sts., San Francisco, (415) 397-3333. • 1 Serramonte Center, Serramonte and Callan Blvd., Daly City, (415) 994-3333. • 115 Hillsdale Mall, El Camino Real and Hillsdale Blvd., San Mateo, (415) 341-3333. • 2838 S. El Camino Real, San Mateo, (415) 341-3333 ext. 406, (furniture, rugs, and mattresses only). • Stanford Shopping Center, El Camino Real and Quarry Rd., Palo Alto, (415) 326-3333. • 200 W. Washington Ave., Sunnyvale, (408) 732-3333. • 2210 Tully Rd., San Jose, (408) 238-3333. • Oakridge Shopping Center, 5411 Thornwood Dr., San Jose, (408) 224-3333. • Valley Fair Mall, 2801 Stevens Creek Blvd., San Jose, (408) 248-3333. Macy's has everything you could possibly want for your home. Go to **The Cellar at Macy's** for an excellent selection of kitchenware, appliances, pots and pans, dinnerware, and glassware. Check around on the other floors for a wide selection of bone china and crystal, towels and bathroom furnishings, bed linen, beds, and a wide range of carpets and rugs.

Pier 1 Imports: 3535 Geary Blvd., San Francisco, (415) 387-6642. • 101 Colma Blvd., Colma, (415) 755-6600. • 2501 El Camino Real, Redwood City, (415) 364-6608. • 1255 W. El Camino Real, Sunnyvale, (415) 969-8307. • 20610 Stevens Creek Blvd., Cupertino, (408) 253-4512. • 1807 Saratoga Ave., San Jose, (408) 255-3533. • 1009 Blossom Hill Rd., San Jose, (408) 978-9555. Pier 1 specializes in wicker baskets and wood furniture, but it also offers basic glassware and dishes, rugs, and so forth. While not as cheap as some other outlets, there's more variety and stylish offerings at Pier 1.

Price Costco: 450 Tenth St., San Francisco, (415) 626-4288. • 451 Airport Blvd., S. San Francisco, (415) 872-2021. • 1340 El Camino Real, San Bruno, (415) 871-0460. • 2200 Middlefield Rd., Redwood City, (415) 369-3321. • 1000 N. Rengstorff Ave., Mountain View, (415) 988-9766. • 150 Lawrence Station Rd., Sunnyvale, (408) 730-1575. • 1600 Coleman Ave., Santa Clara, (408) 988-8516. • 1111 Story Rd., San Jose, (408) 286-5840. • 1900 S. Tenth St., San Jose, (408) 287-5530. The two giants of warehouse shopping, **Costco** and **Price Club**, recently merged to form Price Costco. The transformation is not yet complete, so each store may go by any one of the three names. You have to be a member to shop at Price Costco, but the big plus is the terrific prices, as many things are sold in bulk. Yet the stock, which ranges from stereos to barbecues to dish soap, can be very random. The brand choice is very limited as well. While prices can be low, service is non-existent, as is customer support if something goes wrong with your purchase.

Target: 5001 Junipero Serra Blvd., Colma, (415) 992-8433. • 2485 El Camino Real, Redwood City, (415) 363-8940. • 555 Showers Dr., Mountain View, (415) 965-7764. • 20745 Stevens Creek Blvd., Cupertino, (408) 725-2651. • 3155 Silver Creek Rd., East San Jose, (408)238-7800. • 1811 Hillsdale Ave., West San Jose, (408) 267-7900. Target is a treasure chest of reasonably priced household necessities. Target specializes in cheap towels, pots and pans, plastic anythings, and basic furniture; you can count on them to outfit your bedroom, bathroom, kitchen, and living room (in fact, your whole house) for less money than almost anywhere else. Look for all the kitchen and bathroom accessories you could ever want—plates, glasses, cooking utensils, soap holders, shower caddies, and shower curtains galore. Target's furniture is mostly along the line of shelving units, night stands, and chairs made of either lightweight wood or plastic, mostly unassembled.

Whole Earth Access: 401 Bayshore Blvd., San Francisco, (415) 285-5244. • 3530 Stevens Creek Blvd., San Jose, (408) 554-1500. Whole Earth Access serves as something of a new-age Sears, with a bit of everything the modern family needs to get started, from jeans to housewares to furniture. They stock a small selection of functional, low-priced furniture, with an emphasis on mattresses and home-office items. A trip to Whole Earth Access can yield a cornucopia of stylish housewares: reasonably priced dishware and glasses, cutting boards, Cuisinarts, blenders, and so on. They also have a decent selection of electronics: audio, video, communications, and computers (Apple, IBM, PC clones, and a few laptops).

Specialty Stores

Computers and Electronics

Anderson's: 901 El Camino Real, Redwood City, (415) 367-9400. • 999 El Camino Real, Sunnyvale, (408) 733-9820. • 606 Saratoga Ave., San Jose, (408) 554-1617. Go for the great selection of electronics at decent prices, and go especially for the frequent warehouse sales that'll get you reaching for your wallet.

Circuit City: 303 Gellert Blvd., Daly City, (415) 755-0101. • 1880 S. Grant Rd., San Mateo, (415) 578-1400. • 1250 Grant Rd., Mountain View, (415) 965-3500. • 1825 Hillsdale Ave., San Jose, (408) 723-1500. • 4080 Stevens Creek Blvd., San Jose, (408) 296-5522. • 2217 Quimby Rd., San Jose, (408) 223-1390. Circuit City is a chain store where you'll find low- to mid-end electronics of every kind at competitive prices; check out the huge range of TVs and VCRs. (Ironically, the selection in these huge stores is sometimes somewhat spotty.) Listening rooms for speakers, receivers, and car stereos are available to help with your decision; high-pressure salespeople are unfortunately sometimes a little too available. Circuit City also carries appliances and some computer equipment.

Computer Attic Supercenter: 2750 El Camino Real, Redwood City, (415) 363-8100. This huge store carries Mac, Toshiba, IBM, and Compaq computers, as well as software, books, and hardware accessories galore. Service can be harried but the prices are usually good.

ComputerWare: 343 Sansome St., San Francisco, (415) 362-3010. • 487 S. El Camino Real, San Mateo, (415) 375-5929. • 490 California Ave., Palo Alto, (415) 323-7559. • 3215 Stevens Creek Blvd., Santa Clara, (408) 345-0345. • 520 Lawrence Expwy., Sunnyvale, (408) 732-0200. This local chain specializes in Apple Macintosh computers, monitors, printers, peripherals, accessories, and software. There is also a good selection of Mac software. The staff usually lets you load software on store machines and evaluate it.

CompUSA: 1250 El Camino Real, San Bruno, (415) 244-9980. • 3561 El Camino Real, Santa Clara, (408) 554-1733. This national chain of computer superstores specializes in PC computers, software, and accessories.

Fry's Electronics: 340 Portage Ave., Palo Alto, (415) 496-6000. • 1177 Kern Ave., Sunnyvale, (408) 733-1770. Fry's is a Silicon Valley institution. The former-supermarket-turned-electronics superstore carries Macs, IBMs, countless clones, numerous printers and monitors, and enough parts and accessories to build your own computer. They also carry all kinds of electronics, home stereos, portable stereos, VCRs, TVs, CD players, fax machines, telephones, and answering machines. Look for an especially large selection of telephone equipment and Walkman-type stereos.

The Good Guys: Serramonte Shopping Ctr., Serramonte Blvd. and I-280, Daly City, (415) 301-8855. • 2727 El Camino Real, San Mateo, (415) 574-5100. • 1247 W. El Camino Real, Sunnyvale, (415) 962-0101. • 3149 Stevens Creek Blvd., San Jose, (408) 554-9700. • 5353 Almaden Expwy., San Jose, (408) 978-6664. • 1960 Tully Rd., San Jose, (408) 274-1062. This is a good place to start your foray if you want the biggest choice in mass market consumer goods. The selection of audio/video/communications electronics is unsurpassed, although the store doesn't cater to the audiophile. They do have a 30-day low "advertised" price guarantee, so if you're a bargain hunter you'll want to compare their prices. They also have listening rooms for home and car stereos. The salespeople unfortunately vary from fairly knowledgeable to those with barely adequate information.

Mateo Hi-Fi: 2199 S. El Camino Real, San Mateo, (415) 573-6506. Serious audiophiles might want to check out Mateo Hi-Fi (don't be put off by the funky pawnshop storefront). They specialize in custom home design and installation, as well as mid-fi with some high-fi and specialty products like in-wall speakers. You can always negotiate a good deal with their competent salespeople.

NCA Computer Products: 3825 El Camino Real, Palo Alto, (415) 493-2444. • 1202 Kifer Rd., Sunnyvale, (408) 739-9010. • 962 Blossom Hill Rd., San Jose, (408) 363-4600. Decor and sales assistance are sparse, but prices are absolutely rock bottom at this bare-bones computer supermarket, run in the same style as Fry's but with more focus on computers—mostly PC clones—and hardware components. They have a limited selection of software, mostly CD-ROMs.

Western Audio: 4191 El Camino Real, Palo Alto, (415) 494-2552. Western Audio specializes in high-end stereo and home theater system design and installation. This store is in the "if you have to ask what it costs, you can't afford it" category with brands like McIntosh, Hafler, KEF, and Carver. As you would expect, the salespeople are professional and very knowledgeable; they also have a full service repair department.

Furniture

Cort Furniture Clearance Center: 2925 Meade Ave., Santa Clara, (408) 727-1470. Cort has quality new and used furniture, including some scratch-and-dent stuff.

The Futon Gallery: 2951 El Camino Real, Palo Alto, (415) 322-8193. • 998 El Camino Real, Sunnyvale, (408) 720-8036. The Futon Gallery is a reliable place to buy a futon—they stock an upscale line of futons and frames (with an especially wide selection of frames and covers), and the service is reportedly excellent.

The Futon Shop: 3545 Geary Blvd., San Francisco, (415) 752-9908. • 370 California Ave., Palo Alto, (415) 329-1204. • 3390 Stevens Creek Blvd., San Jose, (408) 296-8989. • 1080 Blossom Hill Rd., San Jose, (408) 978-5696. They have a larger selection than most stores of futons and frames, but the somewhat self-service atmosphere means you should head here only if you feel fairly confident about what you want and how much it should cost.

Harrington Bros. Inc.: 599 Valencia St., San Francisco, (415) 861-7300. Harrington Bros. sells a large selection of used furniture, as do many of the other stores in the Mission district of San Francisco.

Leather Factory: 3555 Geary Blvd., San Francisco, (415) 221-0471. • 4400 Stevens Creek Blvd., Sunnyvale, (408) 244-3664. They sell any furniture that is commonly made with leather, mostly sofas, chairs, love seats, and desks.

Mattress Factory Outlet: 1970 W. El Camino Real, Mtn. View, (415) 969-7580. Mattress Factory has a full line of mattresses, including national brands and discounted products.

Office Depot: 712 DuBuque Ave., S. San Francisco, (415) 742-6700. • 1826 S. Norfolk St., San Mateo, (415) 572-2561. • 910 El Monte Ave., Mountain View, (415) 964-8249. • 121 El Camino Real, Sunnyvale, (408) 746-2040. • 3951 Stevens Creek Blvd., Santa Clara, (408) 241-9382. • 2510 Channing Ave., San Jose, (408) 434-1027. • 932 Blossom Hill Rd., San Jose, (408) 363-8002. As the name implies, the specialty here is office furniture. You'll find a modest selection of desks, shelves, computer stands, files, and chairs. Most merchandise is a step up from white laminated cubes, but low- to moderately-priced nonetheless.

Oprah House: 251 W. El Camino Real, Sunnyvale, (408) 730-1658. Oprah House carries a large selection of new quality oak furniture at bargain basement prices.

Scandinavian Designs: 317 S. "B" Street, San Mateo, (415) 340-0555. • 424 University Ave., Palo Alto, (415) 321-0141. Reasonably priced and good quality furniture, also including kids furniture. The Palo Alto store's third floor is filled with discounted or inexpensive pieces. Most pieces have the laminate look—lots of shelves, desks, dressers, and other basics.

Housewares

Lechters Housewares: 24 Serramonte Center, Serramonte and Callan Blvd., Daly City, (415) 992-5047. • 3251 20th Ave., (415) 759-0528. • 119 Eastridge Center, San Jose, (408) 238-5688. • 137 Oakridge Mall, 5411 Thornwood Dr., San Jose, (408) 365-1703. • 10123 N. Wolfe Rd., Cupertino, (408) 446-5785. Lechters will satisfy your need for anything inexpensive for the kitchen and bathroom. Plates, muffin pans, garlic presses, toothbrush holders, and small rugs abound.

Payless Drug Stores: 3975 Alemany Blvd., San Francisco, (415) 334-9660. • 666 Concar Dr., San Mateo, (415) 573-8161. • 1950 El Camino Real, Redwood City, (415) 599-9130. • 625 El Camino Real, Menlo Park, (415) 326-2701. • 1040 Grant Rd., Mountain View, (415) 968-9401. • 685 San Antonio Rd., Mountain View, (415) 948-6685. • 20580 Homestead Rd., Cupertino, (408) 253-9100. • 2310 Homestead Rd., Los Altos, (408) 774-0131. • 777 E. El Camino Real, Sunnyvale, (408) 738-3611. • 1140 Blossom Hill Rd., San Jose, (408) 264-6460. Here's another great place to stock your kitchen and bathroom inexpensively. You can buy just enough of what you need: one serving spoon, one sharp knife, one frying pan, one egg slicer or matching dishtowel. Payless is also good for things like mops and toilet bowl brushes, even plants.

Strouds: 731 Market St., San Francisco, (415) 979-0460. • 75 Serramonte Center, Serramonte and Callan Blvds., Daly City, (415) 991-9597. • 4 E. Fourth Ave., San Mateo, (415) 342-4743. • 700 El Camino Real, Menlo Park, (415) 327-7680. • 1236 W. El Camino Real, Sunnyvale, (408) 733-0910. • 3111 Stevens Creek Blvd., Santa Clara, (408) 984-6090. • 5353 Almaden Expwy., San Jose, (408) 978-0552. Strouds stores are small but hold an incredible amount of items for the bedroom and bathroom: sheets, comforters, pillows, towels, and bedroom and bathroom accessories. Watch for their frequent sales: if you're going to be spending a lot of money, it may be worthwhile waiting a couple of weeks to see if these items are reduced.

Williams-Sonoma: Stonestown Galleria, 19th Ave. and Winston Dr., San Francisco, (415) 681-5525. • 150 Post St., San Francisco, (415) 362-6904. • Valley Fair Mall, Stevens Creek Blvd. and I-880, Santa Clara, (408) 249-4424. • 10123 N. Wolfe Rd., Cupertino, (408) 257-9044. Visit Williams-Sonoma for the chef in you. Gorgeous copper pots, a wide variety of kitchen gadgetry, tableware and glassware are all featured in this specialty store. Prices tend to be on the high side, but this fabulous stuff is worth it.

Thrift Stores

The thrift shops listed here carry used goods that are usually in decent condition. In general, "thrift" or "charity" stores rely on donated items that vary wildly in quality, but are uniformly low in price; stores subtitled "consignment" or "resale" are more selective, so expect to pay more. The latter group will also sell your unwanted things for a percentage.

Discovery Shop: 1410 Broadway, Burlingame, (415) 343-9100. • 2432 Broadway, Redwood City, (415) 363-2238. • 746 Santa Cruz Ave., Menlo Park, (415) 325-8939. • 142 Main St., Los Altos, (415) 949-0505. • 1451-A Foxworthy Ave., San Jose, (408) 265-5535. If you're in the market for something more like a mink coat or a designer dress, you should visit a Discovery Shop. The wares at these stores are amazingly tasteful and include everything from clothes to furniture to used magazines. Prices are above the usual thrift-store range, but the sales are something out of this world.

Goodwill: 1700 Haight St., San Francisco, (415) 387-1192. • 225 Kenwood Wy., South San Francisco, (415) 737-9827. • 4085 El Camino Way, Palo Alto, (415) 494-1416. • 855 El Camino Real, Mountain View, (415) 969-3382. • 151 E. Washington Ave., Sunnyvale, (408) 736-8558. • 1494 Halford Ave., Santa Clara, (408) 249-1715. • 1125 Saratoga Sunnyvale Rd., Cupertino, (408) 252-3193. • 1579 Meridian Ave., San Jose, (408) 266-7151. • 1080 N. Seventh St., San Jose, (408) 998-5774. This national institution known for its large selection at good prices has many area outlets. The Palo Alto store is chock-full of stuff, all of which is cheap and much of which is in extremely good condition, although clothing and odds and ends are the best find. The Mountain View store is large, basic, and cheap. The Seventh Avenue store in San Jose is a wholesale outlet where junk that won't sell in other Goodwill stores is sold off by the barrel.

Pick of the Litter: 1801 S. Grant St., San Mateo, (415) 345-1024. This store gets its name from its beneficiary, The Peninsula Humane Society, but you won't find many dogs in the merchandise. This big, well-organized store sells it all, from furniture to books and records to clothes to housewares. Prices are low, but look for specials and sales to really save.

Salvation Army: 300 El Camino Real, San Bruno, (415) 583-3589. • 650 El Camino Real, Belmont, (415) 591-5499. • 660 Veterans Blvd., Redwood City, (415) 368-7527. • 4140 Monterey Rd., San Jose, (408) 578-1288. In addition to used clothing, the Salvation Army has secondhand couches, fridges, mattresses, desks, and more, all at very low prices.

Savers: 875 Main St., Redwood City, (415) 364-5545. • 60 S. Dempsey Rd., Milpitas, (408) 263-8338. • 222 Business Cir., San Jose, (408) 287-0591. In Redwood City, you can find furniture on the second floor, while on the main floor you can browse through the huge and well-organized clothing and housewares collection. All the stores offer a good selection. For about $3 you can purchase a Chinese wok; you can get a nice set of glasses for around 99¢ each.

The Second Act: 12882 S. Saratoga-Sunnyvale Rd., Saratoga, (408) 741-4995. Second Act is the type of consignment shop you'd expect to find in a high-rent district like Saratoga, where the cast-off clothes and furniture are nicer than the new purchases down in the Valley. Prices are a good deal compared to what these things cost new, but don't look for any 99¢ racks filled with Polo and Armani jackets.

This'n'That Shop: 1336 Fifth Ave., Belmont, (415) 591-6166. For over 30 years this bargain Mecca has been reselling old clothes, housewares, books, and more to benefit the projects of Good Shepherd Episcopal Church. The store is only open a couple of days a week, but the low prices draw crowds.

Thrift Center: 1060 El Camino Real, San Carlos, (415) 593-1082. Thrift Center is as big and ramshackle a thrift store as you'll find anywhere, with everything from furniture to clothing to appliances. Prices are generally very low.

Flea Markets and Garage Sales

The classified ads in the local papers are another great resource for surprise finds. You'll see listings of secondhand goods, the week's flea markets and garage sales, and sometimes even a freebie section.

Capitol Flea Market: 3630 Hillcap Ave., San Jose, (408) 225-5800. 50¢ per person on Thursday, $1 per person on weekends. • Th 7am-5:30pm; Sa-Su 6am-5:30pm.

De Anza College Flea Market: 21250 Stevens Creek Blvd., Cupertino, (408) 864-8414. No entrance fee, parking $2. Over 800 stalls. • M-F 8:30am-3pm.

The Flea Market Inc.: 1590 Berryessa Rd., San Jose, (408) 453-1110. Plenty of parking. • W-Su 7am-6pm.

OUTLETS

American Tin Cannery: 125 Ocean View Blvd., Pacific Grove, (408) 372-1442. Fish for bargains at **Carole Little** and **Joan and David**, among others.

Crate & Barrel: 1785 Fourth St., Berkeley, (510) 528-5500. The creative Crate and Barrel Outlet offers out-of season, discontinued, and (occasionally) damaged goods from their retail stores. The markdowns are less generous (25%-30%) than most outlets, but they can add up if you're trying to furnish every part of your house.

Esprit Factory Outlet: 499 Illinois St., San Francisco, (415) 957-2550. San Francisco's most dynamic outlet store is filled with high-tech displays and merchandise at prices 30%-75% off department store markups.

Gunne Sax: 35 Stanford St., San Francisco, (415) 495-3326. If formalwear is your object of desire, Gunne Sax's outlet (the biggest user of lace in the country) has elegant evening dresses all ready and waiting for you.

Marina Square in San Leandro: Marina Square, I-880 at Marina Blvd., San Leandro. This East Bay mall has outlet stores for **The Gap** and **Eddie Bauer**, a discount publishers' outlet, and more. There's also a **Nordstrom Rack** clearance center replete with dresses and stylish men's suits—all recent store rejects at great markdowns.

North Face Outlet: 1325 Howard St., San Francisco, (415) 626-6444. • 1238 Fifth St., Berkeley, (510) 526-3530. You can't miss the original North Face Outlet featuring sportswear, outerwear, skiwear, and trustworthy equipment at discounted prices—a place very true to Berkeley's ecological nature. However, there are usually no warranties on outlet goods, something to consider before making any serious investments. You can also check out the new SF sibling store.

Factory Stores at Nut Tree: I-80 at 505 Orange Dr., Nut Tree exit, Vacaville, (707) 447-5755. At this giant collection of outlets you'll find stores such as **Benetton**, **Bugle Boy**, and **Reebok**, along with 50 others.

Pacific West Outlet Store: Hwy 101 at Leavesley Rd. exit, Gilroy, (408) 847-4155. Shopping at the PacificWest Outlet Center in the garlic capital of the world you can find **Liz Claiborne** and the **Nike Factory Store**, as well as 50 designer outlets and a wonderful kitchenware discount store. Come ready to spend the day, and you will find yourself among carloads of people prepared for full-contact shopping; be prepared to spend hours sorting through piles and racks of slightly imperfect items.

Simply Cotton: 1311 Burlingame Ave., Burlingame, (415) 347-7518. Simply Cotton offers the comfortable cotton clothing look, with 50% reductions on past-season merchandise.

Six Sixty Center: 660 Third St., San Francisco, (415) 227-0464. Many places like **Dress Market** and **Carole's Shoe Heaven** sell their goodies in this SoMa outlet center.

RESTAURANTS & CAFÉS

The Acorn $$$ 1906 El Camino Real, Menlo Park, (415) 322-6201. Mediterranean cuisine served in a ritzy lodge setting. Greece, Italy, and France are all represented on the menu, which includes such highbrow fare as sweetbreads with mushrooms in a brandy sauce, moussaka with béchamel, and wilted spinach flambé "performed" at your table. Try the Athenian rack of lamb or the tangy *avgolemono* soup—you won't find Greek cooking of this caliber for miles. • Lunch M-F, dinner daily.

Adriatic Restaurant $$$$ 14583 Big Basin Way, Saratoga, (408) 867-3110. Presided over by Ed Begovic (his wife, Nada, runs things in the kitchen), Adriatic features the cuisine of the couple's native Yugoslavia. Specials include a lemony calamari salad and *burek*, a well-seasoned mixture of chopped veal, lamb, and beef baked in phyllo dough and served with sour cream. Finish off with a strudel and a glass of port. • Dinner Tu-Sa.

Alice's Restaurant $$ 17288 Skyline Blvd., Woodside, (415) 851-0303. You can get anything you want at this Alice's. Eggs, cheeseburgers, and homemade pies are served by day. At night, linens and candles come out, and chops, steak, pasta primavera, and grilled herb chicken are served. Monday is Katmandu night, with Nepalese chefs preparing native specialties, Tuesday is Mexican night, and so on. The rustic interior features mountain-man decor: wood paneling, vintage photos, and a mounted moosehead. The corner location is a popular gathering spot for motorcycle enthusiasts on the weekends. • Breakfast, lunch, and dinner daily.

Allied Arts Guild Restaurant $$ 75 Arbor Rd., Menlo Park, (415) 324-2588. This genteel ladies' lunching spot is located in the lovely Allied Arts Guild compound. The prix fixe menu rotates such vintage fifties fare as melon with strawberries, turkey roulade, and rice pilaf. After lunch you can shop for crafts at the various boutiques housed in the compound and stroll through the well-tended flower gardens. Cash only. • Lunch seatings at noon, 12:30pm, and 1pm, tea w/dessert 2pm-3:30pm M-F, Sa buffet noon-2pm.

Alpine Beer Garden $ 3915 Alpine Rd., Portola Valley, (415) 854-4004. In 1907, Stanford University's first president, David Starr Jordan, tried but failed to convince the county of San Mateo to revoke Zott's (aka Risotti's) liquor license on the grounds of "vileness." Today, the name has changed, but the burgers are still acclaimed all over the Peninsula, and the outdoor picnic tables are a great (if dusty) place to hang with friends. If you're weary of espresso, croissants, sprouts, and tofu, don't despair. Zott's is still around and will probably outlast us all. Cash only. • Lunch and dinner daily.

Amandine $$ 898 Santa Cruz Ave., Menlo Park, (415) 325-4776. Run by friendly Swiss immigrants, this vest pocket–size eatery is done up in high Alpine style—pine paneling, ski chalet-like booths, red tablecloths, and heraldic Swiss emblems on the walls. The menu is simple—fondue, *raclette* (a Swiss concoction of melted cheese, boiled potatoes, and cornichons), and a veal stew in white wine. Salad and a choice of the elaborate desserts from the bakery next door come with the meals. You may feel like yodeling by the end of the meal, so authentic is the ambience. Cash only. • Breakfast and lunch M-Sa, dinner Th-Sa.

Amici's East Coast Pizzeria $$ 69 E. Third Ave., San Mateo, (415) 342-9392. Amici's takes its cue from New York-style pizza parlors, offering thin-crusted pies baked in a wood-burning brick oven for extra crispness. Toppings are straightforward if not pioneering, including fried eggplant, pesto, and three varieties of sausage. Pastas and salads are pizza alternatives: a tangy Caesar antipasto salad makes an inexpensive meal for two. A plus for the late-night crowd: Amici's is one of the few Peninsula restaurants open until midnight every night. • Lunch and dinner daily; open until midnight.

Andale Taqueria $ 6 Santa Cruz Ave., Los Gatos, (408) 395-4244 • 21 N. Santa Cruz Ave., Los Gatos, (408) 395-8997 • 209 University Ave., Palo Alto, (415) 323-2939. Some say these are the best of the fresh-Mex restaurants that are cropping up everywhere. The brightly painted, festive interiors put you in the mood for the first-rate, reasonably priced food. If you're in a burrito rut, try the chicken tamale. Be sure to sip an *agua fresca* through a neon pink straw. Margaritas are made with wine rather than tequila; sangria and beer are also served. Cash only. • Lunch and dinner daily.

Applewood Inn $ 227 First St., Los Altos, (415) 941-9222 • 1001 El Camino Real, Menlo Park, (415) 324-3486. • 989D El Camino Real, Menlo Park, (415) 328-1556. A longtime favorite where the menu is concerned, but you may be less taken with the spare Mom and Pop surroundings. Nevertheless, try the heaped, thick-crusted, lovingly baked specialties: Ever had red caviar on your pizza pie? Polish sauerkraut? One popular model is the Nice with its onions, ricotta, and herb mixture. Also, an amazingly wide selection of imported beers. Across the street at Applewood Pizza 2 Go, you can take out all of the above for dinner. • Lunch and dinner daily.

Armadillo Willy's BBQ $$ 10235 S. De Anza Blvd., Cupertino, (408) 252-7427 • 1031 N. San Antonio Rd., Los Altos, (415) 941-2922 • 2624 Homestead Rd., Santa Clara, (408) 247-1100. The award-winning, slow-smoked mesquite barbecue served at Willy's appeals to hungry, budget-conscious diners. Generous sandwiches are served in addition to the competently executed traditional barbecue fare. Counter service and limited seating with sparse but comfortable surroundings. • Lunch M-Sa, dinner daily.

The Armenian Gourmet $$$ 929 E. Duane Ave., Sunnyvale, (415) 732-3910. You might want to fast in preparation for the feast that awaits you at this simple neighborhood spot. Prices may seem high until the heaping plates of flavorful Mediterranean specialties start to arrive. The savory meats in the sautéed lamb, shish kabob, and *lulleh* kabob (a ground lamb preparation) plates are perfectly cooked. The vegetarian plate features a mound of *tabouli*, a delightful *burek* (a flaky cheese turnover), and an unusual, smoky *baba ganoush*. Good selection of beer and wine. Service is friendly and attentive. • Lunch M-F, dinner W-Sa.

Azuma $$$ 9645 Stevens Creek Rd., Cupertino, (408) 257-4057. Located near Hewlett-Packard, Apple, and Tandem, Azuma attracts a loyal clientele of Silicon Valley engineers at lunch and families at night. The tatami seating, fresh Japanese flower arrangements, and cheerful, kimono-clad servers have a calming influence on the diners—whether they're engineers tired of workplace politics or itchy four-year-olds. Most tables have tatami mats and walls, but you can also sit at the sushi bar or American-style tables. The traditional (but somewhat Americanized) Japanese menu is dependable and features the usual, from California rolls to hot sake. The sushi is fresh and top quality, and the tempura is always hot and crisp. • Lunch M-F, dinner daily.

Babbo's Pizzeria $$ 717 Stanford Shopping Center, Palo Alto, (415) 321-1488. A splendid wood-burning oven roars away, turning out traditional Italian 11-inch single pizzas (about the size of a dinner plate). The toppings are also typically Italian, the crust is thin and crisp, and the atmosphere is 100 percent European. The outdoor seating is something out of downtown Napoli. • Lunch and dinner daily.

Baccarat $$$$$ Hotel Sofitel, 223 Twin Dolphin Dr., Redwood City, (415) 598-9000. Classic French food served with much pomp and circumstance. Ooh la la, the prices will set your head spinning—make this an expense account meal. But the food is excellent. • Dinner M-Sa.

Baccarat Restaurant Club $$$ 1092 E. El Camino Real, Sunnyvale, (408) 261-1234. You may think you've died and been reincarnated as a bit player in *Lawrence of Arabia*. The decor features red velvet, gold tapestries, and a small indoor pond—need we say more? Authentic Persian specialties are the order of the day; choose from an array of dishes including lamb, chicken, beef, and fish kabobs, as well as eggplant and seafood creations. Try the *ghaymeh*, a stew of beef with yellow peas, spices, and french fries. • Lunch and dinner M-Sa; open until 11pm or later.

Bangkok Cuisine $$ 407 Lytton Ave., Palo Alto, (415) 322-6533 • 5235 Prospect Rd., San Jose, (408) 253-8424. The full complement of Thai dishes, with seafood-oriented specialties—savory sautéed shellfish with curry, sweet basil, and coconut milk and whole pompano deep-fried and topped with chili sauce. The portions are smallish and the tables packed too tightly together, but then again the food is well above average. Polite service and inexpensive lunch specials. • Lunch M-Sa, dinner daily.

Bangkok Spoon $$ 702 Villa St., Mtn. View, (415) 968-2038. This small, nicely decorated family restaurant just off Castro Street offers a good variety of Thai dishes. Try the *tom gai kai* or any of the quite palatable curries. The pad Thai, however, is not quite up to snuff. • Lunch M-F, dinner M-Sa.

Barbarossa $$$$ 3003 El Camino Real, Redwood City, (415) 369-2626. There are those who swear by this hushed, Old World restaurant that dates from the time when men were men and women were bored housewives. Waiters cosset you, candles softly flicker, and the table is set with Wedgewood china—you may forget it's the nineties. Luxurious dishes like noisette of lamb with wild rice and fine herbs are the order of the day. Be prepared for high prices: The buckwheat blini with sevruga caviar and smoked salmon breaks the $15-appetizer barrier. • Dinner daily.

Basque Cultural Center $$$ 599 Railroad Ave., South San Francisco, (415) 583-8091. It's worth getting lost to dine at this one-of-a-kind institution, located in the Basque Cultural Center in windy South San Francisco. Simple, delicious Basque-French specialties are served family-style in the comfortable dining room decorated with country French furniture, crisp white tableclothes, and dark wood beams. Meals start off with a tureen of soup, followed by a salad and two entrées, which might include red snapper Basque style or pepper steak with a satisfying black-pepper crust. The portions are huge. Linger over coffee, and don't miss the display of pelota trophies (it's a court game) in the reception hall. • Lunch Tu-F, dinner Tu-Su.

Beauséjour $$$$ 170 State St., Los Altos, (415) 948-1382 • 704 Town & Country Shopping Center, Sunnyvale, (408) 720-0273. A French restaurant with an Asian twist. At the more posh Los Altos location, a quiet fountain at the entrance reflects the Asian influence, but the interior brings to mind a French country house with its burgundy-patterned wallpaper, fresh-cut flowers, and colonial-era prints. The menu showcases standard French openers such as escargot and French onion soup (but try the potato leek soup if it's offered). Entrées are weighted toward seafood, but French traditionalists needn't despair—rabbit, pheasant, duck, and venison are featured, and each comes with a hearty sauce. The Asian influence reappears in the side dishes—the julienned vegetables are delicately bundled and tied like sushi rolls. The Sunnyvale branch does not live up to the original. • Lunch M-F, dinner M-Sa.

Bella Mia $$$ 58 S. First St., San Jose, (408) 280-1993 • 14503 Big Basin Way, Saratoga, (408) 741-5115. Downtown Saratoga's most popular dining spot is located in a historic Victorian where you can enjoy a lazy Sunday brunch, complete with jazz and outdoor seating (weather permitting). The chef competes (and wins) in many of the pasta competitions held in the area. Some of his more stunning creations: salmon ravioli, oven-baked lasagna, and veal or chicken piccata. Indoors, the decor tends toward high Victorian—floral wallpaper, oak furniture, creaky stairs. A favorite pre-prom spot with high schoolers and a popular site for popping the question. A new location in San Jose just opened—the early reports are favorable. • Lunch and dinner daily, brunch Sa-Su.

Bella Vista Restaurant $$$$ 13451 Skyline Blvd., Woodside, (415) 851-1229. High up on top of Skyline Drive, the view from this woodsy retreat is unsurpassed, with the entire Peninsula and bay laid out before you. (Be sure to ask for a table with a view when you make your reservation.) A wood-burning fireplace, lots of rough-hewn wood, and white linen tablecloths create a rustic yet elegant ambience. The menu is classic continental and expensive; the view is worth the price, though. • Dinner M-Sa.

Bellino $$$ 95 S. Market St., San Jose, (408) 277-0690. An arty restaurant and bar that manages to be both to the detriment of neither. The dimly lit bar features live jazz, upscale banquettes with a Miro-esque pattern, and a daily happy hour with free pizza. The adjoining restaurant area is light and open, with a glassed-in section and a small patio overlooking St. Joseph's Cathedral across the street and Mt. Hamilton in the distance. An abundance of abstract paintings and modern statuettes link the two rooms. The menu is conventional Italian, with a few bar appetizers like fried calamari and California oddities, including smoked-salmon pizza with goat cheese and artichokes, thrown in for good measure. • Lunch M-F, dinner M-Sa.

Benihana $$$$ 1496 Old Bayshore Hwy., Burlingame, (415) 342-5202 • 2074 Vallco Fashion Park, Cupertino, (408) 253-1221. High theater at high prices. Inside the immense blue-and-white pagoda, table chefs in towering red toques prepare hibachi meats while juggling their knives to pulsating music. The timid can turn their gaze to the spectacular view of the San Francisco Bay. On weekends, any diners still light on their feet after eating can conclude the evening with a spin on the dance floor. • Lunch M-Sa, dinner daily; open until 11pm F-Sa.

Birk's $$$ 3955 Freedom Circle, Santa Clara, (408) 980-6400. The quintessential upscale California grill for Silicon Valley power lunchers. Birk's features a classic Pat Kuleto design—black-and-white tile, dark wood, and subdued lighting (similar to the Buffalo Grill but without the horns). The menu is big on simple grilled seafood, chicken, and meat, with a heavy emphasis on the steak and ribs; it also covers smoked and sautéed dishes, as well as the ubiquitous pasta. There's a large wine selection and an even better assortment of beers on tap. Check out the local microbrews: we found Tied House Ale. • Lunch M-F, dinner daily.

Bit of England $ 1448 Burlingame Ave., Burlingame, (415) 344-1540. A British pub crossed with a sports bar. The menu covers English peasant fare like shepherd's pie and bangers and mash, old-fashioned American deli sandwiches, and a selection of simple dishes, like pork chops, of no particular derivation. The TV volume is usually mercifully low. • Lunch M-Sa, brunch Su, dinner Tu-Sa.

BJ Bulls $ 3403 Alma St., Palo Alto, (415) 493-7330. Contrary to popular belief, the British have made a respectable contribution to the culinary scene. This place serves delectable homemade meat and vegetarian pies, called pasties. Try the salad and a pasty for lunch or dinner, as well as a homemade fresh fruit pie or cookie for dessert. Large selection of British beers on tap, and also English ales. BJ Bulls sets up shop at the Palo Alto Farmer's Market on Saturday mornings, so you can pick up a pie and some coffee on your way to market. Cash only. • Lunch and dinner M-F.

Black Angus $$$ 1299 Chess Dr., Foster City, (415) 345-9971 • 1011 Blossom Hill Rd., San Jose, (408) 266-6602 • 380 S. Kiely Blvd., San Jose, (408) 261-6900 • 740 E. El Camino Real, Sunnyvale, (408) 245-4501. Part of the Stuart Anderson group that was ranked first among casual dinner house chains in *Consumer Reports*, the four Peninsula locations all feature meaty, large-portioned Western-style entrées such as barbecued ribs, prime rib, T-bone, and porterhouse steak. (The seafood specials and teriyaki options are probably a reflection of health-conscious Bay Area tastes.) The walls are filled with Wild West memorabilia, and the exposed beams and barnlike interior might make you think you're eating in a stable. During happy hours, patrons play trivia games in the bar or watch the big-screen TV while filling up on free appetizers. • Lunch, dinner daily.

Black Forest Inn $$$ 376 First St., Los Altos, (415) 948-5031. Weary of postmodern interiors and organic California cuisine? The Black Forest Inn takes you back in time with its fifties-style linoleum, red-and-white checked oilcloths, and rec-room-style wood paneling. A multitude of beer steins constitutes the decor. Heavy Germanic fare attracts a crowd at lunch and dinner; try the hearty beef *rouladen* with buttered noodles and red cabbage, the Hungarian goulash, or the delicious homemade sausage. On nice days sit outside in the screened-in outdoor beer garden complete with fountain and rock garden. • Lunch and dinner Tu-Sa.

Blue Chalk Café $$$ 630 Ramona St., Palo Alto, (415) 326-1020 The Blue Chalk seats a huge crowd on two airy levels, each with its own bar. For gaming enthusiasts, four small pool tables occupy one room, while upstairs there's a shuffleboard table and dart boards. This isn't your typical pool hall scene: You won't find any surly bartenders or incoherent, Harley-riding patrons. The Cajun-influenced kitchen is run by a top chef. Specialties include a spicy seafood corn chowder, fresh catfish, and grilled-vegetable sandwiches. Small but flavorful beer selection on tap. • Lunch M-Sa, dinner daily.

Blue Sky Café & Flower Bar $$$ 336 Bryant St., Mtn. View, (415) 961-2082. Yes, the delicious spinach salad with warm strawberry vinaigrette comes garnished with a flower, but you may yet acquire a taste for edible flora. The cozy country-style house has plenty of outdoor seating, while indoors there's a romantic and intimate atmosphere with small, candlelit tables. The menu features an impressive range of dishes—from New Zealand lamb wrapped in phyllo pastry and served with two sauces to sautéed tofu and fresh vegetables. Solid brunches, too. • Lunch M-F, dinner Tu-Su, brunch Sa-Su.

Bob's Oak Room $$$ 945 The Alameda, San Jose, (408) 279-1585. Owner Bob Ulloa protects the secret of his salty barbecue recipe with vigilance. You'll arouse the suspicion of his loyal staff if you make the mistake of heading straight back to the dining room—you order in the barroom, and when your meal is ready, a hostess escorts you swiftly past the kitchen and to your table. Hearty souls will delight in the small menu of oakwood-fired meats, but diners with more refined sensibilities had better seek their raspberry glazes and jicama garnish elsewhere. P.S. Dan Quayle would feel at home here—the menu spells *potato* with an *e*. Cash only. • Dinner daily.

Bogie's $$$ 60 E. Third Ave., San Mateo, (415) 579-5911. Buried at the rear of a San Mateo arcade, behind costume jewelry and women's apparel shops, lies a swank, sophisticated throwback to an era when dining was intimate and a restaurant meal constituted an evening out. Bogie's looks like it belongs in a 1940s movie, with romantic lighting, black-and-white photos of old-time film stars, and lots of polished wood and mirrored surfaces. The old-fashioned elegance is not misleading. The service is impeccable and the food is classic. Such continental entrées as lamb medallions in a mustard sauce and chicken-and-vegetable brochettes are the stars of the menu, although the traditional homemade pastas merit a return trip. • Lunch M-F, dinner M-Sa.

Borsalino Saaghi $$$ 801 Hamilton Ave., Campbell, (408) 866-6400. A hot spot for the South Bay's Persian community. The strip-mall facade disguises a glittering interior adorned with gilt-bordered jet black walls, a ceiling flecked with gold dust, and bottles of Australian Cabernet at every table. On the weekend, this restaurant becomes a nightclub with a band of electric instruments playing eastern music, accompanied by a spinning disco ball and the occasional belly dancer. Some of the food seems confused—meals are preceded by pita bread served with sprigs of mint and hunks of raw onion—but the garlicky eggplant entrées and most of the skewered meats hit the spot. A warning for the environmentally sensitive: Smokers dominate the clientele. • Lunch and dinner daily.

Bravo Fono $$ 99 Stanford Shopping Center, Palo Alto, (415) 322-4664. While pasta dishes make up the bulk of the menu, this is a wonderful place to linger over dessert and coffee. An unexpected dimension is the selection of Hungarian specialties. Definitely try the *langos*, a crisp fried bread served with garlic. And as for the tortes and cakes, go full out! • Lunch daily, dinner M-Sa.

British Banker's Club $$$ 1090 El Camino Real, Menlo Park, (415) 327-8769. The fabulously overblown interior of Tiffany lamps and Oriental carpets makes for a Masterpiece Theatre-on-acid effect. A wide selection of English brews on tap and British fare such as bangers and chips (sausage and fries) and Battersea prawns (fried in Bass ale batter) are offered at the bar. If you stay for dinner, you'll be rewarded by a limited menu of well-executed beef, fish, and poultry selections that do occasionally stray from traditional British style. Exemplary table service, although not for the budget-minded. • Lunch and dinner daily, brunch Sa-Su; bar open until 2am.

Bua Thong Kitchen $$ 1320 Broadway, Burlingame, (415) 347-4340. Fairly standard Thai food at incredibly low prices. The atmosphere could use some perking up—the two rows of tables facing each other seem slightly militaristic—but when an order of chicken with mint leaves and chili oil costs just $6, it's hard to complain. • Lunch Tu-F, dinner Tu-Su.

Buffalo Grill $$$ 66 Thirty-first Ave. (Hillsdale Mall), San Mateo, (415) 358-8777. As its name suggests, Pat Kuleto's latest dining sensation departs wildly from his empire of Italian restaurants. The decor of this upscale and perpetually packed diner is over-the-top Western, with faux hunting trophies on the back wall and lighting fixtures shaped like buffalo horns alongside the booths. The food is equally tongue-in-cheek—mock frontier with a Californian flourish. Entrées like grilled chicken club sandwiches with smoked bacon on sourdough and maple-cured pork chops with corn spoonbread and buttermilk onion rings draw a never-ending stream of society mavens and power-lunchers during the day and crowds from all over the Peninsula at night. Anything from the grill is a sure bet, as are the gargantuan homemade desserts (including ten-mile-high devil's food cake with white chocolate ice cream), which two or three diners can happily share. Reservations are a must. • Lunch M–Sa, dinner daily.

Buns $$ 209 Park Rd., Burlingame, (415) 579-2867. The thing to order here is, of course, a burger. Burgers are big and flavorful and come with a choice of toppings. The menu also features huge salads, omelets, fish, and pasta. Wear something you like and comb your hair—mirrors mercilessly surround you. • Lunch M-F, dinner daily.

By-th-Bucket $$ 4565 Stevens Creek Blvd., Santa Clara, (408) 248-6244. A modern, all-American eatery that serves just about everything: pasta, seafood, sandwiches, pizza, meats, chicken, and the namesake buckets of shellfish. By-th-Bucket feels like an upscale Chili's or Denny's—deep booths, cheerful waitrons, light wood, and green carpet. It's popular with Silicon Valley suburbanites—a great place for that office birthday party. (Now if they could just learn to spell *the*.) • Lunch and dinner daily; open until midnight Su-W, until 2am Th-Sa.

Café Fino $$ 544 Emerson St., Palo Alto, (415) 326-6082. An amusing forties-style Art Deco piano bar with a mahogany bar, an antique cash register, and ceiling murals. Festive atmosphere, a campy singer in a vintage gown, and less expensive fare than its more grownup sibling, Maddalenas. Lunch specials of gnocchi gorgonzola or cold salmon salad go for $5—worth checking out. • Lunch M-F, dinner M-Sa.

Café for All Seasons $$$ 50 Third Ave., San Mateo, (415) 348-4996. One of the Peninsula's most celebrated dining spots, with a high, pressed-tin ceiling, blond wood furniture, and colorful prints on the walls. The menu features California/American classics like Cobb salad, hamburgers with excellent fries, and assorted pastas at lunch, and at dinner pork scallops with a mustard cream sauce for a light version of the Germanic standby or chicken with artichoke hearts in light cream. The heavenly desserts include classics like pumpkin pie and triple-chocolate cake. • Lunch and dinner daily, weekend brunch.

Café La Scala $$$ 1219 Burlingame Ave., Burlingame, (415) 347-3035. Over-the-top Tuscan ambience: a large and gregarious staff, faux marble plant beds and urns, Italian opera posters, swaths of lace hanging from ceiling lamps, and a trompe l'oeil view of an Italian countryside complete with peasant maid. The menu itself is less flamboyant— thank heavens—consisting of straightforward but thoughtfully prepared traditional dishes. La Scala is not above offering "ch-ch-chocolate" ice cream cake for dessert. • Lunch and dinner daily.

Café Marcella $$$ 368 Village Ln., Los Gatos, (408) 354-8006. The simple, unpretentious decor here can be a relief after too many visits to restaurants with ocher ombré walls and roaring open brick ovens. White walls are hung with French prints, and light wood chairs and a bar with chrome stools make for a modern feel. The food is well prepared and delicious—try the sensational appetizer plate of brie, smoked salmon, prosciutto, and more. Roast duck, pastas, and pizzas are among the entrée options. A word to the wise: Don't pass up the desserts. • Lunch Tu-Sa, dinner Tu-Su.

Café Pro Bono $$$ 2437 Birch St., Palo Alto, (415) 326-1626. Unfortunately, the food at this charming café isn't given away free for the public good. But come anyway for the spare decor, soft pink light, hushed atmosphere, and light northern Italian food. The homemade tortellini appetizer is heavenly, stuffed with cheese and Swiss chard and topped with a light sage sauce. The well-prepared Caesar salad has a subtle garlic bite and won't ruin your appetite for the courses to follow. Count on the fish being moist with a delicate sauce. The eclectic wine list ranges from Woodside Vineyards to very pricey French. • Lunch M-F, dinner daily.

Caffe Verona $$ 236 Hamilton Ave., Palo Alto, (415) 326-9942. The first and most famous of the great Peninsula cafés—countless businesses and lifelong friendships have been born here. Vagrant, trendy international crowd; brush up on your foreign languages. Pick from plastic mock-ups of Italian dishes; the real McCoys come to your table looking amazingly similar but tasting good. The low-key Euro wait staff generally leaves you alone after seeing to your food and drink. • Breakfast and lunch daily, dinner M-Sa.

California Café Bar & Grill $$$ 50 University Ave., Old Town, Los Gatos, (408) 354-8118 • 700 Welch Rd. (Stanford Barn), Palo Alto, (415) 325-2233 • 2855 Stevens Creek Blvd. (Valley Fair Shopping Center), Santa Clara, (408) 296-2233. A popular chain following the California-cuisine credo: imaginative food, pale drinks, pastel decor, and high prices. The Los Gatos branch is still basking in the glow of Bill Clinton's February 1993 visit. Every moment is documented in a photo collage: Clinton in a disco-style blue shirt, a pale and perspiring Al Gore, a German shepherd police dog sniffing out the premises. Presidential medals for $25 are on sale to commemorate the visit. What did the leader of the free world eat? Dungeness crabcakes with pink grapefruit beurre blanc, arugula, and crispy fried leeks, and for dessert, chocolate whiskey cake with orange sauce and praline cream. • Lunch and dinner daily, Sunday brunch.

California Sushi and Grill $$$ One E. San Fernando St., San Jose, (408) 297-1847. Fresh, creative sushi preparations and fine teriyaki and tempura emerge from the kitchen at California Sushi and Grill, one of downtown San Jose's more pleasant dining spots. The cheerful interior is done up in pink, black, and white, with a few bamboo accents. Sit upstairs and you overlook the Gordon Biersch beer garden. All this and karaoke, too. • Lunch M-F, dinner M-Sa.

Campbell House $$$ 106 E. Campbell Ave., Campbell, (408) 374-5757. Rows of basil plants line the walkway to the Campbell House, located in a classic stucco Spanish-style hacienda. Inside, a country parlor atmosphere prevails, with dried flowers, oak furniture, and dark green tablecloths. Among the inspired creations cooked up by chef Vincent

Brunetto (an alumnus of Le Mouton Noir) are the torta Vincenzo—layers of goat cheese, roasted red peppers, and fresh basil served on a warm olive waffle and drizzled with fresh basil oil—and curry-dusted pan-seared scallops. • Lunch Tu-F, dinner Tu-Su.

Capellini $$$ 310 Baldwin, San Mateo, (415) 348-2296. The high-ceilinged downstairs dining room (designed by Pat Kuleto), with its dark wood bar and gleaming fixtures, reverberates with the din of local patrons. Try to sit on the loft level for a view of the goings on. Bread served with excellent fruity olive oil starts things off; save space for the tasty pastas, salads, and main dishes. Good wine list. • Lunch M-F, dinner daily.

Capriccio $$$ 4546 El Camino Real, Los Altos, (415) 941-1855. The maître d' is jokey and intimate on your very first visit, the bar is discreetly placed to avoid chance encounters, and the dining room is whimsically decorated with sea birds dangling from the ceiling. Sit at one of the curtained booths for extra privacy. When it comes to the menu, Capriccio offers a wide array of splendid dishes. Try the sautéed prawns or any of the divine veal dishes. • Lunch M-Sa, dinner daily.

Carlos Murphy's $$ 10741 N. Wolfe Rd., Cupertino, (408) 255-6240. Sports fans alert: The bar at Carlos Murphy features seven TVs (two are big-screen), so no matter where you sit you're in viewing distance. Done up to resemble a laid-back barrio town in Mexico, the interior is crammed with memorabilia, including road signs and a VW bus. The menu is standard Mexican American; forays into exotica include shark fajitas and grilled fish tacos. • Lunch and dinner daily, Brunch Sa-Su; bar open until 1:30am.

Carpaccio $$$ 1120 Crane St., Menlo Park, (415) 322-1211. A devoted clientele (including couples who refuse to celebrate their anniversaries anywhere else) flocks to this stylish restaurant. The menu features classic Italian antipasti, pizza, pasta fresca, and seafood and veal dishes. Light eaters beware. Pasta portions are generous, and cream sauces are a little heavy, so order carefully. Good, affordable wine list. Incredible desserts, if you have the appetite. Reservations suggested. • Lunch M-F, dinner daily.

Casa Lupe $$ 185 Main St., Los Altos, (415) 941-7390 • 671 S. Bernardo Ave., Sunnyvale, (408) 739-2900. This small Los Altos restaurant is decorated to the nines with Mexican wall hangings, colorful fiesta knickknacks, and piñatas. The menu is undistinguished, featuring the usual combination plates of enchiladas and tacos—but the service is friendly and patient. Casa Lupe 2 opened recently in Sunnyvale. • Lunch M-F, dinner M-Sa.

Casa Vicky $ 792 E. Julian St., San Jose, (408) 995-5488. One of the best values around. The delicious, spicy food at this self-service Mexican restaurant packs a lot of bang for the buck. You can eat solo for $2 to $4—an enormous tamale goes for just $2, and a fiery chile relleno slathered in guacamole and sour cream is $3.50—or feed the entire family for just $13 with a whole mesquite-broiled chicken accompanied by rice, beans, chips, and salsa. Enjoy your meal outside on a nice day. • Breakfast, lunch, and dinner daily.

Caspian Restaurant $$$$ 1063 E. El Camino Real, Sunnyvale, (408) 248-6332. A calmer if pricier introduction to Persian cuisine than Borsalino Saaghi offers. The tasteful interior features white walls, framed Ansel Adams prints, verdigris light fixtures, and subtle background music. Exotic Persian dishes such as *bulanee*, a turnover filled with leek and spicy potato and topped with cilantro sauce, and *fesenjon*, Cornish hen with a walnut pomegranate sauce, are a departure from the usual Middle Eastern offerings. Bargain diner alert: all dishes half-price before 6pm. • Lunch and dinner daily.

Castro Street Bar and Grill $$ 174 Castro St., Mtn. View, (415) 968-7111. Strictly a wingz-and-thingz scene. Buffalo wings come mild, medium, or hot, and are served with blue cheese dressing. (Order a one-pound basket to go for $3.95—not a bad deal.) Other offerings include fried calamari, hamburgers, and club sandwiches. The menu swerves into alien territory with hoisen chicken salad, spicy fettucine jambalaya, and Jamaican jerk chicken. The outdoor seating on the enclosed patio is a must. • Lunch and dinner daily.

The Cats $$ 1733 Highway 17, Los Gatos, (408) 354-4020. An amiable jumble of a roadhouse. Originally a pit stop between Monterey and San Francisco during the logging boom, the Cats preserves its heritage with frontier food like barbecue beef and honey-glazed pork ribs grilled over an oakwood fire (and also with souvenir T-shirts for sale at the bar). The decor is equally low-key—mismatched wooden chairs, Tiffany lamps, and small tables fill the barroom and a separate dining room. The Cats is south of Los Gatos proper—look for the twin stone bobcats just off Highway 17. • Dinner Tu-Su.

Chantilly II $$$$ 530 Ramona St., Palo Alto, (415) 321-4080. An old-style continental restaurant serving a menu heavy on Italian specialties like carpaccio with onions and mustard sauce, *fettucini al salmone* (pasta with golden, red, and black caviar, smoked salmon, scallions, and cream), and divine tiramisu for dessert. Gracious dining rooms with brass chandeliers, intricate wallpaper, pale pink tablecloths, and a single red rose on each table should please traditionalists. • Lunch M-F, dinner M-Sa.

Chao Praya $$ 4300 El Camino Real, San Mateo, (415) 571-9123. Voted Best Thai by the *San Mateo Times*, Chao Praya draws mid-Peninsulans (even from restaurant-laden Palo Alto) to its small dining room. Cozy seating is available in the honeycomb of roomlets left over from a former life as a motel lobby. Lots of good salads to start things off; try the chicken *larb*. For a main course, the *gai prik sod*—chicken sautéed with fresh chili, bell pepper, and onion—is great. • Lunch M-F, dinner daily.

Charley's $$ 244 State St., Los Altos, (415) 948-5700. One of several Chinese restaurants in downtown Los Altos, Charley's sets itself apart with its upscale decor and exceptional service. Teal chairs, a green carpet, and colorful van Gogh prints provide a garden-room feeling, while Lucite panels etched with classical Greek tableaux serve as dividers among the tables—an eclectic combination, to say the least. The food is traditional Chinese, but the portions are large and the service attentive, friendly, and fast. You can even order dishes prepared according to your own recipes. • Lunch M-F, dinner daily.

Chart House $$$$ 115 N. Santa Cruz Ave., Los Gatos, (408) 354-1737 • 8150 Cabrillo Hwy., Montara Beach, (415) 728-7366. Good, simple food, attentive service, and a spectacular sunset view of Montara Beach make the Montara Chart House a popular local and tourist dinner destination. Further south is the Los Gatos branch, located in a Victorian mansion in the center of town. The restaurant buys its excellent beef from Omaha—prime rib and "baseball sirloin teriyaki" (the tenderest part of the sirloin) are the best on the menu. The salad bar features seasonal fruit like fresh raspberries and a garlicky Caesar as well as the more traditional fare. • Dinner daily (lunch M-F for groups of 20 or more).

Chef Chu's $$ 1067 N. San Antonio Rd., Los Altos, (415) 948-2696. Chef Chu's is a Peninsula institution—the kind of place where autographed photos of Brooke Shields and Gerald Ford hang on the wall. For every detractor who claims that standards have slipped, there's an equally adamant defender. But there's much here that's worth ordering, especially those old favorites, moo shu pork and won ton soup. With its landmark status, Chef Chu's is always crowded; expect to wait for a table most nights. • Lunch and dinner daily.

Cheshire Pub and Pizzeria $ 1494 El Camino Real, San Carlos, (415) 592-0607. At first glance, you wouldn't even know they served pizza in this neighborhood bar setting. Try the pancetta con garlic—that's rolled and hand-tied Italian bacon and roasted fresh garlic. Dreamy. Salad bar negligible, but all kinds of imported beers. Guiness and Harp on tap. Handy take-out service and pleasant outdoor patio. Cash only. • Lunch and dinner daily.

Chevy's $$ 979 Edgewater Blvd., Foster City, (415) 572-8441 • 2907 El Camino Real, Redwood City, (415) 367-6892 • 5305 Almaden Expressway, San Jose, (408) 266-1815 • 550 S. Winchester Blvd., San Jose, (408) 241-0158 • 204 S. Mathilda Ave., Sunnyvale, (408) 737-7395. The Peninsula branches of this chain feature the trademark stacks of Corona cartons as furniture and maddeningly cheerful waitrons. Tortilla chips arrive hot off the press and the smoky salsa is top-notch; fajitas are excellent, and quesadillas won't disappoint, especially after a couple of margaritas. A convivial carnival atmosphere on weekends. • Lunch and dinner daily; open until 11pm F-Sa.

Chez Louis $$$$ 4170 El Camino Real, Palo Alto, (415) 493-1660. You know you've entered Gallic territory by the sign that says "The spirit of l'Omelette is alive and well." Classics like *pâté de campagne* and escargot dominate the menu, with rack of lamb roasted with herbs de Provence and prawns à la Provençal rounding out the choices. Ballroom dance lessons are offered free (for two drinks, that is) on Wednesday and Thursdays. The dark, atmospheric bar is the perfect spot for an illicit rendezvous, perhaps with a French can-can dancer. • Lunch M-F, dinner M-Sa; bar open until 2am.

Chez Sovan $$ 2425 S. Bascom Ave., Campbell, (408) 371-7111 • 923 Thirteenth St., San Jose, (408) 287-7619. The original is located in a bleak San Jose neighborhood, but this shining star recently expanded to additional quarters in Campbell. Mme. Sovan, the chef, serves some of the best Cambodian food on the Peninsula. Try the amazing chicken salad crunchy with peanuts, shredded vegetables, and thin noodles in a beguiling sweet and sour hot sauce—you'll crave it for weeks afterward. Curries are fiery and flavorful; beef, pork, and chicken satés are all redolent of Cambodian barbecue-pit flavor. Service is exceptionally friendly. • Campbell, lunch and dinner daily, San Jose, lunch and dinner M-F.

Chez T.J. $$$$$ 938 Villa St., Mtn. View, (415) 964-7466. The interior of this restored Victorian bungalow is strictly Californian—peach walls, contemporary art, glass sculptures. Three prix fixe menus (from the seven-course menu gastronomique to the positively modest four-course menu petit) are offered nightly. Depending on the luck of the draw, you might be offered sea scallops in a potato crust with saffron sauce, venison with three-mushroom ragout, or monkfish in grape leaves. This is the type of place that serves palate-cleansing sorbets. • Dinner Tu-Sa.

China Lion $$ 3345 El Camino Real, Palo Alto, (415) 424-8168. Near many other Asian restaurants along El Camino in Palo Alto, China Lion alone offers comfortable outdoor seating away from the din of the street. The canopied patio is strung with lights that make for a festive atmosphere at night, while inside the dining area is broken into small, cozy rooms. Samsun Chu, the proprietor, is the younger brother of the more famous Larry of Chef Chu's. The lunch menu is standard (portions are large and cheap), but dinner offers a few unusual and full-flavored dishes such as lovers' prawns (half sautéed in rice wine, half cooked in a tomato-garlic sauce) and Chung King crispy chicken (chicken in a spicy ginger and garlic sauce). • Lunch and dinner daily.

Cho's $ 213 California Ave., Palo Alto, (415) 326-4632. Palo Alto's premier venue for inexpensive dim sum. Mr. Cho himself has been serving pot stickers and pork buns to a retinue of regular customers for years, and his tiny store is a local institution. Only two small tables available; get your food to go and sit in the nearby public plaza. Cash only. • Lunch, dim sum and dinner daily.

City Pub $$ 2620 Broadway, Redwood City, (415) 363-2620. Discover the new Old Redwood City and mingle with hip Peninsulan suburbanites in Doc Martens, Chuck Taylors, and cowboy hats as you sample your way through the extensive selection of draught beer—24 varieties at last count, including Tied House Amber, Lighthouse Ale, and Pilsener Urquell. Historic exposed brick walls contrast with the mod curved copper bar and halogen track lights. Decent pub grub with the basic burger/fries, soup/sandwich, pasta/salad selection. Small but reasonably priced wine list compensates for high-priced coffee drinks. • Lunch and dinner daily.

Clark's by the Bay $$$ 487 Seaport Ct., Redwood City, (415) 367-9222. A creative mix of fish and classic American cuisine characterizes this large restaurant overlooking the marina in Redwood City. The atmosphere is a mix of sports-star memorabilia and dark wood; the service is professional and tends to the formal. Fish is well represented on the menu with dishes like Hawaiian *ono* with a light tomato sauce, perfectly grilled and served with lightly steamed summer vegetables. Those seeking comfort food can indulge in braised lamb shanks with garlic mashed potatoes and a blueberry pie that is among the best around. • Lunch and dinner daily.

Clarke's Charcoal Broiler $ 615 El Camino Real, Mtn. View, (415) 967-0851. A self-service barbecue joint with a large following among carnivores. In addition to innumerable variations on the unadorned Clarkesburger, the menu features grilled dogs, ribs, and chicken. The outdoor seating is somewhat removed from the smoky smell and the blaring of the TV inside—whether that's a plus or a minus is up to you. • Lunch and dinner daily.

Clay Oven $$ 78 E. Third Ave., San Mateo, (415) 342-9195. Indian food finally comes to San Mateo's main drag. The lunch buffet is a good deal—for $7, you can sample more than a dozen Indian dishes. Don't miss the spicy *aloo gobhi*, one of 14 vegetarian dishes on the menu (it's also part of the buffet). Your waiter will also brag about the tandoori chicken—trust him. Clay Oven's relaxed atmosphere features skylights, a full bar partitioned from the dining area, and strains of Middle Eastern music. • Lunch M-F, dinner daily.

Coastline Café $$ 411 E. El Camino Real, Sunnyvale, (408) 746-3000. Hidden off El Camino, Coastline Café is a casual eatery where everything is freshly made. Wednesdays is hamburger night, with countless variations on your basic burger, fresh rolls, and homemade french fries. Other nights feature great pasta primavera with garlic butter sauce, a tasty beef stroganoff, and grilled fish. • Lunch and dinner M-Sa.

Coffee Society $ 21265 Stevens Creek Blvd. (Oaks Shopping Center), Cupertino, (408) 725-8091. Nike-clad Apple employees type on PowerBooks inside while their chain-smoking, nose-pierced kids monopolize the tables outside. Weekends and evenings can be packed and loud. Forgo the overpriced coffee drinks and order the delicious apple *chai*—hot apple cider with a shot of Indian *masala chai* tea. The huge slabs of dense carrot cake are an incredible deal; the other muffins and desserts don't measure up. Service can be slow and sloppy, but it's the only lively café in Cupertino. • Breakfast, lunch, and dinner daily; open until midnight.

Coleman Still $$ 1240 Coleman Ave., Santa Clara, (408) 727-4670. Retreat from civilization into the recesses of what looks like a nineteenth-century miner's shack. The menu includes such rustic fare as blackened red snapper and chicken-fried steak as well as bar basics like potato skins and sandwiches. Contemporary California fare like linguini primavera and shrimp scampi is offered for those diners averse to time travel. Stop by at sunrise for a hearty country breakfast. • Breakfast and dinner daily, lunch M-F, brunch Sa-Su.

Colonel Lee's Mongolian Bar-B-Q $$ 304 Castro St., Mtn. View, (415) 968-0381. Everyone should try Mongolian barbecue once. For the uninitiated, it's an all-you-can-eat ritual in which you choose the raw ingredients of your dinner and pile them into a large bowl that is then ceremoniously emptied onto a sizzling surface. The chef whirls around several portions simultaneously to the delight of onlookers. Pick your ingredients carefully, for you have to eat the result of your own recipe. • Lunch M-F, dinner daily.

Compadres $$ 3877 El Camino Real, Palo Alto, (415) 858-1141. Good California-Mexican cooking, although the pitchers of margaritas are the real draw. Combination plates are a high-yield investment, providing a lot of food for a small price. Sitting in the open-air cantina is a social event. All in all, this is one of the most enjoyable places around, with an efficient staff and a varied menu. What more can we say about this all-time favorite? • Lunch and dinner daily.

Country Fare $ 2680 Middlefield Rd., Palo Alto, (415) 326-3802. The menu at Country Fare emphasizes fresh, organic ingredients. Specialties include smoked turkey and brie sandwiches, avocados stuffed with seafood, salmon salad, and Hawaiian Isle french toast. The deli case has dishes like curry tofu salad, couscous, hummus, and *tabouli*. Like the sign says, save room for dessert. Cash only. • Lunch M-Sa, dinner Tu-F.

Country Gourmet $$ 2098 W. El Camino Real, Mtn. View, (415) 962-0239 • 1314 S. Mary Ave., Sunnyvale, (408) 733-9446. Country cooking and a casual atmosphere are the hallmarks at this mini chain, where you can find dolphin-safe tuna salad on the menu alongside pastrami sandwiches and barbecued chicken. The interior features oak furniture, dried flowers, tin milk cans, and a collection of plants. A commercial feel manages to creep in, though. • Breakfast, lunch, and dinner daily.

Crêpe Daniel $$ 12100 S. Saratoga-Sunnyvale Rd., Saratoga, (408) 725-8554. Crêpes, crêpes, and more crêpes. This cozy café serves dozens of variations on the theme: breakfast crêpes are interesting omelet preparations, lunch and dinner specials feature various seafood, meat, and poultry combinations. • Lunch M-F, dinner daily, brunch Su.

Cuban International $$$ 625 N. Sixth St., San Jose, (408) 288-6783. This restaurant was serving tender caramelized plantains long before the neighborhood became overrun by sushi bars. The small dining room is tropically outfitted, complete with a wall-sized poster of a palm-lined beach. The menu focuses on Cuban meat dishes such as *ropa vieja*, chicken stew, and a tasty Brazilian roast pork but also includes several seafood dishes including an extravagant (and costly) paella, as well as the elusive *guarana* fruit drink. Ask for homemade hot sauce with your meal. • Lunch and dinner daily.

Dac Phuc $ 198 W. Santa Clara St., San Jose, (408) 297-5517. Not much to look at either inside or out (the neon beer signs in the windows are misleading—you might mistake this place for a bar), Dac Phuc serves a lunchtime San Jose crowd looking for a bowl of *pho* or a cheap Vietnamese lunch special. The food's adequate, it is right downtown, and beers are just $1.55. Cash only. • Lunch and dinner Tu-Su.

Dal Baffo $$$$$ 878 Santa Cruz Ave., Menlo Park, (415) 325-1588. Haute Italian food served in a hushed, formal (some might stay stuffy) dining room. One of the most expensive Peninsula restaurants—expect to drop a sizable wad. A wine list the size of *Webster's* that according to the *Wine Spectator* is among the best in the world. Pasta and beef dishes are the high points of the menu. A good place for a celebration (say, winning the lottery). Wear your best dress-up clothes. Reservations essential. • Lunch M-F, dinner M-Sa.

Di Cicco $$ 2509 Bascom Ave., Campbell, (408) 377-5850 • 2665 El Camino Real, Santa Clara, (408) 247-6161. This trattoria seems to be suffering from an identity crisis: old-fashioned red leather booths and burgundy red carpet clash with indoor neon advertising cappuccino and espresso. The salad bar is fresh and varied, while the bread tastes like it came from Italy on the slow boat. The menu is extensive—pizza, seafood, and pasta selections abound—while the wine list is minuscule. A first-rate cup of espresso at meal's end adds some zest to a good, if not memorable, traditional Italian dinner. • Lunch and dinner daily; open late Sa only.

Dinah's Poolside Café $ 4261 El Camino Real, Palo Alto, (415) 493-4542. A Palo Alto weekend brunch institution, Dinah's caters to a slightly older crowd than some of its upstart competitors. Although you need a map and a compass to find this unpretentious dining spot (just turn in at the tiny sign and proceed to the rear of the parking lot, down the steps, and around the building), the wait for a table on a Sunday morning is every bit as long as it is at Hobee's. The good news is that the wait is much more pleasant—you can dangle your feet in the water and listen to the birds chirp. The food is solidly American—fresh and plentiful, with a guaranteed lack of surprises. You'll leave satisfied, but it's the pleasant surroundings and cheerful, family-style service that will keep you coming back, not the culinary achievements. • Breakfast, lunch, and dinner daily.

The Dining Room $$$ 1602 S. El Camino Real, San Mateo, (415) 349-5552. A 1907 country cottage plunked down on El Camino in San Mateo. No-nonsense diners might find the lace curtains, floral tablecloths, and china hutch filled with antique dolls precious, but the soft lighting and leisurely paced meals can make a dinner here seem like a romantic getaway even if you live just around the block. The smallish menu is classic continental—veal Oscar, trout amandine, and the like. Start with a glass of Dubonnet or Kir Royal, and forget about city life for the rest of the evening. • Dinner Tu-Sa.

Duke of Edinburgh $$$ 10801 N. Wolfe Rd., Cupertino, (408) 446-3853. This Silicon Valley watering hole for would-be Brits dispenses eight brews on tap—including Watneys, Harp, Fullers, and Newcastle brown ale—and serves quintessential "English Fayre" such as fish n' chips (crispy and not too oily), bangers and mash, and a good ploughman's lunch with chutney and cheddar. The interior was imported from England, from the carpeting to the lamps. On warm afternoons sit on the outdoor patio (an authentic British telephone booth graces one corner) with a a black-and-tan or a shandy. • Lunch and dinner daily.

The Dutch Goose $ 3567 Alameda de las Pulgas, Menlo Park, (415) 854-3245. Push through the creaky screen door for beer, burgers, pool, and some sunshine on the patio out back. The carvings in the tables and peanut shells on the floor let you know that you've found a classic hangout. Have the bartender pull you an Anchor Steam from the tap, try some deviled eggs, toss your peanut shells on the floor, and relax. Cash only. • Lunch and dinner daily until 11:45pm; bar open until 1am.

Ecco Café $$$ 322 Lorton Ave., Burlingame, (415) 342-7355. Self-taught chef Tooraj offers some of the most creative fine dining on the Peninsula. In an intimate dining room, he serves dishes that meld the freshest ingredients into subtle, balanced creations, some laced with lavender. Inventive standouts include a watercress and apricot soup and ahi tuna with an anchovy and olive compote. • Lunch M-F, dinner M-Sa.

840 North First $$$$ 840 N. First St., San Jose, (408) 282-0840. San Jose's power elite flock here at lunchtime—you might spot Mayor Susan Hammer or lawyers on a lunch break from the courthouse. The sophisticated dining room—done up in grays and maroons with quirky modern light fixtures—is the ideal backdrop for business occasions. Italian and Asian influences prevail in the kitchen; pasta choices include shellfish linguine. Prawns with chili paste, sherry, and ginger are featured among the appetizers. The chef's upscale version of surf and turf is sautéed filet mignon with prawns served with sun-dried tomatoes and mushrooms. • Lunch M-F, dinner M-Sa.

El Burro $$ 1875 S. Bascom Ave., The Pruneyard, Campbell, (408) 471-5800. An elaborate two-tiered maze of dining rooms and decorations mocked up like a Spanish villa. The foot-and-a-half-tall menu is as large-scale as the restaurant and surprisingly authentic, with lots of diced pork and California chilies and 16 kinds of enchiladas. More notable is the decor: every inch of the faux stucco interior is painted with trompe l'oeil windows, bricks, and ivy. Innumerable wagon-wheel iron lamps and terra-cotta planters hang from both ceilings, the wait staff's attire is determinedly festive, and thumping Latin music permeates every room. The enormous outdoor patio is equally heavy on the atmosphere and makes a popular gathering spot for local revelers. • Lunch and dinner daily.

El Calderon $$ 699 Calderon Ave., Mtn. View, (415) 940-9533. The oldest and best Salvadorean restaurant on the Peninsula. The food is traditional, and there's a piano player to keep you amused with his renditions of Hollywood classics. Try the *pupusas*—El Salvador's national snack—corn tortillas filled with either cheese, chorizo, or chicken and then fried and served with an *encurtido de vegetales*. Another dish worth trying is the combination plate of *chicharron*, plantains, *pupusas*, rice, and beans. • Lunch M-Sa, dinner daily.

El Maghreb $$$ 145 W. Santa Clara St., San Jose, (408) 294-2243. Lounge on sumptuous sofas and cushions while you feast on delicious Moroccan cuisine served from communal dishes. (In authentic Moroccan style, diners eschew utensils.) The four prix fixe menus feature deliciously spiced lamb and chicken dishes—this is no place for vegetarians—plus eggplant salad, couscous, and fresh fruit and mint tea for dessert. Don't worry if you overindulge—the belly dancers will soon have you shimmying and gyrating the calories off. Tends to be empty midweek and packed on the weekends. Best for a big, festive group. • Dinner daily.

El Pollo Asado $ 1620A Saratoga Ave., San Jose, (408) 866-4204. El Pollo Asado specializes in charbroiled chicken. The economically priced two-piece chicken meal served with side dishes and tortillas is perfect for solo diners. The salsa bar features a variety of condiments to add pizzazz to any meal. Definitely worth a visit. • Lunch and dinner daily.

Emil Villa's Hick'ry Pit $$ 980 E. Campbell Ave., Campbell, (408) 371-2400. A Midwestern-style family diner. The specialty is barbecued beef and pork (bottles of the sauce are available to go), with due attention also paid to omelets and fried side orders. The Naugahyde swivel chairs at the counter afford views of paper-toqued cooks chopping meat. Dessert is homemade pie, naturally. This is the sort of place where the waitresses wear white camp shirts with black A-line skirts and carry pots of coffee at all times. • Breakfast, lunch and dinner daily.

Emile's $$$$$ 545 S. Second St., San Jose, (408) 289-1960. Emile's has ruled the San Jose dining scene for 17 years. Chef/owner Emile Mooser, the dapper Swiss-born and-trained chef, has a flair for public relations (expect to see him canvassing the dining room). The newly remodeled interior has a subdued elegance: an elaborate flower arrangement dominates the dining room, and an intricate, leaflike sculpture decorates the ceiling. Many of the dishes live up to Emile's vaunted reputation: grilled swordfish served with seafood risotto is perfectly cooked, and the osso buco is tender, rich, and flavorful. Finish off your meal with an ethereal Grand Marnier soufflé. • Dinner Tu-Sa, lunch Friday only.

Empire Grill and Tap Room $$$ 651 Emerson St., Palo Alto, (415) 321-3030. This energetic, convivial eatery done up in forest green and lots of burnished wood was a hit the moment it opened its doors. Silicon Valley swingers flock to the long bar to down pints of Red Hook and Anchor Steam and survey the scene. On balmy evenings, the outdoor patio is an ideal spot for a date—the lighting's low, there's enough bustle to fill in the awkward stretches of silence, and the wait staff is discreet and good-humored. The food's good, too, especially the designer pizzas and grilled fish specials. •Lunch M-Sa, dinner daily, brunch Su; bar open until 11:30pm or later.

The English Rose $$ 663 Laurel St., San Carlos, (415) 595-5549. An exceedingly ladylike English tea house with surprisingly delicious food. The rigorously coordinated place settings include lavender napkins, pastel-patterned teacups, and floral tea cozies. Framed paintings of the English countryside, pictures of royalty, decorative plates, and all manner of bric-a-brac line the walls. The menu is inexpensive and authentic, if limited. Luncheon items include quiches, wonderful Cornish pasties, and banger-and-onion sandwiches as well as tea plates and classic ploughman's lunches. Cash only. • Breakfast and lunch M-Sa.

Ernesto's $$$ 14101 Winchester Blvd., Los Gatos, (408) 374-3522. Hidden within a 1950s diner–style exterior and behind a dark, grim-looking barroom, the airy, sparkling-white dining room of Ernesto's takes you by surprise. So does the menu, which includes the usual assortment of burritos, flautas, and tacos served with rice and beans as well as an entrée selection that owes as much to continental Europe as it does to Mexico. Sole and bay shrimp are pan-seared in garlic, lemon, sweet butter, and white wine; medallions of chicken breast are sautéed with a novel mélange of rosemary, thyme, shallots, green olives, and potatoes. Rice pilaf, salad, and vegetables accompany these dishes, and the desserts are wheeled out grandly on a cart. This unique combination of south-of-the-border and Old World cuisines attracts substantial crowds—call ahead for reservations. • Lunch M-Sa, dinner daily.

Esperanza's Restaurant $ 173 S. Murphy Ave., Sunnyvale, (408) 732-3263. Excellent Mexican specialties at low prices. The cheery interior, decorated with trompe l'oeil scenes of Mexico and bright green tablecloths, makes a pleasant setting for a quick meal of fajitas, burritos, tamales, or enchiladas. Try the delicious *chilaquiles*—soft fried corn tortilla with eggs, onions, jalepeños, and tomatoes served with tangy chile verde sauce. • Lunch and dinner daily.

Esposto's Four-Day Café $$$ 1119 S. B St., San Mateo, (415) 345-6443. Next to the B Street Launderette and practically skirting the train tracks, Esposto's is a local favorite you'd never just stumble upon. Nevertheless, this small, dark Italian restaurant is consistently busy the four days it's open, especially on weekends. The ambience and the menu are casually eclectic. Bottles of wine, a rack of candy bars, and even a rubber chicken contribute to the entry display; the pastas and entrées range from northern Italian all the way to Sicilian. The appetizers are bargains: grilled squid with pepperonata and polenta with wild mushrooms each run about $4. Esposto's may not qualify as fine dining, but it's a surprisingly pleasant spot for a laid-back Italian meal. *Note*: Esposto's is also a deli by day. • Lunch (deli) daily, dinner W–Sa.

Eugene's Polish Restaurant $$$ 420 S. San Antonio Rd., Los Altos, (415) 941-1222. The dark, wood-paneled dining room and bar decorated with momentos from Poland quickly transport you from the bright glitter of Silicon Valley to the Old Country. The menu, which features goulash, *pierogi*, and kielbasa, delivers authentic Eastern European flavors. Filling, meat-oriented dishes are the perfect repast on a cold winter evening or dreary rainy day—the hunter's goulash hits the spot. (A vegetarian pierogi platter is offered for nonmeat eaters.) The owners, Eugene and Elizabeth Witkowicz, maintain close ties with the local Polish community, and it's not uncommon to find an impromptu polka jam session going on around you. •Lunch Tu-F, dinner Tu-Su.

Eulipia $$$$ 374 S. First St., San Jose, (408) 280-6161. One of San Jose's trendier spots, Eulipia is done up in high style: sponge-painted walls in shades of ocher, lavender, and gray; an exposed brick wall; and a long, gleaming copper bar. The food is equally high concept; choices range from a Philly cheese steak sandwich with chipotle mayonnaise at lunch to roasted rack of lamb with cabernet demi glace at dinner. One supposed specialty (ordered at the waitress's recommendation) was an ill-conceived combination featuring a slab of brie plopped on a naked chicken breast. • Lunch Tu-F, dinner Tu-Su.

Falafel Drive-In $ 2301 Stevens Creek Blvd., San Jose, (408) 294-7886. Although it looks like a burger joint given a make-over by recent immigrants from the Middle East, Falafel Drive-In has actually been in its present location in the Burbank area of San Jose since 1966. The Drive-In's longevity can be attributed to a simple formula: darn good falafel at working-class prices. Order some fries or onion rings on the side for the perfect vegetarian grease fix. Indoor and outdoor seating is available, and the menu includes burgers for the meat-dependent. • Lunch and dinner daily.

Fiesta del Mar $$ 1005 N. Shoreline, Mtn. View, (415) 965-9354. A bright aqua-and-peach pavilion serving an array of seafood and Mexican specialties, including a few prepararations you might not expect from your usual Mexican restaurant. The seafood selection is the standout, with five different shrimp dinners and one salmon entrée, as well such unexpected à la carte items as poblano chiles stuffed with crab. More traditional pork, chicken, and beef dishes also abound, in a variety of flavorful sauces. • Breakfast, lunch, and dinner daily.

The Fish Market $$$ 3150 El Camino Real, Palo Alto, (415) 493-9188 • 1855 S. Norfolk St., San Mateo, (415) 349-3474 • 3775 El Camino Real, Santa Clara, (408) 246-3474. The El Camino outpost of this chain looks like a nautical warehouse: it features polished brass and wood, photos of fishing piers, and exposed ventilation ducts. The menu offers a huge selection of fresh seafood, mostly mesquite grilled, but also steamed, sautéed, or raw (sushi, ceviche, or half-shell). It's simple, but well done. • Lunch and dinner daily.

Flea Street Café $$$ 3607 Alameda de las Pulgas, Menlo Park, (415) 854-1226. The ambience of a cozy country house and the cooking of enlightened chef and local celebrity Jesse Cool make this a must-visit. An omelet is not just an omelet here, but a concoction of stir-fried greens, roasted garlic, goat cheese, sun-dried tomato cream, and Yucatan sausage. Dinner selections include grilled salmon with mashed buttermilk potatoes. You get the satisfaction of eating organic produce, although healthy comes at a fairly hefty price. Lunches are easier on the pocketbook. • Lunch Tu-F, dinner Tu-Sa, brunch Su.

Florentine $$ 4546 El Camino Real, Los Altos, (415) 949-1235 • 118 Castro St., Mt.View, (415) 961-6543 • 560 Waverley St., Palo Alto, (415) 326-5295 • 2525 El Camino Real, Redwood City, (415) 365-0444 • 745 S. Winchester Blvd., San Jose, (408) 243-4040 • 14510 Big Basin Way, Saratoga, (408) 741-1784 • 460 E El Camino Real, Sunnyvale, (408) 720-1299. Popular, bustling South Bay restaurant chain, though each location has its own look and personality. The portions are large—the three-pasta appetizer is a dinner in itself, and the wedges of pizzalike bread are addictive. Pastas, sadly, tend to be overcooked. The homemade sauces and pasta are available by the pound. • Palo Alto and San Jose, lunch M-F, dinner daily; Saratoga, lunch M-Sa; Redwood City, and Sunnyvale, lunch and dinner daily; takeout only at the Los Altos location.

Fook Yuen $$ 195 El Camino Real, Millbrae, (415) 692-8600. A convenient, commodious, family-oriented restaurant serving high-quality Hong Kong–style cuisine. Fish is uniformly fresh, and barbecued meats are also recommended. Try the fabulous fried whole flounder and the Peking duck done to perfection. At times the brightly lit dining room can be loud and cacophonous, but the service doesn't suffer. Bring Grandma and the kids—no one will look askance. In fact, you'll fit in better. • Lunch, dim sum and dinner daily.

Fresco $$$ 3398 El Camino Real, Palo Alto, (415) 493-3470. It's hard to fathom why the owner chose a former fast food joint as the site of this California-cuisine eatery. This place looks like it belongs in an airport, although it is pleasant and cheery. Try experimental dishes like new-potato skins with prawns, jack cheese, and pesto, or crab and scallop cakes with dill and horseradish. Some work (the skins), some don't (the crabcakes). An eclectic mix of safer dishes like grilled meat and fish, pasta, and sandwiches is available for the less adventurous. • Breakfast, lunch, and dinner daily; open until 11pm.

Fresh Choice $ 1654 S. Bascom Ave., Campbell, (408) 559-1912 • 10123 N. Wolfe Rd., Vallco Fashion Park, Cupertino, (408) 253-1605 • 600 Santa Cruz Ave., Menlo Park, (415) 323-4061 • 555 E. Calveras Ave., Milpitas, (408) 262-6604 • 379 Stanford Shopping Center, Palo Alto, (415) 322-6995 • 1099 El Camino Real, Redwood City, (415) 299-1105 • 1600 Saratoga Ave., Westgate Shopping Center, San Jose, (408) 866-1491 • 1962 El Camino Real, San Mateo, (415) 341-8498 • 3041 Stevens Creek Blvd. Valley Fair Center, Santa Clara, (408) 243-7402 • 1105 W. El Camino Real, Sunnyvale, (408) 732-7788. Now that there's Fresh Choice, you have no excuse not to eat healthy. For $7 ($6 at lunch), you get as many visits to the enormous salad bar as you can manage. Included in the deal are unlimited stop-offs at the soup, pasta, muffin, and dessert bars. Expect lines at peak hours (they move swiftly) but also high turnover of the fresh produce. Keep your eyes open for new locations, which seem to open up on every corner. • Lunch and dinner daily.

Fuji $$ 56 W. Santa Clara St., San Jose, (408) 298-3854. Best known for its Bento boxes (a Japanese sampler of teriyaki, tempura, and sashimi) Fuji provides quick service, fresh ingredients, and a filling meal for a fair price to a downtown lunch crowd. Run by a husband-and-wife team, Fuji offers the usual Japanese menu amid the traditional decor of hanging globe lamps, Oriental prints, and a small sushi bar. • Lunch and dinner M-Sa.

Fuki-Sushi $$$ 4119 El Camino Real, Palo Alto, (415) 494-9383. A giant sushi spot with private tatami rooms—take your shoes off, sit on the floor (dangle your feet in the well), and sip sake served by a waitress in a kimono. Try the Japanese-style fondue called shabu shabu, which is a pot of boiling broth into which you dip cabbage, mushrooms, onions, and thinly sliced meat, and then dip the cooked morsels into a mustard sauce. Finish it off by drinking the broth. Open every day of the year. • Lunch M-F, dinner daily.

Gambardella's $$$ 561 Oak Grove Ave., Menlo Park, (415) 325-6989. Good, hearty southern Italian food served in an atmospheric wood-panelled dining room decorated with hundreds of old wine bottles. Specials might include lobster ravioli with Chardonnay cream sauce or petrale sole with spicy tomato sauce. A welcome respite from rampant trendiness—this place feels like it's been around for years. • Lunch Tu-F, dinner Tu-Su.

Gao Poang $$ 1425 Burlingame Ave., Burlingame, (415) 340-1444 • 275 S. Airport Blvd., South San Francisco, (415) 876-7008. A pretty mauve-and-brass Chinese restaurant over-run with greenery. The menu is ordinary, but the accommodating kitchen will adjust any dish to your liking. Warning: an unappealing smell pervaded the dining room at review time (no explanation was available). You can either hope it was an aberration or hedge your bets by ordering take-out. • Lunch and dinner daily.

Garden City $$$$ 360 S. Saratoga Ave., San Jose (408) 244-4443. Las Vegas comes to San Jose at this legendary South Bay steakhouse. Located on the premises of San Jose's largest gambling and gaming venue, Garden City serves three-inch-thick prime rib, steaks, filets, and grilled fish. Meat-and-potato cuisine is done to perfection here—hence the crowds of loyal patrons. The interior is dimly lit with a nightclub ambience—during dinner hours a jazz band holds forth. • Lunch M-Sa, dinner daily; open until midnight.

Garden Grill $$$$ 1026 Alma St., Menlo Park, (415) 325-8981. Civilized teas are served on the lovely outdoor trellised patio—choose from a "compleat" tea (scones with clotted cream), a cream tea, or a cheese tea. The dining room is on the stuffy side: pastel floral wallpaper, white wrought-iron chandeliers, and lots of grandparents. Classic, well-pre-pared English dishes like prime rib of Angus beef with Yorkshire pudding and horseradish sauce, 14th-century spiced broth with dumplings, and shepherd's pie are served up by the pleasant, efficient wait staff. • Lunch M-F, afternoon tea M-Sa (3pm-5:30pm), dinner M-Sa.

Gaylord India Restaurant $$$ 317 Stanford Shopping Center, Palo Alto, (415) 326-8761. Seekh kabobs, chicken *tikka*, tandoori chicken done to perfection, and garlic *naan* and onion *kulchas* warm from the oven are but a few of the highlights at this elegant, expensive Indian establishment. The elaborate menu covers almost all north Indian dish-es, including a savory lamb curry served with fragrant basmati rice and delectable cucum-ber-yogurt *raita*. Order a Bombay beer to wash it all down and have yourself a dinner fit for a Raj. • Lunch M-Sa, dinner daily, champagne brunch Su.

Germania Restaurant $$$ 261 N. Second St., San Jose, (408) 295-4484. Housed in the 100-year-old Hochburg von Germania historical landmark, this restaurant is filled with Teutonic memorabilia—suits of armor, coats of arms, and antique beer steins. The menu features traditional German dishes prepared with California touches such as tarragon but-ter or spicy pear sauce. The homemade *spätzle* is delicious. Weekends bring live music and dancing in the attached Austrian ballroom. More than 30 German beers are available, and there's an outdoor patio. • Lunch Tu-F, dinner Tu-Su.

Golden Chopsticks $$ 1765 S. Winchester Blvd., Campbell, (408) 370-6610. Learn how to cook Vietnamese at this do-it-yourself restaurant, where the specialties include an entrée of beef, chicken, shrimp, and calamari that you barbecue at your table on a rock heated to more than 450 degrees. The chef prepares the accompanying anchovy sauce and the vegetables wrapped in rice paper. Timid or lazy diners can choose from fried or sautéed beef, poultry, and seafood with accents of lemongrass and fish sauce, as well as a substan-tial variety of vegetarian dishes. The truly intrepid can order fried pigeon or eel soup with rice noodles. Pink fluorescent lights give the dining room a warm glow; the waitresses are in elaborate traditional dress to match. • Lunch and dinner daily.

Golden Wok $$ 895 Villa St., Mtn. View, (415) 969-8232 • Take-out only at 451 California St., Palo Alto, (415) 327-2222. This upholder of the *Fantasy Island*-style of decor serves decent, reasonably priced Chinese food inside or outside on the pleasant patio at lunch. If you're experiencing a surge of bravado, order the shark's fin soup, which actually tastes more like chicken soup with vermicelli noodles. Well-seasoned hot and sour soup is a deal, but skip the pot stickers in favor of the Chinese chicken salad. • Lunch and dinner daily.

Goldie's Oakwood Bar-B-Que $ 1940-C University Ave., East Palo Alto, (415) 321-1019. Finger-licking-good barbecue, traditional down to the Wonder bread it's served on, in a three-table store just off the freeway in East Palo Alto. Mild, tender meats in a tomato-rich sauce with a hot sting. Strictly counter service. • Lunch and dinner daily.

Gombei Japanese Kitchen $$ 1438 El Camino Real, Menlo Park, (415) 329-1799 • 193 E. Jackson St., San Jose, (408) 279-431. You won't find any slimy, fishy things in this Japanese restaurant specializing in simple, light, cooked dishes like teriyaki, tempura, donburi (rice bowls), and udon (noodle soup). A special salad of exotic Asian vegetables was a sculptural triumph one night, with a tangle of seaweed nestled among the various roots and unidentified vegetation. Looking into the open kitchen you'd think the meticulous chefs were assembling Swiss watches instead of meals. The largely Japanese crowd bodes well for the food, but can often mean a wait. Cash only. • Lunch M-F, dinner daily.

Good Earth $$ 2087 Stevens Creek Blvd., Cupertino, (408) 252-3555 • 206 N. Santa Cruz Ave., Los Gatos, (408) 395-6868 • 185 University Ave., Palo Alto, (415) 321-9449 • 3190 Campus Dr., San Mateo, (415) 349-0165 • 2705 The Alameda, Santa Clara, (408) 984-0960. Generous portions of healthy dishes served in an upgraded coffee-shop. There's an ample selection of vegetarian dishes, Mexican entrées retrofitted for suburban Californians, and homemade soups. The restaurant is packed for Saturday and Sunday brunch; sample one of the muffins from the front case before you dig in to your giant bowl of Chinese chicken salad or garlicky Santa Cruz scramble. • Breakfast, lunch, and dinner daily.

Gordon Biersch Brewing Company $$ 640 Emerson St., Palo Alto, (415) 323-7723 • 33 E San Fernando St., San Jose, (408) 294-6785. This upscale beer hall packs them in. The magic formula? Fresh beer brewed on the premises; attractive, on-the-prowl clientele; and an all-around stylish ambience. The long polished wood bar is favored by the young business set, especially on weekend evenings. The California-style cuisine has a mixed reputation, but burgers are always a good wager, and the garlic fries are delicious. • Lunch and dinner daily; bar until 11pm or later.

Great Bear Café and Los Osos Diner $ 19 N. Santa Cruz Ave., Los Gatos, (408) 395-8607. Sensory overload. A rich coffee smell, loud Santa Cruz–style music, and bright oil paintings lining an exposed brick wall set the stage for the strongly flavored dishes at this self-service diner and espresso bar. The menu practically dares you to try a sandwich of spicy Italian sausage and peppers on a sourdough baguette or the garlic pizza with tomatoes, mushrooms, parmesan, and red onions. The glass case at the order counter contains a motley assortment of fruit salads, knishes, and gargantuan slices of truly amazing fruit pie. • Breakfast, lunch, and dinner daily; open until 11pm.

Gulliver's $$$ 1699 Old Bayshore Hwy., Burlingame, (415) 692-6060. A self-styled eighteenth-century English tavern, with an ivy-covered exterior and an interior done up with hanging copper pans and knickknacks galore. "Serving maids" wear scoop-necked bodices, full skirts, and white kerchiefs. The menu mixes pastas, burgers, and sandwiches with Old World standards like prime rib, lamb chops, and broiled steaks; creamed corn accompanies most entrées. Die-hard Anglophiles can finish with English trifle. • Lunch M-F, dinner daily.

Gypsy Cellar $$$ 932 Middlefield Rd., Redwood City, (415) 367-1166. Intimate tables and subdued lighting add to the Old World charm at this Czech/Hungarian restaurant. No caped counts in the vicinity—just a warm welcome and friendly, courteous service. Food is deliciously unique—try the stuffed grape leaves, and be sure to sample the fresh-mint-flavored peas. A pianist and violinist keep you entertained throughout the evening. Regulars in the predominantly forty-something crowd cheerfully gather around the bar for yet another drink and a song. • Dinner Tu-Su.

Hamasushi $$$ 20300 Stevens Creek Blvd., Cupertino, (408) 446-4262. A conspicuous East-meets-West dropout, the former Chez Nous Hama has renounced its French menu to return to its roots as a purveyor of strictly traditional Japanese fare. Perhaps it's for the best—the French-Japanese menu never really worked. The reborn Hamasushi is more elegant than the average sushi joint (although karaoke does make an appearance most nights). • Lunch M-F, dinner daily.

Hangen $$ 134 Castro St., Mtn. View, (415) 964-8881. Call the fire engines—the food at this Castro Street newcomer is flaming hot. The unremarkable interior is bright and noisy, but the food is some of the best Szechuan around. Word is out, though, and dinner lines can be long. Recommended dishes include red oil wontons, heavenly sliced conch salad, tea-smoked duck, eggplant with sliced pork, and Hunan crispy fish. • Lunch and dinner daily.

Hardy's $$ 111 W. Evelyn Ave., Sunnyvale, (408) 720-1531. Generous portions of traditional German fare, including sauerkraut, dumplings, and wurst. Try the warm mushroom salad for a light but satisfying meal. The colorful, Tyrolean cutout dolls lend cheer to the bright, casual interior. There is also seating outside in a pleasant, enclosed courtyard. A bar sports real German Spaten on tap, as well as other bottled German beers; German newspapers and magazines are available for your perusal. • Lunch Tu-F, dinner Tu-Sa.

Henry's $$$ 482 University Ave., Palo Alto, (415) 326-5680. The first visit to Henry's is a surprise. In the back, tucked away behind the neighborhood bar, is a convincing French bistro complete with tiled floor and starched linens. If you find yourself waiting for a table, free popcorn at the bar will tide you over. Generous portions of French-influenced but California-grown dishes await you when you take your seat, as well as good french fries and hamburgers. Fresh fish and meat cuts come with delicious sauces. • Lunch M-F, dinner daily.

Henry's World Famous Hi-Life $$ 301 W. Saint John St., San Jose, (408) 295-5414. Housed in a century-old roadhouse, Henry's is a South Bay institution. Smoky, white-oak barbecue is the specialty—choose from flavorful ribs served with a bowl of spicy sauce, teriyaki steak, or perhaps a side of mushrooms or barbecued onions. Pick a number and wait your turn in the dim, memorabilia-packed bar (an oil portrait of founder Henry Puckett presides over the merriment). • Lunch Tu-F, dinner daily.

Higashi West $$$ 636 Emerson St., Palo Alto, (415) 323-9378. Higashi West's dramatic interior features an indoor waterfall and soaring shoots of black bamboo. The menu is equally striking, featuring many daring East-West preparations. Try the garlic-crusted pork chops with green apple essence and wasabi mashed potatoes, or the Higashi West roll—smoked salmon wrapped around tiger shrimp and baked. The traditional sushi is well prepared and fresh, although pricey. The menu lists 13 varieties of saki, but beware—a few glasses and you may be under the waterfall trying to sober up. • Lunch M-F, dinner M-Sa.

Hobee's Restaurant $ 21267 Stevens Creek Blvd, Cupertino, (408) 255-6010 • 2312 Central Expressway, Mtn. View, (415) 968-6050 • 67 Town and Country Village, Palo Alto, (415) 327-4111 • 4224 El Camino Real, Palo Alto, (415) 856-6124 • 920 Town and Country Village, San Jose, (408) 244-5212. A country-style restaurant chain with a healthy California influence, Hobee's serves up legendary brunches on weekends in a cheery if precious atmosphere. Although breakfast is always available (don't miss the famed coffee cake), take a chance on the delicious daily specials and nonbreakfast standards like the flavorful black bean chili. A favorite breakfast spot of high-tech execs. Ronald Reagan stopped in on a visit to the Valley. • Cupertino, Mtn. View and Town and Country Village, Palo Alto, breakfast, lunch and dinner daily; El Camino Real, Palo Alto and San Jose, breakfast and lunch daily, dinner Tu-Sa.

Hong Fu $$ 20588 Stevens Creek Blvd., Cupertino, (408) 252-2200. Light-handed, Cantonese-leaning seafood specialties served in an elegant, airy dining room decorated with jade statuettes set Hong Fu apart from the run-of-the-mill South Bay Chinese restaurant. Start with minced chicken in a lettuce cup, then try one of the well-prepared seafood dishes such as triple delight in bird's nest—a combination of shrimp, scallops, chicken, and vegetables in a lightly fried potato basket—or dry braised scallops with broccoli. Vegetarians can choose from sizzling tofu Hong Fu style and a variety of braised and sautéed vegetable dishes. All food available for take-out; reserve a table on weekend nights to avoid a wait. • Lunch and dinner daily.

Hong Kong Flower Lounge $$$ 1671 El Camino Real, Millbrae, (415) 588-9972 • 51 Millbrae Ave., Millbrae, (415) 692-6666. A celebrated tile-roofed temple with floor-to-ceiling windows on all three tiers. Ostentatious, yes, even gaudy, but somehow lovable. The Flower Lounge is best enjoyed by a group; reserve one of the round tables by the window. The specialty here is Hong Kong Cantonese seafood: live prawns, crab, lobster, catfish, and ling cod are fished out of huge glass tanks to appear moments later on your plate. The Flower Lounge doesn't stint—if you order prawns with walnut sauce or Szechuan conch and scallops, you'll get a plate piled high. The original location on El Camino is simpler. • Lunch, dim sum and dinner daily.

Hong Truc $ 304 E. Santa Clara St., San Jose, (408) 279-8764. For the adventurous palate, this outpost stands as a beacon. Jellyfish, prawn, and pork salad, perhaps? Have a craving for chicken feet salad? Grilled beef wrapped in Hawaiian tea leaves? The menu is eight pages long, so there's something for everyone. The unremarkable interior features white tablecloths, mirrors, and fake wood paneling. Stick to the classic Vietnamese beef soup pho if you find the choices overwhelming. • Lunch and dinner daily; open until 1am F-Su.

Horky's $$ 1316 El Camino Real, Belmont, (415) 591-7177. Huge servings of satisfying, lovingly prepared Mexican food. The dark but festive dining room features wrought-iron chandeliers with red and yellow lamps and dozens of stone Aztec and Mayan statuettes and carvings. Horky's is easy to spot—look for the carved wooden doors and Aztec stone masks. • Lunch M-F, dinner daily.

House of Cathay & House of Genji $$$ House of Cathay: 1339 N. First St., San Jose, (408) 453-8148 • House of Genji: 1335 N. First St., San Jose, (408) 453-8120. Two neighboring Asian restaurants with a manager in common. The food at House of Cathay is strictly routine Chinese, but the restaurant is invariably packed. At Genji, chefs display elaborate Teppan-style knifework as they prepare Japanese fare cooked to order at your table. • House of Cathay: lunch and dinner daily, House of Genji: lunch M-F, dinner daily.

Hunan Homes $$ 4880 El Camino Real, Los Altos, (415) 965-8818. This unassuming Chinese restaurant serves some of the best hot and sour soup on the Peninsula—the broth is thin and savory, with thin strips of pork and crunchy mushrooms. Also not to be missed are the exceptional wontons in spicy broth. Main courses don't quite live up to the starters, but the quality is generally high. Decor is of the standard-issue Chinese-restaurant-with-pink-walls-and-fish-tank variety. • Lunch, dim sum and dinner daily.

Iberia $$$ 190 Ladera Country Shopper, Alpine Rd., Portola Valley, (415) 854-1746. Regarded as one of the best on the Peninsula, Iberia prepares Spanish specialties in a beautiful setting. Spend a romantic evening in one of the indoor rooms or outside in the garden over large portions of terrific paella or seafood (you don't have to love garlic to love Iberia, but it helps). Many preparations, including dessert flambés, are orchestrated tableside. • Lunch and dinner daily, brunch Su.

Ikenohana $$$ 20625 Alves Dr., Cupertino, (408) 252-6460. This Japanese restaurant in the heart of Silicon Valley features a Zen sand garden out front and a courtyard with a landscaped pond full of large carp and water lilies. The interior has a sleek sushi bar, and a large dining area populated by fuchsia-upholstered chairs. Specialties include lobster (watch them crawl around the fish tank), a variety of teriyaki dishes, and a broad sushi selection. • Lunch M-F, dinner daily.

Il Fornaio Cucina Italiana $$$ 520 Cowper St., Palo Alto, (415) 853-3888 • 302 S. Market St., San Jose, (408) 271-3366. The food is always highbrow, the service surly, and the wait long at the Peninsula's most glamorous restaurant chain. Pioneering pastas, carpaccio with arugula, and the occasional wild-boar ragout attract notables such as Joe Montana, the local Euro set, and anyone else who wants to be seen. The shiny wood bar affords a view of the frantic chefs at work, and the wood-burning ovens emit a delicious aroma—anything off the grill is a good bet. •Breakfast M-F, lunch and dinner daily, brunch Sa-Su; open until 11pm or later.

India Cookhouse $$ 288 Castro St., Mtn. View, (415) 968-8956. Good food at reasonable prices. The tandoori, the lamb or chicken *tikkas*, the hot and spicy vindaloos, as well as the numerous vegetarian entrées are all worth trying. Forgo à la carte options for the dinners, which come with soup, *naan*, basmati rice, vegetables, *raita*, salad, and dessert. • Lunch and dinner daily, open until 10:30pm.

Iron Gate $$$ 1360 El Camino Real, Belmont, (415) 592-7893. Elegant and expensive French cuisine in a romantic if slightly stuffy setting. Take someone special, order the *crevettes bordelaise* or *veau à la saltimbocca* for two, and bask in the glow of the wrought-iron chandeliers. The cocktail lounge, which is nearly as large as the dining room, features live jazz and a happy hour on Thursday evenings. • Lunch M-F, dinner M-Sa.

Isobune $$ 1451 Burlingame Ave., Burlingame, (415) 344-8433. The waterfall outside suggests glamour inside, but Isobune is just a basic sushi bar. Dozens of sushi boats drifting along a blue table-height canal restate the water theme with a more commercial inflection; countless green banners emblazoned with the restaurant's name divide the light wooden booths. • Lunch and dinner daily.

Jasmine $$ 20 S. Santa Cruz Ave., Los Gatos, (408) 395-2373. Homey, cluttered, and inviting, the interior features walls hung with bamboo shades, tropical plants, and Chinese lanterns. Prices are reasonable for downtown Los Gatos. Start with the *pon pon* chicken salad Szechuan style, then move on to the kung pao calamari if you're looking for novelty. • Lunch M-F, dinner M-Sa.

JoAnn's B Street Café $ 30 S. B St., San Mateo, (415) 347-7000. This spin-off of the popular South San Francisco 1950s-style diner finally brings brunch to San Mateo. On weekends, families, couples, and other hungry groups flock to JoAnn's shiny red Formica tables for the most delicious and filling breakfast dishes available for miles. The brunch menu features hearty, no-frills basics with an emphasis on omelets—you can concoct your own by choosing from a list of 29 fillings—as well as thick homemade milkshakes and first-rate burgers. At dinner the selections lean toward burgers, salads, and sandwiches, but you still have a couple of scrambled egg options. Expect a wait during peak hours, and be warned that the service can be slow. • Breakfast, lunch and dinner daily.

JoAnn's Café $ 1131 El Camino Real, South San Francisco, (415) 872-2810. This fabled Bay Area breakfast spot attracts hordes of omelet eaters on the weekends, so be prepared to wait for a table. The bright, airy interior is pleasant—try to snag a booth—and good background music (reggae, rock) serenades you as you peruse the long list of specialty egg dishes. Try the spectacular huevos rancheros or the seasonal berry hotcakes, or create your own omelet from a huge list of ingredients. This is home cooking like your mother never made. A popular spot for breakfast before heading to Candlestick Park for a Giants game. • Breakfast and lunch daily.

Kabul $$ 833 W. El Camino Real, Sunnyvale, (408) 245-4350. Exotic Afghan cuisine with huge portions of kabob: tender chunks of meat charbroiled and served on a skewer with salad, Afghan bread, and rice. Vegetarian entrées, including the notable *challaw gulpi* (cauliflower stew), come with rice, bread, and salad. Despite the elegant atmosphere, jeans are acceptable attire. • Lunch M-F, dinner daily.

Kathmandu West $$ 20916 Homestead Rd., Cupertino, (408) 996-0940. Though the interior of this restaurant will make you think Indian, the menu has Nepalese specialties that you won't find elsewhere. Most of these dishes revolve around lentils, potatoes, and vegetables, which make up the national meal of *dahl bhat* (lentils and rice) many Nepalese eat twice a day. So it's no surprise that the lentil soup is tasty. Other good choices are *chara ko ledo* (chicken stir-fried with ginger and garlic) and the *mismas sekuwa* (marinated grilled meats and seafood). The low-price lunch buffet has plenty of vegetarian offerings as well. • Lunch M-F, dinner daily.

Kazoo $$ 250 E. Jackson St., San Jose, (408) 288-9611. On the corner of Japantown, this eatery boasts an unusually comprehensive display of plastic foods out front—a museum of sushi and tempura—to lure diners in. The interior surroundings are more understated, with the usual wooden shoji screens and Japanese prints. The emphasis is on sushi, and the chef proudly offers $1 sushi orders. The menu also includes curry dishes and chicken cutlets • Lunch and dinner daily.

Khanh's Garden $$ 618 Town & Country Village, San Jose, (408) 241-4940. Together with the ubiquitous rice and noodles, soups form a mainstay of Vietnamese cuisine. At Khanh's, any of the soups make a fine start, but particularly intriguing are the asparagus and crab meat soup and the *pho*, the classic Vietnamese beef soup with rice noodles. Among the extensive gourmet selections, don't miss the spicy lemongrass chicken, served with salad and steamed rice. Another favorite is the *bánh hói chao tôm*, a shrimp cake served with rice paper noodles and vegetables. A small selection of beers, including a Vietnamese one, are offered. In an unusual twist, French desserts are available. • Lunch and dinner daily.

Khyber Kabob House $$$ 4628 Meridian Ave., San Jose, (408) 266-8670. A distinctive hybrid of Middle Eastern and Indian cuisines, Afghan food provides a richly spiced alternative to better-known ethnic foods. The specialty is the well-seasoned kabobs, which lack the fiery burn of Indian food. Look for interesting sauces using yogurt, mint, and cilantro, and myriad varieties of basmati rice with assorted seasonings (variations on rice pilaf). Photos of Afghanistan decorate the walls, sharing space with the mirrors, Moorish arches, and pink highlights. Soft lighting and a single rose on each table make for a romantic feel. • Lunch and dinner Tu-Su.

Kim's Restaurant $$ 368 Castro St., Mtn. View, (415) 967-2707. An authentic Vietnamese restaurant—highlights include the spring rolls, the rice-noodle beef soup, as well as any of the noodle dishes. Cash only. • Lunch and dinner daily.

Kincaid's $$$ 60 Bayview Pl., Burlingame, (415) 342-9844. An enormous seafood-and-chop house overlooking the San Francisco Bay on one side and a small lagoon on the other. Applewood-grilled steaks and shellfish are the stars of the menu; the swank bar features 15 beers, 30 single-malt scotches, and dozens of California wines. The valet parking and long-winded menu descriptions make Kincaid's a good place to impress out-of-town-ers, but if it's a bay view you're after, make sure it's a clear day before you book your reservation. • Lunch M-F, dinner daily.

Kirk's Restaurant $ 361 California Ave., Palo Alto,(415) 326-6159 • 2388 S. Bascom Ave., Campbell, (408) 371-3565 • 1330 Sunnyvale-Saratoga Rd., Sunnyvale, (408) 446-2988. Some of the best, juiciest burgers around are served at these quintessential vinyl and cinder-block burger joints. The purists at Kirk's cook to order over mesquite charcoal and leave the garnishing up to you. Fixings are quirky—there is never lettuce, but always piles of onion and jalapeño peppers. Order a charbroiled steakburger, wash it down with a milk-shake, and call the ambulance. Cash only. • Lunch and dinner daily.

Kisaku $$ 47 E. Fourth Ave., San Mateo, (415) 347-4121. With nearly 200 items on its menu, Kisaku must offer the most extensive selection of any Japanese restaurant on the Peninsula. This includes all the basics along with a comprehensive sushi bar, exotic fare like baked eel, and even children's portions. Perhaps predictably, the quality is inconsistent—the sashimi, for example, is fresh but not always top-grade. Another drawback to the multitude of choices: the service is a bit slow. • Lunch and dinner W-M.

Kitahama $$$ 974 Saratoga-Sunnyvale Rd., San Jose, (408) 257-6449. At this rigorously serene sushi establishment, a spalike ambience pervades the many dining areas. The main room features a light-wood sushi bar with tatami tables on the periphery. Another wing houses private tatami rooms (some with telephones) where a $25 minimum per person is in effect. Yet another room houses a karaoke bar. Waitresses in traditional garb glide quietly through the restaurant, attending to your every need. The authentic, fresh sushi draws a crowd of appreciative Japanese who have made this into a private club of sorts for discriminating expatriates. • Dinner daily.

Kobe $$$ 2086 El Camino Real, Santa Clara, (408) 984-5623. The large wooden bear guarding the door at Kobe is a tip-off that this is a restaurant big on spectacle. Take a moment to admire the suit of Japanese armor on display in the waiting area before taking a seat next to the delightful indoor stream backed by an impressive mural. If you prefer a more practical waterway, belly up to the sushi-boat bar, where sushi-laden craft float by for your perusal. Tables feature fresh-cut flowers, and the staff is friendly and attentive. Kobe offers a full range of Japanese delicacies, including teriyaki, tempura, *udon*, and *soba* noodles, generally very good, although the food doesn't quite hold its own against the decor. If you're in a hurry at lunchtime, certain dishes have been designated "extra quick meals," and bargain hunters can enjoy an early bird dinner special before 6:30. Kobe also features banquet facilities and private dining rooms. • Lunch M-F, dinner M-Sa.

Komatsu $$ 300 Orchard City Dr., Campbell, (408) 379-3000. The dingy screens on the windows and the Hawaiian-vacation-lottery display at the entrance are inauspicious, but the interior of this Japanese restaurant is pleasant, clean, and light. Translucent shoji screens divide one side of the dining room into blond wood tatami booths padded with brightly patterned red and pink cushions. The menu comprises the usual tempura, sushi, and sashimi dishes as well as several surprises: hot tofu with dipping sauce and chicken liver with mushrooms are among the more unusual appetizers, and the slightly upscale selection of broiled meats includes Korean beef, trout, and salmon. Calorie-conscious Californians can request skinless teriyaki chicken. • Lunch Tu-F, dinner Tu-Su.

Krung Thai $$ 1699 W. San Carlos St., San Jose, (408) 295-5508. Adventurous diners in the South Bay are no doubt familiar with the strip-mall genre of Asian restaurants. From the outside, Krung Thai seems a classic example: the cookie-cutter exterior and semi-seedy location promise little. Don't be fooled. There is no better Thai food to be found anywhere (at least on this side of the Pacific). If you don't believe us, ask the customers, most of whom are Thai. The secret is out—long lines snake out the door on weekend evenings and at lunchtime. Inside, the dining room is narrow, crowded, and dimly lit. But once the food arrives, nothing else seems to matter. Fortunately, success hasn't spoiled the serving staff, who are friendly and solicitous. • Lunch and dinner daily.

Kuleto's Trattoria $$$ 1095 Rollins Rd., Burlingame, (415) 342-4922. Is Pat Kuleto taking over the world? After conquering San Francisco, the master restaurateur/designer is making his mark on the Peninsula. The giant sign outside the former Vanessi's in Burlingame announces his latest venture, done up like a huge yellow stucco Italian farmhouse. Inside, signature Kuleto touches abound: tortoise-shell-patterned light fixtures, softly buffed dark wood, and a roaring wood-fired oven. The three-tiered dining area affords views of the sauté chefs juggling pans over leaping flames, and a couple of different bar areas are ideal for solo diners. Chef Robert Montuori, of Kuleto's in San Francisco, reprises old favorites such as smoked-salmon-filled ravioli with asparagus and lemon cream sauce and risotto primavera. The homemade foccacia that comes with lunch and dinner is excellent, but pastas tend to be heavy. • Lunch Su-F, dinner daily; open until 11pm F-Sa.

RESTAURANTS AND CAFÉS

Kyoto Palace \$\$\$ 2500 Pruneyard Shopping Center, Campbell, (408) 377-6456. This enormous temple of Japanese cuisine is two restaurants in one. A light-wood sushi bar occupies one wing, offering teriyaki, sushi, and udon noodle dishes to the health conscious. Meanwhile, a rustic, dark-wooded teppan house draws those with a hankering for tableside drama—grills are inset in long tables, and chefs fire up seafood, meat, and vegetable extravaganzas before your eyes. Carnivores will enjoy the Shogun, a "man-sized steak for meat lovers." • Lunch Tu-F, dinner daily.

La Fiesta \$\$ 240 Villa St., Mtn. View, (415) 968-1364. La Fiesta's drab exterior belies the festive interior, which features sombreros, piñatas, papier-maché birds and fish, and a kitchenful of terra-cotta dishes suspended from the ceiling. A brightly colored, tiled bar occupies the center of the restaurant. Try the mole poblano—breast of chicken served with mole sauce made from ground dried cocoa beans, spices, nuts, and a dash of Mexican chocolate—or the *camarones picantes*—sautéed shrimp in a creamy chipotle and *guajillo* sauce. Portions are large. • Lunch and dinner daily.

La Fondue \$\$\$\$ 14510 Big Basin Way, Saratoga, (408) 867-3332. Just as bell-bottoms and love beads are enjoying renewed popularity, fondue—that staple of the seventies dinner party—is back. The decor at La Fondue is strictly nineties, though—sponge-painted walls, fleurs-de-lis printed banquettes, trompe l'oeil mosaics, and in one of the three dining areas, midnight-blue walls spangled with gold stars and half-moon sconces. Diners can choose from more than 50 fondues prepared tableside, from classic Swiss Emmenthaler to tofu for vegetarians to wild game for meat lovers. Choices include pesto and Cognac fondue and Cajun cheese with shrimp. Be sure to block out a couple of hours—this is not fast food. Ask about specials such as all-you-can-eat nights. • Lunch and dinner daily.

La Foret \$\$\$\$ 21747 Bertram Rd., San Jose, (408) 997-3458. Housed in an old two-story hotel overlooking the Los Alamedos Creek, La Foret is reminiscent of a more peaceful time. The country French atmosphere, with floral curtains, light wood furniture, and crisp white tablecloths, is elegant yet relaxed. The menu changes seasonally, with a rotating selection of fish, poultry, and pasta. All dishes are expertly prepared and simply presented: the ahi tuna is perfectly seared, the pork tenderloin is smooth and tender. For those with a frontiersman's palate, the wild game offerings should appeal. Individual Grand Marnier soufflés are a dramatic ending. When making a reservation, request one of the tables overlooking the creek. • Dinner Tu-Su, brunch Su.

La Hacienda \$ 1377 Laurel St., San Carlos, (415) 591-9711. This Mexican restaurant specializes in take-out and has only seven tables, but it's a great place for a fast, hearty meal. The hot soups are especially popular. The decor is pleasantly low-key, with wrought-iron lamps, rattan chairs, and ceramic-tile tables. • Lunch and dinner M-Sa.

La Locanda \$\$\$ 1136 Broadway, Burlingame, (415) 347-1053. Framed posters of Lucca in the foyer provide culinary foreshadowings—this is traditional northern Italian food, from carbonara to veal parmigiana, in a busy but low-key setting. Objets d'art scattered throughout the small dining room, gilt-framed oil paintings and mirrors, and brass-and-porcelain chandeliers give the storefront restaurant an Old World feel. The pricey entrées reflect La Locanda's insistence on Italian-style multicourse dining: even the à la carte prices include a meat dish, pasta, and vegetables. • Lunch Tu-F, dinner daily.

La Maison du Café \$\$\$\$ 14103 Winchester Blvd., Los Gatos, (408) 378-2233. Making use of a French-blue palette, the owners of this intimate café have created a warm, inviting atmosphere: Blue lattice covers one wall, tables are draped in blue printed cloths, and decorative plates line one wall. The classic French specialties include excellent *escargot à la bourguignon*, grilled salmon Hollandaise, and medallions of veal with morels, to name a few, as well as a delicious, crispy roast duck. Owner Ibrahim Guney will attend to your every whim. A classical guitarist serenades diners from the plant-filled balcony at lunch during the week and at weekend dinners. • Lunch Tu-Su, dinner Tu-Sa, brunch Sa-Su.

La Mere Michelle $$$$ 14467 Big Basin Way, Saratoga, (408) 867-5272. On sunny weekend afternoons the outdoor patio at La Mere Michelle attracts leisurely lunchers with its blue-and-white-striped awning and potted red geraniums. The food is 1950s-style country-club fare—hearts of palm salad, shrimp Louie, and grilled spring lamb chops. Not a place for culinary inventiveness, but for nostalgia's sake a worthy destination. • Lunch and dinner Tu-Su.

La Pastaia $$$ 4233 W. Santa Clara St., San Jose, (408) 286-8686. This stylish restaurant serves northern Italian cuisine in pleasant surroundings. Located in the beautifully restored De Anza hotel, it wins in the design department, with its glamorous dining room. In addition to pasta, the menu includes gourmet pizzas with exotic toppings like roast duck. Be sure to try the melanzane (roast eggplant with goat cheese and sun-dried tomatoes). The linguine alla fantasia—fresh linguine with chopped peppers and tomatoes of every color imaginable—brings Walt Disney Technicolor to the dinner plate. • Lunch M-F, dinner daily.

Late for the Train $$ 150 Middlefield Rd., Menlo Park, (415) 321-6124. Imaginative, delicious vegetarian fare in a countrified interior. The proprietors grow most of their own vegetables and use fresh ingredients in season. Brunch is worth getting out of bed for—try the delicious buttermilk pancakes or one of the spectacular omelets. Outdoor patio seating, weather permitting. • Breakfast and lunch daily, dinner Tu-Sa.

Le Mouton Noir $$$$$ 14560 Big Basin Way, Saratoga, (408) 867-7017. A perennial favorite (and perennial winner of *San Francisco Focus's* Best of Santa Clara County award), Le Mouton Noir serves imaginative French cuisine in a grandmother's-parlor atmosphere. Pink and mauve accents and dried flower arrangements abound. Start off with warm wild mushroom gâteau (sautéed wild mushrooms in a light duck liver mousse) and move on to grilled beef tenderloin served with a mint, soy, and port wine sauce, spicy mashed potatoes, and a green bean and shiitake stir-fry. If you can still see straight after such extravagances, order one of the deluxe desserts. • Lunch Sa, dinner daily.

Le Papillon $$$$ 410 Saratoga Ave., San Jose, (408) 296-3730. A solicitous, tuxedoed maitre d' greets you at the entrance, setting the tone for your meal at this tastefully understated French restaurant. The dining rooms are decorated with framed engravings and feature a neutral palette, and the pleasant bar overlooks a verdant garden. The Asian-influenced French cuisine wins raves from loyal patrons, although the ambience tends toward the corporate (Silicon Valley tycoons frequent the premises). • Lunch M-F, dinner daily.

Le Petit Bistro $$ 1405 W. El Camino Real, Mtn. View, (415) 964-3321. Mountain View's best-kept secret, this charming bistro serves reasonably priced French food. The wine list includes modestly priced French and California wines. Start with one of the delicious soups—a creamy mussel saffron or a fresh purée of spinach and asparagus textured with potatoes and leeks. Sauces are light and distinctive, flavored with cumin, saffron, hazelnuts, or citrus. The enthusiastic three-person staff (the waitress, bus boy, and Jean Michel himself) will minister to your every need. • Lunch Tu-F, dinner Tu-Su.

Le Pot au Feu $$$$ 1149 El Camino Real, Menlo Park, (415) 322-4343. The Gallic charm of this cozy restaurant with country-style decor, traditional French fare, and friendly service will convince you that not all French restaurants are snooty. The menu includes well-prepared versions of such favorites as escargots, brie baked in pastry, and rack of lamb. Lighting is dim for romantic trysts. • Dinner Tu-Su.

Le Tandoor $$ 4546 El Camino Real (at San Antonio), Los Altos, (415) 948-9463. The food here rivals any Indian cuisine around, the service is excellent, and the decor is simple and elegant. In addition to the traditional tandoori dishes (cooked in a clay oven) and lamb entrées, Le Tandoor has an extensive list of vegetarian dishes, rice feasts, and seafood dishes that come sizzling to your table. Try the lamb pasanda with stuffed *naan* (Indian bread) to sop up the sauce. Also don't miss the raita—the serving is generous and thick with cucumbers. • Lunch M-F, dinner daily.

Les Saisons $$$$$ Fairmont Hotel, 170 S. Market St., San Jose, (408) 998-3950. This out-landishly posh continental restaurant, located in San Jose's Fairmont Hotel, is one of the most expensive and extravagant in northern California. The typical entrée will set you back more than $20. If the beluga caviar and blinis wheeled out on a marble cart strike your fancy, add $75. The decor suits the menu: shiny marble and polished wood line the lobby, and the restaurant proper is filled with high-backed tapestry-covered chairs, elabo-rate chandeliers and floral arrangements, and such accoutrements as a harp. The service is predictably stuffy and the food falls short of expectation, but if you can afford to eat here, you won't care. • Dinner daily.

Lion & Compass $$$$$ 1023 N. Fair Oaks Ave., Sunnyvale, (408) 745-1260. This high-tech haunt is starting to look a little faded around the edges, although Silicon Valley movers and shakers still make the pilgrimage at lunch. The white lattice exterior surround-ed by birds of paradise and palm trees has a Florida resort feel. Inside, the tropical theme continues with terra-cotta tile floors, wicker chairs, and lazy ceiling fans. The menu includes such chichi fare as grilled ahi tuna on cucumber strands with ginger and green peppercorn vinaigrette. A good selection of ports by the glass for businesspeople who want to prolong the meal in hopes of closing a deal. • Lunch M-F, dinner M-Sa.

Little Garden $ 4127 El Camino Real, Palo Alto, (415) 494-1230. Excellent Vietnamese food in a Formica-table atmosphere. But where atmosphere is lacking, low prices usually follow, and you can dine sumptuously here on crackly, delicious imperial rolls and curried *kwo* noodle soup bristling with thread noodles and chicken, among other mysterious ele-ments. Lemongrass chicken was a disappointment (the namesake ingredient was unde-tectable), but a healthy portion of moo shu pork made up for the omission. • Lunch M-F, dinner daily.

Los Altos Bar & Grill $$ 169 Main St., Los Altos, (415) 948-4332. Flashing lights, a wide-screen TV, potato skins—this downtown saloon has all the hallmarks of a singles/sports bar. But upstairs is a more formal dining room where an ambitious (if pricey) menu is served, featuring pastas, grilled meats, and seafood. Stick to the simpler prepara-tions such as grilled angus filet with portobello mushrooms or steamed clams with ginger. (Medallions of black horn antelope? No thanks.) Local bands and swingles take over on the weekends. • Lunch and dinner daily, brunch Sa-Su.

Los Gatos Brewing Co. $$$ 130 N. Santa Cruz Ave., Los Gatos, (408) 395-9929. The "No Tank Tops" sign announces that you have arrived at Los Gatos's favorite haunt of beer drinkers and beachgoers alike. Indoors, singles mingle over pints of the brewed-on-site ales, including Dunkles, Los Gatos Lager, and Nut Brown Ale, as well as a rotating sea-sonal specialty. A long bar (salvaged from a St. Louis brothel) dominates one end of the soaring, barnlike space; another wall is occupied by a brick wood-burning oven for pizzas. The faux stone walls painted in earth tones add a rustic note. The menu features designer pizzas, pastas, and grilled meats, but beer is the draw here. • Lunch and dinner daily; open until midnight F-Sa.

Luceti's $$$ 109 W. Twenty-fifth Ave., San Mateo, (415) 574-1256. A cozy, old-fashioned neighborhood restaurant and bar presided over by transplants from North Beach. The menu is northern Italian/continental, with various omelets, frittatas, and Americanish sandwiches thrown in at lunch and an expanded veal and fish selection at dinner. A plate of fettucine with veal, prosciutto, and mushrooms in a cream sauce served in the comfort-ably cluttered dining room is guaranteed to please. • Lunch M-F, dinner daily.

Mabel's Lantern House $$ 39 N. Santa Cruz Ave., Los Gatos, (408) 354-1844. Kung pao calamari and red snapper are the standouts on the otherwise routine Chinese menu. Mabel's fills lots of take-out orders, but the redwood cane chairs, pink tablecloths, and paintings mounted on pink matting make for a pleasant if unexceptional atmosphere. • Lunch M-Sa, dinner daily.

Mac's Tea Room $$$ 325 Main St., Los Altos, (415) 941-0234. Actually a restaurant and bar, with American meat dishes and only one kind of tea. The dry-aged steak is Mac's signature; meatloaf and roast pork are more casual entrées. The kitchen whips up a hearty feast of roast turkey and lamb on Sundays. Live music enlivens the lounge four nights a week. • Lunch and dinner daily.

MacArthur Park $$$ 27 University Ave., Palo Alto, (415) 321-9990. Housed in a beautiful, rustic barn designed by Julia Morgan. Fidgety diners can doodle with crayons on the paper-draped tables as they wait for giant platters of ribs or mesquite-grilled chicken, sausages, or fish. Fish entrées are fresh and cleanly grilled, while barbecue options from the oak-fueled smoker require a dentist-style bib. Entrée accoutrements are excellent; grilled pork loin is served with sautéed red cabbage and a delightful apple compote. Plentiful Sunday brunch buffet. • Lunch M-F, dinner daily, brunch Su; open Su-Th until 10:30pm, open F-Sa until 11pm.

Maddalena's $$$$ 544 Emerson St., Palo Alto, (415) 326-6082. One of the more formal restaurants in the mid-Peninsula, done up in dark wood paneling, antiques, and crystal chandeliers—the whole nine yards. Popular with the Silicon Valley expense account crowd as well as the Stanford elite. Solicitous waiters in tuxes serve up luxury fare like rack of lamb, duck, and filet mignon. • Lunch and dinner daily.

Mandarin Chef $$$ 14572 Big Basin Way, Saratoga, (408) 867-4388. White-linen-clad tables, fresh flowers, and country-style decor distinguish the Mandarin Chef. Try the excellent (not too sweet) honey-roasted walnut prawns or the Mandarin Chef's special beef if it's available. Start off with the generous *pu pu* platter. • Lunch and dinner daily.

Mandarin Gourmet $$$ 420 Ramona St., Palo Alto, (415) 328-8898 • 5560 Santa Teresa Blvd., San Jose, (408) 281-8898. Don't be intimidated by the sleek appearance of these restaurants—prices do not match the swank decor. The chicken salad, a mélange of shredded chicken with lettuce and crispy rice noodles tossed with sesame dressing, is divine, as is the fiery hot and sour soup. Waiters are big on theatrics; nearly every dish seems to require tableside hocus-pocus. Observe the attention devoted to the art of folding—from the napkins to the moo shu pork pancakes that are individually wrapped for you to the artfully sealed take-home parcels. • Lunch and dinner daily.

Mango Café $$ 435 Hamilton Ave., Palo Alto, (415) 325-3229. Settle back in one of the huge fanbacked wicker chairs, order a dragon's mouth (tamarind, lime, and ginger) smoothie, and imagine you're in the West Indies. The spicy cuisine of Jamaica and Trinidad and Tobago is unusual and delicious. Try one of the patties (meat turnovers with a curried crust), a jerked joint (very spicy marinated drummettes), or a delicate hearts of palm salad. For dessert, get the best bread pudding, an exemplary rendition of the old classic. The background music is reggae and the service is friendly and hip. No liquor; cash only. Cash only. • Lunch and dinner M-Sa.

Mariani's Inn $$ 2500 El Camino Real, Santa Clara, (408) 243-1431. This Santa Clara landmark has been dishing up classic Italian food for as long as anyone can remember. Mariani's operates a hotel on the same property, and you get the feeling the same interior designer is responsible for the restaurant—lots of mauve and beige, and carpeting everywhere. Opinions differ on the quality of the food, but Mariani's maintains a devoted clientele. • Breakfast, lunch, and dinner daily; open until 11pm F-Sa.

Martha's Restaurant $$$$ 1875 S. Bascom Ave., The PruneYard, Campbell, (408) 377-1193. Hailed as one of the most creative chefs on the Peninsula, Steve Chan dazzles diners with his East-West cuisine. An informal café menu is served on the outdoor garden patio, while indoors a more elaborate (and more expensive) menu is offered. Chan works wonders with seafood: Try his baked salmon in phyllo pastry with shrimp mousse for a delicate balance of flavors and textures. Exotic meats find their way onto the menu as well: venison stir-fry is an intriguing concept. • Lunch M-F, dinner M-Sa.

Marvin Gardens Alehouse and Grill $ 1160 Old County Rd., Belmont, (415) 592-6154. As the wall of cans behind the bar attests, this is a place that caters to people who take beer, burgers, and pizza seriously. Seventeen bottled beers, eight on draft, eight specialty pizzas, and burgers grilled any which way should offer something for everyone. Despite its unlikely location in a semi-industrial block, Marvin Gardens is aptly named: until a train passes you're likely to forget that the spacious, trellised beer garden in the back borders the railroad tracks. Cash only. Cash only. • Lunch and dinner daily.

Max's Bakery and Kitchen $$ 111 E. Fourth Ave., San Mateo, (415) 344-1997. Gargantuan portions are the hallmark of this busy New York–style deli and bakery. From the football-size stuffed potatoes to the sandwiches stacked so high with corned beef that you can hardly fit your mouth around them, everything on the menu at Max's is calculated to make you feel positively Lilliputian. Save room for dessert, though—this is where the mammoth sweets for all the Max's restaurants in the Bay Area are baked. Buy some cheesecake or *rugalach* by the pound to take with you if you've overindulged. Outdoor seating is available. • Lunch and dinner daily, brunch Sa-Su.

Max's Opera Café $$$ 711 Stanford Shopping Center, Palo Alto, (415) 323-6297. 1250 Bayshore Hwy., Burlingame, (415) 342-6297. Deli decor has never had it so good. In Palo Alto, the soaring ceilings, singing waitrons, and shelves stacked with cans of olive oil attract a done-to-the-nines crowd. The Burlingame locale is a bit more suburban. The brassy, boastful menu starts with New York-deli-style chopped liver and corned beef sandwiches and then goes ballistic with sweet and sour duck. Not everything works perfectly, but it's always tasty and interesting. Best to take a doggie bag for the main course to save room for Sweet Max's larger-than-life desserts. • Lunch and dinner daily.

Mei's $$ 71 E. Third Ave., San Mateo, (415) 347-2722. Modern, vaguely European decor and a leisurely feel distinguish this Chinese restaurant from most others in the area. French doors open onto an outdoor patio bordered by beds of multicolored flowers; the airy interior features track lighting and a full bar adorned with vases of white orchids. Old standards such as kung pao chicken are reliable, but for a real treat order the more exotic entrées, like the green-shell mussels in a delicious black bean sauce or roast game hen with garlic and ginger. The slightly Westernized side dishes and desserts include fried calamari, tiramisu, and coffee fudge ice cream. • Lunch and dinner daily.

Menara Moroccan $$$ 41 E. Gish Rd., San Jose, (408) 453-1983. You might wonder if this place is even open from its uninviting exterior. But once inside you'll think you've wandered on to the set of *Aladdin*. Be sure to go when the belly dancers are on duty—the audience participation can be almost as entertaining—or request them for parties by calling well in advance. The food is standard Moroccan. *Caution*: seating is Indian style, so this is not a place for the weak of knee or stiff of joint. • Dinner Tu-Su.

Michael's $$$$ 830 El Camino Real, Sunnyvale, (408) 245-2925. The long oak bar and leather wing chairs bring to mind a men's club, while the dining room features leather banquettes, plants, and etched-glass panels for a Belle Epoque supper-club feel. "New England seafood specialties" are advertised, but the menu features Australian lobster tail, Maryland soft-shell crabs, and crabmeat and shrimp cannelloni—not what you'd find at your average Maine clam house. Meat eaters will be relieved to find a New York steak sandwich and various veal preparations on the menu. • Lunch M-F, dinner daily.

Ming's $$$ 1700 Embarcadero Rd., Palo Alto, (415) 856-7700/7701. Ming's is one of the most well-regarded Chinese restaurants on the Peninsula, with a special room for power-lunching businesspeople. Everybody else dines in an elegant room done up in soft pink, green, and white, though the din during dim sum (try the crab claws and stuffed mushrooms) can be deafening. Hong Kong chefs prepare the southern Chinese cuisine according to traditional recipes, and the waiters assemble the final dishes before your very eyes. Don't miss the famous chicken salad. • Lunch, dim sum, and dinner daily.

Mio Vicino $$ 1290 Benton St., Santa Clara, (408) 241-9414. A neighborhood joint where the smart-aleck staff joke among themselves and with guests (who are separated from the kitchen only by a small counter) and happily try to accommodate special requests. Most important, the exotic pizzas and pastas are prepared to mouth-watering perfection. Mio Vicino is a bright corner space with lots of windows, simple yellow brick walls, and cheerful green-and-white checked tablecloths. The restaurant doubles as a hangout for students at Santa Clara College, which is also a steady supplier of wait staff. • Lunch M-F, dinner daily; open until 11pm F-Sa.

Mistral $$$ 370-6 Bridge Pkwy., Redwood Shores, (415) 802-9222. High California cuisine: sun-dried tomatoes, shiitake mushrooms, contrived pizzas, and the inevitable garlic mashed potatoes. The barren dining room and bar overlook the water (a lagoon, to be exact), but for full romantic effect sit outside on the deck. Occasional special events like a Halloween costume contest cater to bored singles. The restaurant is brand-new—maybe it will acquire some character in time. • Lunch M-F, dinner daily.

Miyake $$ 10650 S. De Anza Blvd., Cupertino, (408) 253-2668 • 261 University Ave., Palo Alto, (415) 323-9449. There's always a line stretching out the door at Miyake—sushi hounds flock here for the riotous atmosphere created by barking chefs, screaming waiters, and slap-happy clientele. Inflatable globes dangle from the ceiling and a general atmosphere of insanity prevails. Little boats in the mini moat around the bar float by laden with sushi—patrons grab when the urge hits. Lots of fun, but the fish isn't always the freshest. • Lunch and dinner daily.

Mondello Ristorante Italiano $$$ 20343 Stevens Creek Blvd., Cupertino, (408) 257-2383. Named for a Sicilian seaside town but located in a Cupertino strip mall, Mondello looks more South Bay than southern Italian, with a palette of grays and mauves and black-and-white photos of Italy lining the walls. The menu, however, reflects the heritage of owner Mario Landino. Risotto Milanese is a good choice, as is linguine *verdaiulo*—prepared with tomatoes, basil, garlic, and olive oil. • Lunch M-F, dinner M–Sa.

Motomachi $$ 1036 Castro St., Mtn. View, (415) 960-3484. Motomachi may be on the wrong side of the tracks, but it's a welcome change from the Japanese restaurants of downtown Castro Street. Insiders come here for the pleasant, spacious interior, the attentive service, and the convenient parking. The food is good, too, especially the lunch specials. • Lunch M-F, dinner M–Sa.

Mount Everest $$$ 412 N. Santa Cruz Ave., Los Gatos, (408) 354-2427. Indian food in Los Gatos? It can be found. Mount Everest may be buried in a down-at-the-heels strip mall along Winchester Boulevard, but it's worth discovering. The atmosphere is unexpectedly cheerful, considering the surroundings, with glittery fans hung upside-down on the soft pink walls and dense rows of track lighting adding a modern touch. The menu is traditional Indian, but that's unique in Los Gatos. • Lunch M-Sa, dinner daily.

The Mountain House $$$ 13808 Skyline Blvd., Woodside, (415) 851-8541. Located amid the redwoods of Skyline Boulevard, the Mountain House faces west into the woods and is best visited when there's still some daylight left. Stop off after a hike or bike ride and huddle by the giant fieldstone fireplace with a hot toddy; the delightful smell of wood smoke permeates the lodgelike bar area. Good bar menu in the front, with more traditional continental dishes in the dining room. • Dinner W-Su; bar opens Su at noon.

Mr. D's & Sons Barbeque $ 1038 E. El Camino Real, Sunnyvale, (408) 749-9213. A small eat-in or take-out barbecue operation that focuses on the essentials. Dishes are named after sixties sitcom characters—Clamp's pork ribs, Granny's laid-back chicken, Professor's catfish, and Skipper's red snapper. Go figure. But the dishes are strongly flavored, and the sweet potato pie is a find. • Lunch and dinner daily.

Mumtaj $$ 126 Castro St., Mtn. View, (415) 961-2433. A haven for the bargain hunter, Mumtaj serves an extensive north Indian lunch buffet. Dinner waits are long and service is mediocre, but the food is authentic and tasty. Highlights include boneless chicken curry and *rogan josh* (lamb with spinach), while *baingan bharta* (roasted eggplant with peas) and *channas* (garbanzo beans) are good vegetarian dishes. • Lunch and dinner daily.

Nataraja $$$ 117 University Ave., Palo Alto, (415) 321-6161. Nataraja serves up heavenly curries, tender meat, and some great vegetarian options amid an appealing ambience: comfortable, roomy booths (which make the restaurant a cozy place for a date) and unobtrusive Indian music playing in the background. The service is attentive and friendly, and the lunch buffet is one of the best around. Good entrée choices include prawn curry or any of the tandoori meats. • Lunch and dinner M-Sa.

Nicolino's Garden Café $$$ 1228 Reamwood Ave., Sunnyvale, (408) 734-5323. Fernheavy, elaborately decorated Nicolino's is the most ambitious of the D'Ambrosio brothers' restaurant group (which also owns Frankie, Johnnie & Luigi Too and Giorgio's Pizza). Located in a high-tech office park, Nicolino's stages lots of business lunches, celebration dinners, and banquets. The food is formal Italian from the Puglia province—hearty portions of meats and seafood with tomato and cream sauces. The big excitement is on Saturday nights, when Nicolino's presents Italian Showcase—live performances of Italian opera arias and Neapolitan love songs. Thursday and Friday evenings feature live piano music, and there is a happy hour weekdays from 4-7pm. • Lunch M-F, dinner M-Sa.

Nina's Café $$$ 2991 Woodside Rd., Woodside, (415) 851-4565. *Très français*, from the charming bistro-style handwritten menus ("Bon Appetit from Nicole and Henri") to the flowered curtains to the classic French onion soup. The back porch is a choice venue for an alfresco meal. Start with seafood bisque in puff pastry with garlic dip, move on to excellent roast Petaluma duck or sweetbreads flambéed in brandy and served in puff pastry, and by dessert you'll be singing "La Marseillaise." • Lunch and dinner Tu-Sa.

94th Aero Squadron $$$ 1160 Coleman Ave., San Jose, (408) 287-6150. Located next to the runway at San Jose International Airport, this restaurant has gone all the way with its World War II aviator theme. Antique planes are parked on the lawn of the Tudor-style structure, and inside sandbags line the stairway and flying memorabilia festoon the walls. Window tables overlook the runway and feature headphones broadcasting the happenings from the nearby air-traffic control tower. After you've paid for your meal, the waiter returns with a folder marked "Discharge Papers" containing your receipt and informs your party that you're honorably discharged. The menu features seafood, steaks, and pasta along with burgers for the kids, but no one comes here for the food, which ranges from OK to bad (as does the service—waiters have been known to go AWOL in the middle of a meal). Patrons come back year after year, though, to watch the planes and revel in the goofy charm. • Lunch and dinner daily, brunch Su.

North Beach Pizza $ 240 E. Third Ave., San Mateo, (415) 344-5000. The suburban outpost of San Francisco's celebrated pizza parlor is loud and energized, with lots of families and large groups in attendance. Toppings are sometimes hidden beneath the cheese, which can make for some surprises. The menu includes other Italian favorites, but stick to the pizza—pastas are only fair and tend to be salty. The green, red, and white color scheme is true to the Italian flag, and booth seating provides a modicum of intimacy. Service is good, though it can be rushed when the place is packed and lines are long. • Lunch and dinner daily; open until midnight.

Nouveau Trattoria $$$ 541 Bryant St., Palo Alto, (415) 327-0132. When you can't face the trendy crowd at Il Fornaio, the Nouveau Trattoria offers an old-style European dining experience. Wine bottles line the walls, the lights are low, and the gracious wait staff won't make you feel like a cretin if you mispronounce the wine. Italian specialties like *penne al quattro formaggi* and *linguine alle vongole* never disappoint, but owner Annie Nunan adds a flip side featuring French classics such as *pâté de foie, salade Nicoise,* and an excellent *steak au poivre.* Thursday evenings are dedicated to something different—Basque specialties. • Lunch Tu-F, dinner Tu-Su.

The Oasis $ 241 El Camino Real, Menlo Park, (415) 326-8896. This is the ultimate hang-out—a slightly grubby and cheap old-fashioned sports bar, with hacked-up wooden booths (go ahead, add your initials), peanut shell–strewn floors, and a long bar for leaning, scoping, and imbibing. Hamburgers do the job, pizza has its share of devotées, and the beer list is long and eclectic. Good TV-to-window ratio, and video games for the antisocial. Those under 21 years old are relegated to a small, heated outdoor patio equipped with picnic tables. Show up early if you plan to watch major sporting events. • Daily 11am-1:15am; bar open until 2am.

Okoyama $$ 565 N. Sixth St., San Jose, (408) 279-9920. A pyramid scheme finally pays off at this low-key Japanese restaurant, where the best deals are the so-called pyramid dinners—various three-item combinations at low prices. The smallish, bare tables are closely spaced—no tatami rooms or shoji screens separate them—but rice-paper window screens shield diners from the outside world, and the piped-in Japanese music will relax all but the most pressured business luncher, who can grab a Bento box to go. • Lunch M-Sa, dinner daily.

Osteria $$ 247 Hamilton Ave., Palo Alto, (415) 328-5700. An always-bustling, attractive trattoria in the heart of downtown Palo Alto with solid Italian fare and reasonable prices. Contemporary paintings hang in the somewhat cramped but pleasant dining area. The menu features classic pastas, veal dishes, salads. Try the excellent Caesar salad, but avoid the gummy spinach ravioli. Can be noisy; tables are mercilessly close to each other. • Lunch M-F, dinner M-Sa.

Pacific Gourmet Pizza $$ 1080 Shell Blvd., Foster City, (415) 570-2253. Extravagant combinations are the glory of this haute cuisine pizza parlor. Go gourmet with a chicken and pesto combination, or go all-out ethnic with the Bangkok chicken pizza with vegetables in a peanut sauce or the chicken with tomatillo-chile sauce and Jack cheese. You can also assemble your own pizza from an exhaustive list of crusts, sauces, cheeses, and toppings. Pretty good pasta for those who prefer their combinations on noodles instead of a crust. • Dinner daily.

Pagoda $$$$ Fairmont Hotel, 170 S. Market St., San Jose, (408) 998-3937. Located in the downtown Fairmont Hotel, this dark, elegant restaurant is done up in lots of glamorous black lacquer. A framed antique kimono hangs in the bar area, and design flourishes abound: even the enormous, jet-black service plates are eye-catching. In addition to well-executed, tasty Chinese dishes, a few Mongolian selections—lamb sautéed with leeks and served with onion bread, and a lamb satay—appear on the menu, as well as a few unusual choices—tea-smoked trout and a shark's fin soup for $20. Yes, there is take-out. • Lunch M-F, dinner M-Sa.

The Palace $$$ 146 S. Murphy Ave., Sunnyvale, (408) 739-5179. Big-city glitz comes to Silicon Valley in this swanky supper club, which recently began offering dinner as well as weekend jazz and musical events. Located in a restored Art Deco movie theater, the soaring two-tiered interior is an architectural extravaganza, with biomorphic silver-painted columns, wrought-iron accents, and sponge-painted orange walls. The ambitious tapas menu features ahi tuna carpaccio with deep-fried onion rings and sesame-ginger-soy vinaigrette, crispy coconut prawns with mango mustard, and a soup de nuit. The perfect setting for modern romance. • Dinner W-Sa.

Palermo $$$ 452 University Ave., Palo Alto, (415) 321-9908 • 380 S. Second St., San Jose, (408) 297-0607. Big bites of garlic and ripe tomato punctuate most of Palermo's southern Italian dishes—this is not subtle cuisine. The San Jose and Palo Alto locations differ wildly: The gargantuan San Jose facility encompasses three private banquet halls, a ballroom, a breezy outdoor courtyard, and even a wedding chapel, while the Palo Alto interior is small and rather cramped. • Lunch M-F, dinner M-Sa.

Palo Alto Sol $$ 408 California Ave., Palo Alto, (415) 328-8840. Fresh, authentic Mexican food served up by a congenial staff in a cheerful storefront setting. The à la carte selection may well be the largest of any mid-Peninsula Mexican restaurant—where else could you find rice-and-bean burritos with mushrooms and tomatoes, or chicken mole enchiladas with 20 spices and sesame seeds? The decor is equally colorful, from the artwork and climbing greenery that adorn the white stucco walls to the brightly painted wooden fish dangling from the ceiling. • Lunch and dinner M-Sa.

Paolo's $$$$ 333 W. San Carlos St., San Jose, (408) 294-2548. Among the notables who have dined on Paolo's acclaimed and inventive food are Joe DiMaggio, the Reagans, Frank Sinatra, and JFK. The chilled breast of rabbit stuffed with salsa verde and radicchio is one of the most novel concoctions, but innovative touches enliven even the more staid dishes, like beef tortellini in a béchamel sauce and veal scaloppine with wilted spinach. In its new location (the decorating bill ran into the millions), Paolo's features European artwork on ocher sponge-painted walls and vaguely classical interior architecture. The atmosphere is more corporate than glitzy—at lunchtime there's even a *menu al professione*. Upstairs, you can enjoy an aperitif in the wine room or on the patio. • Lunch M-F, dinner M-Sa.

Paradise Persian Cuisine $$ 1350 Grant Rd., Mtn. View, (415) 968-5949. Exotic Persian cuisine at bargain prices, served in unpretentious surroundings. Try the *fesenjon*, an intriguing stew of chicken, pomegranate juice, walnuts, and spices. Kabobs and vegetarian specialties are dependable as well. • Lunch and dinner daily.

Pasand $$ 3701 El Camino Real, Santa Clara, (408) 241-5150. Never tried Indian food? Try Pasand's First Timer Special for an affordable introduction to some accessible dishes. The menu also features a large selection of curries and *dosas* as well as tandoori items and north Indian *pooris*. This link in the Bay Area chain is bright and airy, with white tiles and tablecloths, high ceilings, and large windows. Eat to the accompaniment of live Indian music on weekends. • Lunch and dinner daily.

Pasquale's $$$ 476 S. First St., San Jose, (408) 286-1770. Southern Italian food served in flamboyantly decorated surroundings. Antipasti and salads are especially popular—try the memorable spinach salad dressed up with pears and goat cheese and the roasted vegetables. Classics like *linguine con vongole* and veal piccata are among the entrée choices, and a well-chosen wine list and powerful espresso drinks round out the offerings. The dining room has the cluttered feel of an antique shop, with stained-glass panels, Tiffany lamps, and abundant knickknacks. A sign declaring "Italians Only" points to the pleasant patio, which is replete with lush greenery, a waterfall, and a small-scale *David*. • Lunch M-F, dinner daily.

Passage to India $ 1100 W. El Camino Real, Mtn. View, (415) 964-5532. This is one of the least expensive of the major Indian restaurants in the area, and the portions are huge. The decor has been updated, but the focus is still on quality food and service. Go for the lunch buffet heaped with 25 selections—all you can eat for just a few bucks. You won't be disappointed. • Lunch M-F, dinner daily.

Pasta Moon $$$ 315 Main St., Half Moon Bay, (415) 726-5125 • 425 Marina Blvd., South San Francisco, (415) 876-7090. The South San Francisco branch of this Half Moon Bay favorite is located in the brand-new Oyster Point Marina complex. Overlooking the marina, the dining room is bright and comfortable, if a little institutional looking. (Outdoor tables overlooking the boat basin are preferable.) The original location in Half Moon Bay is small and quaint, albeit a bit cramped, with casual, small town hospitality. Start with the antipasti plate, which might include generous servings of grilled eggplant, roasted peppers, frittatas, and more. Pastas are always a good bet, as are the seafood dishes, but avoid some of the more elaborate offerings. • Half Moon Bay, lunch and dinner daily, South San Francisco, lunch M-F, dinner M-Sa.

Pedro's Cabo Grill $$ 316 N. Santa Cruz Ave., Los Gatos, (408) 354-7570. A festive Mission-style Mexican restaurant with a perpetual din from the enthusiastic patrons, who range from large families to margarita-loving singles. The portions are filling and the ingredients are fresh, but the menu doesn't break any new ground. Relax during the weekday happy hour from 4-6pm. • Lunch and dinner daily, brunch Su; open until 11pm F-Sa.

Peking Duck Restaurant $$ 2310 El Camino Real, Palo Alto, (415) 856-3338. The contemporary interior lacks the usual Chinese artifacts—no gold-encrusted dragons here. The menu borrows from the different regions of China and mixes in a little California cuisine. Try the delicious sautéed prawns with mango. The chefs will prepare anything you suggest, so bring your imagination. Not surprisingly, the specialty is Peking duck, and it's prepared right at your table with a flourish. • Lunch and dinner daily.

Peninsula Fountain & Grill $ 566 Emerson St., Palo Alto, (415) 323-3131. You may experience the eerie feeling that you've stumbled onto the set of *Happy Days*. The food is fifties-style: juicy, enormous burgers, golden onion rings (delicious, if sometimes a bit on the greasy side), and tuna melts. The towering pies actually taste good (the apple in particular). Though the neon clock says, "Eat and Get Out," the owners and the youthful wait staff are friendly to a fault. Service is snappy, the music is sock-hop cheery, and you can buy Pixie Stix at the cash register. • Breakfast, lunch, and dinner daily; open until 11pm.

Petaluma's Rotisserie Chicken $ 703 Town & Country Village, Palo Alto, (415) 326-9484. From the couple behind the Fresh Choice salad-bar chain, a similar approach to chicken: fast, inexpensive, and abundant in variation. The menu offers roast chicken in a pot pie, in a barbecue sandwich, in a pesto salad, or whole for take-out. But just chicken, so vegetarians and red-meat carnivores both should steer clear. The blatantly faux ceramic tiles and simulated marble refrigerator case give Petaluma's something of a fast-food feel, but the restaurant is clean and the service is friendly. • Lunch and dinner daily.

Pho Hua $ 735 The Alameda, San Jose, (408) 286-3481. *Pho* is the classic Vietnamese beef noodle soup, and this unpretentious diner serves it in style. Each order comes in a huge bowl, along with fresh herbs and hot sauce so that you can doctor it up to your own specifications. The Vietnamese owners have set up shop inside an old fast-foot drive-in just up the street from the new San Jose Arena. Stop by and try something new on your way to a Sharks game. • Breakfast, lunch and dinner daily.

Piatti $$$ 2 Stanford Shopping Center, Palo Alto, (415) 324-9733. The seventh restaurant in a chain with branches in the wine country and the Bay Area, Piatti is spacious and bright, decorated with murals of giant vegetables and done up in warm shades of terra-cotta. Chef Aram Chakerian, from the Sacramento Piatti, prepares homemade pastas in garlicky sauces, pizzas from the wood-burning oven, and rotisserie chicken. A worthy player in the Peninsula Italian dining scene. Sit outdoors on the eminently pleasant patio—beware, though, you may find yourself surrounded by a horde of smokers. • Lunch and dinner daily.

Piccolo Mondo $$$ 4926 El Camino Real, Los Altos, (415) 968-5450. On the site of a former nightclub, vestiges of Piccolo Mondo's former life linger—a boarded-up ticket booth, a marbleized mirror, a huge brass chandelier. Upstairs is an understated dining room with stucco walls, light wood beams, private booths, and a display case for desserts. The menu is strictly Italian, featuring homemade pastas (try the fusilli Genovese with Swiss chard, pine nuts, and garlic for an inspired variation on classic pesto) and grilled meats and fish. • Lunch M-F, dinner M-Sa.

Pigalle $$$ 27 N. Santa Cruz Ave., Los Gatos, (408) 395-7924. Murals of Parisian street scenes cover every inch of the walls, transporting you to the City of Light. The authentic Gallic specialties add to the illusion. Opt for the prix fixe menu; you get a mixed green salad, an entrée, vegetables, and dessert for far less than you would pay in Paris. A la carte specialties include a delicious grilled *entrecôte* with three-peppercorn port wine sauce and rabbit with mustard sauce. An abundance of Gallic charm makes for a memorable dining experience. • Lunch and dinner daily, brunch Su.

Pizz'a Chicago $ 1576 Halford Ave., Santa Clara, (408) 244-2246. A pizza parlor that all but renounces its Bay Area location. The wall-to-wall Chicago memorabilia proclaims its true loyalties (don't dis da Bears if you expect to walk out alive), as does the delicious deep-dish pizza with olive oil–based tomato sauce. More novel tributes to Chicago include soft drinks served in mason jars and wait staff attired in White Sox and Cubs uniforms. What more could you want? Monday-night football specials? You got it. • Lunch and dinner daily; open until 11pm F-Sa.

Pizzeria Uno $$ 19930 Stevens Creek Blvd., Cupertino, (408) 973-1466 • 2570 El Camino Real, Santa Clara, (408) 241-5152. More Chicago-style deep dish pizza, served in a bustling diner. Those who don't like the thick, flaky Chicago crust can opt for thin-crust "pizzettas." The menu also includes pasta, salad, and burgers, but the big attraction is the pizza. Beware: The large number of children makes for a high noise level. • Lunch and dinner daily; open until 11pm F-Sa.

The Plumed Horse $$$$$ 14555 Big Basin Way, Saratoga, (408) 867-4711. This renowned Saratoga restaurant opened in 1952—a century ago in Silicon Valley time—on the site of a former stable. The plush dining rooms hark back to another era, when dining out involved steamship rounds of roast beef and tuxedo-clad waiters. High rollers will gravitate to the $75 appetizer of beluga caviar, the $45 baked Australian lobster tail with black Perigord truffle sauce, and the $600 bottle of Romanée-Conte. Next to these extravagances, the $25 entrées start to look reasonable. Choose from salmon in parchment with julienne of leeks, carrots, and romaine; filet mignon; or roast tenderloin of pork with sun-dried bing cherries. • Dinner M-Sa.

Pollo's $ 1040 Grant Rd., Mtn. View, (415) 962-1800 or (415) 969-8244 • 543 Emerson St., Palo Alto, (415) 473-0212. The latest participant in the fresh-Mex craze, with self-service, pulsating Latin music, and low, low prices. Succulent mesquite-roasted chicken, accompanied by hand-cut salsa and whole beans, is the centerpiece of the menu, which also features the by-now customary assortment of salads, no-lard burritos, and *agua frescas*. The crowds, the eclectic decor, and the music make for a festive atmosphere, but the noise can be a little overwhelming—we recommend the outdoor seating. • Lunch and dinner daily.

Pup and Hound $$ 1100 Holly St., San Carlos, (415) 592-8853. A country-style family restaurant with an emphasis on quantity: All dinners include soup, salad, vegetables, pasta, and bread. The entrées are seriously meat oriented—roast lamb, veal with marsala sauce, top round, turkey, garlic chicken, various steaks, and fish. A few pedestrian pastas round out the menu. A plus for frazzled families: a substantial children's menu. • Breakfast, lunch and dinner daily.

Quadrus Café $$ 2400 Sand Hill Rd., Menlo Park, (415) 954-2342. Part of a conference facility near Stanford, this is a bright, airy spot for lunch in the Palo Alto area. The menu reflects various multicultural influences: Look for fresh pasta dishes and Asian-inspired chicken or noodle salads. Pizza with imaginative toppings is a reliable standby, and for the grand finale, try a fruit cobbler. Arrive before the crowds of Stanford staff and scientists descend for their midday break. • Lunch M-F.

Quoc Te $ 155 E. Fernando St., San Jose, (408) 289-8323. Now ten years old, Quoc Te is the granddaddy of the Vietnamese restaurants popping up like mushrooms everywhere, and it's still one of the best. The menu is long and crammed with unfamiliar-sounding dishes, but there is little chance of going wrong. Try the delicious *banh xeo* (pancake) or *banh hoi thit nuong* (fried noodles) for appetizers. Any of the *lau canh's* (fiery stews with flavorful broths) make outstanding meals. A house specialty is *bo bay mon*—seven courses of beef. Don't let the carnivorous orientation put you off—each variation is subtly flavored, and plenty of vegetables accompany the meal. • Lunch and dinner daily; open Su-Th until 11pm; open F, Sa until 3am.

Ramona's $ 541 Ramona St., Palo Alto, (415) 326-2220 • 2313 Birch St., Palo Alto, (415) 322-2181. Ranked high among pizza aficionados. Interesting varieties (Cajun, Thai, Stromboli) abound, the crust is thick but not overly doughy, and the restaurant is always swinging. Ramona's Too on Birch is mostly takeout. • Lunch M-Sa, dinner daily.

Rangoon $$ 565 Bryant St., Palo Alto, (415) 325-8146. Rangoon hedges its bets by including Chinese cuisine along with its namesake Burmese; in fact, the menu consists mostly of familiar Chinese dishes. It works because it's well made, but the Burmese food is more exciting. The samosas make a good lead-off, followed by the *onh no kaw soi* noodles, a delicious coconut chicken noodle soup. The soft yellow walls with the modified Buddhist temple motif make for a welcome, if slightly upscale, change from the usual spartan decor at such establishments. Attentive service. • Lunch and dinner M-Sa.

Red Sea Restaurant $$ 684 N. First St., San Jose, (408) 993-1990. Housed in a homey California bungalow, the Red Sea is attractively decorated with African crafts and tapestries. The excellent East African food is served in big colorful mounds on top of a tangy, spongy bread called *injera*. You tear off a piece and use it to scoop up a serving of meat, lentils, greens, or mixed vegetables. The injera salad is especially good. The drink menu is fun, including Ethiopian honey wine and some obscure African beers (try Ngoma, a pilsener from Togo). Lots of good vegetarian options. Service is friendly. • Lunch and dinner M-Sa.

Redwood Café and Spice Co. $$ 1020 Main St., Redwood City, (415) 366-1498. Blink and you might miss this gem, which is tucked away in a tiny Victorian in downtown Redwood City. It offers scrumptious omelets—try the one with smoked salmon and cream cheese—but not much for non-egg-eaters. All breakfasts are served with a basket of delicious, piping hot bread and muffins. Service is friendly and homey. Small gift shop sells teas, jams, spices. • Breakfast and lunch Tu-Su.

Rico's Place $$ 920 El Camino Real, San Carlos, (415) 592-7863. This self-styled American trattoria transforms itself at midday. The breakfast menu includes a decidedly un-Italian selection of pancakes, cereals, and a variety of omelets to rival Joanne's. At 11:30, the kitchen shifts to elaborate pasta dishes and meats. Burgers and grilled sandwiches are available all day. An American touch: Rico's sponsors numerous events and deals, including early-bird and late-bird specials, senior citizen discounts, Sunday champagne brunches, ladies' nights with complimentary drinks and flowers, and rented videos with breakfast. • Breakfast, lunch and dinner daily.

Ristorante Piacere $$$ 727 Laurel St., San Carlos, (415) 592-3536. A relaxed alternative to the glitzy Italian restaurants of Palo Alto and the city. The pastas and appetizers are all familiar, but a few of the *secondi*, like baked duck in a Grand Marnier sauce and veal scaloppine stuffed with ham and provolone in a red wine sauce, are more novel. • Lunch M-Sa, dinner daily.

Ritz Seafood $$ 1528 S. El Camino Real, San Mateo, (415) 571-6213. Everything else plays second fiddle to the seafood dishes at this popular Chinese restaurant on El Camino (look for the neon whale in the window). Though the non-seafood offerings are just fine, the most extensive and inspired portion of the menu is devoted to such dishes as sautéed scallops with pine nuts and a variety of steamed whole fish. The brightly lit interior features fish tanks that assure diners their entrées are fresh. Ritz also serves dim sum and has a full bar. • Lunch, dim sum and dinner daily.

Rock 'N Taco $ 131 W. Santa Clara St., San Jose, (408) 993-8230. The best thing about Rock 'N Tacos is that it's open until 3am on weekends—a miracle in sleepy Silicon Valley. The second best thing about this hyper-neon taqueria is its fresh, healthy approach to Mexican fast food. Choose from fish tacos, skinless chicken cooked without oil, plentiful vegetarian selections including lard-free beans, and homemade salsa. Warning: it's not called *rock'n* for nothing—the music is on the loud side, to put it mildly. • Lunch and dinner daily; Su-W open until midnight, Th-Sa 3am.

Roman's Deli $$$ 7173 Washington St., Santa Clara, (408) 296-3864. From the outside, you wouldn't guess that a gourmet Italian restaurant lurked in the back of this storefront deli, and we suspect that the owners want to keep it that way. Roman's is a real neighborhood restaurant, where the proprietors know the customers by name and remember their favorite dishes. There's no menu to speak of, just daily specials, which are uniformly good. Accompany your meal with any of the wines in the store or one of the extensive selection of beers. • Lunch daily, dinner W-Sa.

Rooh's Café Salsa $$ 15525 Los Gatos Blvd., Los Gatos, (408) 358-7664 • 650 Castro St., Mtn. View, (415) 969-6363 • 1171 Homestead Ave., Santa Clara, (408) 246-2455. The concept here is low-fat—sometimes no-fat—Mexican cooking. Burritos, enchiladas, and nachos are available, along with entrées like the trademarked *paparosa*—a baked potato covered with beef, chicken, chili, or lentils and topped with beans, cheese, tomatoes, and olives—and triple-layer tortilla pizza. • Lunch and dinner daily.

Rosita's Taqueria $ 175 Fifth Ave., Redwood City, (415) 364-9685. Rosita's is one of many simple yet outstanding Little Mexico taquerias. The menu is practically identical to those of several nearby spots, yet many locals profess that Rosita's is the best. The portions are large and all food can be eaten in the cozy, recently remodeled dining area or packaged for take-out. • Breakfast, lunch, and dinner daily.

Royal Palace $$ 4320 El Camino Real, Los Altos, (415) 941-8818. One of the best places around for good dim sum on a weekend morning. Despite its huge dining room, the place gets crowded, so make sure you arrive early, when the food is freshest. Dinners are OK but don't compare to the dim sum. A wonderful touch at the end of the meal is the small bowl of red-bean soup, instead of fortune cookies. • Lunch, dim sum, and dinner daily.

Rue de Paris $$$$ 19 N. Market St., San Jose, (408) 298-0704. Behind the floral-print curtains in this old-style dining room, an array of couples at various stages of romance—from first date to fiftieth anniversary—bill and coo. The menu, lettered in elaborate script, lists an array of French specialties, from *escargots de Bourgogne* to filet mignon with bérnaise sauce, with a few Italian standbys like fettucine Alfredo thrown in. Order a glass of fine old port to prolong your meal. • Lunch M-F, dinner M-Sa.

Sand Dabs $$$ 4926 El Camino Real, Los Altos, (415) 968-1030. Although a fish net adorns the dining room walls, the trappings here are more sophisticated than your average surf-and-turf restaurant—peach walls, light wood furniture, piano music. Seafood, predictably, gets star billing (try the panfried sand dabs), although steak and chicken have cameos. Sit outdoors on the pleasant patio on warm afternoons or evenings. • Dinner Tu-Sa.

Santini's $$ 510 El Camino Real, Belmont, (415) 592-2300. Volume eaters gravitate here on Mondays to consume all the spaghetti they can for just $6. The bar and big TV provide the perfect backdrop for a football feast. Santini's also features an inordinate number of traditional Italian dishes, from ten types of veal to innumerable pizza combinations. • Dinner daily until 10:30pm.

Savera $$ 1146 S. Saratoga-Sunnyvale Rd., San Jose, (408) 446-3390. The square white building along Saratoga-Sunnyvale Road that houses Savera has seen more past lives than Shirley MacLaine. Only time will tell if this incarnation will outlast its predecessors. The tandoori chicken and other tandoori items are delicious, as is the lamb *palak*, a mild lamb curry in a creamy spinach sauce. The lunch buffet, however, is woefully underseasoned, and even items labeled spicy on the menu, such as chicken masala, are bland. Dinner is pricier, but it includes an immense amount of food, from *dal* to dessert. • Lunch and dinner daily.

Scott's Seafood Grill and Bar $$$ 2300 East Bayshore Rd., Palo Alto, (415) 856-1046 • 185 Park Ave., San Jose, (408) 971-1700. An elegantly furnished restaurant with tasteful maritime art on the walls and plenty of room between tables to allow for private conversation or just serious concentration on the well-stocked menu. The Massachusetts fisherman's stew could feed a minor fleet, while the cornmeal-grilled catfish jambalaya will please the most finicky seafood connoisseur. Service is relaxed, to put it kindly, but you'll be glad for the extra time to savor every tender morsel. • Lunch M-F, dinner daily.

71 Saint Peter $$$ 71 N. San Pedro St., San Jose, (408) 971-8523. This intimate downtown spot manages to be rustic and elegant at the same time, with brick walls, exposed rafters, linen tablecloths, and flowers on every table. Chef Mark Tabak conjures up specialties such as filet mignon with bleu cheese, pork loin with an herb crust, and excellent polenta. The perfect setting for a romantic rendezvous. • Lunch M-F, dinner Tu-Sa.

Shigemasu $$$ 1190 Broadway, Burlingame, (415) 347-4944. Traditional Japanese food in a rather untraditional setting. Formica luncheon tables and slightly stuffy booths replace the usual tatami rooms, wood screens, and sushi bar. The menu covers the usual dishes, as well as more exotic fare like 18 types of sashimi, and oyster and lobster tail teriyaki. Lunch prices are considerably lower than dinner. • Lunch M and W-F, dinner W-Tu.

Siam Garden $$ 1143 Crane St., Menlo Park, (415) 853-1143. Popular, passable Southeast Asian food served in a prototypical Thai atmosphere—booths, pink napkins, extremely friendly service. Try the tart soups and fragrant curries. • Lunch M-Sa, dinner daily.

Siam Thai Cuisine $$ 220 E. Main St., Los Gatos, (408) 354-1019. Attention culinary daredevils: The term *medium hot* is relative here. Fiery green chiles, garlic, and red curry paste season almost everything on the menu, from the acclaimed soups to the extensive seafood selection. The desserts, which emphasize coconut, are soothing but no less flavorful. The decor features mauve banquets, matching napkins, and diaphanous white curtains. • Lunch M-F, dinner daily.

Smitty's $ 199 Old Middlefield Rd., Mtn. View, (415) 968-5883. Where the beef is. Mostly oakwood-barbecued burgers, to be more precise, with every imaginable combination of toppings, but also ribs and chicken, all served up by a jovial staff. The accompaniments—salad, potatoes—are nothing to write home about, but Clara Peller wouldn't have dared pose that famous question if she had been anywhere near a full-pound Smitty burger. • Lunch and dinner daily.

Sousa's $$$ 1614 Alum Rock Ave., San Jose, (408) 926-9075. In the middle of the Latin district on Alum Rock, Sousa's provides a festive respite from an otherwise pedestrian area. Inside, a doorway framed by an enormous guitar (Guinness Book of World Records material?) connects two large dining rooms. The Portuguese menu features a variety of homemade, flavorful dishes from the old country. If octopus stew is too exotic for your first visit, try the beef stew or marinated pork—both are standouts. • Lunch and dinner Tu-Su.

Spencers Jambalaya and Ribs Shop $$ 5721 Cottle Rd., San Jose, (408) 365-7728. The South Bay is home to some pretty fierce barbecue competition, but Spencers has managed to distinguish itself with its flaming hot sauce. The claim is that more than 40 spices go into the fiery sauce, which is liberally applied to cuts of pork, beef, and chicken. The jambalaya is also spicy—you can specify the degree of heat you can tolerate. Spencers is a little out of the way for most folks—south of Blossom Hill—but it's worth the trip to satisfy a barbecue craving. Cash only. • Lunch and dinner M-Sa.

RESTAURANTS AND CAFÉS

Spiedo's $$$ 223 E. Fourth Ave., San Mateo, (415) 375-0818. This spacious San Mateo restaurant had a rocky start as the Fourth Avenue Café. Now owner Hamdi Ugur is trying something new: reasonably priced, hearty northern Italian fare. Most notable are the mesquite-grilled entrées, including fresh fish, lamb chops, prawns, and more. Pastas and pizzas are also featured, as well as a wide selection of appetizers. The interior is bright and attractive and the service assiduous. • Lunch M-F, dinner daily.

Spoons $$ 1555 S. Bascom Ave., Campbell, (408) 559-7400 • 725 Fair Oaks Ave., Sunnyvale, (408) 720-0136. Whoever dreamed up the Spoons concept hit pay dirt with the sports bar/taqueria theme. This chain draws crowds on weekend nights with its festive frat-party atmosphere, "mugaritas" (frozen margaritas served in mugs), and abundant selection of bar food. The taproom is decked out with sports pennants and athletically inclined patrons, and the dining room is done up in high-Mexican knickknack, with bright-colored tin lamp shades and ceramic-tile tables. In addition to Tex-Mex staples like fajitas, you'll find everything from Buffalo wings to burgers to Philly cheese steak to brownies with ice cream on the menu. Party on. • Lunch and dinner daily.

Sports City Café $$ 10745 N. De Anza Blvd., Cupertino, (408) 253-2233 • 150 S. First St. (in the Pavilion), San Jose, (408) 291-2233. Don't be fooled by the name—this is no typical sports bar. Yes, there are framed photos of athletes on the walls and a few televisions, but there are also ocher-sponged walls, white tablecloths, skylights, and tiled floors. A popular spot for business lunches, Sports City serves basic upscale California fare along with dressed-up bar food. The renditions of popular California cuisine—mesquite-grilled seafood or poultry, fresh pastas, and sandwiches—are unexciting, and the service can be excruciatingly slow. Sports City Café features a full bar, banquet and meeting facilities, and brunch on Sundays. • Lunch and dinner daily, brunch Su.

Steamers Fish Again $$$ 50 University Ave., Old Town (Los Gatos), (408) 396-2722. This festive seafood spot has a lively atmosphere. An aroma of garlic greets you at the door, foreshadowing good things to come. A glass block bar dominates the dining area, and curved wooden banquettes accommodate locals who come for well-prepared seafood specialties like grilled salmon, teriyaki mixed-fish grill, and steamed clams by the pound. • Lunch and dinner daily; open until 11pm F-Sa.

Stoddard's Brewhouse $$$ 111 S. Murphy Ave., Sunnyvale, (408) 733-7824. Opened by Bob Stoddard, former brewmeister at the Tied House, the soaring two-story space houses a long, polished wood bar, wicker seating area, a downstairs dining room, and an upstairs aerie for quieter dining. Out back there's a beer garden in case you're restless. For starters, the hummus and eggplant with flatbread has become a quick success while the roast chicken with garlic mashed potatoes and roasted corn is a good bet for an entrée. And oh, yes, the fresh-brewed ales are delicious. • Lunch and dinner daily.

Su Hong $$ 1037 El Camino Real, Menlo Park, (415) 323-6852 • 630 Menlo Ave., Menlo Park, (415) 322-4631 • 4101 El Camino Way, Palo Alto, (415) 493-3836, take-out (415) 493-4664. Su Hong sports tasteful cream and lilac walls for a soothing environment. The food is standard spicy Chinese, but it's extremely popular, especially the hot and sour soup, the pot stickers, and the rolled lettuce minced chicken with plum sauce. There's usually a wait on weekends, but with Kepler's Books across the street, killing time is no problem. If you're in a hurry, Su Hong's take-out station is just behind the restaurant. In Palo Alto, there is a new Su Hong just off El Camino. Same good food, but served in a more modern decor. • Lunch and dinner daily. 630 Menlo Ave is takeout only.

Subaru Restaurant $$ 867 W. Dana St., Mtn. View, (415) 960-6876. A complete selection of Japanese cuisine, including *gyoza* (Japanese pot stickers) and udon noodle soups. The sushi selection is not as extensive here as at some other places, but what is available is fresh and high quality. The chicken and beef teriyaki dinners are excellent. Bright and airy, casual atmosphere. • Lunch M-F, dinner M-Sa; food served until 11pm, bar open until 2am.

Sue's Indian Cuisine $$$ 216 Castro St., Mtn. View, (415) 969-1112 • 895 Willow St., San Jose, (408) 993-8730. The waiters with their pensive, piercing black eyes seem to have just stepped out of a Sartre story, but they'll forget their existential angst long enough to serve you any of Sue's delicious tandoori specialties, complete with *pilau* rice, vegetables, and *naan*. Order a variety of main dishes and share them around the table. Warning: The *gulab jaman* (fried milk balls in rose flavored syrup) are overly sweet, even for an Indian dessert. The background music adds an authentic feel to the dining atmosphere. • Lunch Tu-F, dinner daily.

Sun Sun $$ 867 E. El Camino Real, Mtn. View, (415) 961-4030. A devoted clientele descends on Sun Sun for the Szechuan specialties and the dim sum lunch on weekends. The decor is standard-issue Chinese. Formica tables, wood paneling circling the dining room, Chinese prints, and a bar area with droning TV may lead you to expect chop suey–style cuisine, but the food is better than the decor would suggest. • Lunch and dinner daily, dim sum Sa-Su.

Super Taqueria $ 1095 S. White Rd., San Jose, (408) 848-8543 or (408) 292-3470 • 476 S. Tenth St., San Jose, (408) 292-3470. Fast, authentic Mexican food with a fanatical following. The menu contains only five basic items—a taco, a burrito, and so on—but the selection of meat fillings, which runs from barbecued pork to beef cheeks and tongue, provides sufficient variety. Colorful Latino murals make for a lively atmosphere. The speedy service, hefty portions, and low prices endear Super Taqueria to San Jose State students, who occupy at least a couple of tables at any given time. • Lunch and dinner daily.

Sushi on the Run $ 114 N. Santa Cruz Ave., Los Gatos, (408) 354-1125. An eight-seat sushi bar on Los Gatos's main drag notable chiefly for its decor. The menu is printed in reverse type on the wall behind you; to read it, consult the wall-length mirror in front of you. An electronic bulletin board advertises the daily specials. • Lunch and dinner Tu-Sa.

Sushi Ya $$ 380 University Ave., Palo Alto, (415) 322-0330. This tiny sushi bar serves excellent, still-quivering sushi and sashimi and is a favorite with visiting Japanese businessmen. If you're a sushi novice let Toshi, the sushi master, lead the way. He creates innovative presentations, and he'll put together a stunning sushi box to take out. There are only a few tables, so be prepared to wait or sit at the sushi bar. • Lunch M-F, dinner M-Sa.

Taj India $$ 899 E. El Camino Real, Sunnyvale, (408) 720-8396. The exotic ambience provides a welcome escape from suburban tedium—wonderful curry smells fill the air, and carved wooden screens, prints of India, and white linen tablecloths adorn the dining room. Start with lamb *samosas* and any of the *roti*—freshly baked Indian breads. The tandoori dishes are a good bet, and the wide selection of vegetarian specialties will please nonmeat eaters. • Lunch and dinner daily.

Tao Tao Café $$ 175 S. Murphy Ave., Sunnyvale, (408) 736-3731. The softly lit dining area is divided into several rooms with ceiling-high screens and plush brown carpet for a warm, intimate ambience. Food is high quality: meats are a cut above the usual tough and fatty grades used by many Asian restaurants, and the ginger beef and pressed almond duck are especially tasty. Start things off with a shredded chicken salad. • Lunch M-F, dinner daily.

Taqueria La Bamba $ 2058 Old Middlefield Way, Mtn. View, (415) 965-2755. Huge burritos the size of a small loaf of bread and a limited menu with a Salvadoran touch are La Bamba's trademarks. The best strategy is to start with a *pupusa* (small corn tortilla stuffed with pork and cheese) and move on to the first half of a hard-to-find vegetarian burrito. Save the other half for your next meal. Expect a brief wait during the lunchtime rush—you may have to scramble for one of the few chairs. • Lunch and dinner daily.

Tasty Chinese Cuisine $$ 2318 S. El Camino Real, San Mateo, (415) 341-1918. Philip Lo, the original chef at the celebrated Hong Kong Flower Lounge in Millbrae, has moved south. The food at his newest restaurant is less adventurous—unpretentious traditional

Cantonese dishes—but the quality is nearly as high. And though the drab brick exterior isn't glamorous, the dining rooms are less crowded and the waits much shorter than at the Flower Lounge. The service is friendly and prompt. • Lunch and dinner daily.

Teske's Germania House $$$ 255 N. First St., San Jose, (408) 292-0291. An authentic German beer hall in San Jose? Strange but true. Teske's delivers a hunting lodge atmosphere—dark wood, stuffed birds, antlers, wagon-wheel lights, and an electric train running around the bar. The menu features heavy German specialties such as Wiener schnitzel and sauerbraten, as well as an alarming-sounding barbecued piglet. During happy hours an oompah band holds forth. Sit in the lovely beer garden out back on warm evenings. • Lunch M-F, dinner M-Sa; bar open late.

Thai Best $$ 1500 El Camino Real, San Carlos, (415) 594-1097. An extremely popular restaurant in a lavender shack on El Camino. The menu is classic Thai, with lots of curry, coconut milk, and lemongrass, and the decor is simple—a couple of glittery objects of art on the wall and a fireplace in one corner. • Lunch M-F, dinner daily.

Thai City $$ 3691 El Camino Real, Palo Alto, (415) 493-0643. The aggressively red carpet and tablecloths might make you think you're at a Chinese restaurant, but the elegantly folded pink napkins tell you it's Thai all the way. The richly flavored sauces are pungent with spice but won't burn even a timid palate. While the soups are a joy, the curries can be heavy. A large menu covers a variety of tastes at an equally wide range of prices. Vegetarians are catered to: the chef will substitute tofu, egg, and vegetables in any dish. • Lunch M-Sa, dinner daily.

Thanh Da $$ 253 E. Maude Ave., Sunnyvale, (408) 245-1342. A mix of Vietnamese, Thai, and Chinese cuisine is served within this unexceptional-looking storefront restaurant. The steamed rolls filled with pork and shrimp, the "delights noodles" (grilled pork and steamed rice noodles with herbs), and the sesame-beef noodle dishes are fresh and tasty. If it's available, be sure to try the special shrimp wrapped in sugar cane. • Lunch and dinner M-Sa.

Thanh's Restaurant $ 3151 Middlefield Rd., Redwood City, (415) 367-0567. Thanh's offers authentic Vietnamese and Chinese food—start with the barbecued quail, flambéed before your eyes, and imperial rolls, the Vietnamese version of egg rolls. The beef and prawns in a clay pot is a great hands-on meal: roll them in rice patties, along with fresh mint, pickled garlic, and other vegetables. Other entrées worth trying are the coconut curried chicken and the spicy lemongrass chicken. Don't be put off by the no-nonsense linoleum floors and brown checked tablecloths. • Lunch M-Sa, dinner M-Tu, Th-Sa.

Thepthai $$ 23 N. Market St., San Jose, (408) 292-7515. A roaring success. The decor at this modest downtown restaurant is minimal—a few Christmas lights and a pagoda-like folly. The food is the point here, though, with some of the most delectable Thai dishes around emerging from the kitchen (the restaurant was voted best Thai in the *Metro*). Pad Thai is the specialty—crunchy red cabbage, sprouts, cilantro, and lime distinguish this rendition. Other hits are the fried tofu appetizer with peanut sauce, the ginger chicken, and all the soups. • Lunch and dinner daily; open late F-Sa.

The Tied House Café and Brewery $$ 945 Villa St., Mtn. View, (415) 965-BREW • 65 N. San Pedro, San Jose, (408) 295-BREW. An always-crowded beer hall big enough to accommodate an entire fraternity. A big-screen TV, darts, shuffleboard, kegs to go—what more could a frat brother ask for? Bar food, of course. Garlic onion rings, oyster shooters, and buckets of steamed clams (all mediocre) can be found on the menu, along with pizzas and pastas (borderline edible). Let's face it, though, the food is secondary to the brews here. Eight beers are served on tap, from Alpine Pearl Pale to Ironwood Dark. Order a sampler if you can't decide. • Lunch and dinner daily; late-night menu until 1:30am Th-Sa.

Tien Fu $$ 176 Castro St., Mtn. View, (415) 968-6699. This reliable spot for Mandarin and Szechuan cuisine is one of the few Chinese restaurants around with outdoor seating (in this case, on pleasant Castro Street). Peach walls and mirrors make for a disco effect in the dining room. Try Ants Climbing Up the Tree—a flavorful mélange of bean thread noodles topped with finely minced pork, water chestnuts, and cloud ear mushrooms—or one of the spectacular sizzling dishes served on a hot platter, ranging from tofu to lamb. • Lunch and dinner daily.

Tokie's $$ 1058 Shell Blvd., Foster City, (415) 570-6609. The basics, plain and simple. What this unassuming strip-mall restaurant lacks in atmosphere it makes up for with satisfying, traditional Japanese fare: teriyaki, udon, donburi, and sushi with all the usual accompaniments. Despite the crowds of business lunchers on weekdays, the booths and tables are well spaced and you never feel rushed. The prices are low, the service is cheerful, and the food is fresh. • Lunch Tu-F, dinner Tu-Su.

Tony and Alba's Pizza and Italian Food $ 619 Escuela, Mtn. View, (415) 968-5089 • 3137 Stevens Creek Blvd., San Jose, (408) 246-4605. These are the most authentic of authentic Italian pizza parlors. Everything you expect in a family-run pizza hangout: sports-blasting TVs, photos, pictures, and posters all over the walls; friends partying over pitchers; whole families chowing down; lovers sharing slices and ashtrays; and lots and lots of noise. So much of it, in fact that many loyal customers prefer to take their pizza out. The crust is floppy, and the toppings are piled high. • Lunch and dinner daily.

Tour Eiffel $$ 200 State St., Los Altos, (415) 917-1328. Though the name *Tour Eiffel* may conjure up memories of tourist traps in Paris, the sign hanging on the door—"Vietnamese Food & French Bakery"—brings you back to the California melting pot. This bright café in Los Altos does a brisk breakfast and lunch business. The quiches, soups, and pastries are the highlights of the French section of the menu, while the Vietnamese dishes are substantial and flavorful. The egg rolls are crisp and the vermicelli dishes (chicken, tofu, or prawn) come in a large bowl heaped full of ingredients. • Breakfast, lunch, and dinner M-Sa.

29 East Main $ 29 E. Main St., Los Gatos, (408) 395-4889. An artsy, casual café in downtown Los Gatos, with bare wood floors, modern lighting fixtures, and rotating artwork. Inviting dishes like Thai and eggplant pizza emerge from the open kitchen. All that's missing are the starving, goateed artists. • Lunch and dinner M-Sa.

2030 $$$ 2030 Broadway, Redwood City, (415) 363-2030. Giant portions are the hallmark at this chic Redwood City dining spot. (One waitress explained that the chef is "a big guy who likes to eat a lot.") Entrées include a salad and a soup, so appetizers are irrelevant. Lamb loin chops with garlic and herbs are outstanding, as are the prawns with prosciutto, spinach, and mushrooms served over linguine. If you have room for dessert, try the vanilla bean crème brulée. • Lunch M-F, dinner daily.

Two Pesos Taqueria $ 787 Franklin St., Santa Clara, (408) 249-9225. If you're not a student at Santa Clara U, you probably haven't noticed this new entrant to the fresh-Mex food craze. But Two Pesos is noteworthy for its large and tasty vegetarian burritos, freshly cooked black and pinto beans, good selection of Mexican beers, and Monday night all-you-can-eat deal. • Lunch and dinner daily.

231 Ellsworth $$$$ 231 Ellsworth St., San Mateo, (415) 347-7231. Critics and patrons alike rave about this San Mateo restaurant, which serves some of the most innovative cuisine on the Peninsula. The two-tiered interior, done up in passé pink and aqua pastels, is uninspired. But the food more than makes up for any design lapses, and the four-course $30 prix fixe menu brings the menu within reach of mere mortals. Appetizers in particular shine—try the sautéed sweetbreads if they're available. Main courses include imaginatively prepared seafood, grilled meats, and homemade pasta. Order the luscious chocolate cake for dessert—it's heavenly. • Lunch and dinner M-Sa.

Valeriano's Ristorante $$$ 160 W. Main St., Los Gatos, (408) 354-8108. A former bank on Los Gatos's main drag extravagantly transformed into a restaurant serving northern Italian cuisine. The soaring ceilings, terra-cotta walls, abundant brass accents, and hanging tapestries give a postmodern luxuriousness to the surroundings. Among the offerings are carpaccio, prosciutto with melon, designer pizzas, and brick-oven roasted chicken or game hen. Imaginative pasta preparations include *gnocchi alla salsa salvia*—gnocchi with fresh sage, Parmesan, and dry ricotta. A nice selection of California and Italian wines. • Lunch and dinner daily.

The Vans $$$ 815 Belmont Ave., Belmont, (415) 591-6525. One of the Bay Area's top ten places to pop the question, according to a recent poll. This hilltop restaurant and bar earned its romantic reputation largely for its breathtaking views of the East Bay hills and Mt. Diablo, softly illuminated by the Japanese lanterns outside. The Vans has a colorful past, as befits the oldest bar on the Peninsula: It was built in 1915 as a Japanese tea house in San Francisco, barged down the Bay to Belmont, and then transformed by turns into a speakeasy and gambling den during Prohibition, a legal saloon in the thirties, and a full-scale restaurant in the forties. The food today is classic continental/American, with an emphasis on mesquite-broiled meats and elaborate weekend brunches. • Lunch and dinner daily, breakfast Sa-Su.

Vic's $ 1125 San Carlos Ave., San Carlos, (415) 595-2606. The breakfast hot spot of San Carlos. Every day hungry locals cluster around the lunch counters and in the leatherette booths to feast on hefty omelets and slog down institutional coffee. Vic's is almost as popular for lunch and dinner, when burgers, grilled sandwiches, and simple pastas and meats dominate the gargantuan menu. • Breakfast and lunch daily, dinner M-Sa.

Vienna Woods $$ 14567 Big Basin Way, Saratoga, (408) 867-2410. Hidden in the back of the Plaza del Roble off Big Basin Way, Vienna Woods is a respite from the High Church restaurants nearby. Order take-out or sit around café tables in the pleasant courtyard and enjoy well-prepared German specialties such as hot bratwurst or *leberkase* (veal loaf). Homemade soups round out the menu. Cash only. • Lunch and dinner daily.

The Village Pub $$$$ 2967 Woodside Rd., Woodside, (415) 851-1294. Don't let the folksy name deceive you, this is haute cuisine at the kind of high-rent prices you'd expect in Woodside. The interior is California-cottage style, with whitewashed walls and discreet framed prints. The menu changes daily, but it might include such highly evolved fare as sautéed crabcakes with corn relish and pepper essence, or steamed Penn Cove mussels with chipotle chili broth and cilantro. • Lunch M-F, dinner daily.

White Lotus $$ 80 N. Market St., San Jose, (408) 977-0540. The menu at this Chinese restaurant sends mixed messages, proclaiming that "all food items are meatless" and yet listing dishes like spicy pork with lemongrass and meatloaf with shredded tofu over rice. But perplexed vegetarians can breathe easy: all the "meats" at White Lotus are merely substitutes fashioned from tofu, wheat gluten, and vegetables. Several more traditional dishes with no pretensions to animal origins will satisfy purists who object even to imitation flesh, and vegetarians who prefer meat-free diner food to meat-free Chinese food can enjoy the mock ham sandwiches and beef stew. *Note*: the fish tank at the back is purely decorative. • Lunch and dinner Tu-Sa.

Willow Street Wood Fired Pizza $$ 1072 Willow St., San Jose, (408) 971-7080. Yuppie pizzas emerge from the roaring ovens at this bustling neighborhood dinner spot. Toppings include goat cheese and barbecued chicken, plus upscale versions of the basics, like plum tomatoes and basil. Pastas round out the offerings. Finish off your meal with an excellent tiramisu. • Lunch and dinner daily, brunch Su.

Windy City Pizza $$ 35 Bouet Rd., San Mateo, (415) 591-9457. Unbelievably deep-dish Chicago-style pizza, along with smoky barbecued ribs and hot links. Allow some time to choose from the zillions of toppings—there's even a dessert pizza with cream, chocolate, cheese, and fruit. Stick to the basics, though, for the most expert execution. Windy City offers a comfortable blue-collar atmosphere and the friendliest wait staff for miles. We advise passing on the free delivery, which can make for soggy pizza. • Lunch and dinner daily, open until 11pm F-Sa.

The Wine Cellar $$$ 50 University Ave., Los Gatos, (408) 354-4808. A sunken medieval-looking tavern with a slightly upgraded diner menu. The stone tile floor, dim reddish lighting, and meat-oriented bill of fare will make you forget you're in the Golden State. The entrées consist chiefly of burgers and sandwiches, with a few half-hearted gestures in the direction of California cuisine, like fettucine with chicken, Italian sausage, sun-dried tomatoes, and fresh herbs. Live music is featured Thursdays and Saturdays. • Lunch and dinner daily; open until midnight F-Sa.

Woodside Bakery & Café $$ 3052 Woodside Rd., Woodside, (415) 851-7247. Squeezed into a small shopping center across from Robert's Market, this upscale eatery serves excellent pastries and lattés as well as light lunches. The patrons have a country-gentry look, but prices are reasonable. Try a gourmet pizza (prosciutto, mozzarella, capers, and romano cheese are among the toppings) from the giant wood-burning oven. A favorite stopping-off point for cyclists and Sunday drivers. • Daily 7am-6pm.

Woodside Thai Spot $$ 593 Woodside Rd., Redwood City, (415) 365-4079. Despite the unpromising exterior (in a former life this establishment could have been a biker bar), excellent, fiery Thai food served on white linen tablecloths is found within. *Tom kha kai*—hot and sour soup with chicken, lemongrass, and coconut milk—is a masterpiece. *Yum ta lay*—silver noodles with shrimp, chicken, red onion, peanuts, and chili in a lemon dressing—will have you calling the fire engines. Weekend nights can be busy, so be patient—there is only one harried waiter. • Lunch M-F, dinner daily.

Yet Wah $$ 1026 Foster City Blvd., Foster City, (415) 570-7888. A link in a Mandarin megachain that ventures far afield of the usual bill of fare. Where else can you find Mongolian lamb, curry lobster, barbecued spareribs, fried chicken wings, and old standbys like beef chow mein on the same menu? The businesspeople who descend on Yet Wah at lunchtime contribute to a rather staid atmosphere, although a fireplace and a view of one of the Foster City lagoons relieve the corporate feel. The full bar in the back accommodates serious schmoozers who don't want to bother with food. • Lunch and dinner daily.

Yiassoo $ 2180 Bascom Ave., Campbell, (408) 559-0312 • 10660 S. De Anza Blvd., Cupertino, (408) 253-5544. Greek grub at low prices. A few genuinely exotic dishes supplement the usual selection of gyros, spanakopita, and the like. The blue-and-white tiled interior is bright and clean, although a fast-food ambience prevails. Yiassoo is a fun spot for a quick meal—just don't expect to be transported to a Greek isle. Cash only. • Lunch and dinner daily.

Yu Shan $$ 1330 S. Mary St., Sunnyvale, (408) 245-1222. Hidden behind a nondescript storefront of colorless shades and haphazardly strewn white blinking lights is a tastefully decorated Szechuan restaurant. Potted trees, an abundance of cut flowers, and festive Chinese prints provide Yu Shan with a quick counter to any dreary first impression. The daily menu features the usual offerings, but the house specialties are spicier and more flavorful—try the Hunan lamb, empress shrimp, and sizzling three-delicacy. • Lunch and dinner daily.

Yuen Yung $$ 639 Santa Cruz Ave., Menlo Park, (415) 323-7759 • 7273 Bark Ln., San Jose, (408) 252-6144. Excellent Chinese food in a larger-than-life setting—soaring ceilings, white tablecloths, and speedy service from the helpful wait staff. The menu is extensive, with a good selection emphasizing Cantonese and Shanghai cuisine. Check out the minced chicken wrapped in iceberg lettuce moo shu style. The clay pot, seafood, and black bean sauce dishes also shine, as does the whole fish. Sadly, hot and sour soup is only so-so. • Lunch, dim sum and dinner daily.

CITY INDEX

BELMONT
Horky's
Iron Gate
Marvin Gardens
Santini's
The Vans
Windy City Pizza

BURLINGAME
Benihana
Bit of England
Bua Thong Kitchen
Buns
Café La Scala
Ecco Café
Gao Poang
Gulliver's
Isobune
Kincaid's
Kuleto's Trattoria
La Locanda
Shigemasu

CAMPBELL
Borsalino Saaghi
Campbell House
Chez Sovan
Di Cicco
El Burro
Emil Villa's Hick'ry Pit
Fresh Choice
Golden Chopsticks
Komatsu
Kyoto Palace
Martha's Restaurant
Spoons
Yiassoo

CUPERTINO
Armadillo Willy's BBQ
Azuma
Benihana
Carlos Murphy's
Coffee Society
Duke of Edinburgh
Fresh Choice
Good Earth
Hamasushi
Hobee's Restaurant
Hong Fu
Ikenohana
Kathmandu West
Miyake
Mondello Ristorante
Pizzeria Uno
Savera
Sports City Café
Yiassoo

EAST PALO ALTO
Goldie's Oakwood BBQ

FOSTER CITY
Black Angus
Chevy's
Pacific Gourmet Pizza
Tokie's
Yet Wah

LOS ALTOS
Applewood Inn
Armadillo Willy's BBQ
Beauséjour
Black Forest Inn
Capriccio
Casa Lupe
Charley's
Chef Chu's
Emil Villa's Hick'ry Pit
Eugene's Polish Restaurant
Florentine
Hunan Homes
Le Tandoor
Los Altos Bar & Grill
Mac's Tea Room
Piccolo Mondo
Royal Palace
Sand Dabs
Tour Eiffel

LOS GATOS
Andale Taqueria
Café Marcella
California Cafe
The Cats
Chart House
Ernesto's
Good Earth
Great Bear Café and Los
    Osos Diner
Jasmine
La Maison du Café
Los Gatos Brewing Co.
Mabel's Lantern House
Mount Everest
Pedro's Cabo Grill
Pigalle
Rooh's Cafe Salsa
Siam Thai Cuisine
Steamer's Fish Again
Sushi on the Run
29 East Main
Valeriano's Ristorante

MENLO PARK
The Acorn
Allied Arts Guild
Amandine
Applewood Inn
British Banker's Club
Carpaccio
Dal Baffo
The Dutch Goose
Flea Street Café
Fresh Choice
Gambardella's
Garden Grill
Gombei
Late for the Train
Le Pot Au Feu
The Oasis
Quadrus Café
Siam Garden
Su Hong
Yuen Yung

MILLBRAE
Fook Yuen
Hong Kong Flower Lounge

MOUNTAIN VIEW
Bangkok Spoon
Blue Sky Café
Castro Street Bar & Grill
Chez T.J.
Clarke's Charcoal Broiler
Colonel Lee's Mongolian
    Bar-B-Q
Country Gourmet
El Calderon
Fiesta del Mar
Florentine
Golden Wok
Hangen
Hobee's Restaurant
India Cookhouse
Kim's Restaurant
La Fiesta
Le Petit Bistro
Motomachi
Mumtaj
Paradise Persian Cuisine
Passage To India
Pollo's
Rooh's Café Salsa
Smitty's
Subaru Restaurant
Sue's Indian Cuisine
Sun Sun
Taqueria La Bamba
Tied House
Tien Fu
Tony and Alba's Pizza

PALO ALTO
Andale Taqueria
Babbo's Pizzeria
Bangkok Cuisine

84

BJ Bulls
Blue Chalk Café
Bravo Fono
Café Fino
Café Pro Bono
Caffe Verona
California Café
Chantilly II
Chez Louis
China Lion
Cho's
Compadres
Country Fare
Dinah's Poolside Café
Empire Grill and Tap
Fish Market, The
Florentine
Fresco
Fresh Choice
Fuki-Sushi
Gaylord India Restaurant
Golden Wok
Good Earth
Gordon Biersch
Henry's
Higashi West
Hobee's Restaurant

Il Fornaio Cucina Italiana
Kirk's Restaurant
Little Garden
MacArthur Park
Maddalena's
Mandarin Gourmet
Mango Café
Max's Opera Café
Ming's
Miyake
Nataraja
Nouveau Trattoria
Osteria
Palermo
Palo Alto Sol
Peking Duck Restaurant
Peninsula Fountain
Petaluma's
Piatti
Pollo's
Ramona's
Rangoon
Scott's Seafood
Su Hong
Sushi Ya
Thai City

PORTOLA VALLEY
Alpine Beer Garden
Iberia

REDWOOD CITY
Baccarat
Barbarossa
Chevy's
City Pub
Clark's by the Bay
Florentine
Fresh Choice
Gypsy Cellar
Mistral
Redwood Café and Spice Co.
Rosita's Taqueria
Thanh's Restaurant
2030
Woodside Thai Spot

SAN CARLOS
Cheshire Pub and Pizza
The English Rose
La Hacienda
Pup & Hound
Rico's Place
Ristorante Piacere
Thai Best
Vic's

$ RATINGS

Rating the price of a restaurant meal isn't a science: two groups can go to the same establishment and leave with wildly different checks. Do you order an appetizer, a dessert, or alcohol? These items can double the price of the meal.

Our ratings are based on what it might cost each person to have a reasonable dinner (breakfast or lunch if that's all the restaurant serves) including tax and tip. This means neither splurging nor skimping: Maybe enjoy one drink, split an appetizer, order an entrée, and share a dessert.

$ A filling meal for $8 or less. In most cases, this refers to taquerias, burger joints, and other take-out places.

$$ $8 to $15 each for dinner. Typically, places that only serve brunch and lunch, ethnic restaurants, and other eateries where main dishes are under $10.

$$$ You can get away with spending as little as $15 for dinner or easily go up to $25. Mostly places serving pasta, sushi, or moderately priced meat and seafood dishes.

$$$$ Meals run from $25 to $40 per person. Restaurants where there is no escape from ordering entrées priced in the teens, most items are à la carte, and every table has a bottle of wine.

$$$$$ There is no cap on the amount you could spend at these fine dining establishments, but we have them starting at $40 per person. For that blow-out celebration meal (or when someone else is paying).

LOCAL RESTAURANTS

SAN JOSE
Bangkok Cuisine
Bella Mia
Bellino
Black Angus
Bob's Oak Room
Bold Knight Cattleman's
California Sushi and Grill
Casa Vicky
Chevy's
Chez Sovan
Cuban International
Dac Phuc
840 North First
El Maghreb
El Pollo Asado
Emile's
Eulipia
Falafel Drive-In
Florentine
Fresh Choice
Fuji
Garden City
Germania Restaurant
Gombei
Gordon Biersch
Henry's World Famous Hi-Life
Hobee's Restaurant
Hong Truc
House of Cathay & House of Genji
Il Fornaio Cucina Italiana
Kazoo
Khanh's Garden
Khyber Kabob House
Kitahama
Krung Thai
La Foret
La Pastaia
Le Papillon
Les Saisons
Mandarin Gourmet
Menara Moroccan
94th Aero Squadron
Okoyama
Pagoda
Palermo Ristorante
Paolo's
Pasquale's
Pho Hua
Quoc Te
Red Sea Restaurant
Rock 'N Taco
Rue de Paris
Scott's Seafood
71 Saint Peter

Sousa's
Spencers Jambalaya & Ribs
Sports City Café
Sue's Indian Cuisine
Super Taqueria
Teske's Germania House
Thepthai
Tied House
Tony and Alba's Pizza
White Lotus
Willow Street Pizza
Yuen Yung

SAN MATEO
Amici's E. Coast Pizzeria
Bogie's
Buffalo Grill
Café for All Seasons
Capellini
Chao Praya
Clay Oven
Dining Room, The
Esposto's Four-Day Café
Fish Market, The
Fresh Choice
Good Earth
JoAnn's B Street Café
Kisaku
Luceti's
Max's Bakery
Mei's
North Beach Pizza
Ritz Seafood
Spiedo's
Tasty Chinese Cuisine
231 Ellsworth

SANTA CLARA
Armadillo Willy's BBQ
Birk's
By-th-Bucket
California Café
Coleman Still
Di Cicco
The Fish Market
Fresh Choice
Good Earth
Kobe
Mariani's Inn
Mio Vicino
Pasand
Pizz'a Chicago
Pizzeria Uno
Roman's Deli
Rooh's Cafe Salsa
Two Pesos Taqueria

SARATOGA
Adriatic Restaurant
Bella Mia
Crêpe Daniel
Florentine
La Fondue
La Mere Michelle
Le Mouton Noir
Mandarin Chef
The Plumed Horse
Vienna Woods

SOUTH SAN FRANCISCO
Basque Cultural Center
Gao Poang
JoAnn's Café
Pasta Moon

SUNNYVALE
The Armenian Gourmet
Baccarat Restaurant
Beauséjour
Black Angus
Casa Lupe
Caspian Restaurant
Chevy's
Coastline Café
Country Gourmet
Esperanza's Restaurant
Florentine
Fresh Choice
Grand Palace
Hardy's
Kabul
Lion and Compass
Michael's
Mr. D's & Sons BBQ
Nicolino's Garden Café
The Palace
Spoons
Stoddard's Brewhouse
Taj India
Tao Tao Café
Thanh Da
Yu Shan

WOODSIDE
Alice's Restaurant
Bella Vista Restaurant
The Mountain House
Nina's Café
The Village Pub
Woodside Bakery Café

TYPES OF CUISINE

AFGHANI & NEPALESE
Kabul
Kathmandu West
Khyber Kabob House

AMERICAN
Alice's Restaurant
Allied Arts Guild Restaurant
Blue Chalk Café
Blue Sky Café
Buns
By-Th-Bucket
Castro Street Bar & Grill
City Pub
Clark's by the Bay
Coastline Café
Coffee Society
Coleman Still
Country Gourmet
Dinah's Poolside Café
Flea St. Café
Garden City
Great Bear Café & Los Osos
    Diner
Gulliver's
JoAnn's B Street Café
JoAnn's Café
Kim's Café
Mac's Tea Room
Max's Bakery and Kitchen
Max's Opera Café
94th Aero Squadron
Peninsula Fountain & Grill
Petaluma's Rotisserie
Pup & Hound
Quadrus Café
Spoons Grill & Bar
Sports City Café
Tied House
Vans
Vic's
Wine Cellar

BARBECUE
Armadillo Willy's BBQ
Bob's Oak Room
Cats
Emil Villa's Hick'ry Pit
Goldie's BBQ
Henry's Hi-Life
Mr. D's & Sons
Smitty's Oak Bar-B-Q
Spencer's Jambalaya & Ribs
    Shop

BASQUE
Basque Cultural Center

BREW PUBS
Gordon Biersch
Los Gatos Brewing Co.
Stoddard's Brewhouse
Tied House

BURGERS
Alpine Beer Garden
Buns
Cheshire Pub and Pizzeria
Clarke's Charcoal Broiler
Coastline Café
Dutch Goose
Kirk's Restaurant
Marvin Gardens
Oasis Beer Garden

BURMESE & CAMBODIAN
Chez Sovan
Rangoon

CALIFORNIA
Birk's
Buffalo Grill
Café for All Seasons
Café Marcella
California Café Bar & Grill
840 North First
Empire Grill and Tap Room
Eulipia
Fresco
Gordon Biersch
Henry's
Kincaid's
Los Gatos Brewing Co.
MacArthur Park
Martha's Restaurant
The Palace
Stoddard's Brewhouse
2030
Village Pub

CARIBBEAN & CUBAN
Cuban International
    Restaurant
Mango Café

CHINESE
Charley's
Chef Chu's
China Lion
Colonel Lee's Mongolian BBQ
Fook Yuen
Gao Poang
Golden Wok
Hangen
Hong Fu

Hong Kong Flower Lounge
House of Cathay
Hunan Homes
Jasmine
Jing Jing
Mabel's Lantern House
Mandarin Chef
Mandarin Gourmet
Mei's
Ming's
Pagoda
Peking Duck Restaurant
Quoc Te
Ritz Seafood
Royal Palace
Su Hong
Sun Sun
Tao Tao Café
Tasty Chinese Cuisine
Tien Fu
White Lotus
Yet Wah
Yu Shan
Yuen Yung

CONTINENTAL
Acorn
Amandine
Bella Vista
Bogie's
Café Fino
Campbell House
Chez TJ
Dal Baffo
The Dining Room
Ecco Café
Hardy's
La Fondue
Lion and Compass
Los Altos Bar & Grill
Maddalena's
Mountain House
Vans

EASTERN EUROPEAN
Adriatic Restaurant
Bravo Fono
Eugene's Polish Restaurant
Gypsy Cellar

ENGLISH
Bit of England
BJ Bulls
British Banker's Club
Duke of Edinburgh
English Rose
Garden Grill

LOCAL RESTAURANTS

FRENCH
Baccarat
Barbarossa
Beauséjour
Chantilly II
Chez Louis
Crepe Daniel
Emile's
Iron Gate
La Foret
La Maison du Café
La Mere Michelle
Le Mouton Noir
Le Papillon
Le Petit Bistro
Le Pot au Feu
Les Saisons
Mistral
Nina's Café
Nouveau Trattoria
Pigalle
Plumed Horse
Rue de Paris
Tour Eiffel
231 Ellsworth

GERMAN
Black Forest Inn
Germania Restaurant
Teske's Germania House
Vienna Woods

GREEK
Acorn
Yiassoo

HEALTHY/VEGETARIAN
Country Fare
Fresh Choice
Good Earth
Hobee's
Late for the Train
White Lotus

INDIAN
Clay Oven
Gaylord India Restaurant
India Cookhouse
Le Tandoor
Mount Everest
Mumtaj
Nataraja
Pasand
Passage to India
Savera India Restaurant
Sue's Indian Cuisine
Taj India

ITALIAN
Babbo's Pizzeria
Barbarossa
Bella Mia
Bellino
Bravo Fono
Café La Scala
Café Pro Bono
Caffè Verona
Capellini
Capriccio
Carpaccio
Dal Baffo
Di Cicco's
Esposto's Four-Day Café
Florentine Restaurant
Gambardella's
Il Fornaio Cucina Italiana
Kuleto's Trattoria
La Locanda
La Pastaia
Luceti's
Mariani's Inn
Mio Vicino
Mondello Ristorante
Nicolino's Garden Café
Nouveau Trattoria
Osteria
Palermo Ristorante Italiano
Paolo's
Pasquale's
Pasta Moon
Pasta Moon/Oyster Point
Piatti
Piccolo Mondo
Rico's Place
Ristorante Piacere
Romans Deli
Santini's
71 Saint Peter
Spiedo's
Tony and Alba's
Valeriano's Ristorante

JAPANESE
Azuma
Benihana of Tokyo
California Sushi and Grill
Fuji
Fuki Sushi
Gombei Japanese Kitchen
Hamasushi
Higashi West
House of Genji
Isobune
Kazoo
Kisaku
Kitahama
Kobe
Komatsu
Kyoto Palace
Miyake
Motomachi
Okayama
Shigemasu
Subaru Restaurant
Sushi on the Run
Sushi-Ya
Tokie's

LATIN/MEXICAN
Andalé Taqueria
Carlos Murphy's
Casa Lupe
Casa Vicky
Chevy's
Compadre's
El Burro
El Calderon
El Pollo Asado
Ernesto's
Esperanza's Restaurant
Fiesta del Mar
Horky's
La Fiesta Restaurant
La Hacienda
Palo Alto Sol
Pedro's Cabo Grill
Pollo's
Rock 'N Tacos
Rooh's Café Salsa
Rosita's Taqueria
Spoons Grill & Bar
Super Taqueria
Taqueria La Bamba
Two Pesos Taqueria

MIDDLE EASTERN
Armenian Gourmet
Falafel Drive-In

MOROCCAN & ERITREAN
El Maghreb
Menara Moroccan
Red Sea Restaurant

PERSIAN
Baccarat Restaurant Club
Borsalino Saaghi
Caspian Restaurant
Paradise Persian Cuisine

PIZZA
Amici's East Coast Pizzeria
Applewood Inn
Babbo's Pizzeria
Cheshire Pub and Pizzeria

Il Fornaio Cucina Italiana
Marvin Garden
North Beach Pizza
Oasis Beer Garden
Pacific Gourmet Pizza
Pizz'a Chicago
Pizzeria Uno
Ramona's
Santini's
Tony and Alba's
29 E. Main Café
Willow Street Pizza
Windy City Pizza
Woodside Bakery & Café

SEAFOOD
Black Angus
Castro Street Bar & Grill
Chart House
Clark's by the Bay
Fiesta del Mar
Fish Market
Garden City
Michael's
Ritz Seafood
Sand Dabs
Scott's Seafood Grill and Bar
Steamer's

SPANISH & PORTUGUESE
Iberia
Sousa's

THAI
Bangkok Cuisine
Bangkok Spoon
Bua Thong
Chao Praya
Krung Thai
Siam Garden
Siam Thai
Thai Best
Thai City
Thepthai
Woodside Thai Spot

VIETNAMESE
Dac Phuc
Golden Chopsticks
Hong Truc
Khanh's Garden
Kim's Restaurant
Little Garden
Pho Hoa
Quoc Te
Thanh Da
Thanh's Restaurant
Tour Eiffel

SPECIAL FEATURES

BREAKFAST/BRUNCH
Alice's Restaurant
Bella Mia
Blue Sky Café
British Banker's Club
Café for All Seasons
Caffe Verona
California Café
Carlos Murphy's
Casa Vicky
Coffee Society
Coleman Still
Country Gourmet
Crêpe Daniel
Dinah's Poolside Café
Empire Grill and Tap
Fiesta del Mar
Flea Street Café
Fresco
Good Earth
Hobee's Restaurant
Il Fornaio Cucina Italiana
JoAnn's B Street Café
JoAnn's Café
La Foret
La Maison du Café
Late for the Train
MacArthur Park
Mariani's Inn
Max's Bakery
Peninsula Fountain
Pigalle
Redwood Café and Spice
Rico's Place
Sports City Café
Tour Eiffel
The Vans
Vic's

GOOD FOR CHILDREN
Chevy's
Fresh Choice
Hobee's Restaurant
MacArthur Park
Peninsula Fountain
Pizzeria Uno

DELIVERY
Amici's E. Coast Pizzeria
Borsalino Saaghi
Castro Street Bar & Grill
Compadres
El Calderon
Flea Street Café
Fresco

Fuji
Gao Poang
Gaylord India Restaurant
Germania Restaurant
Golden Wok
Good Earth
MacArthur Park
Ming's
Mr. D's & Sons BBQ
Nataraja
North Beach Pizza
Pizz'a Chicago
Ramona's
Su Hong
Tien Fu
Tony and Alba's Pizza
Vienna Woods
Windy City Pizza
Yuen Yung

DIM SUM
Cho's
Fook Yuen
Hong Kong Flower Lounge
Hunan Homes
Ming's
Ritz Seafood
Royal Palace
Sun Sun
Yuen Yung

ENTERTAINMENT
Baccarat
Baccarat Restaurant & Club
Bella Mia
Bit of England
Borsalino Saaghi
British Banker's Club
Café Fino
The Cats
Chez Louis
City Pub
El Maghreb
Eugene's Polish Restaurant
Garden City
Germania Restaurant
Gordon Biersch
Gypsy Cellar
Iron Gate
La Maison du Café
Les Saisons
Los Altos Bar & Grill
Mac's Tea Room
Maddalena's
Max's Opera Café
Menara Moroccan
Nicolino's Garden Café
The Palace

LOCAL RESTAURANTS

Pasand
Teske's Germania House
Tied House

OPEN LATE

Amici's E. Coast Pizzeria
Baccarat Restaurant & Club
British Banker's Club
By-th-Bucket
Caffe Verona
Carlos Murphy's
Chevy's
City Pub
Coffee Society
Duke of Edinburgh
The Dutch Goose
El Burro
Emil Villa's Hick'ry Pit
Florentine
Fresco
Garden City
Gordon Biersch
Great Bear Café and Los
    Osos Diner
Hong Truc
Il Fornaio Cucina Italiana
Khanh's Garden
Kincaid's
Kuleto's Trattoria
Los Gatos Brewing Co.
MacArthur Park
Mariani's Inn
Marvin Gardens
Mio Vicino
North Beach Pizza
The Oasis
The Palace
Pedro's Cabo Grill
Peninsula Fountain
Pizz'a Chicago
Pizzeria Uno
Quoc Te
Rock 'N Taco
Santini's
Spoons
Sports City Café
Steamer's Fish Again
Thepthai
Tied House
Tony and Alba's Pizza
The Vans
Willow Street Pizza
Windy City Pizza

OUTDOOR SEATING

Adriatic Restaurant
Alice's Restaurant
Allied Arts Guild

Alpine Beer Garden
Andale Taqueria
Armadillo Willy's BBQ
Babbo's Pizzeria
Bella Mia
Bellino
Bit of England
BJ Bulls
Blue Chalk Café
Blue Sky Café
British Banker's Club
Café La Scala
Café Pro Bono
California Café
Castro Street Bar & Grill
Cheshire Pub and Pizza
China Lion
Cho's
City Pub
Clarke's Charcoal Broiler
Coffee Society
Compadres
Dinah's Poolside Café
Duke of Edinburgh
The Dutch Goose
El Burro
Empire Grill and Tap
Falafel Drive-In
Fresh Choice
Garden Grill
Germania Restaurant
Gordon Biersch
Hardy's
Iberia
Kirk's Restaurant
La Mere Michelle
Late for the Train
Los Altos Bar & Grill
Martha's Restaurant
Nina's Café
The Oasis
Paolo's
Pasquale's
Pedro's Cabo Grill
Piatti
Redwood Café and Spice
Rooh's Cafe Salsa
Sand Dabs
Stoddard's Brewhouse
Teske's Germania House
Tied House
Tien Fu
Vienna Woods

ROMANTIC

Alice's Restaurant
Barbarossa

Bella Vista Restaurant
Blue Sky Café
Café Fino
Café Pro Bono
Capellini
Carpaccio
Chantilly II
Chez T.J.
Dal Baffo
The Dining Room
Emile's
Flea Street Café
Gambardella's
Garden Grill
Gaylord India Restaurant
Iberia
Iron Gate
La Fondue
La Foret
La Maison du Café
Le Mouton Noir
Le Pot Au Feu
Maddalena's
Mandarin Gourmet
Mistral
The Mountain House
Nina's Café
Nouveau Trattoria
The Plumed Horse

VIEW

Bella Vista Restaurant
Chart House
Clark's by the Bay
Kincaids
La Foret
The Mountain House
Pasta Moon
Scott's Seafood
The Vans

ARTS AND ENTERTAINMENT

AMUSEMENTS

Action Zone Indoor Paintball Center: 111 Uranium Dr., Unit A, Sunnyvale, (408) 738-2255. Enjoy this modern game of two teams battling with guns that fire exploding sacs of paint. The Center has lots of hidden corners, a three-story castle, and even a 50-foot slide to make the combat scene more adventurous. • Tu-Th 6pm-midnight; F 6pm-1am; Sa noon-1am; Su noon-midnight. $10/first hour (including equipment); $5 for each additional hour.

Almaden Billiards: 4700 Almaden Expwy., San Jose, (408) 266-POOL. Another addition to the upscale pool hall scene. This one has a suburban angle: it's open to all ages and has darts and an arcade for when you're tired of being hustled.

Bay Meadows: 2600 S. Delaware St., San Mateo, (415) 574-7223. Is Custer's Revenge going to place or show in the fourth? Will Semiahmoo Slew cream the field if the track condition is muddy? Put your money where your mouth is. When the sun shines and the field is tight, you can't beat the fun and excitement: only a crowd with money on the line can cheer like this one does. Live horse racing throughout the year, but call for schedule (racing alternates with sister track Golden Gate Fields in Berkeley). Watch a simulcast when they're not running live.

Belmont Iceland: 815 County Rd., Belmont, (415) 592-0532. Call after 1:30pm for nightly session schedule. Admission $5; skate rental $2.

Eastridge Ice Arena: 2190A Tully Rd., San Jose, (408) 238-0440. M-Th 7:30pm-9:30pm; F-Sa 8pm-10pm. Admission $5; skate rental $2.

Great America: Great America Pkwy., Santa Clara, (408) 988-1800. (Take Hwy 101 South to Great America Parkway exit.) For man-made vertigo, you'll want to go to Great America, a full-blown amusement park in Santa Clara. The steely-stomached won't want to miss the Vortex, an enormous rollercoaster that you ride standing up, or the 360-degree Tidal Wave rollercoaster. For those more likely to lose their lunch, there's Rip Roaring Rapids, a simulated white-water rafting ride (you do get wet), and completely unstrenuous attractions like an ice skating rink, singing and dancing performances, a dolphin show, and a seven-story movie screen. Munchkins will enjoy meeting the Smurfs and other cartoon characters in the kids' areas, Smurf Woods and Fort Fun. Great America occasionally hosts rock concerts. They raise the admission price slightly that day, but for the price you get not only the concert but also all the rides. • Open March-October. Summer: Su-F 10am-9pm; Sa 10am-11pm. Spring and fall: Sa-Su 10am-8pm. $23.95 ages 7-54; $11.95 ages 3-6; free ages 2 and under; $16.95 seniors. Season passes $49.95. Parking $4.

Ice Capades Chalet: 2202 San Mateo Fashion Island, San Mateo, (415) 574-1616. Call for session schedule. Admission $5; skate rental $2.

Ice Center of San Jose: 1500 S. Tenth St., San Jose, (408) 279-6000. New, dual-ice rink. Call for session and lesson information. General skating: $5.50 adults; $4.50 children; $2.50 skate rental.

Ice Oasis: 3140 Bay Rd., Redwood City, (415) 364-8090. This indoor rink was formerly the Golden Gate Ice Arena, and has benefited greatly from a change in ownership. The ice, glass, and boards are all new, the locker rooms and lobby have been redone, and everything has been tastefully repainted and redecorated. They'll be hosting a new Friday night public skate at 9:45pm, complete with a DJ. They also have a skating school for all levels and adult and youth hockey leagues. Call for session schedule. • $6 adults; $5 children 12 and under. Skate rental $2.

Keystone Family Entertainment Center: 451 W. El Camino Real, Mountain View, (415) 964-7117. Stock up on loose change and check out the Keystone Family Entertainment Center, chock-full of video games, pinball machines, air hockey, and pool tables. • Su-Th 10am-11pm; F-Sa 10am-midnight.

Lake Cunningham: 2305 South White Rd., San Jose, (408) 277-4319. Next to Raging Waters, but operated separately from the water park. Here water fun is in the form of boating and fishing. • 8am-30 min. past sunset daily.

Magic Edge: 1625 Shoreline Blvd., Mountain View, (415) 254-7325. Where else but Silicon Valley could you expect to find a virtual reality restaurant and bar? Look out Red Baron—pray the flight simulators don't make you air sick. Reservations recommended. • M noon-11pm; Tu-Th 11am-11pm; F 11am-1am; Sa 10am-1am; Su 11am-10pm. $12.75–$19.95 depending on length of flight and time of day. Flights 12 or 20 minutes.

Malibu Castle: 320 Blomquist St. and Seaport Blvd., Redwood City, (415) 367-1905. (Hwy 101 to Seaport Blvd., exit east to Blomquist). Rent some clubs and take a whack at the 18-hole miniature golf course or grab a bat and take a few practice swings in the electronic batting cages. Replenish your energies for another round of putt-putt at the snack bar; hot dogs and Velveeta-covered nachos never tasted so good. Malibu Castle also has a mini-prix for kids between 4'6" and 3'2". • M-F 10am-10pm; Sa 9am-midnight; Su 9am-10pm. $5.95 adults; $4.95 ages 14 and under; $3.95 seniors.

Malibu Grand Prix: 340 Blomquist St., Redwood City, (415) 366-6442. A dream come true for would-be Indy 500 racers (and fun for everyone else as well). Malibu has a fleet of turbo-charged go-carts and several different tracks of varying difficulty for child drivers and regular cars for older speed demons. After you've satisfied the speed demon in you, wander inside and regress for a while in the video arcade. • M-Sa 10am-midnight; Su 10am-10pm. Requirements: 8 years old and 4'6" for go-carts; 18 years old and valid driver's license for regular cars.

Marine World Africa: I-80 and Hwy 37, Vallejo, (707) 643-6722. For zoological entertainment, take a trip to Marine World Africa USA in Vallejo, sort of a combination Sea World and zoo. Learn about dolphins, whales, seals, and other sea life as you wander through the aquarium and tide pools. Their much-touted Shark Experience does give you a new angle on these solemn, graceful creatures as you walk along a Plexiglas walkway right under them. The park also has hundreds of land-roaming animals like monkeys, tigers, and elephants; not to mention the airborne ones like parrots, toucans, and cockatoos. In addition to the furs and fins, check out the water-ski and boat show. Some of the world's best skiers excite and delight daily with cuts, jumps, tricks, and flips in their own style of high-octane water ballet. • Winter W-Su 9:30am-5pm; summer 9:30am-6:30pm. $24.95 adults; $16.95 ages 4-12; free ages 3 and under; $20.95 seniors. Parking $4. Accessible via Blue & Gold ferry and BART.

Moonlight Lanes: 2780 El Camino Real, Santa Clara, (408) 296-7200. Check out their Saturday night rock and bowl: all the balls you can bowl from 10pm to 1am with full rock-club sound and light. Regular bowling the rest of the week.

Raging Waters: Lake Cunningham Regional Park, San Jose, (408) 270-8000. If it's summer and you're looking for a way to cool off, head to Raging Waters in San Jose. This water park with lots of neon bathing suits and teeny-boppers is especially fun with a large group of people. Slides with names like White Lightning, Blue Thunder, Rampage, and Serpentine will twist you, turn you, and finally throw you into a huge pool. Changing rooms, showers, and lockers available. • Hours vary from spring to fall. General admission $15.50; children under 42″ $11.50. After 3pm all admission $9.95; free ages 3 and under.

Santa Clara Billiards: 4525 Stevens Creek Blvd., Santa Clara, (408) 296-333. Su-W noon-2am; Th-Sa noon-4am.

Taps: 661 Walsh Ave., Santa Clara, (408) 748-1188. Morbidly named paintball arena. Offers introductory sessions for new players and a practice shooting range, all for the full SWAT team feel. • Tu-F 5pm-1am; Sa noon-1am; Su noon-10pm.

Winchester Mystery House: 525 S. Winchester Blvd., San Jose, (408) 247-2101. A taste of the bizarre. This 160-room maze underwent 24-hour-a-day construction at the behest of firearms heiress Sarah Winchester, who was convinced that this non-stop construction would appease evil spirits she held responsible for the deaths of her husband and baby daughter. • Daily 9am-8pm. $12.50 adults; $6.50 ages 6-12; free ages 5 and under. Admission includes hour-long guided tours.

The Winter Lodge: 3009 Middlefield Rd., Palo Alto, (415) 493-4566. The only outdoor ice rink west of the Sierras is to be found right in Palo Alto. Call for session and lesson information. • Open October–April. Admission $5; skate rental $1.

Pro Sports

If the baseball and hockey strikes haven't squelched your enthusiasm, the Bay Area is ripe with opportunities to heckle, boo, and do the wave. Grab a hot dog and prepare to experience the rivalry of East Bay, San Francisco, and Peninsula teams (try the A's and the Giants, or the Cal Bears and the Stanford Cardinals). On rare occasions, the towns unite in support of one team, like the 49ers, Warriors, or Sharks, making for a non-confrontational good time. Whatever your preference, there are many stadiums along the Peninsula and East Bay, and plenty of home teams to fill them.

Baseball

Oakland Athletics: Oakland Coliseum, Oakland, (I-880 to Hegenberger Rd. exit or BART to Coliseum station), (510) 638-0500.

San Francisco Giants: Candlestick Park, Daly City, (Hwy 101 to Candlestick exit), (415) 467-8000.

Basketball

Golden State Warriors: Oakland Coliseum, Oakland, (I-880 to Hegenberger Rd. exit or BART to Coliseum station), (510) 382-2305.

Football

San Francisco 49ers: Candlestick Park, Daly City, (Hwy 101 to Candlestick exit), (415) 468-2249.

Hockey

San Jose Sharks: San Jose Arena, W. Santa Clara St. and Autumn St., San Jose, (800) 366-4423.

Soccer

San Francisco Bay Blackhawks: Spartan Stadium, Seventh St. at Alma Ave., San Jose State Univ., San Jose, (800) 677-4295.

ENTERTAINING CHILDREN

The Bay Area holds plenty of old-fashioned ways to keep the little ones amused. Below is a selective sampling of free or low-cost activities (for kids and adults) that get everyone out of the house and away from the Nintendo or TV. Look for many more activities listed in other sections of the *Guide*. Many Bay Area museums provide excellent children's activities. In particular, try San Jose's Children's Discovery Museum, Tech Museum of Innovation, and Rosicrucian Egyptian Museum; the Palo Alto Junior Museum and Barbie Doll Hall of Fame; Coyote Point Museum of Environmental Education in San Mateo; the Academy of Sciences, Exploratorium, and National Maritime Museum in San Francisco; and the Bay Area Discovery Museum in Sausalito. The Monterey Bay Aquarium (*Monterey* section) is a favorite family destination, as is Año Nuevo State Park (*Parks and Open Space* section), along with the many other beautiful parks in our area. Many of the activities listed in the *Amusements* section are sure-fire kid pleasers, or you can always rely on a trip to the old ball park to catch your favorite sport, along with plenty of pretzels and hot dogs.

Ardenwood Historical Farm: 34600 Ardenwood Blvd. at Hwy 84, Fremont, (510) 796-0663. An historic California farm where you can learn about California in the early days of European settlement. Staff and volunteers wear Victorian clothing and cultivate the same crops that were grown 100 years ago; visitors can see demonstrations of farm chores and ride in horse-drawn trains and wagons. • April–November: Th-Su 10am-4pm, plus Memorial Day, Independence Day, Labor Day, and the first weekend in December. Admission: $6 adults; $3.50 ages 4-17; $4 seniors.

Discovery Zone: 280 Metro Center, 123 Colma Blvd., Colma, (415) 992-7777. • 2541 S. El Camino Real, Redwood City, (415) 568-4386. • 648 Blossom Hill Rd., San Jose, (408) 225-4386. Children absolutely love these indoor fun centers. Each is filled with a variety of soft, brightly colored structures that kids can jump on, crawl through, slide down, or play with. Toddlers even have their own area. There is also an arcade for less strenuous stimulation, and a snack bar to recharge with pizza and popcorn. Socks are required. • Su-Th 10am-8pm; F 10am-9pm; Sa 9am-9pm. Weekdays pay child's age up to $4.99; weekends $2.99 ages 2 and under, $5.99 ages 3-12. Free for parents.

Happy Hollow Park and Zoo: 1300 Senter Rd., San Jose, (408) 295-8383. Part of Kelley Park, right in the heart of the city. You'll find a miniature train and a few other rides, a Japanese tea garden, a small petting zoo, and a play area where kids can go wild. Also within Kelley Park is the San Jose Historical Park, where you can visit a re-creation of San Jose's original main street, inspect an old firehouse, or sip a soda at O'Brien's Candy Factory—the place that served the first ice cream soda west of Detroit. • Happy Hollow: Daily 10am–5pm. $3.50. Historical Park: M-F 10am-4:30pm; Sa-Su noon-4:30pm. $4 adults; $2 ages 4-17; $3 seniors.

Hidden Villa: Rhus Ridge Rd. (off Moody Rd.), Los Altos Hills, (415) 949-8660. An educational working farm nestled on the edge of Rancho San Antonio Open Space Preserve. Check out the crops, learn how farms work, and pet the animals. Also houses an AYH Youth Hostel and a multi-cultural summer camp. • W-Su 9am-dusk; $3-$7 fee requested.

Lawrence Hall of Science: Middle Centennial Dr., Berkeley, (510) 642-5133. Perched high on the hill behind UC Berkeley like an ancient Greek temple paying worship to the gods. Views of the Bay and civilization below are spectacular. Inside, the first things to command the youngsters' attention are the special robotics exhibitions (in the past they've included huge insects and dinosaurs which stamp, screech, and roar). Other highlights of this interactive science museum are hairy tarantulas that crawl on your arm (kids like this), computers that psychoanalyze, and electricity globes that make anyone's hair fit for the 1970s. • Daily 10am-5pm. $6 adults; $2 ages 3-6; $4 students and seniors.

Oakland Zoo: 9777 Golf Links Rd., Oakland, (510) 632-9523. Stresses the presentation of animals in their natural habitat. It features an island habitat for monkeys, an acre of roaming territory and a mud bath for the elephants, and a eucalyptus grove for the romping lions. There's also a train ride, picnic areas, and a great sky ride. • Daily 10am-4pm. $4.50 adults; $3 ages 2-14 and seniors; $3 parking.

Oak Meadow Park: Blossom Hill Rd. at Garden Hill Dr., Los Gatos, (408) 354-6808, (408) 395-RIDE. Attached to Vasona Lake County Park. Ride the restored carousel and the steam railroad. • $1 rides; $5 parking.

San Francisco Zoo: Sloat Blvd. at 45th Ave. (next to Lake Merced), (415) 753-7061. This zoo features animals in recreations of their natural habitats, although some claim the cages are on the small side. The Primate Discovery Center is a centerpiece of the zoo, although, by flaw or fluke, there seems to be an escape every few years. Other highlights include penguins, lions, tigers, and koala bears (oh my!). A train ride gives a quick overview. • Daily 10am-5pm. $6.50 adults; $1 ages 6-11.

Serra Park: 730 The Dalles Ave., Sunnyvale, (408) 730-7506. Local park with soft lawns, a wading creek, and an excellent playground with monkey bars, slides, and tubes galore. The spray pool is a hot weather highlight.

MOVIE THEATERS

Like anywhere else, multiplexes dominate the mainstream-movie scene, and the multiplexes keep dividing into more and smaller screens that sell out more and more quickly. Next to San Francisco, the Palo Alto area has the most theaters showing alternative flicks: foreign, independent, art, or classic. Those who can wait a while after hot new movies are released can see them at a substantial discount at many theaters. Both individual theaters and chains such as Landmark Theaters sell discount cards entitling purchasers to a discount on movies—although most discounts don't apply to Friday and Saturday night shows, nor to blockbuster hits. In an effort to cope with sellouts, many theaters are allowing customers to purchase tickets in advance over the phone using a credit card. Fortunately, theaters have also made great advances in providing access for the disabled and devices for the hearing impaired. Call your local theater for additional information on these programs. You can also always dial (415) 777-FILM for a quick and handy computer listing of the next and nearest showtime of your favorite flick, yours without even finding the paper. Finally, don't forget to check out movies playing in alternative venues like universities, libraries, and churches: you may find movies well beyond the mainstream, often at bargain prices.

Daly City to San Bruno

AMC Serramonte Six: Serra Blvd. east of I-280, Daly City, (415) 756-6500. Discount theater showing first-run movies with a family bent after they've opened at the larger chains. $1.75 admission every show.

Century Plaza 8: 410 Norr Ave. (off El Camino Real north of I-380 and Tanforan), South San Francisco, (415) 742-9200. First-run multiplex. $7.

Tanforan Discount: Tanforan Shopping Ctr., El Camino Real, San Bruno, (415) 588-0291. Discount first-run multiplex. $3.75.

UA Metro Center: 200 Colma Blvd., Colma, (415) 994-1065. First-run multiplex. $7.

Millbrae to San Carlos

Belmont Arts Cinema: 100 El Camino Real, Belmont, (415) 591-5349. First-run films and Rocky Horror at midnight on Saturdays. $6.50.

Burlingame Drive-In: Burlingame Ave. off Old Bayshore Hwy., Burlingame, (415) 343-2213. A funky, penny-wise option. Double features of first-run films play at this relic for the outmoded price of $4.95, for those who are willing to forego state-of-the-art sound. $4.95 general admission.

Century Hyatt 3: 1304 Old Bayshore Hwy., Burlingame, (415) 340-1516. First-run multiplex. $7.

Fashion Island 6: Fashion Island Mall, San Mateo, (415) 341-6166. Discount theater showing first-run movies after they've played at the larger chains. $1.50 all seats.

Hillsdale Cinema: 3011 S. El Camino Real, San Mateo, (415) 349-4511. First-run multiplex. $7.

Redwood City to Mountain View

Aquarius Cinemas: 430 Emerson St., Palo Alto, (415) 327-3240. Just off University Ave., Aquarius shows those esoteric foreign films that are hard to track down elsewhere. $3.75 first show Sa-Su. $7.

Century Cinema 16: 1500 N. Shoreline Blvd., Mountain View, (415) 960-0970. Huge, first-run multiplex. Parking lot fills up and popular movies frequently sell out. $7.

Century Park 12: 557 E. Bayshore Rd. (at Whipple Ave.), Redwood City, (415) 365-9000. First-run multiplex. $7.

Guild Theater: 949 El Camino Real, Menlo Park, (415) 323-6760. Shows artsy and foreign films in a slightly down-at-the-heels art-deco auditorium adorned with frayed velvet curtains and giant chevrons (bring a sweater on a cool night—this theater is mercilessly underheated). $7.

Palo Alto Square: 3000 El Camino Real (El Camino and Page Mill Rd.), Palo Alto, (415) 493-1160. A spacious duplex showing a mix of commercial and art-house flicks, Palo Alto Square is the South Bay's participant in the San Francisco International Film Festival held each spring. $7.

Park Theater: 1275 El Camino Real, Menlo Park, (415) 323-6181. Almost identical to its neighbor the Guild. $7.

The Stanford Theater: 221 University Ave., Palo Alto, (415) 324-3700. The remodeled Stanford Theater presents double features of classic movies (along with a few old clunkers) in an elaborate art deco setting complete with live organ music. Showings follow monthly themes—Garbo, for example—and features change every few nights. $6 for double feature.

UA Redwood Six: 305 Walnut St., Redwood City, (415) 367-9090. First-run multiplex. $6.75.

Sunnyvale to San Jose

Almaden Twin: Willow Glen Shopping Ctr., 2306 Almaden Rd., San Jose, (408) 265-7373. Discount older first-run films. $2 all ages, all times.

AMC Oakridge Six: Oakridge Mall, 913 Blossom Hill Rd., San Jose, (408) 227-6660. First-run multiplex. $6.

AMC Saratoga Six: El Paseo Shopping Ctr., Campbell and Saratoga Aves., Saratoga, (408) 374-3324. First-run multiplex. $6.

AMC Sunnyvale Six: Sunnyvale Town Ctr., McKinley and Mathilda Aves., Sunnyvale, (408) 746-3800. First-run multiplex. $6.

AMC Town & Country: Town & Country Shopping Ctr., Stevens Creek Blvd. at Winchester Blvd., San Jose, (408) 243-4262. First-run multiplex. $6.50.

Camera One: 366 S. First St., San Jose, (408) 998-3005. Art and foreign flicks. $6.75.

Camera Three: 288 S. Second St., San Jose, (408) 998-3300. Art and foreign flicks. $6.75.

Capitol Drive-In: Capitol Expwy. and Monterey Rd., San Jose, (408) 226-2251. Double features of first-run films with FM radio sound. $4.95 per person.

Campbell Plaza 4: 2501 Winchester Blvd., Campbell, (408) 378-2425. Discount first-run multiplex. $3.

Century Almaden: 5655 Gallup Dr., San Jose, (408) 265-7111. Discount first-run multiplex. $1.50-$3.

Century 10 Berryessa: 1171 N. Capitol Ave. (at Berryessa Rd.), San Jose, (408) 926-7091. First-run multiplex. $7.

Century 21-24: 3161 Olsen Dr. (at Winchester Blvd.), San Jose, (408) 984-5610. First-run multiplex. $7.

Century 25: Westgate Shopping Ctr., Campbell and Saratoga Aves., San Jose, (408) 984-5610. First-run multiplex. $7.

Gould Cinema: 1019 E. Capitol Expwy., San Jose, (408) 226-5040. Discount older first-run films. $1.50.

Los Gatos Cinemas: 41 N. Santa Cruz Ave., Los Gatos, (408) 395-0203. Art, independent, and foreign flicks (part of the Camera chain). $6.75.

Meridian Six: 4400 Stevens Creek Blvd., San Jose, (408) 246-6710. First-run multiplex. $5.75.

Oaks Five Cupertino: 21275 Stevens Creek Blvd., Cupertino, (408) 446-1134. Shows older first-runs films to members with a pass for $1.50 Monday through Thursday, and $3 on the weekends. Membership $2.

Towne Theatre: 1433 The Alameda, San Jose, (408) 287-1433. Art, independent, and foreign flicks (part of the Camera chain). $6.75.

UA Pruneyard: 1875 S. Bascom Ave., Campbell, (408) 371-3020. First-run multiplex. $7.

San Francisco

Several San Francisco film houses are worth the drive or train ride.

AMC Kabuki 8: 1881 Post St. (at Fillmore), San Francisco, (415) 931-9800. In early spring, Japantown's Kabuki 8 takes part in the **San Francisco International Film Festival**, which showcases foreign, political, independent, and short films. Tickets sell out days or even weeks in advance; call (415) 567-4641 for details.

Castro Theater: 429 Castro St. (at Market), San Francisco, (415) 621-6120. A beautiful, historic theater which screens a broad spectrum of classic, art, and foreign films—often director's cuts—shown on a gloriously wide screen and often preceded by live organ music on a stupendous Wurlitzer. The Castro is also home to the **Annual Gay and Lesbian Film Festival** every June and the annual **Tournee of Animation** in the fall. $3.50 first show each W, Sa, Su.

Red Victorian Movie House: 1727 Haight St., San Francisco, (415) 668-3994. A Haight Street institution that shows a well-chosen variety of classic, cult, and rerun films; your first ticket includes a voucher for a dollar discount on all subsequent shows. The theater is renowned for its funky bench seats and popcorn condiment bar, which features brewer's yeast, garlic, tamarind, and dill, as well as salt and butter. $5.50 for first ticket.

Roxie Cinema: 3117 16th St., San Francisco, (415) 863-1087. The Roxie shows narrow-release political and avant-garde films. Admission is $6; $5 with $5 membership card.

MUSEUMS

Bay Area museums range in scope from local to international to galactic. San Francisco and San Jose claim the Bay Area's major art and science museums, as well as a wealth of smaller museums devoted to specific cultures, crafts, and historical topics. While the selection of museums in the mid-Peninsula is considerably narrower, the area offers several intriguing specialty museums, focusing predominantly on the environment and technology. In San Francisco, **Golden Gate Park** is home to the M.H. de Young and Asian Art Museums, and the Academy of Sciences. (Museum frequenters note: membership in the **Museum Society** entitles you and a friend to a year's free admission to both the de Young and Asian Art museums.) **Fort Mason** houses several smaller museums that spotlight particular cultures, while the **Yerba Buena Center for the Arts** in the South of Market area is the city's new and comprehensive home for the arts. The Center grounds, abundantly flowered and peaceful, are the site of free spring and summer outdoor concert series. In January of 1995, the San Francisco Museum of Modern Art reopened in a new facility nearby. With the Center for the Arts Theater next door, and The Friends of Photography and Ansel Adams Center just around the corner, this area is truly becoming a hub of artistic and cultural activity.

Peninsula and South Bay

American Museum of Quilts and Textiles: P.O. Box 1058, San Jose, 95108-1058, (408) 971-0323. Full of rotating exhibits on contemporary and traditional quilt making and textile design, the American Museum is the only one of its kind in the state. The museum is in the process of relocating; call for information on interim temporary exhibits.

Barbie Doll Hall of Fame: 433 Waverley St., Palo Alto, (415) 326-5841. Come examine one of the most famous of contemporary cultural icons in a newly expanded collection of over 16,000 pieces. Check out nearly every Barbie product created since 1959 (the year of her birth), and see how the world of Barbie reflected almost every change in our popular culture. • Tu-F 1:30pm-4:30pm; Sa 10am-noon & 1:30pm-4:30pm. $4.

Children's Discovery Museum: 180 Woz Way (between Almaden and San Carlos), San Jose, (408) 298-5437. Get involved in the wonderful world of science in this participatory science museum. Includes a walk-through model of San Jose's city streets and underground, complete with traffic controls and waste-disposal systems that children can operate. • Tu-Sa 10am-5pm; Su noon-5pm. $6 adults; $4 ages 2-18; children under 2 free. Parking $2.

Coyote Point Museum for Environmental Education: Coyote Point Dr., San Mateo, (415) 342-7755. Includes the two-acre Wildlife Habitat filled with badgers, otters, and other native animals; and the Environmental Hall, an 8000-square foot simulated walk from the San Francisco Bay to the Pacific coast. This museum also pays tribute to its California setting with computer games designed to educate players about the environment. • Tu-Sa 10am-5pm; Su noon-5pm. $3 adults; $1 ages 6-17, children under 6 free. Free first W of month. $4 vehicle fee.

Museum of American Heritage: 275 Alma St. (at Everett), Palo Alto, (415) 321-1004. Historically minded Silicon Valley denizens will love this showcase of pre-computer technology. Travel through the past in their 1930s kitchen, turn-of-the-century attorney's office, and 1920s grocery store. The museum is staffed entirely by volunteers, so if the history bug bites you on your visit, inquire about positions. • F-Su 11am-4pm, or by appointment. Free during regular hours.

Palo Alto Cultural Center: 1313 Newell St., (415) 329-2366. Displays contemporary local artwork. • Tu-Sa 10am-5pm; Th 7pm-9pm; Su 1pm-5pm. Free.

Palo Alto Junior Museum: 1451 Middlefield Rd., Palo Alto, (415) 329-2111. Features a zoo of small animals representative of each phylum of the animal kingdom, as well as rotating exhibits on topics like forests and underwater life. Trainers show off the animals on weekends. • Tu, Th-Sa 10am-5pm; W 1pm-8pm; Su 1pm-4pm. Free.

Rosicrucian Egyptian Museum: Park and Naglee Ave., San Jose, (408) 947-3636. Ancient history buffs and anyone who still believes in King Tut's curse will want to explore this museum, which contains more than 4,000 artifacts from Egypt, Assyria, and Babylonia. Highlights include human and animal mummies and a full-size replica of a nobleman's tomb. The museum also houses a planetarium. • Daily 9am-5pm. $6 adults; $3.50 ages 7-15; children under 7 free. Free tours.

San Jose Institute of Contemporary Art Galleries: 451 S. First St. and 2 N. Second St., San Jose, (408) 283-8155. Gallery space for changing exhibitions of cutting-edge visual artists. Look for exhibits like a multimedia depiction of "What Heaven Looks Like." • Tu-Sa noon-5pm. Free.

San Jose Museum of Art: 110 S. Market St., San Jose, (408) 294-2787. Focuses on art from the 20th century. Houses only a small permanent collection, but hosts some spectacular traveling exhibitions in its new 45,000-square foot wing. The first Sunday of every month kids and their escorts get in free. • Tu, W, F-Su 10am-5pm; Th 10am-8pm. $5 adults; $3 students; $3 ages 6-17; children under 5 free. Free first Th of month.

Stanford Museum and Gallery: Stanford Univ., (415) 723-4177. The museum, which houses one of the world's largest collections of August Rodin's works, is closed indefinitely due to damage from the 1989 Loma Prieta Earthquake. However, the adjacent **Rodin Sculpture Garden** is still open and features numerous works by the namesake sculptor, including the haunting "Gates of Hell." Visit at night when lighting dramatizes the sculptures. Other famous Rodin sculptures are scattered around campus, including one of the world's nine replicas of "The Thinker." The Stanford Gallery features exhibitions by artists ranging from Ansel Adams to Richard Diebenkorn to the graduating class of art students.

Tech Museum of Innovation: 145 W. San Carlos St., San Jose, (408) 279-7150. A Silicon Valley highlight designed to help visitors understand how technology works. Visitors can drive a Land Rover over a simulated Martian landscape, man the controls of life-size robots, and perform calculations on a nine-foot-square computer chip. • Tu-Su 10am-5pm. $6 adults; $4 ages 6-18; children under 6 free.

Triton Museum of Art: 1505 Warburton Ave., Santa Clara, (408) 247-3754. Modern museum hosting a variety of changing exhibitions. Focuses on works by contemporary California artists but also shows art from all over the world. • Tu 10am-9pm; W-F 10am-5pm; Sa-Su noon-5pm. Admission varies.

San Francisco

Academy of Sciences: Tea Garden Dr., Golden Gate Park, San Francisco, (415) 750-7145. Morrison Planetarium: (415) 750-7141. Laserium: (415) 750-7138. San Francisco's main science museum. The attractions include a "safe quake," a simulation of the 1906 earthquake; a frozen great white shark and the Discovery Room for Children, which is filled with interactive exhibits. Academy admission includes entry to the **Steinhart Aquarium** located in the same building. Watch dolphins, seals and thousands of other fish and aquatic creatures cruise in tanks. Call for animal feeding schedules. The Academy also houses the **Morrison Planetarium**, which features celestially oriented planetarium shows and entertainment oriented Laserium shows. Admission to Planetarium is separate. • Daily 10am-5pm. $7 adults; $4 ages 12-17; $1.50 ages 6-11; children under 6 free. Free first W of month. Morrison Planetarium: $2.50 adults; $1.25 ages 6-17; children under 6 free. Laserium: Th-Su evenings, call for times and matinee shows. $7 adults; $5 ages 6-12; $5 matinee.

African-American Historical and Cultural Society: Bldg. C, Fort Mason, San Francisco, (415) 441-0640. Displays African, African-American, and Caribbean artwork. • W-Su noon-5pm; first W of month noon-8pm. $2 adults; $1 seniors; 50¢ children.

Asian Art Museum: Tea Garden Dr., Golden Gate Park, San Francisco, (415) 668-8921. Located in the same building as the de Young, the Asian Art Museum contains an important permanent collection of paintings and ceramics from all the Asian countries. Because of limited space, only a small portion of the collection is on display at a time, so exhibits are frequently rotated. • W-Su 10am-5pm; first W of month 10am-8:45pm. $5 adults; $2 ages 12-17; children under 12 free. Free first W and 10am-noon first Sa of month.

Bay Area Discovery Museum: 557 E. Fort Baker Rd., Sausalito, (415) 332-7674. It's in Sausalito, not San Francisco, but it is a worthwhile destination for parents with children. Activities include crewing on a child-size fishing boat and guided nature walks through seven acres of land. • Labor Day-Memorial Day W-Su 10am-5pm; Memorial Day-Labor Day Tu-Su 10am-5pm. $5 adults; $3 ages 2-17; children under 2 free. Free first Th of month.

Cable Car Museum: 1201 Mason St., San Francisco, (415) 474-1887. A tiny museum which houses three antique cable cars, including the world's first (built in 1873), and the cable winding machinery that's still used to run the cars. • Daily 10am-6pm. Free.

Cartoon Art Museum: 665 Third St., San Francisco, (415) 546-3922. A collection of · newspaper strips, animation stills, comic books, and political cartoons illustrating the history of the craft, from a Hogarth engraving to present-day "funnies." • W-F 11am-5pm; Sa 10am-5pm; Su 1pm-5pm. $3 adults; $2 students; $1 children under 12.

Chinese Cultural Center: 750 Kearny St. (3rd floor of Holiday Inn), San Francisco, (415) 986-1822. Features changing exhibits of everything from Chinese-American history to calligraphy. Visit especially during Chinese New Year's. • Tu-Sa 10am-4pm. Free.

Exploratorium, Palace of Fine Arts: Marina and Lyon Sts., San Francisco, (415) 561-0360. The City's other major science museum is located in the Marina District, dangerously close to the road that leads you without return onto the Golden Gate Bridge. (Check your map before going.) It houses more than 650 fascinating hands-on exhibits that will enchant minds of all ages. You can see wind funnels, play with light beams, compose songs, and watch animals. Crawl your way through the completely dark Tactile Dome guided by only your sense of touch (advance reservations are required for this popular exhibit). • Tu, Th-Su 10am-5pm; W 10am-9:30pm. $8.50 adults; $6.50 students and seniors; $4.50 ages 6-17; $2 ages 3-5; children under 3 free. (They refuse no one due to financial hardship.) Free first W of month. Tactile Dome: $7 (includes Exploratorium admission).

The Friends of Photography and Ansel Adams Center: 250 Fourth St., San Francisco, (415) 495-7000. Houses works by Adams and also exhibits works by other photographers. • Tu-Su 11am-5pm. $4 adults; $3 students; $2 ages 13-17 and seniors; children under 12 free.

Jewish Museum: 121 Steuart St., San Francisco, (415) 543-8880. Features changing exhibits of Jewish art and artifacts from all over the world. • Su 11am-6pm; M-W noon-6pm; Th noon-8pm. Admission varies with the exhibition.

Mexican Museum: Bldg. D, Fort Mason, San Francisco, (415) 441-0404. A 9000-work collection divided into galleries on pre-Hispanic, colonial, folk, Mexican, and Mexican-American art. • W-Su noon-5pm; first W of month noon-8pm. $3 adults; $2 students; children under 10 free. Free first W of month.

Musée Mecanique: Cliff House, 1090 Point Lobos Ave., San Francisco, (415) 386-1170. A re-creation of a tacky, turn-of-the-century arcade, where the mechanical attractions include fortune tellers, elaborate moving toothpick architecture constructed by Alcatraz inmates, and hysterical laughing ladies. (Warning: racist caricatures abound.) • M-F 11am-7pm; Sa, Su, Hol 10am-8pm. Free.

Museo Italo Americano: Bldg. C, Fort Mason, San Francisco, (415) 673-2200. Contains a permanent collection of Italian and Italian-American modern art, and also presents four special exhibits a year. • W-Su noon-5pm. $2 adults; $1 students; free ages 12 and under.

Maritime National Historical Park: San Francisco, (415) 556-3002. Museum: Beach St. and Polk St. The outdoor historic park extends from Aquatic Park at Polk Street to Fisherman's Wharf at Taylor Street. Within the park, the **Maritime Museum** at the northern foot of Polk Street houses models and photos of historical ships. Outside, at the **Hyde Street Pier**, explore three nineteenth-century ships—a sidewheel ferry, a lumber schooner, and a square rigger. • Museum: Daily 10am-5pm. Free. Hyde Street Pier: Labor Day-Memorial Day, Daily 9:30am-5pm; Memorial Day-Labor Day, Daily 10am-6pm. $3 adults; $1 ages 12-17; free under 12 and seniors.

M.H. de Young Memorial Museum: Tea Garden Dr., Golden Gate Park, San Francisco, (415) 863-3330. The de Young, 44 galleries strong, features a recently expanded collection of American art from the colonial period to the mid-twentieth century, along with exhibits featuring the arts of Africa, Oceania, the Americas, and England. The de Young also offers tours, workshops, children's classes, and occasional films, often free. • W-Su 10am-5pm; first W of month 10am-8:45pm. $5 adults; $2 ages 12-17; free ages 11 and under. Free first W and 10am-noon first Sa of month. Free Walkman-guided tours.

San Francisco Craft and Folk Art Museum: Bldg. A, Fort Mason, San Francisco, (415) 775-0990. The only museum of its kind in Northern California, this San Francisco original hosts six exhibitions a year on subjects ranging from African-American quilt making to Haitian steel-drum sculpture. • Tu-F 11am-5pm; Sa 10am-5pm; Su 11am-5pm. $1 adults; 50¢ seniors and ages 12-17; free ages 11 and under.

San Francisco Museum of Modern Art: 151 Third St., San Francisco, (415) 357-4000. The permanent collection includes works by virtually every major twentieth-century artist, including Calder, Klee, Matisse, and Pollack. The fascinating array of visiting exhibits range from visions of futuristic cities created by Japan's leading architects to a pop sculpture of Michael Jackson and his chimpanzee created by art whiz Jeff Koons. The museum has recently moved to the Yerba Beuna Center in SoMa and reopened in a large and stunning new home. • Tu, W, F, Sa, Su 11am-6pm; Th 11am-9pm. $7 adults; $3.50 students. Half-price Th 5pm-9pm; free first Tu of month.

Stamp Francisco: 466 Eighth St., San Francisco, (415) 252-5975. The only rubber stamp museum in the world, Stamp Francisco houses the largest collection of antique rubber stamps in the U.S. and a gallery dedicated to performance art, eraser carvings, rubber stamp art, and mail art. Limited-edition, hand-bound stamp art books and 1,800 rubber stamps are manufactured in the on-site factory and sold in the adjacent shop or by mail order. • Tu-F 10am-5pm; Sa 11am-3pm. Free.

Tattoo Art Museum: 841 Columbus St., San Francisco, (415) 775-4991. The country's only museum devoted to body graphics displays tattoo equipment, flashes (advertisements), and exhibits on tattoo use in other cultures. • M-Sa noon-10pm; Su noon-8pm. Free.

U.S.S. Pampanito: Pier 45, Fisherman's Wharf (at Taylor St.), San Francisco, (415) 929-0202. Explore a World War II submarine in this part of the National Maritime Historic Park. Labor Day-Memorial Day: Su-Th 9am-6pm; F-Sa 9am-8pm. Memorial Day-Labor Day: Daily 9am-9pm. $5 adults; $4 ages 6-12 and seniors; free ages 5 and under. $15 family rate includes 2 adults and 4 children.

Yerba Buena Center for the Arts: 701 Mission St., San Francisco, (415) 978-ARTS. The Center for the Arts Gallery is bright, open, and spacious. There is no permanent collection, so exhibits change regularly. The gallery shares its elegant space with a screening room for documentaries, films, and video presentations, a café, and a gift shop selling goods made by local and international artisans. • Tu-Su 11am-6pm; first Th of month 11am-8pm. $4 adults; $2 students and seniors. (More for special events.) Free first Th of month 6pm-8pm.

NIGHTLIFE

The Bay Area features a huge array of nightspots that cater to the many different tastes of its eclectic residents. On the Peninsula, mellow neighborhood pubs dominate the scene. San Jose and San Francisco offer a wider range of hipper places, many with dancing and live music. Beer drinkers rejoice—there are a surprising number of peanuts-and-beer joints. A growing number of bars brew their own beer, and many others serve great selections on tap—you can even find places without indulging in peanut shells and sports.

Closing time is 2am (although some places somehow stay open later) and the legal drinking age in California is 21 (most bars and clubs check identification religiously). Some night spots, especially those with live entertainment, have "All Ages" nights, when the age requirement drops to 18; those over 21 can get their hands stamped to purchase liquor.

Clubs, Bars, and Beer

Alpine Beer Garden: 3915 Alpine Rd., Portola Valley, (415) 854-4004. A former stage-coach stop and longtime standby that's still known primarily by its old nickname, Zott's (it was also formerly known as Risotti's). Gather up ten of your closest friends and plant your-selves at one of the dusty outdoor tables with a couple of pitchers some Saturday afternoon.

Antonio's Nut House: 321 California Ave., Palo Alto, (415) 321-2550. For knee-deep nutshells on the floor, peek into Antonio's Nut House (it's unclear whether the name refers to the snacks or the clientele). Snarl hello to barmaid Monica and drink a beer while watching the big-screen TV or take in a game of pool—if the regulars will let you play.

Blue Chalk Café: 630 Ramona St., Palo Alto, (415) 326-1020. One of downtown Palo Alto's most popular hangouts, The Blue Chalk has something to keep everyone enter-tained all night. The airy, two-level hall features an excellent restaurant, pool tables rented by the hour (or one "challenge" table for the hustlers in the crowd), dart lanes, a shuffle-board table, and a sports TV section. If all this activity makes you hungry, sit down for a delicious meal of updated Southern cuisine. A good mix of singles-scene energy and neigh-borhood hangout comfort.

Britannia Arms: 5027 Almaden Expwy., San Jose, (408) 266-0550 • 1087 Saratoga-Sunnyvale Rd., Cupertino, (408) 252-7262. A pair of British theme pubs catering to the pints-and-darts crowd. You won't forget you're in the Valley, but with a good band and a delicious black and tan, you might be comfortable hanging out awhile.

British Bankers Club: 1090 El Camino Real, Menlo Park, (415) 327-8769. At the BBC, you can lounge in plush sofas and wingback chairs amid tapestries and chandeliers while sipping a cocktail in genteel fashion. Don't be intimidated by the somewhat older and obviously wealthier crowd that gathers here; the atmosphere can be a refreshing change from the noise of other bars, although it does occasionally get jolted up by live blues bands.

City Pub: 2620 Broadway, Redwood City, (415) 363-2620. A hip and happening hangout in Redwood City's revived Old Downtown, where you can mingle with trendy Peninsulans sporting the latest Doc Martens and Gap flannels. Designer lighting high-lights the restored brick, warm fireplace, and mod copper bar. Decent pub grub and an excellent selection of beer on tap.

Compadres Mexican Bar and Grill: 3877 El Camino Real, Palo Alto, (415) 858-1141. Summer or winter, people are always packed around the courtyard tables at Compadres, munching chips and salsa while downing huge, frosty margaritas (some of the best around). Check it out on your birthday and you're apt to walk away with a piñata and a photo of yourself in an oversized Mexican sombrero.

Dicey Riley's Irish Pub: 221 Park Rd., Burlingame, (415) 347-7656. Dicey Riley's is more of a Blue-collar American bar than an Irish pub, sporting a long bar and plenty of Naugahyde. It's big on sports and beer, and features live music—including traditional Irish.

The Dutch Goose: 3567 Alameda de Las Pulgas, Menlo Park, (415) 854-3245. A dark hole-in-the-wall with pinball machines, pool tables, and a small patio in the back. Eclectic menu mixing bags of peanuts, deviled eggs, burgers, and reasonably priced pitchers of good beer. The Goose is also the favorite hangout of Sun Microsystems' CEO Scott McNealy.

Fibbar MaGee's: 156 S. Murphy Ave., Sunnyvale, (408) 749-8373. This cozy, new, Irish pub, complete with stone fireplace and plenty of beer on tap, provides an alternative for those not feeling up to its hip and trendy neighbors, The Palace and Stoddard's.

Gordon Biersch Restaurant/Brewery: 640 Emerson St., Palo Alto, (415) 323-7723 • 33 E. San Fernando St., San Jose, (408) 294-6785. $8-$10 cover charge on Su. • 2 Harrison St. (at Embarcadero), San Francisco, (415) 243-8246. One of the first of the Peninsula brew-pubs and the first catering right to the yuppie market. Rampant competition has cut the crowds a little, but no one else attracts as many suits after work. Beer brewed on the premises is fresh and delicious, and the upscale food is pretty good, especially in San Jose. San Jose has live jazz most nights.

Oasis Beer Garden: 241 El Camino Real, Menlo Park, (415) 326-8896. Generations of graffiti carved into the hardwood tables and booths of The O attest to this bar's longtime popularity, especially with Stanford students. Beer by the pitcher and several TVs eternally tuned to sporting events make the Oasis a great place to hang out any night of the week. Also popular with local softball teams.

Paddy's Irish Pub: 31 E. Santa Clara St., San Jose, (408) 293-1118. Two bars in one: downstairs is a typical Irish pub for drinking pints at the bar. Upstairs, couch potato sports fans can vegetate in front of a big screen.

Prince of Wales Pub: 106 E. 25th Ave., San Mateo, (415) 574-9723. San Mateo's oldest pub, with darts, foosball, and plenty of beer. Complete with outdoor patio for warm weather lounging.

Rose & Crown: 547 Emerson St., Palo Alto, (415) 327-ROSE. Friendly and authentically smoky English pub setting, complete with British ales on tap, pub fare, and darts.

South First Billiards: 420 S. First St., San Jose, (408) 294-7800. The San Jose outpost of San Francisco's successful South Beach Billiards follows the same formula: a clean, well-lit pool hall renting tables by the hour, serving up decent bar food, and pouring lots of good beer from the tap.

Stoddard's: 111 S. Murphy Ave., Sunnyvale, (408) 733-7824. Former Tied House brewmeister Bob Stoddard created this soaring monument to yuppie South Bay culture. This trendy brewpub gleams with polished wood, Jackson Pollock wall paint, and singles heating it up after work. Excellent beer and good (if pricey) food. There's also a beer garden out back.

Tied House Café and Brewery: 954 Villa St., Mountain View, (415) 965-BREW • 65 N. San Pedro St., San Jose, (408) 295–BREW. One of the best brewpubs around. Their beers are absolutely delicious, and you can watch the creation of these tasty brews in giant gleaming vats. Tied House features seasonal beers and such libations as passion fruit ale, wheat beer, and stout. Pub grub is passable (stick to the basics). The kitchen here stays open later than many other places on the Peninsula.

Town Club: 180 Castro St., Mountain View, (415) 367-2425. If you really want to get down and dirty in the bar scene, remember the Town Club. A veritable dive bar in a land sadly without them, Town Club has a pool table, juke box, and all kinds of local characters.

Beer Brewed by the Bay

Since the mid-1980s, Northern California has been a leader in providing its residents with quality suds from local microbreweries. It's a throwback to the turn of the century, when every city had its own brewery. The oldest microbrewery in the Bay Area is San Francisco's **Anchor Brewing Company**, started during the Gold Rush. Nearly bankrupt in the early 1970s, Anchor was revived after its purchase by Fritz Maytag (heir to the appliance fortune) and today creates five different types of beer. Make a reservation for one of their free tours—they're great fun. Producing somewhere around 70,000 barrels of brew each year, Anchor has now far outgrown the "micro" in microbrewery. A few breweries small enough to fit the "micro" name can still be found in Northern California: Boonville's **Anderson Valley Brewing Co.**, Modesto's **St. Stan's**, Hopland's **Mendocino Brewing Co.**, and Nevada City's eponymous **Brewing Company**. (Chico's **Sierra Nevada** once belonged to this group, but it has been growing rapidly.) They all have retail operations on-site.

Brewpubs are another species created by the evolution of Northern California beer culture. A brewpub is similar to a microbrewery but manufactures even smaller quantities of premium brew, and usually sells it only in its own bar, pub, or restaurant. Some newer brewpubs are decidedly yupscale, such as **Gordon Biersch** (see *Bar* listing). **The Tied House** (see *Bar* listing) is another popular multi-location brewpub. The **San Francisco Brewing Company**, found in San Francisco between the Financial District and North Beach, is a wood-bar and burgers-and-fries brewpub; live music entertains while you enjoy your pint. Slightly hipper is the popular **20 Tank Brewery**, located in San Francisco's SoMa area and frequented by young flannel-clad single types.

In the East Bay, check out the Berkeley institution that inspired 20 Tank: **Triple Rock**, located on Shattuck Avenue, is a favorite all-day student hangout and all-around great place—you can even pull in some sun on the small rooftop deck. Just down the street, **Jupiter** has quickly become a popular place to eat and drink with friends in an incredibly comfortable indoor (cozy pub) and outdoor (lovely courtyard) atmosphere. **The Bison Brewery** on Telegraph Avenue is a straight-ahead place with great happy-hour beer specials and some chess games for those with mellower things in mind. Judy Ashworth at **Lyon's Brewery** in Dublin serves Northern California's best selection of micro-brewed beer on tap in a big, dark hall with loud music and plenty of pool tables (although she doesn't serve her own beer).

Anchor Brewing Company: 1705 Mariposa St., San Francisco, (415) 863-8350.

Bison Brewing Company: 2598 Telegraph Ave., Berkeley, (510) 841-7734.

Jupiter: 2181 Shattuck Ave., Berkeley, (510) 843-8277.

Lyon's Brewery: Town & Country Shopping Ctr., 7294 San Ramon Rd., Dublin, (510) 829-9071.

San Francisco Brewing Company: 155 Columbus Ave., San Francisco, (415) 434-3344.

Triple Rock: 1920 Shattuck Ave., Berkeley (510) 843-2739.

20 Tank Brewery: 316 11th St., San Francisco, (415) 255-9455.

Live Music

As with bars, there is wide selection of live music throughout the Bay Area, with a few clubs on the Peninsula, a bigger selection in San Jose, and the cutting edge in San Francisco. Great sources for finding out what's happening each weekend are *The Metro*, the "Eye" section in Friday's *San Jose Mercury News*, Sunday's *San Francisco Chronicle* "Pink Pages," the *Bay Guardian*, and the *SF Weekly*. You might want to call **BASS Tickets** at (510) 762-2277 or (408) 998-2277 for information on ticket availability for bigger shows and a listing of events.

Major Bay Area Venues

Concord Pavilion: Ygnacio Valley Rd., Concord, (510) 676-8742; for tickets call BASS. Large outdoor amphitheater featuring major label performers spring through fall. Attracts country western acts in addition to traditional rock. Capacity: 8,700.

Cow Palace: Geneva Ave. and Santos St., San Francisco, (415) 469-6065. Large all-purpose venue (from rodeos to concerts). Not a common site for shows anymore. Capacity: 15,000.

Fillmore: 1805 Geary St., San Francisco, (415) 346-6000. The San Francisco legend, home to innumerable psychedelic concerts in the 60s, has finally reopened after being badly damaged in the 1989 Loma Prieta quake. The mid-sized theater now hosts a good mix of rising local and national rock acts like Counting Crows and Cracker. Capacity: 1,100.

Great American Music Hall: 859 O'Farrell St., San Francisco, (415) 885-0750. A traditional theater—complete with balcony, table seating, cocktail and bar food service, good acoustics, and lots of smoke—now used for contemporary music shows. Arrive early for good seating to see the really hot acts. Presents a varied parade of musical genres, including rock, traditional jazz, blues, international, folk, and zydeco. Capacity: 600.

Greek Theatre: Gayley Rd. between Hearst Ave. and Bancroft Way, UC Berkeley Campus, (510) 642-0527. As the name implies, the Greek is both elegant and old, and also a very pretty outdoor amphitheater located on the UC Berkeley Campus. Hosts a popular spring and summer concert series featuring major-label acts, with an emphasis on folkrockers like the Indigo Girls. The seating is designed so that each audience member has a killer view of the stage. Bring a blanket to cushion the concrete seats. Capacity: 8,500.

Kaiser Arena: 10 Tenth St., Oakland, (510) 238-7765. A fairly large arena that used to feature the Grateful Dead's famous New Year's shows and now highlights standbys like Little Feat and Tower of Power. Capacity: 8,000.

Lively Arts at Stanford: Stanford Univ., (415) 723-2551. The Stanford Concert Network brings professional bands like Shawn Colvin to campus every year, usually at very low prices. The small, outdoor **Frost Amphitheater** holds occasional concerts, but most well-known groups play at gloomy **Memorial Auditorium** when they come to campus. Capacity: Frost 3,000; Memorial Auditorium 1,700.

Mountain Winery: 14831 Pierce Rd., Saratoga, (408) 741-5182. Spectacular outdoor amphitheater in the former Paul Masson Winery hosts popular summer music series featuring an eclectic mix of jazz, folk, country, and comedy. Capacity: 1,500.

Oakland Coliseum and Stadium: 7000 Coliseum Way, Oakland, (510) 639-7700. Major Bay Area concerts come to the Oakland Coliseum (the indoor basketball arena) and the Oakland Stadium (the huge outdoor baseball stadium). As big and impersonal as you would expect. Accessible via BART. Capacity: Arena 15,000; Stadium 50,000.

San Jose Arena: W. Santa Clara St. and Autumn St., San Jose, (408) 287-9200. Recently completed home to the NHL's San Jose Sharks also plays host to a variety of popular acts, from Eric Clapton to Boyz II Men. Capacity: 18,000.

Shoreline Amphitheatre: Shoreline Blvd. at Amphitheatre Pkwy., Mountain View, (415) 967-4040. Large outdoor amphitheater hosting a varied lineup of major acts performing spring through fall. Reserved seating down low, general admission on the lawn further back, with large video monitors set up so you can see the band. Generally pleasant, but it was built on landfill and you can occasionally smell it. Capacity: 20,000.

Villa Montalvo: 15400 Montalvo Rd., Saratoga, (408) 741-3421. Smaller outdoor amphitheater on historic estate. Hosts a variety of summer performances, from music to drama to children's shows. Capacity: 800.

The Warfield: 982 Market St., San Francisco, (415) 775-7722; hotline (415) 775-9949. One of the best places in the area to see a show. A small, recently-remodeled venue with old-style decor, food and cocktails delivered to the tables on the floor, and traditional theatre seating (reserved) in the balcony. The Warfield presents everything from Dylan to Dinosaur Jr. If your ticket is General Admission you should get there at least an hour early to guarantee a good seat. Capacity: 2,000.

Zellerbach Auditorium: UC Campus, Zellerbach Hall; box office (510) 642-9988. This small auditorium on the UC Berkeley campus is a showplace for well-known musicians appealing to eclectic smaller crowds. Most acts are part of the excellent Cal Performances series, which embraces Cecilia Bartoli as well as the traditional Irish sounds of the Chieftains. Capacity: 2,000.

Rock/Pop/Alternative

Peninsula and San Jose Clubs

The following places regularly feature live music. In addition, many bars and restaurants offer occasional live music ranging from cocktail piano players to full bands. You'll be especially lucky with the night spots listed under *Dance Clubs*. Look for listings in the local papers.

Boswell's: Pruneyard Shopping Ctr., 1875 S. Bascom Ave. and Campbell Ave., Campbell, (408) 371-4404. In Campbell, you shouldn't be surprised to find your bars in shopping centers, although the slightly run-down Anglophile yard-sale theme differentiates Boswell's from its surroundings. Sibling to Woodside's venerable Pioneer Saloon, Boswell's anonymous local bands keep the joint jumping with solid rock covers.

Cactus Club: 417 S. First St., San Jose, (408) 986-0866. SOFA (South of First Area) dance club, with live rock and alternative music part of the week and DJ dance music the other days covering the usual mix of hip hop, disco, house, top 40, and techno. Admission without alcohol for those 18-21. Live music: M, W, F, Sa; DJ dance music: Tu, Th, Su.

The Edge: 260 California Ave., Palo Alto, (415) 324-EDGE. Primarily a dance club playing modern rock of the Live-105 variety (dress in black if you really want to fit in), The Edge also puts on occasional concerts by hip local bands like American Music Club or national groups like Hole. Though this is one of the few places where the under-21 set can go for a good time, it's surprisingly not an exclusively teeny-bopper hangout.

Fanny & Alexander: 412 Emerson St., Palo Alto, (415) 326-7183. Authentic re-creation of a Scandinavian bar, with gleaming hardwood floors, lots of open space, and a spacious back patio. Weekends feature live music and lively crowds, and the food is not to be missed.

Fogg's Tavern: 303 Bryant St., Mountain View, (415) 390-9696. A cool bar with indoor and outdoor seating and lots of beer on tap and in bottles. Live music mixes rock, reggae, and more.

JJ's Blues Café, JJ's Downtown, JJ's Blues Lounge: 165 El Camino Real, Mountain View, (415) 968-2277 • 14 S. Second St., San Jose, (408) 286-3066 • 3439 Stevens Creek Blvd., San Jose, (408) 243-6441. The JJ's are the South Bay's premier blues clubs. The Mountain View locale is tucked into an obscure corner of a shopping center on El Camino. The 50s decor—except for the disco ball above the postage stamp-sized dance floor—gives this place a character all its own. The downtown version is a more traditional space, a narrow brick-walled blues bar. Nightly drink specials and terrific blues bands, both local and national, keep all three joints jamming.

The Los Altos Bar & Grill: 169 Main St., Los Altos, (415) 948-4332. This neighborhood venue is all things to all people and plays everything from jazz to dance music seven nights a week.

Mountain Charley's: 15 N. Santa Cruz Ave., Los Gatos, (408) 395-8880. Another hot spot for trendy rockers to hear local modern rock bands.

Pioneer Saloon: 2925 Woodside Rd., Woodside, (415) 851-8487. One of the best of the local joints, the Pioneer features a different band every night, and the tiny dance floor is usually packed with urban cowboys. Cover charge is around $3, but the beer is cheap and the atmosphere is relaxed.

Rosie's Down Under: 2401 Broadway, Redwood City, (415) 363-2041. A throwback to the days when rock and roll clubs were all basement operations. Thursdays through Saturdays, local bands churn out rock covers, reggae, and country. The atmosphere is minimal and low-key with plenty of good beer on tap.

Toon's: 52 E. Santa Clara St., San Jose, (408) 292-7464. A downtown club featuring live music and a sense of humor. Lots of early drink specials. Wednesdays feature the popular local band The Gents.

San Francisco (and Beyond) Clubs

San Francisco has many rock venues, each with its own great character and charm. San Francisco is also the Bay Area's hub for up-and-coming underground bands and genres. (The Mission is rapidly replacing the Haight as *the* scene for alternative concerts.) More places are mentioned in the *San Francisco Neighborhoods* section. The East Bay, not surprisingly, is the best place to catch world music and jazz.

Ashkenaz: 1317 San Pablo Ave., Berkeley, (510) 525-5054. Basically a big friendly shed where you and your friends can enjoy such interesting programs as a "Flamenco Open Stage," African rhythms, or zydeco.

Bimbo's 365 Club: 1025 Columbus Ave., San Francisco, (415) 474-0365. A unique venue, this huge, swanky, 40s-style nightclub features an eclectic line-up, everything from zydeco concerts to rock benefits.

Bottom of the Hill: 1233 17th St., San Francisco, (415) 626-4455. A Potrero Hill alternative to the Mission scene, featuring a wide variety of touring bands largely signed with independent record labels. With its Pee Wee's Playhouse decor, Bottom of the Hill is a popular spot, although it sometimes gets claustrophobic (especially if the band's hot).

Caribee Dance Center: 1408 Webster St., Oakland, (510) 835-4006. International sounds, ranging from reggae to Brazilian pop.

Club Chameleon: 853 Valencia St., San Francisco, (415) 821-1891. A funky Mission area venue offering a variety of experimental bands.

DNA Lounge: 375 11th St., San Francisco, (415) 626-1409. Long-time SoMa standard hosts alternative bands in an industrial bar.

Elbo Room: 647 Valencia St., San Francisco, (415) 552-7788. Upstairs is an ultra-hip place to catch Bay Area talent, from hip-hop and acid jazz to spoken word.

Eli's Mile High Club: 3629 Martin Luther King Jr. Way, Oakland, (510) 695-6661. Where great blues bands sound off to a mixed and interesting crowd.

Jack's: 1601 Fillmore St., San Francisco, (415) 567-3227. It's not the down-home bar it used to be, but then the Fillmore isn't the Western Addition anymore. Still, the best branch of this growing chain of blues bars still packs in enough sweat, smoke, beer, and loud blues to make you forget that your woman done left you and remember how to dance.

Paradise Lounge: 1501 Folsom St., San Francisco, (415) 861-6906. Still the anchor of the SoMa live music scene, and the best place to glimpse San Francisco's hard-working bands struggling to make it. With up to three bands playing simultaneously on different stages in separate rooms, you can mellow to Bud E. Luv if the aggro-grunge in the other room is too loud, or go upstairs and play pool while listening to the latest in spoken word.

Slim's: 333 11th St., San Francisco, (415) 621-3330. Rocker Boz Scaggs' club, Slim's, is a fun SoMa arena for acts ranging from King Sunny Ade to Digable Planets to the Meat Puppets. If you're headed for Slim's, be ready to be on your feet for the entire show, because the venue is laid out to accommodate about 600 on a flat floor intended for a standing (and, if the music permits, dancing) audience.

Jazz and Folk

Well-known national jazz acts play at most of the major Bay Area venues listed above, especially the **Great American Music Hall**, **Zellerbach Hall**, **Villa Montalvo**, and the **Mountain Winery**. The Lively Arts at Stanford frequently features well-known jazz groups.

To check out less well-known musicians in a more intimate environment, look for a wide array of talent at many local bars and clubs. While San Francisco has a good selection of jazz bars, the Bay Area's two premier jazz venues, **Yoshi's** and **Kimball's East**, are in the East Bay. Some bars such as **Gordon Biersch** in San Jose feature live jazz most nights. Many other bars have live jazz more sporadically: check the listings in your local papers to see who's playing in your neighborhood. The following list should get you started.

Ajax Lounge: 374 S. First St., San Jose, (408) 298-2529. Live jazz most nights in this hip new club.

Blue Lamp: 561 Geary St., San Francisco, (415) 885-1464. Provides a true grungy, jazz-dive experience.

Café Claude: 7 Claude Ln., San Francisco, (415) 392-3505. Charming French bistro located in a picturesque downtown alley and featuring traditional jazz trios.

Café du Nord: 2170 Market St., San Francisco (415) 861-5016. Ultra-cool subterranean hangout at the edge of the Castro. Come for hip company, crowds, and jazz.

Café Quinn: Oaks Ctr., 21269 Stevens Creek Blvd., Cupertino, (408) 252-CAFÉ. Live folk and jazz in an airy bistro café. Food and service are quirky, but tall windows and an outdoor patio make it a winner in warm weather.

Fairmont Jazz at the New Orleans Room: 950 Mason St., San Francisco, (415) 772-5259. The ultimate red-plush jazz lounge in this historic Nob Hill hotel has such cool atmosphere that you wouldn't be surprised if James Bond dropped by for a smoke and a smirk. Look for mellow jazz and high ticket prices.

Freight and Salvage: 111 Addison St., Berkeley, (510) 548-1761. Folk musicians, Irish duets, and swing-inspired groups, as well as your standard acoustic troubadours, play at this coffeehouse every night.

Giannotti's: 34 S. B St., San Mateo, (415) 579-2534. A small suburban cocktail lounge featuring live jazz from big band to local lounge lizard Bud E. Luv.

Iron Gate: 1360 El Camino Real, Belmont, (415) 592-7893. A large cocktail lounge attached to a French restaurant. The live jazz Thursday through Saturday is mostly traditional and swing.

Kimball's East: 5800 Shell Mound St., Emeryville, (510) 658-2555. The San Francisco original has been experiencing difficulties, but the East Bay sibling continues to present world-class jazz performers. Downstairs Kimball's Carnival brings in Latin jazz acts.

La Peña Cultural Center: 3105 Shattuck Ave., Berkeley, (510) 849-2568. Berkeley's Latin American Cultural Center hosts a wide range of world music and jazz in a festive setting.

Palm Room: 302 S. Market St., San Jose, (408) 295-2000. Il Fornaio operates both the restaurant and lounge within the renovated Hotel St. Claire. The plush Palm Room may feel more like a hotel lobby than a jazz club, but the live music will quickly have you up and swinging.

Pasand: 3701 El Camino Real, Santa Clara, (408) 241-5150 • 2284 Shattuck Ave., Berkeley, (510) 848-0260 • 1875 Union St., San Francisco, (415) 922-4498. Serves hot jazz and spicy Indian food to packed crowds at a trio of Indian restaurants with jazz clubs.

Phoenix Jazz Club: 325 S. First St., San Jose, (408) 279-2271. A recently opened club featuring a mix of traditional acoustic jazz, fusion, and salsa.

St. Michael's Art House Café: 806 Emerson St., Palo Alto, (415) 326-2530. This warm, homey café has been hosting talented local performers with a folk/bluegrass bent since the Warlocks played for Ken Kesey and the Merry Pranksters.

Up and Down Club: 1151 Folsom St., San Francisco, (415) 626-2388. Hosts a variety of jazz acts every night of the week.

Yoshi's Nitespot: 6030 Claremont Ave., Oakland, (510) 652-9200. An Oakland jazz house and Japanese restaurant that opens its doors to all ages. Yoshi's regularly brings top national acts to the Bay Area for multi-night engagements. Yoshi's is moving to Jack London Square at the beginning of 1996.

Dance Clubs

Most of the bars that host live music also have dancing going on. The following places get most of their music from DJs, but they do occasionally feature live bands. The Peninsula has very little to offer in the way of dance clubs. San Jose's SOFA (South of First Area) has become quite a nightspot. And, of course, San Francisco has all you would expect from a major cultural center (look for more places under the *San Francisco Neighborhoods* section). Clubs are notorious for coming and going quickly, so check your local paper for the evening's events.

Alberto's Club: 736 W. Dana St., Mountain View, (415) 968-3007. A top spot for an introduction to Latin American dance music, Alberto's has live salsa on Thursdays (lessons are included with the cover charge for early arrivals). Other nights you might find DJ dancing to salsa or occasionally other live music from reggae to samba.

Club Oasis: 200 N. First St., San Jose, (408) 292-2212. Not to be confused with Menlo Park's Oasis bar, this SOFA sibling of The Edge in Palo Alto has lively dancing to modern mix, house, etc., as well as occasional live music. Look for a variety of promotions and cheap drink specials.

Covered Wagon Saloon: 917 Folsom St., San Francisco, (415) 974-1296. Fills up with dancers ready to groove to the funky sounds of the 70s.

F/X: 400 S. First St., San Jose, (408) 298-9796. Formerly a movie theater, now one of the hippest clubs in San Jose's SOFA district. Features DJ dancing Wednesday through Saturday to new wave oldies, modern mix, house, techno, and acid jazz. You might even catch an occasional live show. Look for various deals on cover charges and drinks throughout the week.

Jose's Caribbean Restaurant: 2275 El Camino Real, Palo Alto, (415) 326-6522. Relatively new to the dance scene, Jose has renovated his empanada factory with a colorful new dance floor where you can party to live and DJ Brazilian, salsa, and reggae beats.

Nickie's BBQ: 460 Haight St., San Francisco, (415) 621-6508. Boogie by Nickie's, a lower Haight dive club. Nickie's features a different musical genre nightly (from Grateful Dead to hip hop), and can often get as hot as a sauna when large crowds fill up the small space.

The Palace: 146 S. Murphy Ave., Sunnyvale, (408) 739-5179. Swanky supper club in a restored art deco movie theater featuring biomorphic silver-painted columns, wrought-iron accents, and sponge-painted orange walls. Live jazz Thursday nights, DJ dancing Friday and Saturday, and live Salsa Orquesta music on Wednesdays.

Saddle Rack: 1310 Auzerais Ave., San Jose, (408) 286-3393. Urban cowboys and real rednecks meet at the Saddle Rack, a country-western club that features a mechanical bull and free dance lessons. Rumor has it they once brought in a real bull, but it escaped and ran wild down the streets of San Jose.

St. James Infirmary: 390 Moffett Blvd., Mountain View, (415) 969-0806. A bar known primarily for its street signs, sleds, and other odd adornments, including a 25-foot Wonder Woman statue which you can dance around at night when St. James turns into a dance club.

La Tropicana: 47 Notre Dame Ave., San Jose, (408) 279-2340. Huge downtown hotspot for Mexican *Banda* music and dancing.

Zanzibar: 842 Valencia St., San Francisco, (415) 695-7887. A funky Mission District club known for its deep-house DJs.

Gay and Lesbian Clubs

Most of the Bay Area's gay and lesbian clubs are located in San Francisco. The popular clubs change names depending on the weeknight and the crowd they're hosting. Check the local free weeklies for current DJs and themes; try the *Bay Area Reporter* (BAR), the *Sentinel*, or *Odyssey Magazine*, which has separate listings for men's and women's parties and bars. Most men's clubs generally feature go-go boys or erotic dancers at some time during the night (or morning). Also look for plenty of gays and lesbians at the city's innumerable raves. To find out the location of these all-night dance fests, just look for a flyer posted on nearly every telephone pole in the city.

For literature and current rave and party postings go to **A Different Light Bookstore** at 489 Castro Street in San Francisco (415/431-0891), just down the street from the Castro Theater. For pre-club fun, check out **Lavender Lounge**, the cutting edge of queer TV, on Tuesday nights, channel 45, at 10pm (in San Francisco only).

The Box: 715 Harrison St., San Francisco, no phone. The most notable party catering to the entire homosexual community, last held at 715 Harrison. (There's no phone or club name, so you might want to research this in a weekly paper.)

B-Street: 236 S. B St., San Mateo, (415) 348-4045. A Peninsula club open every night. Dancers (and strippers on Thursdays) of both genders party to a great music mix, from country to deep house to disco.

Café: 2367 Market St., San Francisco, (415) 861-3846. Another good bet formerly known as Café San Marcos. This hangout is a great place to go on Friday and Saturday nights when the mixed crowd boogies to upbeat music on the open deck. Enjoy both bars and the pool table, or simply soak up the flavor of the Castro.

The Endup: 401 Sixth St., San Francisco, (415) 543-7700. A major dance club in San Francisco's SoMa district with different events each night from Thursday through Monday. Call for the ever-changing details, including information on early morning (6am) dancing. Th: Kit Kat Club; F: Madhouse; Sa: The Girlspot; Su: Tea Dance and Family Affair; M: Chill House during the day, Club Dread at night.

Family Affair: See The Endup. At Family Affair (Sunday nights at The Endup) you can gawk at go-go boys gyrating in cages, step outside to cool off by the club's own waterfall, or join the young and lively crowd on the dance floor.

The Girlspot: See The Endup. For women, the Girlspot (Saturday nights at The Endup) is one of the best places to dance and mingle. DJ Exotica lays down the grooves every Saturday at this dance club.

Hamburger Mary's: 170 W. Saint John St., San Jose, (408) 947-1667. Of the South Bay gay clubs, Hamburger Mary's (formerly Club St. John and The Saint) is the largest, with an outdoor patio, pool tables, and a good-sized dance floor. Wednesday is prime dance night, and strippers show up on Sundays. Call for current happenings on other nights.

Lion Pub: Divisadero and Sacramento Sts., San Francisco, (415) 567-6565. Wednesday is Macho Night at the Lion Pub, a small, hidden, neighborhood hangout in Pacific Heights.

Pleasuredome: 177 Townsend St., San Francisco, (415) 974-6020. Sundays at the SoMa club Townsend. Pleasuredome's front dance bar caters to the "boy"-ish crowd with house music and "smart drinks." Travel through the black lycra time tunnel to the back dance bar, which sports a spinning, mirrored ball and mustaches. (Need we say more?)

Pussy Cat: The City's best undressed women can be found at the Pussy Cat on Sunday nights. The club's strippers do their thing at 9pm. Since this party roams around the city, check the numerous flyers floating around for each week's location.

The Rawhide II: 280 Seventh St., San Francisco, (415) 621-1197. The friendliest club—they sponsor free country-western dance lessons Monday through Thursday at 7:30pm and Saturdays at 6:30pm.

Shouts Bar and Grill: 2034 Broadway, Redwood City, (415) 369-9651. Redwood City's only gay bar, offering dining and dancing, free pool Monday through Wednesday, and $1 schnapps on Thursdays.

Spread: (415) 431-BOYS. Currently shut down, but try the same phone number for future happenings.

The Stud: 399 Ninth St., San Francisco, (415) 863-6623. A San Francisco institution. Don't miss Oldies Night on Wednesdays, when college students pack the place.

Tea Dance: See The Endup. The return of the ever popular all-day Sunday institution. Finish your weekend with a bang, and enjoy the patio when the weather is good.

A Tinker's Damn: 46 Saratoga Ave., Santa Clara, (408) 243-4595. A Tinker's Damn is complete with dance floor, pool table, and friendly Silicon Valley patrons.

Comedy Clubs

What could be more fun than laughing the night away? The Bay Area, spawning ground for such major-league stars as Robin Williams and Whoopi Goldberg, boasts stand-up comedians worth an ovation. Remember, however, that you must be 21 or older to enter most clubs. This doesn't mean that the humor is always risqué; it mainly means that a two-drink minimum is required of all who pass by the bouncer (based on the theory that liquor adds fuel to an audience's fire). It isn't, however, a general rule that everyone must consume something alcoholic; two diet sodas will do. Appetizers are often included.

Another rule of the comedy club routine is the cover charge, although there are alternatives: during the week many establishments offer discounts or complimentary admissions. Discounted tickets are sometimes available for groups. To improve your chances of receiving free admission offers, ask to be placed on mailing lists.

Make sure you're familiar with the scheduled comedian, or at least call ahead to ask about his or her sense of humor—there's nothing worse than expecting dry wit and getting raunchy humor. Since many performers extend their routines into the audience, you might not want to sit near the stage—get there early enough to snag the seats of your choice.

Bay Area Theatre Sports: BATS hotline (415) 824-8220. While you won't find traditional stand-up comedy here, Bay Area Theatre Sports, an avant-garde musical troupe, performs an array of daring routines, including comedy acts—call their hotline for a schedule of events.

Cobb's Comedy Club: 2801 Leavenworth St. in the Cannery, San Francisco, (415) 928-4320. Cobb's, a San Francisco giant in the comedy arena, is so popular that they even let you in if you're under 21 (provided your ID proves you're 18 and you're escorted by an adult). They also offer free validated parking, a real plus in the busy Fisherman's Wharf.

Comedy Sportz: 3428 El Camino Real, Santa Clara, (408) 985-LAFF. The Family Feud of comedy clubs: watch improvisational comics compete for the best audience reaction.

Knuckleheads: 150 S. First St., San Jose, (408) 998-4242. A struggling newcomer in the local comedy scene, appeals to a younger audience with featured performers from MTV. Currently experimenting with foregoing the minimum drink requirement, but that may change.

Last Laff: 29 N. San Pedro St., San Jose, (408) 287-5233. Large, multi-level club with sparse decor but good views of the stage. Limited food, but good happy hours. Most nights feature three comedians—two locals and a national act.

Punchline San Francisco: 444 Battery St., San Francisco, (415) 397-7573. The Punchline is a major-leaguer, usually with three comedians per night; they serve dinner and boast big-name marquees.

Rooster T. Feather: 157 W. El Camino Real, Sunnyvale, (408) 736-0921. A medium-sized club with good visibility and layout, though it can get noisy next to the bar. Typically two or three comedians perform each night, usually a local comedian followed by one or two well-known or national performers. There's a two-drink minimum. Reservations are recommended three to five days in advance, but you can sometimes squeeze in if you arrive 45 minutes before the show and get on the waiting list.

PERFORMING ARTS

Few places in the country possess the cultural riches of the Bay Area. An hour's drive can bring you to an almost unparalleled selection of performances, including San Francisco's lively and expansive arts scene and San Jose's big names like Pavarotti and Streisand. We've compiled a sampling of performing arts companies and venues throughout the area. Please note that many companies play at a variety of venues, choosing whichever one best fits each performance. For detailed information, check your local paper or call the **San Jose Events Hotline** at (408) 295-2265. For a bit of adventure or a budget evening out, don't forget the smaller performances at the many schools and churches in the area.

Classical Music and Opera

California Youth Symphony: (415) 325-6666. For over 40 years the Youth Symphony has maintained a variety of programs training future stars. The award-winning group performs three times a year, primarily in the San Mateo Performing Arts Center and the Flint Center, with an additional free concert at Foothill College in December.

El Camino Youth Symphony: (415) 327-3369. A training ground for aspiring professional musicians; check out their popular holiday concert in December.

Nova Vista Symphony: Foothill College Theater, 12345 El Monte Rd., Los Altos Hills, (408) 245-3116. Performs four Sunday afternoons a year at the Foothill College Theater.

Oakland East Bay Symphony: 1999 Harrison St., Ste. 2030, Oakland, (510) 446-1992. This symphony now calls the gorgeous art-deco Paramount Theatre home. Tickets run $10-$30, and if you plan on going more than once per season, inquire about three-and four-concert subscription tickets for students and families, which amount to half-price performances. Rush tickets are also available at the door for students and seniors. Performances are from January through April.

Opera San Jose: Montgomery Theatre, W. San Carlos and S. Market Sts., San Jose, (408) 437-4450. At the Montgomery Theatre you can attend the performances of Opera San Jose, a company developing young professional talent by producing classical works by composers such as Verdi, Rossini, and Mozart. • Box office M-F 9am-5pm.

Palo Alto Chamber Orchestra: (415) 856-3848. An excellent group of young Peninsula musicians that performs chamber and symphonic works.

Peninsula Civic Light Opera: San Mateo Performing Arts Center, 424 Peninsula Ave., San Mateo, (415) 579-5568. A very popular community theater appearing at the San Mateo Performing Arts Center.

Peninsula Symphony Orchestra: (415) 574-0244. Performs alternately at the Flint Center and the San Mateo Performing Arts Center.

Pocket Opera: Temple Emanu-El, 2 Lake St., San Francisco, (415) 989-1853; tickets 989-1855. Performs contemporary English renditions of short operas, such as Mozart's "Bastien and Bastienne," as well as full-length operas.

Redwood Symphony: Cañada College (exit I-280 at Farm Hill Blvd.), Redwood City, (415) 366-6872. Based at Cañada College, the Redwood Symphony performs their casual brand of orchestral music throughout the area.

San Francisco Opera: 301 Van Ness Ave., San Francisco, (415) 864-3330. Arguably one of the best opera companies in the world, and certainly one of the best in the country. The ticket prices reflect this status: single seats run from about $35 to well over $100. Performances take place in the grand War Memorial Opera House, where the sound is good even in the least expensive seats far in the back and on the sides. Supertitles projected above the stage make it easy to follow the plots of foreign-language operas, and opera glasses are available for rent.

San Francisco Symphony: Louise M. Davies Symphony Hall, 201 Van Ness Ave., San Francisco, (415) 431-5400. The excellent San Francisco Symphony performs a full and varied schedule and attracts several world-class soloists and guest conductors each season. The least expensive tickets cost around $20, but you can also get standing-room tickets (available two hours before performances) and student rush tickets (available one hour before performances, space permitting). Acoustics are generally better in the center seats of elegant Davies Symphony Hall, which also plays host to some of the greatest orchestras in the world, including the Leipziger Gewandhaus Orchestra and the Boston Symphony. Tickets to guest orchestras usually cost more than San Francisco Symphony performances. Bay Area residents can also take advantage of the free summer performances given by the Symphony in Stern Grove every weekend.

San Jose Symphony: (408) 288-2828. Attracts excellent soloists and guest conductors, and tickets tend to be a little less expensive than those for the San Francisco Symphony. Performances alternate between the Flint Center in Cupertino and the San Jose Center for the Performing Arts.

San Jose Chamber Orchestra: (408) 286-5111. San Jose's resident chamber music company.

Stanford University: Braun Music Center, Stanford University, (415) 723-3811. Stanford plays host to an entire city's worth of performing groups. Look for a delightful Midsummer Mozart festival. For home-grown talent, the **Stanford Symphony Orchestra** and the **Symphonic Chorus** are excellent groups, particularly when they perform together. The **Chamber Chorale** is a smaller chorus that performs chamber music of every period from the Renaissance to the 20th century; most of the university's best singers have been involved with this outstanding group at one point or another.

West Bay Opera: (415) 321-3471. The West Bay Opera appears at the Lucie Stern Theatre in Palo Alto. The highly acclaimed company performs for two long weekends every October, February, and May. Watch for student discounts on Thursday nights.

Dance

Berkeley City Ballet: 1800 Dwight Way, Berkeley, (510) 841-8913. This multiracial performing arts organization runs a ballet school and also graces the Zellerbach stage during the December *Nutcracker* performance. The young dancers perform chamber works commissioned from New York and beyond, in addition to the classics. In the spring, the company performs at the Berkeley Community Theater.

Cal Performances: (510) 642-9988. Cal Performances at UC Berkeley showcases some of the world's top artists and companies; past highlights have included performances by Baryshnikov and the companies of Alvin Ailey and Twyla Tharp. • Box office M-F 10am-5:30pm; Sa-Su 10am-4pm.

Dimensions Dance Theatre: Alice Arts Center, 1428 Alice St., Ste. 300, Oakland, (510) 465-3363. Traces the evolution of contemporary African-American dance. Live musicians accompany compositions by director Deborah Vaughan and company members. Tickets $8-$10.

Janlyn Dance Company: (408) 255-4055. This modern dance company performs 20-35 times a year, makes guest appearances around the Peninsula, and has a special children's program for area schools.

Lively Arts at Stanford: Press Courtyard, Santa Teresa St., Stanford University, (415) 723-2551. The **Lively Arts at Stanford** routinely brings such well-known and innovative groups as MOMIX, Bebe Miller Dance Company, and Pilobolus to various venues on campus. Also, the Dance Division of the Stanford Athletics Department presents ballet, modern, jazz, and ethnic dance concerts throughout the year; the annual Spring Migration is a popular highlight. • Information M-F 8am-5pm.

Oakland Ballet: Paramount Theatre, 2025 Broadway, Oakland, (510) 452-9288. Performs at Oakland's beautifully restored Paramount Theatre and occasionally at the Concord Pavilion and Berkeley's Zellerbach Hall. The company is known for its unique style, which combines elements of classical European ballet with American and ethnic dance influences. Tickets range from $10 to $30, and discounts are given to students and seniors. Performances are from September through December.

Peninsula Ballet Theatre: San Mateo Performing Arts Center, 600 N. Delaware St., San Mateo, (415) 343-8485. The only professional ballet company in the mid-Peninsula area draws consistently good notices for favorites such as *The Nutcracker* and *Giselle*.

San Francisco Ballet: 455 Franklin St., San Francisco, (415) 861-5600. The War Memorial Opera House is home to the San Francisco Ballet, a major company that draws mixed reviews favoring the more contemporary pieces. The American Ballet Theatre and other world-class touring ballet companies, such as the Kirov and Joffrey, also make frequent appearances at the Opera House. You can get standing-room tickets two hours before performances; student rush tickets may be purchased one hour beforehand if space is available.

San Jose Cleveland Ballet: Center for the Performing Arts, Almaden Blvd. and Park Ave., San Jose, (408) 288-2800. A joint venture between the cities of San Jose and Cleveland which has received critical acclaim for its performances of new ballets and elegant renditions of the classics. The company performs from September to May at the San Jose Center for the Performing Arts.

Western Ballet School: 2028 Old Middlefield Way, Mountain View, (415) 968-4455. This Palo Alto school presents its students to the public in major ballet productions twice a year at the Mountain View Center.

Theatre

Peninsula and South Bay

City Lights Theater Company: 529 S. Second St., San Jose, (408) 295-4200. Produces contemporary plays.

Manhattan Playhouse: Manhattan Ave. and W. Bayshore Rd., E. Palo Alto, (415) 322-4589. This on-site company mounts only two shows a season, but it is worth the visit.

Menlo Players Guild: Burgess Theater, 601 Laurel St., Menlo Park, (415) 322-3261. Mounts productions at the Burgess Theatre that improve with each season.

Mountain View Center for the Performing Arts: Mercy and Castro Sts., Mountain View, (415) 903-6000. Hosts community theater, professional touring companies, and international artists and attractions.

Palo Alto Players: (415) 329-0891. The oldest group around; they put on six shows a year, notable for their consistent quality and reasonable ticket prices.

San Jose Civic Light Opera: Center for the Performing Arts, 255 Almaden Blvd., San Jose, (408) 453-7108. Performs traditional Broadway musicals on a large scale at the San Jose Center for the Performing Arts.

San Jose Repertory Theatre: (408) 291-2255. A professional outfit producing a combination of classics, old favorites, and also some original plays.

San Jose Stage Company: Old Town Theater, 50 University Ave., Los Gatos, (408) 283-7142. Performing in the Old Town Theatre in Los Gatos, this is a semi-professional group specializing in contemporary works.

Saratoga Drama Group: (408) 255-0801. This group has been putting on two musicals a year for the past three decades and has developed a considerable following.

Stage One Theatre: (408) 293-6362. Produces cutting-edge contemporary theatre. Highlights include the South Bay premiere of *Jeffrey*.

Stanford University Department of Drama: Memorial Hall, Stanford University, (415) 723-2576. The Drama Department mounts several productions a year, directed by graduate students, in the Little Theatre in Memorial Hall and the Nitery in Old Union. Tickets are $5 for students for Little Theatre productions and usually less for shows in the Nitery. **Ram's Head Theatrical Society** (415-723-0801) puts on three shows a year.

TheatreWorks: (415) 903-6000. TheatreWorks is a highly regarded and extremely popular local company that produces everything from Broadway musicals to staged readings of new works. Performs primarily at the Lucie Stern in Palo Alto.

San Francisco

TIX Bay Area (formerly STBS): Union Square, Stockton St. between Post St. and Geary St., (415) 433-7827. This small kiosk is a full-service box office serving most of the city's theatres and performances. It also offers day-of-show half-price tickets to many events. Half-price tickets are cash only, and any tickets for Sunday and Monday shows must be purchased by Saturday. • Tu-Th 11am-6pm; F-Sa 11am-7pm.

ACT (American Conservatory Theater): 450 Geary St., San Francisco, (415) 749-2228. Maintains the Stage Door Theater on Mason and the Marine Memorial Theater on Sutter, each with its own specialty, and also presents staged readings. Expect controversial productions from ACT's director Carey Perloff.

Beach Blanket Babylon: 678 Beach St., San Francisco, (415) 421-4222. Steve Silver's beloved San Francisco institution offering ever-changing, highly-polished musical revues poking fun at contemporary popular culture. Reserve tickets far in advance.

Curran Theater: 445 Geary St., San Francisco, (415) 474-3800. The Best of Broadway series brings traveling Broadway productions such as *The Phantom of the Opera* to the Curran Theatre.

Lorraine Hansberry Theater: 620 Sutter St., San Francisco, (415) 474-8800. This small theatre primarily produces African-American productions from standards like *The Colored Museum* to comical and biting contemporary pieces.

Magic Theatre: Building A, Fort Mason Center, Buchanan St. at Marina Blvd., San Francisco, (415) 441-8822. One of the best places to catch contemporary experimental theatre in the City. Look for high-quality productions of works by playwrights like Sam Shepard (before *The Right Stuff*).

San Francisco Mime Troupe: 855 Treat St., San Francisco, (415) 285-1717. Park information: (415) 285-1720. The world-renowned troupe is not precisely mime, comedy, theater, or performance art, but combines elements of each. Check out the entertaining and socially relevant shows seen outdoors in various Bay Area parks during the warmer months. • Show times 2pm.

Theatre Artaud: 450 Florida St., San Francisco, (415) 621-7797. Presents a good mix of avant-garde and contemporary dance, drama, and multimedia performance. Those prone to acrophobia might not appreciate the scaffolding-like seating.

Theatre Rhinoceros: 2926 16th St., San Francisco, (415) 861-5079. San Francisco's premier gay theatre.

Venues

Burgess Theater: 601 Laurel St., Menlo Park, (415) 323-9365.

City Lights Theater: 529 S. Second St., San Jose, (408) 295-4200.

Cubberley Theatre: 4000 Middlefield Rd., Palo Alto, (415) 329-2418.

Flint Center: 21250 Stevens Creek Blvd., De Anza College, Cupertino, (408) 864-8816.

Foothill College: 12345 El Monte Rd. (at I-280), Los Altos, (415) 948-4444.

Fox Theatre: 2215 Broadway, Redwood City, (415) 363-0149.

Hillbarn Theatre: 1285 E Hillsdale Blvd., Foster City, (415) 349-6411.

Los Altos Conservatory Theatre: 97 Hillview Ave., Los Altos, (415) 941-5228.

Lucie Stern Theatre: 1305 Middlefield Rd., Palo Alto, (415) 329-2623.

Manhattan Playhouse: Manhattan Ave. at W. Bayshore Rd., E. Palo Alto, (415) 322-4589.

Montgomery Theater: Market and San Carlos Sts., San Jose, (408) 277-3900.

Mountain View Center for the Performing Arts: Mercy and Castro Sts., Mountain View, (415) 903-6000.

San Jose Performing Arts Center: 255 Almaden Blvd., San Jose, (408) 277-3900.

San Mateo Performing Arts Center: 600 N. Delaware, San Mateo, (415) 348-8243.

Santa Clara University Theatre: Mayer Theater, Santa Clara Univ., (408) 554-4015.

Saratoga Civic Theater: 13777 Fruitvale Ave., Saratoga, (408) 867-3438.

Sunnyvale Performing Arts Center: 550 E. Remington Dr., Sunnyvale, (408) 733-6611.

SPORTS AND THE GREAT OUTDOORS

ADVENTURE SPORTS

Sometimes you just want to do something really weird and really stupid. When this mood hits you, try out one of the many adventure sports available in the Bay Area. Imagine the tension released when you leap off an 11-story bridge and are snatched from the jaws of death by the equivalent of a rubber band on steroids. Imagine how petty everyday concerns become when you're hanging from the strut of a plane, 3,000 feet above the ground, wearing a glorified bedspread on a string. But fear not: these sports are all taught and practiced by professionals, under whose guidance the apparently insane is, in all probability, quite safe. In fact, you're more likely to be seriously injured while driving to the site of the sport than you are once you get there. So tighten down your straps, click on your helmet, and go jump off something!

Bungee Jumping

Bungee jumping is sort of the quick-fix of adventure sports. You don't have to have any skills, any preparation, or even any brains. (In fact, some would argue that bungee jumpers are distinctly lacking in the last category.) The basic concept is to get some significant distance above the ground (at least 100 feet), attach yourself firmly to a very strong elastic band, and then jump from this suicidal height in the hopes that the elastic will stop you before the ground does. In practice, the launching platform is a crane, a balloon, or a bridge. The elastic band is actually multiple strands of a cord originally designed to absorb the shock of a tank parachute—in other words, these are damn strong cords. The cords are attached to the jumper by both a chest and pelvis harness system. The net result of all the redundancy (one cord could work, but four to six are used) and overkill is that although bungee jumping is one of the craziest-looking of the thrill sports, in many ways it is probably the safest, at least at the beginner level.

Now that your brain is convinced that bungee jumping is totally safe, try telling that to your body when it's teetering over a 100-foot drop with only a fat string to save it from going "splat." Even if you *know* it's safe, bungee jumping is still a huge rush.

Bungee Adventures: 2218 Old Middlefield Way (at the Shoreline Amphitheater), Mountain View, (415) 903-3546. The granddaddy of the business is owned by the Kockelman brothers of the banned Reebok commercial fame. They specialize in crane jumps. The latest, something called the ejection seat, is essentially a giant slingshot: the victim or victims (it can accommodate two) are strapped into a chair attached to the cord and catapulted into space. • Sa 10am-3pm and before most concerts. $49 for 150-foot jump; $69 for 220-foot jump. $10 extra for ankle harness.

Icarus Bungee: (510) 521-5867. Run by Dan Roza out of his Alameda home, although you'll have to travel a little farther than Alameda to jump with this bonzai bungee master. Mr. Roza specializes in bridge jumping. Despite what you might think, Mr. Roza also strongly emphasizes safety. Dissatisfied with the quality of bungee cords on the market, he has his cords custom manufactured specifically for his purposes. • $85 for two jumps off 100-foot bridge spring and summer; $75 winter and fall; group discounts.

Hang Gliding and Paragliding

For those who haven't seen paragliding, it looks like hang gliding with a rectangular parachute. Unlike hang gliding, paragliding equipment doesn't require complicated setup procedures or special roof-racks. You can pack all the gear necessary for gliding—a harness, glider, and helmet—in a pack that's smaller than most camping packs. Preparation time is negligible: it takes 10 minutes to find yourself soaring aloft among our feathered friends.

So how do you get involved? There are a variety of gliding schools around San Francisco that teach paragliding to the beginner. It takes about four days to soar and from five to eight days to get a "class one" rating that officially entitles you to fly solo. Even if you have no intentions of pursuing the sport, the first day is nonetheless great fun and well worth the effort. You get to glide just like the experts, but not for quite as long.

What hang gliding demands in skill and preparation it gives back in speed and maneuverability. Paragliders go 20-25 miles an hour, while the speed of a hang glider can approach 65 or 70. Where paragliders float, hang gliders soar and swoop. When the wind becomes too strong for paragliders, the hang gliders are just coming into their element.

The first day of hang gliding is a lot like the first day of paragliding. Cast aside those fears of launching off sheer cliffs; as a novice, you'll be learning on gently sloping sand dunes where you'll reach an altitude of no more than a few feet. After learning the rudiments of flight, you'll progress to larger and larger hills and glides until you can finally soar off cliffs, usually after around 10 days of training.

Air Time of San Francisco: 3620 Wawona St., San Francisco, (415) 759-1177. Offers lessons for paragliding (never more than three people), a ground school to understand how it all works, and sells paragliding and hang gliding equipment. Reservations required for all lessons. • M, W-F 11am-6pm; Sa 10am-4pm. One-day lesson $160, five-day package $700, tandem flight $129.

A Place of Wings: (408) 736-1222. Gregg Pujol, the owner, recognizes the need for small classes, so he guarantees no more than four to a class. Classes include "ground school" where principles of flight and aerodynamics are taught in order to give students the best understanding of the intricacies of paragliding. • Call for appointment.

Chandelle: 1595 E. Francisco Blvd., San Rafael, (415) 454-3464. One of the oldest flying schools around, Chandelle teaches both paragliding and hang gliding, and also maintains a retail shop. Classes limited to three to five people. • M, Tu, Th, F 10am-6pm; Sa 10am-4pm. Half-day intro lesson $100, six-day lesson package $750. Tandem flights by appointment.

Mission Soaring: 1116 Wrigley Way, Milpitas, (408) 262-1055. Mission Soaring, one of the most complete hang gliding shops anywhere, offers lessons for beginners at competitive rates and throws in extensive ground-school training. The shop also sells, rents, and services equipment. • Shop hours: W 11am-5:30pm; Th 11am-9:30pm; F 11am-6:30pm; Sa 9am-6:30pm. Hang gliding on weekends and most weekdays. Free orientation Sa 10am-11:30am. One-day lesson $120, five-lesson package $500.

Skydiving

Skydiving may be the granddaddy of all airborne adventure sports, but don't think that it's been overtaken by its younger relatives. The total terror generated by hurling yourself out of a speeding plane miles off the ground is still unmatched. And perhaps because skydiving is older and more established, or perhaps because it really *is* dangerous, the preparation involved is much greater than that for the above-mentioned thrill sports, especially considering the actual time elapsed during the sport. When you sign up to "do a jump," you're in for a half-day of thorough training. After four hours of land training, which includes working with a simulated chute and learning every possible emergency procedure, you strap on the gear, crawl into a tiny plane, and take off for your drop.

Note that there are essentially three approaches to the first day of skydiving. The basic approach is the **solo static-line jump**, which means that when you finally leave the safety of the plane your rip-cord (which activates the chute) is attached by a 30-foot cord to the plane. The second approach is the **accelerated free-fall jump**. This jump involves six rather than four hours of training, but it allows you to jump solo and to free-fall for about 60 seconds. You are not simply left to survive on your own, however; two instructors jump with you. The final approach is a **tandem-freefall jump**. You and an instructor strapped to your back free-fall for about 60 seconds. You don't pull your own rip-cord, and the tandem-jump does not directly lead toward becoming certified. Skydiving is not taught in population centers (for obvious reasons), so teaching areas are a trek.

Adventure Center: Hollister Airport, Hollister, (408) 636-0117. The closest and the most expensive place to go, but people who have learned here seem satisfied with their experience. • M, W, F-Su 9am-sundown. Static line $190 for first jump, extra jumps $75 each. Accelerated free-fall $270 first jump or $1,200 for seven-lesson package. Groups of ten or more $245 each for first jump. Tandem $160 per jump; groups of ten or more $145 each. Certified jumpers $17 per jump and $15 for rig rental.

Parachute Center: 23597 N. Hwy 99, Acampo, (209) 369-1128. Located at a private airport way out in Lodi. They recommend their bargain-rate tandem jumps for the first time to get you acquainted with skydiving and see if you're really interested. • M-Su 10am-sundown. Static line $135 for first jump, $35 thereafter. Tandem jumps $100. Accelerated freefall $900 for seven jumps. Certified jumper $3 plus $1 for every 1,000 feet ($16 from 13,000 ft.). $10 for equipment rental.

Skydance Skydiving: Davis Airport, Davis, (800) 752-3262. Run by Alasdair Boyd, an Englishman who treats jumpers in a most civilized fashion. Skydance features substantial group discounts. • W-Su 8am-sundown. Static line $148 first jump, $64 thereafter. Groups of eight or more $125 each for first jump. Accelerated free-fall $268 first jump, $1,034 for seven-lesson package. Tandem (9,000 feet) $148 per jump.

MOUNTAIN BIKING

The good news for mountain bikers is that the surrounding area is loaded with parks and open space preserves with extensive, well-maintained trail networks. The bad news is that mountain bikers are not welcome in many of these areas. San Mateo County is by far the least friendly toward mountain bikers, limiting them to major service roads with few exceptions. California State Parks limits bikes primarily to fire roads; however, bikes are allowed on some trails. The Mid-Peninsula Open Space District and Santa Clara County allow bikes on many of their single-track trails.

The following rides are just a sampling of what's available locally. In Marin, the trails surrounding Mt. Tamalpais are extremely popular, and the East Bay hills offer many possibilities. But to really enjoy long rides without all the bothersome regulations and speed limits and whining hikers and equestrians, head far from the city to someplace like Tahoe.

Long Ridge Open Space Preserve

This preserve offers some of the best legal single-track riding on the Peninsula. The trail rolls along a ridge parallel to Skyline Boulevard between Page Mill Road and Hwy 9, through a mix of oak-filled canyons and grassy knolls, reaching an overlook with terrific views.

Parking and the trailhead are on the west side of Skyline Boulevard, three miles south of Page Mill. Look for the Long Ridge/Peters Creek trail and head down to the stream crossing, then turn left and follow the creek up through lush ferns into an open meadow. Take the trail to your right up to the ridge through an oak forest. Keep climbing until you reach the spectacular view at the ridge top. The trail winds and rolls along the ridgetop to an intersection with Skyline Boulevard.

Montebello Road

The views on this ride are spectacular. Park at Stevens Creek Reservoir off Stevens Canyon Road in the hills above Cupertino. From the parking lot, Montebello Road is a sharp right turn off Stevens Canyon Road another quarter mile up. The first stretch is a good indicator of what lies ahead: grades as steep as 15 percent. Nestled among the acres of vineyards at the top is Ridge Winery, vintner of some of California's best reds. The paved portion of Montebello comes to an end not far above the winery, and gives way after a few bends to real dirt. The trail climbs approximately 2,000 feet in eight miles up to the top of Black Mountain, one of the highest points on the Peninsula.

To return, continue along Montebello to a junction with the Indian Creek Trail—a long, bumpy traverse down a steep hillside. At the bottom turn left on the Canyon Trail toward Stevens Canyon and Saratoga Gap. The final thrill of this trail is where it cuts across a washed-out section of old Stevens Canyon Road. Crossing really isn't difficult, but don't look down until after you're across. A short way down you'll hit paved Stevens Canyon Road—a great wind-down road along a shaded creek. The road joins Mt. Eden Road, which cuts sharply off to the right. Turn left to stay on Stevens Canyon.

Upper Stevens Creek County Park

This park offers steep canyons in a remote and beautiful valley. Park at the Grizzly Flat trailhead on the east side of Skyline three miles north of Hwy 9. The two-mile, 1000-foot vertical descent down the Grizzly Flat Trail is a beautiful glide through a canopy of mixed evergreen and hardwood forest; look out for some tricky rocks and ruts that cut across the wide trail. At the bottom pass a lovely clearing and cross Stevens Creek. Turn right on the Canyon Trail and begin your loop back via Table Mountain Trail to Charcoal Road. At the top of Charcoal Road, turn right on a connector trail to get back to Skyline.

ROAD BIKING

Perhaps no other sport is so closely associated with Northern California: on any given weekend, hundreds of road bikers swarm the streets of the Peninsula.

Cañada Road

Flat, expansive Cañada Road is a cruising ground for beginners and a proving ground for triathletes and time trialists. Running parallel to I-280 from Hwy 84 in Woodside north to Hwy 92 near San Mateo, this out-and-back route clings to the eastern edge of the San Andreas Rift with views of the Santa Cruz mountains and Crystal Springs Reservoir. (15 miles to Hwy 92). Begin at Woodside Road (Hwy 84) about one mile west of I-280. Cañada Road is closed to cars on the first and third Sunday of the month from April to October, making it a fine stretch for an exhaust-free ride.

Kings Mountain Road

Kings Mountain Road climbs to Skyline Boulevard from Woodside to the north of Hwy 84. It is ideal for fast descents and relaxed climbs. Begin on Hwy 84 in Woodside and head west until you see Kings Mountain Road branching off to the right (about 0.7 miles). The climb begins after you pass the historic Woodside Store at Tripp Road, and winds upward past hidden mansions and through Huddart Park. From the summit at Skyline, descend the way you came or consider taking Skyline five miles south to Hwy 84.

Old La Honda Road

An area favorite, narrow Old La Honda Road climbs from Portola Valley to Skyline Boulevard. It heads west from Portola Road about a mile south of Sand Hill Road, making a twisting ascent through stands of oak and redwood to Skyline. Minimal traffic and patched, uneven pavement combined with dense vegetation make for a peaceful, if strenuous, climb. At the top, enjoy panoramic views of the bay and ocean from Windy Hill (0.3 miles south on Skyline), then continue north on Skyline to Hwy 84. Turn right on Hwy 84 to Portola Road (first right at the bottom) back to your starting point. (19 miles)

Old La Honda Road (west)

This route makes either a short, rustic loop on its own or an extension to any of the other rides that pass by. From the intersection of Skyline Boulevard and Hwy 84, take Hwy 84 west approximately three miles. Look for Old La Honda Road on the left (when you see a big red barn you've just missed it). The ascent back to Skyline from the West is dramatic, with a view over the surrounding hills to the ocean. (5.5 miles round-trip)

Portola Valley Loop

Probably the area's best-known cycling route, the Portola Valley loop is a pleasant, mildly hilly circuit passing along the stables and woods of this tranquil community. Due to its popularity, Portola Road's wide shoulders generally whir with the passage of shiny, spandex-clad cyclists. Start at the intersection of Alpine Road and Sand Hill Road. Follow Sand Hill west across I-280 and around the western edge of Jasper Ridge Preserve, where it merges into Portola Road. Pass through Portola Valley and go left onto Alpine Road, which leads back to Sand Hill Road. (12 miles)

GOLF

Golfers the world over maintain that playing the courses of Northern California is an experience just this side of heaven. The Monterey Bay area is home to some of the most famous courses: Pebble Beach, Cypress Point, and Spyglass. The courses listed below are mostly public—pay a fee, wait your turn, and fore! The private clubs require you to buddy up to someone who is a member, and even then the greens fees are still pretty frightening.

Blackberry Farm Golf Course: 22100 Stevens Creek Blvd., Cupertino, (408) 253-9200. A nine-hole par three course; short and tight, but enjoyable. It's ideal for beginners, but you'll feel at home whatever your level of expertise. • Public, 9 Holes, Par 29. Greens fee: M-F $7.50; Sa-Su $9.25; seniors, juniors (16 and under) $1 off weekdays.

Crystal Springs Golf Club: 6650 Golf Course Dr., Burlingame, (415) 342-4188. A public course located at the edge of the Santa Cruz Mountains overlooking the San Francisco Watershed. • Public, 18 holes, Par 72. Greens fee: M-F $40; Sa-Su $50. Cart Fee: $24.

Deep Cliff Golf Course: 10700 Clubhouse Lane, Cupertino, (408) 253-5357. Perfect for the golfer who wants to graduate from his or her first nine-hole experience. Yet this course has some interesting holes and can still capture the interest of the more experienced golfer. It tends to play rather slow on weekends. • Public, 18 Holes, Par 60. Greens fee: M-F $21; Sa-Su $28. No carts available.

Del Monte Golf Course: 1300 Sylvan Rd., Monterey, (408) 373-2436. Semi-private course with public play accepted. The oldest course this side of the Mississippi (dating back to the 1870s), Del Monte has recently been improved. The greens are small, but you have to be dead center to sink those putts! It has some very interesting and difficult holes, as well as good package deals with privileged tee times for hotel guests. • Public, 18 Holes, Par 72. Greens fee: $55. Cart fee: $10/person.

Half Moon Bay Golf Links: 2000 Fairway Dr., Half Moon Bay, (415) 726-4438. This public course is a favorite of all who've played it—expensive, but worth it. Located on the coast, it meanders by beautiful homes and is well-known for its final hole running downhill on the cliffs along the ocean. On a windy day this hole will challenge any level of golfer, as will the par three 17th where you hit towards the ocean. Truly a pleasure to play. • Public, 18 Holes, Par 72. Greens fee: M-Th $74; F $84; Sa-Su, holidays $94. Prices include cart fee.

Pacific Grove Golf Links: 77 Asilomar Blvd., Pacific Grove, (408) 648-3175 or 648-3177. A fun public course with two different nines. With some noteworthy holes along the ocean, Pacific Grove is reasonably priced compared to its close neighbors on 17-Mile Drive. • Public, 18 Holes, Par 70. Greens fee: M-Th $24; F-Su, holidays $28. Cart fee: $23. Reservations taken 7 days a week beginning at 6:50am.

Palo Alto Golf Course: 1875 Embarcadero Rd., Palo Alto, 856-0881. On the Bay next to the Palo Alto Baylands, this moderately-priced municipal course is for long hitters. Like a number of courses in this area, it often takes on a totally different character in the afternoon when the wind can really blow. If you don't like high winds, play in the morning—especially in a tournament! Greens fee: M-F $19; Sa, Su $23. Cart fee: $20.

Pebble Beach Golf Links: 17-Mile Dr., Pebble Beach, (408) 624-6611. A public resort course. Words cannot really do justice to the experience of playing this world-famous course. With eight holes skirting the ocean, lush fairways, tough and very fast greens, and breathtaking scenery, golfers travel from all over the world to fulfill their dreams of playing at Pebble. Probably the only course in the world where the experience is more important than the score! • Resort/Public play accepted, 18 Holes, Par 72. Greens fee: $175 guests, $245 non-guests. Price includes cart fee. Reservations recommended.

Shoreline Golf Links: 2600 N. Shoreline Blvd., Mountain View, 969-2041. A moderately-priced public course which takes on another character when the afternoon winds blow. This course, with two different nines, can be tough. The tenth hole skirts the beautiful windsurfing lake. Public, 18 Holes, Par 72. Greens fee: M-F $30; Sa, Su $42. Cart fee: $24.

(The Links at) Spanish Bay: 2700 17-mile Dr., Pebble Beach, (408) 624-6611. The newest addition to the wonders of the 17-Mile Drive. This public course was designed in the style of the famous British links courses. If you like a difficult course, with lots of sand, wind and rough, a game here is a must. There are plenty of accommodations for vacations or overnight stays. Public/Resort, 18 Holes, Par 72. Greens fee: $125 for guests, $155 non-guests. Prices include cart fee. Reservations recommended two months in advance.

Spyglass Hill Golf Course: Stevenson Dr. and Spyglass Hill Rd., Pebble Beach, (408) 624-6611. Part of the renowned trio from the old Crosby Clambake (together with Pebble Beach and Cypress Point), Spyglass Hill is semi-private, with public play accepted. From challenging holes to very fast tricky greens, to say nothing of the weather, this course can humble the best. A must for the avid golfer. • Semi-Private/Resort. 18 Holes, Par 72. Public play accepted. Greens fee: $150 guests, $195 non-guests. Price includes cart fee.

Stanford University Golf Course: 198 Junipero Serra Blvd., Stanford University, (415) 323-0944. A green splash set in the Foothills. This private course ranks with the best; each hole is distinctive. It's a course you'll remember and to which you'll certainly want to return—a true but fair test of your golfing prowess. Members, students, and faculty can invite guests for $30 or $40. • Private, 18 Holes, Par 71. Guest fees: M-F $30; Sa-Su $40; w/ Stanford I.D. 7 days a week $18. Cart fee: $24.

Sunnyvale Golf Course: 605 Macara Ln., Sunnyvale, (408) 738-3666. This municipal course is one of the best values around, and one of the most played. Recently improved, this course is forgiving and favors the uncontrolled fade (slice). It's also fun to play and good for the intermediate golfer. • Municipal, 18 Holes, Par 69. Greens fee: M-F Sunnyvale residents $17, non-residents $22.50; Sa-Su residents $22, non-residents $28. Cart fee: $22.

SEA KAYAKING

Sea kayaking is a sport that you can do safely with a minimum of instruction—sea kayaks are both stable and easy to paddle. If you already know what you're doing, check out the sites listed below. If you want to try it out before committing, many operators have basic programs that will put you and your friends out on the water with a minimum of hassle. As you improve, you can join organized trips to a variety of destinations throughout Northern California. The full moon trips are particularly popular!

Kayaking Sites

With the Ocean and the Bay all around us, kayaking sites are abundant. For beginners, the sheltered bays and coves of San Francisco Bay are convenient starting points. The generally quiet waters of **Richardson Bay** between Sausalito and Tiburon and the **Oakland Estuary** both work well. Other typically calm areas include **Bolinas Lagoon** (near Stinson Beach in Marin) and **Tomales Bay** (by Point Reyes). Also look for kayaking operations on the **Russian, Gualala, Albion,** and **Big Rivers.** From these sites you can move on to more exposed parts of the bay and ocean. Yet don't overestimate your ability: the huge swells, ripping tidal currents, and huge ships all pose a formidable challenge. **Half Moon Bay** has a core group of enthusiasts. In **Santa Cruz**, the ocean is beautiful: blue, clear and almost warm. One of the most popular kayaking destinations, **Monterey Bay**, offers excellent opportunities to view the area's abundant wildlife.

Kayak Rentals and Instruction

Adventure Sports: 303 Potrero St., Santa Cruz, (408) 458-DO-IT. Rents kayaks, along with other water toys, and offers lessons for paddlers of all levels. Beginners are required to take an introductory class in basic paddling and safety before going out. • M-F 11am-7pm; Sa noon-6pm; Su noon-5pm. Rentals $25/day for experienced kayakers.

BlueWaters Ocean Kayak Tours: P.O. Box 1003, Fairfax, (415) 456-8956. BlueWaters specializes in tours and don't rent their boats for any other purpose, but their tours include trips throughout most of California and special moonlight paddles. • Hours vary. Tours $45-$65/day; discounts for groups of 6 or more.

Cal Adventures: Office located at 2301 Bancroft Ave., Berkeley, (510) 642-4000. Rowing center at South Basin of the Berkeley Marina. Cal Adventures offers instruction and equipment for reasonable prices, a variety of classes for all levels, and even off-site rentals. Introductory classes are offered almost every weekend and cover basic equipment, safety, paddling techniques, and rescues. • Call for class dates and times. Prices $5/students to $65/community. Reservations recommended.

California Canoe and Kayak: 409 Water St., Oakland, (510) 893-7833. Also provides instruction and equipment for reasonable prices, a variety of classes for all levels, and off-site rentals. Introductory classes are offered almost every weekend, which cover basic equipment, safety, paddling techniques, and rescues. Classes given on the Bay for all levels. Then take one of their guided group paddles, especially to Angel Island. $65 intro safety class required for renting. Reservations accepted. • M-Sa 10am-8pm; Su noon-6pm.

Gualala Kayak: 39175 Hwy 1, Suite E (behind Don Berard Associates, east side of Hwy 1), Gualala, (707) 884-4705. Located in the middle of Gualala, this outfit offers river or ocean kayaking with self-guided tours that include kayaks, paddles, and life vests. • Daily 8:30am-5:30pm. Rates $25/person and up; mid-week and group discounts available.

Monterey Bay Kayaks: 693 Del Monte Ave., Monterey, (800) 649-KELP. Offers excellent instruction and a full line of kayaks for rental or purchase. Classes are designed to elevate you beyond mere paddling to enjoying the water and wildlife. The company also organizes special outings—whale watches, trips to bird and wildlife sanctuaries, and camping trips. • M-F 10am-6pm; Sa-Su 8:30am-6pm. $25/day with 20 min. orientation. Reservations recommended on weekends.

Sea Trek Ocean Kayaking Center: Schoonmaker Point Marina, Sausalito, (415) 488-1000. Will qualify you to paddle at any kayaking location after a full day of lessons. They teach formal safety lessons on the quiet Richardson and Tomales Bays; from there you can move on to novice and expert daytime trips and night tours of the Bay on the full moon. • Hours vary. Full-day lessons $80; tour prices vary.

PARKS & OPEN SPACE

The Peninsula has some of the Bay Area's most extensive open space, offering a wide variety of terrain from deep redwood forests to sere, grassy slopes. To the west, you can enjoy beautiful coastline and beaches and redwood forests. To the east, abundant and exotic waterfowl live on the shores of the San Francisco Bay. Many parks are linked by connecting trails which allow visitors to explore miles of parkland without interruption. Area Parks fall roughly into four classes: City Parks, County Parks, Regional Open Space Preserves, and State Parks. Each government agency has its own rules and the different classes of parks have different levels of development—highest in State Parks and lowest in Regional Open Space Preserves.

The following information covers some of the major parks in the Peninsula area, but there are always more gems out there. For more information, you can contact any of the managing agencies or the **Trail Center** at 3921 E. Bayshore in Palo Alto, (415) 968-7065 (open M, Tu, Th, F 10:30am-2:30pm); they can tell you all about local trails and trail activities, and also sell you some excellent maps. Most of our daytrips and weekend getaways (see *Tahoe, Peninsula Coast,* etc. sections) include information on outdoor excursions beyond the immediate area. A final word of caution: poison oak grows abundantly in most of these parks. Learn to recognize it!

City Parks

In addition to the many local neighborhood parks (check the front of your yellow pages for more information), some cities maintain larger parklands with regional appeal. Please remember, Palo Alto's Foothills park is open only to Palo Alto residents and their guests.

Alum Rock: Alum Rock Ave. or Penitencia Creek Rd., San Jose (east of I-680), (408) 259-5477. Mineral springs, picnicking, hiking, biking, and horseback riding through dry ranchland all beckon park visitors to this 700-acre canyon east of San Jose.

Foothills Park: 3300 Page Mill Rd. (entrance between Altamonte and Moody Rds.), Palo Alto, (415) 329-2423. Located halfway up Page Mill Road, this 1,400-acre nature preserve is *open only to Palo Alto residents and their guests.* Nature trails, hiking, picnicking, fishing, playing fields, car camping, and an interpretive center make Foothills a popular spot. Day use fee is $3 per automobile, $1 per bicycle.

Hakone Gardens: 21000 Big Basin Way, Saratoga, (408) 867-3438. One of the Emperor's former gardeners built this city park in 1917 as an exact rendition of a Japanese Zen garden.

Palo Alto Baylands: Left at the east end of Embarcadero Rd., Palo Alto, (415) 329-2506. A beautiful spot for an easy walk or bicycle ride through 2,000 acres of salt marsh and sloughs. There is an astonishing variety of bird life here, and the sight of a great blue heron is impressive and far from rare. An interpretive center shows you what to look for.

Shoreline Park: 3070 N. Shoreline Blvd., Mountain View, (415) 903-6392. Small manmade park on a reclaimed landfill with Shoreline Amphitheatre, a golf course, a sailing lake, and many trails along the bay.

County Parks

Most County parks include picnic areas, bathrooms, a visitors center or park headquarters, comprehensive maps, the occasional playing field or playground, and readily-available rangers. **San Mateo County Parks and Recreation Department**, which covers the northern portion of the Peninsula and most of the coast north of Santa Cruz, can be reached at 590 Hamilton St., Redwood City, (415) 363-4020; reservations 363-4021; TDD 368-7807. **Santa Clara County Department of Parks and Recreation**, encompassing San Jose and the southern Peninsula, can be reached at 298 Garden Hills Dr., Los Gatos, (408) 358-3741; reservations (408) 358-3751.

Coyote Point County Recreational Area (San Mateo): Coyote Point Dr. from N. Bayshore Blvd., San Mateo, (415) 573-2592. A small, bayside park with swimming, trails, a marina, boat ramp, and nature museum. Parking fee is $4.

Huddart County Park (San Mateo): King's Mountain Rd. 2 mi. west of Hwy 84, Woodside, (415) 851-1210. Once the hub of an extensive logging operation, Huddart Park is now heavily forested with second-growth redwoods. Shady trails wind through steep redwood canyons, evergreen and oak forests, and flat chaparral and meadows. There are picnic grounds with barbecue pits, and a unique playground designed for the physically handicapped. Other attractions include hiking, equestrian trails, a whole-access trail, and hike-in group campsites. No dogs.

Memorial Park (San Mateo): Pescadero Rd., 6 mi. west of Alpine Rd., (415) 879-0212. Tiny Memorial Park is arguably one of the most beautiful of the inland coast-side parks. Particularly inviting is the swimming hole made from Pescadero Creek, which is kept stocked with trout during the spring and summer. Enjoy the hiking, biking, and equestrian trails, as well as picnicking and car camping areas and a nature museum.

Pescadero Creek County Park (San Mateo): Camp Pomponio Rd. off Alpine Rd. west of Skyline Dr. (trails connect with Memorial and Sam McDonald County Parks and Portola State Park), (415) 879-0212. By far the largest of this cluster of three county parks with 7,500 acres. The hillsides are quite steep and feature lush redwood groves and open ridgetops with views of the ocean. Bicycles are allowed on fire roads. Trail camping is first come, first served.

Sam McDonald County Park (San Mateo): Pescadero Rd., 3 mi. west of La Honda, (415) 879-0212. Sam McDonald borders **Heritage Grove**, a stately 27-acre stand of old-growth redwood, and offers hiking and camping (car and trail). This park offers hiking on 42 miles of trails, biking on some fire roads, picnicking, and camping. The **Sierra Club Hikers' Hut** is a great place for group overnights (book far in advance through the Sierra Club, 415-390-8411).

San Pedro Valley County Park (San Mateo): Linda Mar Blvd. east to Oddstad Blvd., Pacifica, (415) 355-8289. Small park in a deep canyon just inland from Pacifica. Informational visitors center and hiking, including whole-access trails. Fee $3 summer only.

Sanborn Skyline County Park (Santa Clara): Skyline Blvd. between Hwy 9 and Hwy 17, (408) 867-9959. Steep forested slopes set the background for hiking, biking, camping, an outdoor theater, and a youth hostel.

Stevens Creek County Park (Santa Clara): Stevens Canyon Rd., Cupertino, (408) 867-3654. Wooded canyons surrounding a reservoir offer good hiking, biking, horseback riding, and picnicking.

Upper Stevens Creek County Park (Santa Clara): Skyline Blvd., 1.5 mi. north of the Hwy 9 intersection, (408) 867-9959. Offers 1,200 otherwise undeveloped acres with trails descending from Skyline Boulevard into Stevens Canyon and adjoining Open Space Preserves. Trails are open for hiking, biking, and horseback riding.

Open Space Preserves

There is an extensive green belt stretching along Skyline Boulevard (Hwy 35) from Hwy 92 west of San Mateo to Los Gatos. Trails run through grassy plains and scrub oaks and descend to chaparral, pine and madrone forests, and redwood-filled canyons. Trail maps can be obtained at the **Midpeninsula Regional Open Space District Office** at 330 Distel Circle in Los Altos, (415) 691-1200 (open weekdays 8:30am-5pm). Or you can try **The Trail Center** in Palo Alto at 3921 E. Bayshore, (415) 968-7065 (open M, Tu, Th, F 10:30am-2:30pm). There are two classes of preserves. Group A Preserves have fully-developed parking areas, well-maintained trails, and good signs. Printed brochures and maps are available at the preserve entrance. Group B Preserves have little or no developed parking facilities and trails are limited; maps are available only from the District Office. Preserves are located outside of city limits, so park addresses do not include a city.

El Corte de Madera (B): Skyline Blvd. (4 mi. north of Hwy 84), parking at Skeggs Point Overlook. Boasts a massive sandstone outcropping (accessible only on foot) and the Methuselah Tree, one of the oldest redwoods in the area. Due to recent logging, many of the trails here are dead-ends, and signage is insufficient at best, so prepare for a potentially long and confusing—but definitely beautiful—outing.

Long Ridge (B): Skyline Blvd. (3 mi. north of the intersection of Hwy 9 and Skyline Dr.), parking on the east side of Skyline or the southeast corner of the intersection of Hwy 9 and Skyline. The rolling terrain along Skyline has a mix of oak, madrone, and fir, as well as grasslands with spectacular views of surrounding parklands. (And don't forget some of the best legal single-track mountain biking trails in the area.)

Los Trancos (A): Page Mill Rd., parking 1 mi. east of Skyline Blvd. on the north side of Page Mill. Small preserve with deep woods, rolling grasslands, and great views from San Francisco to Mt. Diablo. Enjoy the hiking and equestrian trails—the most famous is the San Andreas Fault Trail, which features a self-guided explanation of earthquakes.

Monte Bello (A): Page Mill Rd., parking 1 mi. east of Skyline Blvd. on the south side. The largest MROSD preserve can boast excellent views of Santa Clara Valley from Black Mountain, which at 2,800 feet is the highest peak on the mid-Peninsula. The sag ponds formed along the San Andreas fault by the 1906 earthquake are no less admirable. A sign in the Page Mill parking area will help you identify local summits, while a nature trail will help you identify natural inhabitants. Reservations required for the trail camp near Black Mountain.

Purisima Creek Redwoods (A): Skyline Dr., parking 4 mi. south of Hwy 92, parking for disabilities-access trail 6 mi. south of Hwy 92. (Alternate access from Hwy 1, one mile south of Half Moon Bay on Higgins-Purisima Rd.) Offers two magnificent redwood-filled canyons facing Half Moon Bay and a quarter-mile handicapped-access trail with restrooms and picnic tables.

Rancho San Antonio (A): Cristo Rey Dr. off Foothill Rd. (south of I-280), parking at Rancho San Antonio County Park. Accessible through Rancho San Antonio County Park, this preserve has excellent hiking trails up the foothills, with spectacular views of the Santa Clara Valley from the grassy plains at the summit. Bicycling is not permitted.

Skyline Ridge (B): Skyline Blvd. (just south of Alpine Rd.), parking less than 1 mi. south of Page Mill Rd. This park along Skyline features an interpretive center, wheelchair-accessible trails, excellent mountain biking trails, ponds, and a Christmas tree farm.

Windy Hill (A): Skyline Blvd., parking 2 mi. south of Hwy. 84 on the east side. The most prominent bald spot along Skyline Ridge, the grassy knolls atop this park feature spectacular views of both the ocean and the bay. Hike one of three trails down the steep hillside into the lush creekside valley above Portola Valley.

State Parks

State Parks are the most well-known, visited by tourists and locals alike, and provide all the amenities required by the RV set. Expect campsites, tour buses, well-maintained visitors centers, comprehensive maps, and guided tours. The agency responsible for these parks is the **California Department of Parks and Recreation**, P.O. Box 2390, Sacramento, 95811, (916) 653-6995. They also have local district offices: (415) 726-8800 and (408) 429-2850. Reservations for camping at these parks or for other restricted programs are generally handled by **Mistix**, (800) 444-7275 or (619) 452-1950. Trail camps are usually first come first served, otherwise reservations are made directly through the park.

Año Nuevo State Reserve: Hwy 1, 30 mi. south of Half Moon Bay, (415) 879-0227. Between December and March, Año Nuevo is the breeding ground for a large colony of northern elephant seals. Guided tours are necessary during these months: park officials don't want tourists wandering freely while bull elephant seals as large as mini-vans fight for territory. Walks last over two hours and cover three miles; tickets must be purchased in advance through Mistix. During the off-season, elephant seals are less numerous and more sedate, and the preserve provides excellent birdwatching, fishing, and surfing. Parking is $5.

Big Basin Redwoods State Park: Hwy 236 (runs right through the park), headquarters 9 mi. south of Boulder Creek, (408) 338-6132. Big Basin is California's first state park, now comprising 18,000 acres of magnificent old-growth redwoods. There is a hiking trail connecting Big Basin to Castle Rock State Park, 14 miles to the northeast, and another trail leading from the park headquarters down a rough but scenic drop to the ocean (together forming the Skyline to the Sea Trail). Another long hike leads to idyllic Berry Creek Falls. The park also offers camping (car and trail), a visitors center, and food service. Parking is $5.

Butano State Park: Cloverdale Rd., 3 mi. east of Hwy 1 and 5 mi. south of Pescadero, (415) 879-2040. Nearly 2,200 acres of steep coastal canyon with redwood forests, banana slugs, and chaparral ridges. Hiking here can be strenuous: the Año Nuevo trail (not for the weak of heart) leads to an overlook with a panoramic view of the ocean and Año Nuevo Island. The park offers camping (car and trail), picnicking, and hiking trails. Parking is $5.

Castle Rock State Park: Skyline Blvd., 2 mi. south of the intersection with Hwy 9, (408) 867-2952. Located on the crest of the Santa Cruz Mountains, Castle Rock boasts amazing sandstone formations popular with rock climbers, waterfalls, and canyons. It also has trail camping on a first come, first served basis. Day use fee runs $3 per vehicle.

Henry Coe State Park: Dunne Ave. east from Hwy 101 in Morgan Hill, (408) 779-2728. An enormous park of over 80,000 acres of great views over rugged ranchland in mountains east of Morgan Hill. The large size makes it good for mountain biking. The park has a friendly ranger station, a small museum, and first come, first served camping (car and trail). Day use fee is $5 per vehicle.

Portola State Park: Portola State Park Rd., off Alpine Rd. 3 mi. west of Skyline Dr., (415) 948-9098. Deep in the folds of the Santa Cruz mountains, wander among second-growth redwoods in this isolated park. Features include hiking, camping (car and trail), picnicking, a nature trail, museum, and visitors center. Parking is $5.

Hiking

Los Trancos Open Space Preserve: The parking lot and main entrance of the preserve are on the north side of Page Mill Road 7 mi. west of I-280. Grab a brochure at the parking lot and start on the San Andreas Fault Trail, which offers a self-guided tour of the fault zone. Follow the yellow markers and read up on plate movements. On your way back, turn right onto the Franciscan Loop Trail, which leads into a densely wooded hollow. Head left on the Lost Creek Loop to Los Trancos Creek and then reconnect with the Franciscan Loop Trail. Continue eastward, staying to the right will return you to the Fault Trail.

Pescadero Creek Park: The hiking trails in the Pescadero Creek area are almost matchless in their tranquillity. Take Hwy 84 west past La Honda, then follow Pescadero Road south, passing through Sam McDonald Park, until you reach Wurr Road, and go left. The Old Haul Road Trailhead is 0.3 miles down on the left. Because of the complexity of the trail network, hikers are strongly advised to pick up a map at the trailhead or at the ranger station, located just a little past Wurr Road on Pescadero Road. Begin by heading east on the Old Haul Road Trail, along a valley floor next to Pescadero Creek. To the right, Butano Ridge Trail makes a long, hard climb—about 1,400 feet—through redwoods to the top of a ridge. While you strain from the top to catch ocean views through the trees, don't forget to look down for banana slugs. At the ridgetop, turn left on the Butano Ridge Loop Trail and continue east parallel to the Old Haul Road, then turn left on the Butano Ridge Loop Trail to rejoin the Old Haul Road near the valley floor. Turn left and return to your starting point four miles).

Purisima Creek Redwoods O.S.P.: The preserve's 2,519 acres of forested canyons and ridges host a mere 13 miles of trails, making hiking here perhaps the closest thing in this area to experiencing the wilderness. The preserve is on the west side of Skyline Drive, less than half a mile north of Kings Mountain Road and Tunitas Creek Road. Purisima Creek Trail drops rapidly down from the ridge to wind westward along the banks of Purisima Creek. On your descent you'll pass lumberman's clearings now filled with lilacs and tan oak trees. When you reach the preserve's western entrance, turn right to take Harkins Trail up to chaparral-covered Harkins Ridge, then turn right on Soda Gulch Trail to return to Purisima. Turn left and climb back to your car. (10 miles round-trip)

Windy Hill Open Space Preserve: This loop hike provides a good walk through a variety of terrain, from shady woods to windy grasslands. Park in the Windy Hill parking lot on the east side of Skyline Drive, two miles south of Highway 84 and five miles north of Page Mill Road. Climb the Anniversary Trail to the very top of Windy Hill's bald knobs and admire the view of the entire Bay Area. Head northwest down to Spring Ridge Trail, then east down the grassy slope. At the bottom, turn right onto Eagle Trail and start back up the valley. Turn right on Hamm's Gulch Trail and climb up to Skyline under a leafy canopy of trees. At the fork near the top, turn right and follow the connector trail parallel to Skyline back to the parking lot. (8.5 miles)

Camping

The region's many parks offer a variety of camping opportunities, from drive-in areas with showers and flush toilets to backpacking camps with no facilities. Trail camps rarely have a water supply, so you'll have to pack in what you'll need. Campground policies and fees vary from park to park; call for up-to-date details. Many parks require reservations, especially for car camping during the summer. Trail camps are more frequently first come first served, and much less likely to fill up.

Big Basin Redwoods State Park: (408) 338-6132.

Butano State Park: (415) 875-0173.

Castle Rock State Park: (408) 867-2952.

Coyote Lake County Park: (408) 842-7800.

Foothills Park: (415) 329-2423.

Half Moon Bay State Beach: (415) 726-8820.

Henry Cowell Redwoods State Park: (408) 335-4598.

Henry W. Coe State Park: (408) 779-2728.

Joseph D. Grant County Park: (408) 274-6121.

Memorial County Park: (415) 879-0212.

New Brighton State Beach: (800) 475-4850.

Portola State Park: (415) 948-9098.

Sanborn-Skyline County Park: (408) 867-9959.

Seacliff State Beach: (800) 688-3222.

Sunset State Beach: (408) 724-1266.

Uvas Canyon County Park: (408) 779-9232.

RIVER RAFTING

The first questions of rafting are which rivers and which seasons to choose. All rivers are rated on an international scale of rafting difficulty from one to five (Class One means "barely moving" and the Class Five is for experts only). The rafting season as a whole extends from March or April until September or October, depending on snow melt and reservoir release. Trips can run from an afternoon to a month, and multiple-day trips often combine rafting with camping, hiking, or other wilderness activities. No matter what kind of trip you take, reservations should be made well in advance. In preparation, talk to your guide about what you'll need to pack.

Access to Adventure: (800) 441-9463. This outfit offers special theme tours, such as Western, Romance, and Polynesian Luau, as well as discounts on their runs through Northern and Central California. • $69-$320; group discounts available.

All Outdoors Whitewater Trips: 2151 San Miguel Dr., Walnut Creek, (510) 932-8993, (800) 247-2387. A large, interesting outfit with trips to the Grand Canyon, Oregon, and ten rivers in Northern California. Local trips combine bed-and-breakfast stays and wilderness camping with runs on the American, Stanislaus, Klamath, Merced, Toulumne, and Salmon Rivers. • $74-$1,785; group discounts available.

Beyond Limits Adventures: (800) 234-RAFT, (209) 869-6060. Beyond Limits runs tours in California's "Gold Country" on the American, Stanislaus, and Yuba Rivers. • $49-$296; group and midweek discounts available.

Cal Adventures: 3201 Bancroft Way, Berkeley, (510) 642-4000. Cal Adventures always has competitively priced trips, including a one-day trip to the South Fork of the American River. It can get overcrowded, but the well-trained guides will maneuver your boat through any sticky situation. • $76-$86; group discounts available.

Environmental Traveling Companions (ETC): Fort Mason Center, Bldg. C, San Francisco, (415) 474-7662. This fascinating all-volunteer operation organizes a variety of water adventures for people with disabilities (as well as the able-bodied), ages 12 and up. ETC will take you on trips all over Northern California as well as Colorado and Utah. • $45 and up; reservations required.

OARS: (800) 446-7238, (209) 736-4677. OARS is a well-reputed outfit with rafts on many rivers throughout the western United States, such as the Tuolumne, Merced, Kern, and Rogue Rivers. • $49-$2,250.

Tributary Whitewater Tours: (916) 346-6812. Rafts on most of the California rivers. They have a special Easter trip that covers most of the major Northern California waterways. Student and group discounts are available. • $60-$330.

Whitewater Connections: (800) 336-7238, (916) 622-6446. Unusual trips combining rafting with sailing, horseback riding, parasailing, and hot-air ballooning. They will arrange a charter bus for Bay Area groups. • $59-$449; group discounts available.

SAILING

Where to Sail

The Bay Area provides some of the best sailing in the world. The Bay's major **harbors— San Francisco, Sausalito, Alameda, Berkeley, Richmond**—provide the best access to the central part of the bay. Richmond has better access to San Pablo Bay, which is shallower and less windy. Alameda presents some challenges—including a lengthy estuary and a large wind hole just south of the Bay Bridge. South of the Bay Bridge, try **South Beach** (slightly south of the Bay Bridge), **Oyster Point** (South San Francisco), **Coyote Point** (San Mateo), and **Redwood City**. On the East Bay shore, check out the **Bollena Bay Harbor** just south of the Alameda Naval Air Station, and the **San Leandro Harbor** further to the south.

Some protected areas of the Bay and outlying lagoons are ideal for sailing smaller boats: **Shoreline, Parkside Aquatic,** and the **Leo Ryan Parks** on the Peninsula; **Berkeley Marina's South Sailing Basin;** and Oakland's **Lake Merritt.**

Bay Area **yacht clubs** are operated for the benefit of members and their guests. **Private sailing clubs** own boats which are available for charter, either skippered or bareboat. With a skippered charter, the charter company supplies both the skipper and boat. Experienced skippers can reserve a bareboat charter, which lets you control your own day on the bay. The least expensive charters are those which take place at regularly scheduled times and set their prices on a per-person basis. **Sailing schools** that aren't club-affiliated also provide a viable introduction to sailing, although they are typically reserved for small boats (ideal for learning the basics). One of the best ways to get plugged into the local sailing network is to pick up an edition of *Latitude 38* (415-383-8200).

Resources

U.S. Coast Guard NorCal Region: Yerba Buena Island, (415) 399-3400.

Note: Clubs and associations should be contacted before visiting in person. Most operate around the clock, with main business hours M-F 8am-6pm.

Universities

UC Berkeley's Cal Adventures: 2310 Bancroft Ave., Berkeley, (510) 642-4000. Their flexible and inexpensive programs are open to all, even non-students. Classes and rentals are available through the UC Aquatic Center (at the Berkeley Marina); the rental program is open to those who have completed their intermediate course or the equivalent. Sailing privileges are open to graduates of more advanced courses.

UC Santa Cruz: Office of Physical Education, Santa Cruz, (408) 459-2531. Similar to Cal Adventures, UC Santa Cruz also allows certified skippers to bring along guests for a small fee.

Private Sailing Clubs and Schools

Cass Charters and Sailing School: 1702 Bridgeway, Sausalito, (415) 332-6789. They offer lessons on 22- to 27-foot boats, and offer rentals on a range of sizes.

Chardonnay Charters: 400 Beach St., Santa Cruz, (408) 423-1213. They rent the Santa Cruz 70 and do not offer lessons.

Foster City Recreational Department: 650 Shell Blvd., Foster City, (415) 345-5731. The department holds small-boat sailing classes during the summer months. Classes are taught in the nicely landscaped Leo Ryan Park, although they are not offered as frequently as those run by outfits solely dedicated to sailing, and they do not provide a rental service.

Lake Merritt Sailboat House: 568 Bellevue St., Lakeside Park, Oakland, (510) 444-3807. Located on Lake Merritt in Oakland's Lakeside Park, this quaint setting seems totally removed from the nearby downtown. There's a year-round rental program for small boats.

Pacific Yachting: 333 Lake Ave., Santa Cruz, (408) 476-2370. This club has a fleet of 17 sailing yachts ranging from 26 to 43 feet that certified sailors can take out bareboat. (You can also rent skippered charters for any occasion.) The club offers various instruction programs that will take a non-experienced sailor through to certification. One of the most popular programs is the six-day live-aboard instructional vacation.

Spinnaker Sailing Mountain View: 3160 N. Shoreline Blvd., Shoreline Regional Park, Mountain View, (415) 965-7474. Spinnaker offers rentals, children's sailing camps, and small-boat courses at Shoreline Park in Mountain View.

Spinnaker Sailing Redwood City: One Uccelli Blvd., Pete's Harbor, Redwood City, (415) 363-1390. This is the place where Spinnaker teaches big-boat sailing courses and rents charters on the bay.

Spinnaker Sailing San Mateo: 1 Seal St., Parkside Aquatic Park, San Mateo, (415) 570-7331. In San Mateo, look for rentals, children's sailing camps, and small-boat courses at Parkside Aquatic Park.

UC Sailing Club: Berkeley Marina, (510) 642-4000. This organization is run by volunteers, so call for details. Their membership rates are excellent, they give lessons, and discounts are given to students.

Yacht Clubs

Berkeley Yacht Club: 1 Seawall Dr., Berkeley, (510) 540-9167, (510) 649-0216.

Coyote Point Yacht Club: Coyote Point Dr., San Mateo, (415) 347-6730.

Saint Francis Yacht Club: Marina Blvd., San Francisco, (415) 563-6363.

San Francisco Yacht Club: 98 Beach Rd., Belvedere, (415) 435-9133.

Santa Cruz Yacht Club: 244 Fourth Ave., Santa Cruz, (408) 425-0690.

Sequoia Yacht Club: 455 Seaport Ct., Redwood City, (415) 361-9472.

Equipment

North Sails: 2415 Mariner Sq., Alameda, (800) 626-9996. M-F 8am-6pm.

West Marine Products: 850 San Antonio Rd., Palo Alto, (415) 494-6660. M-Sa 9am-8pm, Su 9am-5pm • 2200 Livingston St., Oakland, (510) 532-5230. M-F 8am-7pm; Sa 8am-6pm; Su 8am-5pm • 295 Harbor Dr., Sausalito, (415) 332-0202. M-W, F 8am-7pm; Th 8am-8pm; Sa 9am-6pm; Su 9am-5pm • 2450 17th Ave., Santa Cruz, (408) 476-1800. M-W 9am-6pm; Th-F 9am-8pm; Sa 9am-6pm; Su 10am-5pm • 608 Dubuque Ave., South San Francisco, (415) 873-4044. M-W 9am-7pm; Th-F 9am-8pm; Sa 9am-6pm; Su 9am-5pm.

SCUBA DIVING

Some of the world's best diving can be found off the Northern California coast—the water, rich in nutrients carried by upwellings and currents, supports a wide variety of marine life. Our giant kelp forests are famous throughout the world, and there's even a good chance that a friendly seal might bump into you on your next dive.

General Information

Monterey Bay Harbormaster: (408) 646-3950.

Mistix State Park Reservation System: (800) 444-7275.

Where to Dive

Some of the best and most convenient dive sites are in Monterey, Pacific Grove, and Carmel. Don't forget to pick up a copy of *California Diver* at local dive shops.

Shore Diving

Point Lobos State Reserve, four miles south of Carmel on Hwy 1, is a great place to begin diving. The shore entry into **Whaler's Cove** is easy, and the cove itself has a nice kelp bed and wonderful trough covered with invertebrates. **Bluefish Cove** is right nearby, a very nice, deeper dive. Diving in the Reserve is limited, so reservations are recommended—call the Mistix State Park Reservation System. The cost is $3 per diver.

Another calm spot to dive in Monterey is the **Breakwater**, but it is often crowded. At its deepest, it descends to about 60 feet off the rock reef down to the sandy sea floor, and is teeming with life—sea lemons are a common sight. To get there, go to Foam Street at the start of Cannery Row. Parking is available at the dock and costs only $1. **Lover's Point** is one of the safest and easiest dives in the Monterey Bay Area, although no diving is allowed after 11:30am in the summer, making it a popular night diving spot. There are three places to enter from the beach, but Lover's Point Beach is the safest and easiest entry and exit.

Only those experienced with surf entries and exits should try **Monastery Beach**. There is a large kelp forest community at both ends of this reef, and a plenitude of wildlife, but absolutely don't dive if it's rough and choppy.

Boat Diving

If you can't find a protected entry and are tired of braving the surf and the surge, most of the area dive shops have boat trips or listings for companies operating in the area.

Wharf #2 and the **Eel Grass Bed** is an easy shallow dive at the north end of Figueroa Street. Access is by boat only and requires the permission of the Harbormaster. Be sure to check out the Eel Grass Beds, which are some 30 feet from the pilings.

Located between Pescadero Point and Cypress Point, **the Pinnacles** is a boat dive site regarded as one of the best in the area. On a sunny day, the combination of kelp and rocky pinnacles make the scenery quite dramatic. The area is part of the Carmel Bay Ecological Reserve, so no collecting or spear fishing is permitted.

Equipment and Lessons

Prices listed at end of each listing are for weekend scuba rental (all gear included).

Any Water Sports: 1130 Saratoga Ave., San Jose, (408) 244-4433. Offers certification classes that last from two to five weeks. M-F 10am-8pm; Sa 9am-5pm. $69.

Aquarius Dive Shop: 32 Cannery Row, The Breakwater, Monterey, (408) 375-6605. M, Th, F 9am-noon, 1pm-6pm; Sa-Su 7am-6pm • Rental: 2240 Del Monte Ave., Monterey, (408) 375-1933. M-F 9am-6pm; Sa-Su 7am-6pm. A good supply of rentals, though reservations are recommended for weekend use. They sponsor a chocolate abalone dive each March. $65.

Bamboo Reef: 614 Lighthouse Ave., Monterey, (408) 372-1685. • 584 Fourth St., San Francisco, (415) 362-6694. The oldest dive shop in northern California carries a complete spectrum of diving gear. They offer instruction certified by both NAUI and PADI, and continuing diving programs for advanced divers. • Monterey: M-F 9am-6pm; Sa-Su 8am-6pm. San Francisco: M-F 10am-7pm; Sa 10am-5pm. $61-$90.

Monterey Bay Wetsuits: 207 Hoffman Ave., Monterey, (408) 375-7848. Monterey Bay makes custom wet and drysuits for all water sports, and even does repairs and mending. They also sell "no-name" equipment manufactured by leading international brands at bargain prices. • M-F 10am-6pm; Sa 10am-5pm.

Scuba Discoveries: 965 Brewster Ave., Redwood City, (415) 369-DIVE. • 651 Howard St., San Francisco, (415) 777-DIVE. A PADI five-star Instructional Dive Center with classes ranging from entry-level to Instructor Level Certification. The center carries one of the broadest ranges of scuba equipment in the Bay Area, and also features well-maintained rental equipment and repair services. • M-F 10am-7pm; Sa 9am-5pm; Su noon-6pm. $55.

Wallin Dive Center: 517 E. Bayshore Rd., Redwood City, (415) 369-2131. A fairly large shop with a good equipment selection, regulator service, and bookings for trips in Monterey and more exotic locales. • M-F 10:30am-8pm; Sa 9:30am-5pm; Su 11am-5pm. $66.

Wet Pleasure: 2245 El Camino Real, Santa Clara, (408) 984-5819. The folks at Wet Pleasure can help you get PADI and NAUI certification or show you one of the largest lines of scuba gear in the area. Ask about their annual gear swap. • M-F 11am-8pm; Sa 11am-6pm. $69-$94.

WINDSURFING

Few areas in the United States have as many breezy days as the Bay Area, which provides ideal conditions for the avid windsurfers who regularly color our waters. (Not to mention the abundant launch spots, terrific views, and well-stocked windsurfing shops.) As a general rule, winds pick up in mid-to late-afternoon and die down as the sun starts to set. The summer season (May-July) sees the best wind. You'll need a wetsuit year-round in the Bay and the Pacific, as water temperatures are frequently low enough to induce hypothermia.

Places to Sail

Most of the beginner and intermediate spots listed will have good wind on clear days in the late spring and summer. On those days when San Francisco's famous fog just refuses to recede, you'll have better luck finding the breezes inland.

Beginning to Intermediate

Alameda's Crown Memorial State Beach: This sheltered location with side-onshore winds that push you back to shore has an easy launch that leads directly to the sandy-bottomed sailing site—a great place to practice waterstarts. From I-880 exit west on High St. Take a right on Hwy 61, then a left on Shoreline Dr., which turns into Westline Dr. Crown Beach is on the left side of the road.

Lake Del Valle State Park (Livermore): A beginner's paradise with rentals, lessons, and facilities on-site. Take I-580 east to Livermore Avenue, which turns into Tesla Road. Go right at Mines Rd. and follow the signs.

Intermediate to Advanced

Berkeley Marina: A tricky launch from the sheltered pier at the Marina leads to the main sailing area. Full facilities and plenty of parking can be found at the west end of University Ave. in Berkeley, with on-site lessons and rentals by **Cal Adventures**. Launch from the piers adjacent to the Cal Adventures yard (follow the signs).

Candlestick Point: The flat-water speed sailing conditions here are ideal for learning and refining jibing technique, although the gusty winds that tend to blow side-offshore can be hazardous. Take Candlestick Park exit off Hwy 101 and stay right until you see the entrance. The sailing area is at the end of the parking lot.

Coyote Point Regional Park: Some of the most consistent winds in the bay, with conditions that vary from moderate winds and flat water near shore to powerful wind-driven chop further out. Excellent facilities with a $4 per car entry fee. Hwy 101 to the Dore Ave. exit., left at off-ramp and follow signs to entrance.

Crissy Field: Expect to contend with frigid waters, strong tides, howling winds, and immense ships. This is a thrilling spot to sail with large swells and amazing views of the city, the Marin headlands, and the Golden Gate Bridge. Enter the Presidio in San Francisco from Marina Blvd. across from the St. Francis Yacht Club and continue straight. Once inside the gate, take the first street to your right and follow it to the beach.

Rio Vista/Windy Cove: This warm-weather, fresh-water sailing spot gets crowded at early morning. The best winds blow from dawn to 10am, and again in the late afternoon. Take I-580 east to Hwy 24 east through the Caldecott Tunnel. Then to I-680 north, to Hwy 242 west, to Hwy 4 west toward Antioch/Stockton. Cross the Antioch toll bridge and continue until the next bridge (Brannan Isld. State Bridge). Windy Cove is located just across this second bridge on the left side of the road.

San Luis Reservoir: Expect extreme (15 to 40 knots) winds from 5am to 10am at this popular freshwater site. The reservoir is approximately 20 mi. east of the Hwy 101/152 interchange in Gilroy; just follow the signs.

Waddell Creek State Park: Check out one of Northern California's most celebrated wavesailing playgrounds. Only advanced sailors should try, and even they pay an admission fee from Memorial Day through Labor Day. Located about 45 min. south of Half Moon Bay on Hwy 1; watch for the signs.

Lessons and Retail Shops

ASD: 302 Lang Rd., Burlingame, (415) 348-8485. Caters to the high-end sailor with custom board manufacturing and repairs.

Cal Adventures: 2301 Bancroft Way, Berkeley, (510) 642-4000. One of the best buys in the area, Cal Adventures is located on campus but opens all courses to the public at low prices. After completing a beginners' course, students are eligible to buy a two-month, $80 pass that provides unlimited use of all equipment during recreational hours.

City Front Sailboards: 2936 Lyon St., San Francisco, (415) 929-7873. A small but well-stocked shop with custom and retail equipment.

Delta Windsurf Company: 3729 Sherman Island Rd., Rio Vista, (916) 777-2299. A great retail store and launch site on the shore of one of Rio Vista's most popular sailing spots.

Helm Ski & Windsurf: 333 N. Amphlett Blvd., San Mateo, (415) 344-2711. A full-service shop that hosts swap meets in the summer.

San Francisco School of Windsurfing: Lake Merced (off of 19th Ave.), San Francisco (beginner and intermediate); or Candlestick Park (advanced), (415) 750-0412 office, (415) 753-3235 dock. A complete range of lessons are available, as well as demo days and windsurfing camps. Completion of the basic course earns you WIA beginner's certification.

Spinnaker Sailing: Shoreline Lake, Shoreline Park, Mountain View, (415) 965-7474 • Pete's Harbor, Redwood City, (415) 363-1390 • Parkside Aquatic Center, San Mateo, (415) 570-7331. Complete WIA certification facilities with a great rental program, beginning through advanced lessons, and instructor-certification courses. If you don't pass the test after the first course, you may repeat it until you do.

Windcraft Sailboard Center & Academy: 17124 Sherman Island Rd., Rio Vista, (916) 777-7067. A full-service shop with a windsurfing academy that holds beginner's classes at Rancho Seco Lake and intermediate to advanced lessons on the windy delta waters.

Windsurf Bicycle Warehouse: 428 S. Airport Blvd., S. San Francisco, (415) 588-1714, (800) 878-SURF. Production and hybrid equipment, high-end hardware, and an attentive staff.

Windsurf Del Valle: 391 Livermore Ave., Livermore, (510) 455-4008. Beginning and intermediate sailors are taught in lessons geared to new participants of the sport.

MARIN

Marin County is just north of San Francisco, extending from the Golden Gate Bridge up the coast to Bodega Bay and inland to the wine country. With the most hot tubs per-capita in the U.S., one of the highest per-capita income levels, and notable residents like the Grateful Dead and LucasFilms Productions, Marin has earned a reputation for being quintessentially Californian. It is also home to some of the most stunning scenery in the Bay Area. With such abundant open space and natural beauty, outdoor activities dominate the list of things to do in Marin.

General Information

Area Code: 415

Golden Gate National Recreation Area: National Park Service, Building 201, Fort Mason, San Francisco, 556-0560. M-F 9:30am-4:30pm.

Marin County Visitors Bureau: 30 N. San Pedro Rd. #150, San Rafael, 472-7470. M-F 8:30am-5pm.

Marin State Parks District Office: 1455A East Francisco Blvd., San Rafael, 456-1286. M-F 8am-5pm. **Samuel Taylor State Park:** Sir Francis Drake Blvd., Lagunitas, 488-9897. Su-Th 8am-8:30pm; F, Sa 8am-10pm.

Mill Valley Chamber of Commerce: 85 Throckmorton Ave., Mill Valley, 388-9700. M-F 11am-4pm.

Sausalito Chamber of Commerce: 333 Caledonia St., Sausalito, 332-0505. M-F 9am-5pm.

Getting There

Take I-280 north until it becomes 19th Avenue, and follow 19th Avenue through the western side of San Francisco, Golden Gate Park, and the Presidio to the Golden Gate Bridge. You can also take Hwy 101 to San Francisco and exit at Van Ness Avenue. Follow Van Ness to Lombard Street, take a left and follow signs to the Golden Gate bridge.

To get to Marin from San Francisco, you can take the ferry (see below) or jump on a bus. Bus service from San Francisco to Marin is provided by Golden Gate Transit. The schedules are geared to suit commuters' needs, and serve most Marin cities and towns, and even some beaches. San Francisco has a city bus, the #76, which goes to the Marin Headlands on Sundays.

Ferries

Golden Gate Transit: Embarcadero Ferry Building, 332-6600, 453-2100. Ferries leave from the Ferry Building on the Embarcadero at the foot of Market Street, and go to Sausalito ($4.25 o/w) and Larkspur ($2.50 M-F, $4.25 Sa-Su). Commuter-oriented, running most frequently M-F during rush hour.

Red and White Fleet: Pier 43 1/2, Fisherman's Wharf, 546-2896. Tourist-oriented ferries from Pier 43 1/2 on Fisherman's Wharf to Sausalito ($5.50 o/w), Tiburon ($5.50 o/w), and Angel Island ($9 r/t). Commuter-oriented ferries from Ferry Building at Embarcadero to Tiburon M-F ($5.50 o/w). Also serves Alcatraz Island.

Tiburon-Angel Island Ferry: 21 Main St., Tiburon, 388-6770, 435-2131. Family-run ferry. In addition to Tiburon-Angel Island route, offers sunset cruises, charters, and other special trips. Round-trip tickets: adults $5, children ages 5-11 $3, bikes $1.

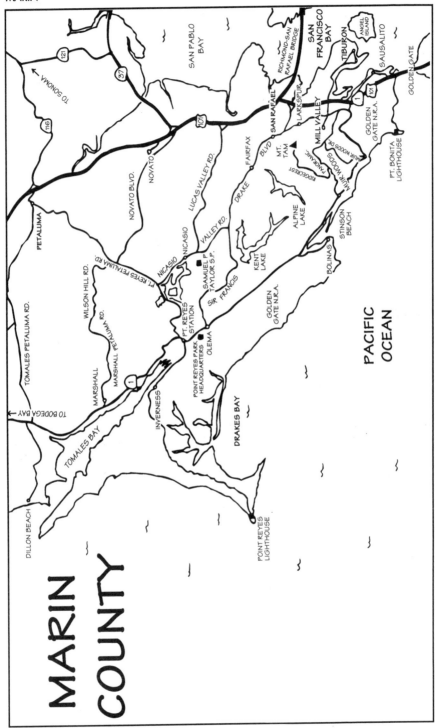

MARIN COUNTY

MARIN HEADLANDS

Encompassing most of the hills and valleys inland from the Pacific Coast north of the bridge, the **Marin Headlands'** grassy hills offer amazing views, while the valleys are filled with wildflowers and wildlife.The Headlands are a war legacy, home to military installations active through WWII—battlements and bunkers still dot the hilltops.

Take Hwy 101 to Alexander Avenue, the first exit north of the Golden Gate bridge.Go left under the highway and follow Conzelman Road up the hill. Bear left at the Y-intersection and continue to the top and **Battery 129**, a typical military relic. Hike up to the top of **HawkHill** for great views, but if it's a sunny weekend, expect a crowd. Halfway up Conzelman Road, a dirt road on the left leads hikers and bikers down to **Kirby Cove**—a secluded beach almost under the bridge. **The Park Service** (556-0560) allows group camping here.

Continue west down the other side of Hawk Hill to **Point Bonita**. The still-functioning **Point Bonita Lighthouse** was one of the first to be built on the West Coast. The footpath leading to the lighthouse was washed out during the 1993 rainy season; call the Park Service for current information.

After visiting Point Bonita, go to the nearby **Marin Headlands Visitors Center** (331-1540). Newly renovated, it houses engaging hands-on exhibits in the historic Fort Barry Chapel. **Rodeo Lagoon** and **Rodeo Beach** are nearby, as is the **Marine Mammal Center** (289-SEAL), a hospital for marine critters that allows visits from the public.

SAUSALITO

Sausalito lies across Hwy 101 from the Headlands. Originally a fishing village and then an artists' retreat, Sausalito is now a typical tourist town. Located on the edge of the Bay, it has a marina and a main commercial street lined with a variety of cafés, waterfront restaurants, galleries, and T-shirt shops. Ferry service from S.F. makes it particularly convenient for tired bikers looking for a shortcut back to the City.

Take Hwy 101 to Alexander Avenue and follow it into town. Downtown offers shops and a boardwalk. On the water a little north of town sits a fascinating collection of **houseboats**, more house than boat (locals call them floating homes). Nearby at 2100 Bridgeway, there's the **San Francisco Bay Model** (332-3870), a working facsimile built by the Army Corps of Engineers to study the Bay's features. You can rent mountain bikes at **Wheel Escapes'** (332-0417) behind the wharf at 30 Liberty Ship Way, and head along the shore of the Bay or into the hills above.

Nearby, at 85 Liberty Ship Way, **Sea Trek Adventures** (488-1000) launches ocean kayaks for tours of Sausalito Harbor and beyond. Their Full Moon Tour is a favorite. In the same building, **Open Water Rowing** (332-1091) offers lessons to all, and equipment rentals for the experienced. If you prefer sailing, try **Cass' Rental Marina** at 1702 Bridgeway (332-6789). For more information, see the *Sailing and Kayaking* sections.

Restaurants and Entertainment

Angelino's $$$: 621 Bridgeway, 331-5225. Down-to-earth Italian fare. Specialties include fresh seafood and pasta. Lunch and dinner daily. Reservations advised on weekends.

Bar (with no name) $: 757 Bridgeway, 332-1392. Popular local spot for drinks, sandwiches, and live music. Pleasant covered patio out back. There is no sign, as the name, or lack thereof, implies. Daily 10am-2am. Cash only.

Caffé Trieste $: 1000 Bridgeway, 332-7770. Decent pizza and pasta; fantastic cappuccino and cheesecake. Daily 7am-1am.

Casa Madrona $$$/$$$$: 801 Bridgeway, 331-5888. California/French cuisine served on an outdoor patio or in a romantic dining room. Spectacular views. Lunch M-Sa, dinner daily, Su brunch.

Cat n' Fiddle $$: 681 Bridgeway, 332-4912. Simple lunches and dinners, and great views of the bay. Lunch and dinner daily.

Chart House $$$: 201 Bridgeway, 332-0804. Pleasant outpost of the upscale surf and turf chain. Dinner daily.

Fred's Coffee Shop $: 1917 Bridgeway, 332-4575. Simple breakfasts and diner-style lunches enjoyed by locals and tourists alike. Breakfast and lunch daily.

Gatsby's $: 39 Caledonia St., 332-4500. No mint juleps here, Daisy. Just good pizza (and whole-wheat crust for the health-conscious). Lunch F-Su, dinner daily.

TIBURON

Spanish for "shark," Tiburon lies on a fin-shaped peninsula north of Sausalito. There isn't much in the way of tourist attractions; most people go to eat at one of the restaurants with a view of the bay and San Francisco. A small waterfront park has great views of S.F. and soft grass for picnics. The stores and galleries on **Ark Row** at the west end of Main Street will happily deplete your savings. **Windsor Vineyards** (800-214-9463) has a tasting room and sales outlet at 72 Main Street, where Rodney Strong began making wine in his basement.

Take Hwy 101 to Tiburon Boulevard east. A small pay-parking lot at the very end of the road is the best place to ditch your car. If you bike from S.F., you can follow a lovely bike path, which begins along Bridgeway in Sausalito and goes north along the bay to Tiburon Boulevard. A right turn leads you to town. There is also ferry service from San Francisco (see *Ferries* section above).

Restaurants and Entertainment

Il Fornaio $: 1 Main St., 435-0777. Indulge in their famous baked goods and panini in their corner cafe, or eat them on the lawn outside. M-F 6am-10pm; Sa 7am-10pm; Su 7am-8pm.

Guaymas $$/$$$: 5 Main St., 435-6300. Serves up good (though pricey), fresh Mexican grill food. Excellent views from its patio. Get anything with shrimp. Lunch and dinner daily.

New Morning Café $: 1696 Tiburon Blvd., 435-4315. Healthy fare of sandwiches and salads. M-F 7am-2:30pm; Sa-Su 7am-4pm.

Sam's Anchor Café $$/$$$: 27 Main St., 435-4527. Has a huge waterfront deck where the Corona Beer crowd comes to hang out and scarf burgers, fries, and deep-fried seafood; its location also makes it a popular place for yachters to dock for snacks. At night, the seafood menu gets more serious. Lunch and dinner daily, brunch Sa-Su till 3pm.

Sweden House Bakery $: 35 Main St., 435-9767. Delicious, authentic, and pricey Swedish baked goods, plus more substantial breakfasts and sandwiches. M-F 8am-5pm; Sa-Su 8am-6pm, later in summer.

ANGEL ISLAND

Angel Island, the largest island in the San Francisco Bay, sits in the bay across from Tiburon. The **Visitor's Center** (435-1915) has historical displays documenting the military use of the island from the Civil War to its days as a Japanese internment camp in WWII. Today, Angel Island is best known for its hiking and biking. **Mt. Hamilton** rises 800 feet, and offers excellent views of the area from a number of trails. The island is a great spot for a picnic away from the crowds. Other than the new **Cove Cafe**, there are few amenities available, so bring your own supplies. The Red and White Fleet ferries service Angel Island from San Francisco; the Tiburon-Angel Island Ferry, from Tiburon. See *Ferry* information above.

LARKSPUR

Larkspur, a bucolic town nestled at the eastern base of Mt. Tam, was once a wild summer playground for city-weary San Franciscans. Turn-of-the-century visitors flocked to Larkspur's Rosebowl dances, saloons, prizefights, and bowling alleys. Their "summer shacks" eventually became year-round residences. Today, Larkspur is known for its historic architecture and impressive array of eateries.

From Hwy 101, take Paradise Drive/Tiburon Boulevard west, then take a right onto Magnolia Avenue and continue into the heart of Larkspur. (Warning: the ferry docks at Larkspur Landing, a large, colonial style shopping center which is different than Larkspur.) Bike rentals are available at **Wheel Escapes** (332-0218), at 1000 Magnolia Avenue.

Restaurants and Entertainment

Fabrizio's $$$: 455 Magnolia Ave., 924-3332. Well-done, classic Italian fare in a simple, bright space. Lunch and dinner daily.

Java $: 320 Magnolia Ave., 927-1501. A hip new coffeehouse and restaurant in an old brick depot. Offerings include salads, light entrees from quesadillas to lasagna, and occasional live music. M-Th 8am-10pm; F-Sa 8am-11pm; Su 8am-8pm.

Lark Creek Inn $$$$: 234 Magnolia Ave., 924-7766. Serves fabulous, innovative California cuisine with views of the surrounding redwoods. (Despite the name, Lark Creek Inn has no accommodations.) Lunch M-F, dinner daily, Su brunch. Reservations usually required.

Marin Brew Company $$: 1809 Larkspur Landing Cir., Larkspur Landing, 461-4677. Large, immensely successful brewpub offering high-quality microbrew and an eclectic menu ranging from wood-fired pizza to oriental salads to pub-grub. Huge hall with large patio and dart lanes. Lunch and dinner daily.

Pasticceria Rulli $: 464 Magnolia Ave., 924-7478. Cappuccino, gelato, panini, and gourmet Northern Italian pastries in a cozy parlor. Su-M 8am-6pm, Tu-Th 7:30am-10pm; F- Sa 7:30am-11pm.

MILL VALLEY AND MT. TAMALPAIS

Mill Valley, once home to the mill that processed the huge trees used to build San Francisco, is now quintessentially Marin: a hip bedroom community with cute cottage houses, good food, coffee, lots happening in the arts, and the world's first Gap store. Each autumn the **Mill Valley Film Festival** (383-5256) brings the town to life. Mill Valley is also a convenient base of operations for expeditions to Mt. Tam, which rises to the west.

Mt. Tam (2,600 feet) dominates the landscape and offers spectacular views of the Bay Area plus an enormous trail system. Within its vast expanse lie **Mt. Tamalpais State Park** (388-2070), **Muir Woods National Monument** (see below), and the **Marin Municipal Water District** (924-4600, or 459-5267). The diverse terrain includes redwoods, oak, and grassland.

Take Highway 101 to Tiburon Boulevard/East Blithedale exit and go west, following the signs to downtown Mill Valley. A quick way to sample Mt. Tam is to drive to the top. Take Hwy 101 to Hwy 1. Bear right on Panoramic Highway following signs to Mt. Tam and Muir Woods. At Pantoll Road, turn right and wind your way to the top. From the parking lot, walk up a short, steep dirt road for the ultimate view.

The extensive trail network on all sides of the mountain offers endless possibilities for exploring and lets you approach from any angle. Limited camping is also available. Bikes can be rented in San Anselmo at **Caesar's Cyclery**, 29 San Anselmo Avenue (258-9920). The Olmstead Bros. map *Trails of Mt. Tamalpais and the Marin Headlands* is an excellent map available in most bike and bookstores.

Close to the summit you will find the **Sydney B. Cushing Memorial Theater**, a 5,000-seat outdoor amphitheater which hosts excellent musical productions by the **Mountain Play Association** (383-1100) on the last two Sundays of May and the first four Sundays in June. Advance ticket purchases are usually necessary.

Restaurants and Entertainment

Avalon $$$: 639 E. Blithedale Ave., 381-6284. A fresh new import from Lahaina, Maui, serving wildly creative concoctions based on Hawaiian and Asian ingredients. Big, breezy restaurant with a patio. Lunch M-Sa, dinner daily.

Avenue Grill $$$: 44 E. Blithedale Ave, 388-6003. Upscale American food. Dinner daily.

Buckeye Roadhouse $$$/$$$$: 15 Shoreline Hwy., 331-2600. Belongs to the same people who own the Fog City Diner in San Francisco, and serves the same expensive "new American" cuisine—although not quite as good—in an old hunting lodge. Lunch and dinner daily, Su brunch.

Cactus Café $$: 393 Miller Ave., 388-8226. Highly-rated, inexpensive Mexican food goes beyond basics with green chile polenta and posole. Simple, diner-like setting. Lunch and dinner daily.

Cantina $$: 651 E. Blithedale Ave., 381-1070. The Cantina chain of Mexican restaurants originated here, and boasts potent margaritas and live mariachi bands; one violinist is the father of rock guitarist Carlos Santana. Lunch and dinner daily.

Depot Bookstore and Café $: 87 Throckmorton Ave., 383-2665. Tiny cafe in a charming old train station in center of town; local slackers play hackey-sack out front. Some locals feel success has led to high prices and negligent service. Daily 7am-10pm; food till 8:30pm.

Dipsea Café $: 200 Shoreline Hwy., 381-0298. Home-cooked brunches, salads, and sandwiches in country cottage hall. Breakfast and lunch daily.

Jennie Low's Chinese Cuisine $$: 38 Miller Ave., 388-8868. Watch your upscale Chinese food being prepared through a window on the kitchen while Jennie herself works the crowd. Lunch M-Sa, dinner daily.

Mill Valley Coffee Roastery $: 2 Miller Ave., 383-2912. Friendly local hangout for cappuccino and pastries. M-Th 7am-9pm; F 7am-10pm; Sa 8am-10pm; Su 8am-9pm.

Mountain Home Inn $$$: 810 Panoramic Hwy., above Mill Valley, 381-9000. On the slopes of Mt. Tam, the rustic Mountain Home Inn feeds hungry hikers and tourists great breakfasts on the weekends and dinners all week. Enjoy the view from their outdoor deck during the day and their cozy fireplace at night. You pay for the wonderful atmosphere, but the food is quite good. Lunch and dinner daily, breakfast and Sa, Su brunch. (Closed Mondays during winter).

Perry's Deli $: 246 E. Blithedale Ave., 381-0407. Great place for picnic supplies. M-F 7am-7pm; Sa 9am-7pm; Su 10am-5pm.

Phyllis' Giant Burgers $: 72 E. Blithedale Ave., 381-5116. The name says it all. Daily 11am-9pm.

Sweetwater: 153 Throckmorton Ave., 388-2820. A small saloon which hosts excellent live music, ranging from jazz to folk to Cajun. National acts, with prices to match. Daily 12:30pm-1am.

MUIR WOODS

One of the only places you can find old-growth, coastal redwoods in Northern California, Muir Woods is the forest primeval. The towering, thousand-year-old trees block out most of the sunlight, leaving the narrow valley lush and tranquil. **The Visitors' Center** (388-2595) is open daily 8am-sunset.

Take Hwy 101 to Hwy 1. Bear right on Panoramic Highway, then turn left down Muir Woods Road. The park is about a mile down the road on your right.

Muir Woods attracts a well-deserved crowd; you can avoid the throngs somewhat by going during the week or in the winter, when the creeks are filled with water. A short loop winds its way along a stream bed among towering redwoods; this walk of less than an hour is what most visitors choose to explore. Even on weekends, you can find solitude by taking the steeper trails away from the valley floor.

MUIR BEACH AND STINSON BEACH

These two very different beaches west of Mt. Tam are part of the Golden Gate National Recreation Area. **Muir Beach** is located in an isolated, semi-circular cove cut into the cliffs, with horse ranches and rugged hills in the background.

Stinson Beach is a very happening place; a wide spit of sand perfect for running, Frisbee, or sand castles. The parking lot has sheltered picnic spots, and a small settlement at the entrance includes shops and restaurants where you can fill out your picnic, rent a surfboard, or pop down oysters and beers under an umbrella. **Off the Beach Boats** (868-9445) rents open-top kayaks for experts to use in the surf and the rest of us to use in Bolinas Lagoon; rates are about $20 for 2 hours, $35 all day. Be forewarned—Stinson Beach has a huge following. On hot weekends, traffic gets backed up for miles. You can avoid the crowds and find parking if you go early.

Both beaches can be reached by getting off Hwy 101 at Hwy 1 and following the signs. After six miles on Hwy 1 you will see the **Pelican Inn**. To reach Muir Beach turn left. To reach Stinson Beach, continue straight past the Pelican Inn for six miles and follow the signs to the left.

Restaurants and Entertainment

Parkside Cafe and Snack Bar $$: 39 Arenal Ave., 868-1272. Basic but fresh breakfasts and lunches, with inexpensive family Italian and seafood dinners. Close to the beach. Large patio. Breakfast and lunch daily, dinner Th-M.

Pelican Inn $$$: Hwy 1 at Muir Beach, 383-6000. A rambling Tudor-style B&B with an authentic British pub and rather formal dining room. Stop for a pint and some darts on your way back from the beach. Lunch and dinner Tu-Su, Su lunch buffet.

Sand Dollar $$/$$$: 3466 Hwy 1, 868-0434. All-American beach restaurant with sandwiches, burgers, seafood, and pasta. Cozy bar inside is local hangout, while patio can be a scene. Lunch and dinner daily, Su brunch.

Stinson Beach Grill $$/$$$: Hwy 1, 868-2002. Burgers, seafood, Southwest, and Italian cuisine in a beach house with a big deck. Lunch and dinner daily, Su brunch.

POINT REYES NATIONAL SEASHORE

At the northern edge of Marin lies Point Reyes National Seashore, a spectacular park ideal for hiking, camping, and beachcombing. The 75,000-acre expanse contains numerous well-marked trails through forest and coastal territory, while the ten-mile stretch of beach is full of caves, cliffs, waterfalls, and windy headlands.

To get there, take Hwy 101 to Sir Francis Drake Blvd. to Hwy 1, turn right and then immediately left and follow the signs to the Park Headquarters. Information is available at the **Bear Valley Visitors Center** (663-1092). If you want to bike in Point Reyes, you can rent mountain bikes at **Trailhead Rentals** in Olema, 88 Bear Valley Rd, (663-1958). Bike rentals are $6/hr or $20/day M-F; $24/day Sa-Su. Call ahead for reservations and information. In addition to bikes, they also rent tents, cameras, and binoculars.

The **Visitors' Center** is a good place to begin your visit by picking up maps or walking through the exhibits on park wildlife. Nearby is the **Earthquake Trail**, a **Miwok Village** re-creation, and **Morgan Horse Ranch**. The **Bear Valley Trail** is a popular trail that leads hikers through four fairly flat miles to Arch Rock. From Arch Rock you can enjoy the beautiful view of the ocean, or take the lower trail to the beach and walk through Miller Cave if it's low tide. For a strenuous 3-mile hike, take Bear Valley Trail to the Sky Trail which ascends Mt. Wittenberg, the highest point in Point Reyes. From there, you can continue down to the coast; then return either via the same route, or, to avoid Mt. Wittenberg, along the beach to Arch Rock and back.

Point Reyes lighthouse sits at the very tip of the Point Reyes peninsula. It's the perfect spot for watching California gray whales during their bi-annual migrations. Late November through early January is best for sighting whales cruising south, while March and April are best for spotting them moving north. The lighthouse, located down a long set of stairs on a steep cliff, is open Th-M 10am-4:30pm; it is closed when the wind is too strong. The weather can be cold, foggy and extremely windy, but when it is clear the views are spectacular. To reach Point Reyes Lighthouse take Sir Frances Drake Boulevard to the end.

Drake's Bay Beach (watch for the left turn off Sir Francis Drake a few miles before the lighthouse) is located on the south side of the Point Reyes peninsula; the beach is backed by towering cream-colored cliffs. Along the way to the peninsula, you'll pass through the sleepy town of **Inverness**, which has bed-and-breakfasts, restaurants, and a grocery store. Alongside is Tomales Bay—calm, flat, and undeveloped.

Restaurants

Bovine Bakery $: 11315 Hwy 1, Pt. Reyes Station, 663-9420. Pastries, scones, muffins, cookies, and other desserts. M-F 6:30am-5pm; Sa-Su 8am-5pm.

The Cheese Factory$: Petaluma-Pt. Reyes Rd., Petaluma,(707)762-6001. They make the Rouge et Noir brand of Camembert, Schloss, and Brie cheeses, sold along with other picnic foods. The factory and farm is set on a bucolic picnic area situated around a pond. Daily 9am-5pm; tours 10am-4pm.

Drake's Bay Beach Café $/$$: Drake's Bay Beach, Pt. Reyes, 669-1297. Warm and cozy, serving fried, barbecued, and stewed Johnson's oysters, along with more typical seaside café favorites. Daily 10am-6pm.

Gray Whale Pub & Pizzeria $: 12781 Sir Francis Drake Blvd., Inverness, 669-1244. Pizza, beer, coffee drinks, and a variety of cakes, pies, and pastries. M-F 11am-9pm; Sa, Su 10am-9pm.

Johnson's Drake Bay Oysters $: 17171 Sir Francis Drake Blvd., Inverness, 669-1149. Six miles past Inverness on the way to the lighthouse. You can see how these delicacies are cultivated, then buy some to take home. Shucked oysters are sold by the pint or the quart; oysters in the shell go by the dozen or the thousand. Tu-Su 8am-4pm.

Knave of Hearts $: 12301 Sir Francis Drake Blvd., Inverness Park, 663-1236. Budget-priced meals and baked goods. Tu-Su 8am-5pm.

Manka's $$$$: Corner of Callendar and Argyle Rds., Inverness, 669-1034. California wild-game menu that draws rave reviews. The building is an old hunting lodge that captures the feel with roaring fires, open grill cooking, over-stuffed chairs, and board games from another era. Dinner M-Th.

Olema Inn $$$: Corner of Sir Francis Drake Blvd. and Hwy 1 in Olema, 663-9559. Romantic diners will appreciate the intimate lunch and dinner atmosphere. Pretty good seafood, pasta, and salads. Lunch and dinner daily, Su brunch. Reservations required on weekends.

Palace Market $: Main St. in Pt. Reyes Station (next to Bank of America), 663-1016. Features a wide selection of fresh breads and cheeses, as well as soups, sandwiches, and salads to go. Su-Th 8am-8pm; F-Sa 8am-9pm.

Point Reyes Station Café $$/$$$: 11180 Hwy 1, Pt. Reyes Station, 663-1515. Warm and homey, a favorite for wholesome preparations featuring local ingredients—especially fresh seafood and delicious brunch. Breakfast, lunch, and dinner daily. Reservations suggested on weekends.

Taqueria La Quita $: Third St. and Shoreline Hwy, Point Reyes Station, 663-8868. Budget-priced burrito shop. W-M 11am-9pm.

Tony's $: Hwy 1, Marshall, 663-1107. A down-home place to slurp oysters (raw, barbecued, or fried). F-Su noon-8pm. Cash only.

Vladimir's $$$$: Sir Francis Drake Hwy, Inverness, 669-1021. Features Czech dishes and maintains a loyal following. Lunch and dinner Tu-Su.

Places to Stay

Camping

Camping is available on most of the public lands in Marin, including Point Reyes, the Marin Headlands, Angel Island State Park, and Samuel Taylor State Park. Many of the sites are walk-in, and most require reservations. **Marin State Parks District Office:** 1455A East Francisco Blvd., San Rafael, 456-1286, supervises local State Parks: Samuel Taylor, Angel Island, and Mount Tamalpais. Open M-F 8am-5pm. For reservations, call Mistix.

Mistix: State Park Reservations (800) 444-7275.

Point Reyes National Seashore: Bear Valley Visitors Center, Bear Valley Rd. just west of Olema, 663-1092. Backpack sites only. Coast camp is shortest hike (2 miles each way). Wildcat Camp is also near beach. Glen Camp and Sky Camp lie inland. Reservations required. For reservations, call M-F 9am-noon. Free.

Samuel Taylor State Park: Sir Francis Drake Blvd., Lagunitas, 488-9897. Typical state park car camping: closely packed loops under the trees, plenty of facilities. Open Su-Th 8am-8:30pm; F, Sa 8am-10pm. For reservations, call Mistix.

Hostels

Point Reyes Youth Hostel: Limantour Rd., Pt. Reyes National Seashore, 663-8811. Located two miles from the ocean in a secluded valley near hiking trails and the estuary. You'll probably want to cook your own food here, but shop before you arrive, since the stores are an eight-mile trek from the hostel. Call for reservation information 8am-9:30am; 4:30pm-9:30pm. $10 adult, $5 children.

Steep Ravine Environmental Cabins: Mount Tamalpais State Park, Hwy 1, 1 mi. south of Stinson Beach. Rustic cabins on bluff overlooking ocean, with platform beds, wood stoves, and pit toilets. Water nearby, but no electricity. Camping allowed. (For reservations, call Mistix first thing in morning, exactly eight weeks in advance.) $30 per cabin, $9 per campsite.

Hotels, Motels, Bed and Breakfasts

Be aware that some places require two-night stays on weekends.

Bear Valley Inn Bed and Breakfast: 88 Bear Valley Rd., Olema, 663-1777. Three-room Victorian ranch house in Olema 1/2 mile from the Pt. Reyes National Seashore. The staff promises to pamper guests with great food and old-fashioned hospitality. Rents Mtn. bikes, too. $70-$125; $10 off midweek.

Blackthorne Inn: 266 Vallejo Ave., Inverness, 663-8621. A unique lodging experience in a beautiful hand-crafted treehouse, complete with fireman's pole and spiral staircase, tucked in a secluded wooded canyon adjacent to the park. There are five rooms, a deck, a hot tub, and full breakfast served every morning. Hiking trails are nearby. $105-$185.

Casa Madrona: 801 Bridgeway, Sausalito, 332-0502. Deluxe, (mostly) historic inn built into hill above town. $105-$250.

Coastal Lodging of West Marin: 485-2678 & 663-1351. Referrals for bed-and-breakfasts.

Inns of Pt. Reyes: 485-2649 or 663-1420. Referrals for bed-and-breakfasts.

Inverness Lodge/Manka's: Corner of Callendar and Argyle Rds., Inverness, 669-1034. Hunting lodge-style rooms and cabins, some with decks overlooking Tomales Bay. $85-$145, breakfast extra.

Mountain Home Inn: 810 Panoramic Hwy., above Mill Valley, 381-9000. Charming old lodge on slopes of Mt. Tam. Some rooms offer fireplace and Jacuzzi. $131-$215.

Pelican Inn: Hwy 1, Muir Beach, 383-6000. Cozy, English-style pub, at entrance to Muir Beach. $140-155 (includes full English breakfast); call 4-6 months in advance for Sa reservations!

Pt. Reyes Seashore Lodge: 10021 Hwy 1, Olema, 663-9000. 21-room reproduction of a turn-of-the-century lodge. Some rooms have fireplaces, whirlpools, decks, or patios, and all guests are served a continental breakfast. Located near the park. $95-$195.

Ten Inverness Way: 10 Inverness Way, Inverness, 669-1648. Built in 1904, a quaint four-room inn with a stone fireplace, a hot tub, a sun room, and a flower garden. Full breakfast is served. $110-$140.

West Marin Vacation Rentals: 11150 Sir Francis Drake, Pt. Reyes Station, 663-1776. Vacation home rentals.

MENDOCINO

MENDOCINO & FORT BRAGG

Mendocino is the jewel in the crown of the Northern California coast. Built on a wide bluff, the town juts out into the ocean and has dramatic views of the gorgeous, rocky coastline on three sides. The town looks like a Maine fishing village, with its white New England-style houses and clapboard church. In keeping with its old-fashioned charm, few establishments post their street numbers, so pick up a good map of town before exploring. During the summer and holiday weekends, the town fills up with tourists; so off-season visits are the most pleasant (and less socked in with fog), though many services may be closed during midweek. Ten miles north of Mendocino is **Fort Bragg**, a large town catering to the lumber industry. Fort Bragg lacks the charms of its southern neighbor, but provides many of the practical services that are either unavailable or high-priced in Mendocino.

General Information

Area Code: 707

Fort Bragg-Mendocino Chamber of Commerce: (800) 726-2780 or 964-3153.

Getting There

To see as much as possible, take Hwy 1 in one direction and Hwy 101 the other. (Avoid taking Hwy 1 north in the late afternoon—the sun can be a formidable adversary.) To see the most north of San Francisco, take the San Anselmo/Sir Francis Drake exit off Hwy 101 and go west on Sir Francis Drake Boulevard until hitting Hwy 1 in Olema. Then head north for about three hours until you hit Mendocino (see the *Inland Mendocino* section for inland directions).

Sights and Attractions

Parks and Preserves

There are several state parks in and around Mendocino. Right in town is the **Mendocino Headlands State Park**, which wraps around the southwest side of the town, preserving its spectacular landscape. **Van Damme State Park**, about five miles south of town, has excellent camping, a small beach for swimming, and several hiking trails that wind through pygmy forests, dense fern thickets, and a skunk cabbage bog (the Fern Canyon Trail is best). North of Mendocino is **Russian Gulch State Park**, home to the Devil's Punch Bowl, a blowhole that sends the surf shooting skyward when the ocean is stirred up. Camping is available, and from the park's headlands it is possible to watch migrating whales in the winter months.

Further north on Hwy 1 is the **Jug Handle State Reserve**, home to the ecological staircase trail that traces the geological and natural history of the area, from the beach to the redwoods. For information about these and other parks, contact **Mendocino State Parks**, 937-5804.

A few miles further north of town, at 18220 N. Hwy 1, is the **Mendocino Coast Botanical Gardens** (964-4352), an ideal place to explore the ecologically-rich coastal environment. For the admission fee of five dollars, you can enjoy the well-manicured gardens (with over 10,000 plant varieties) and spectacular bluff views in an hour's stroll, but spend an afternoon if you have time.

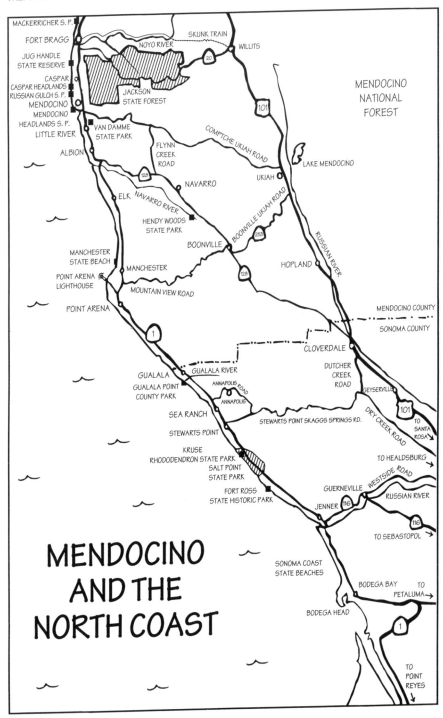

MENDOCINO
AND THE
NORTH COAST

Outdoor Activities

Just south of Mendocino off Comptche-Ukiah Road is **Catch a Canoe & Bicycles, Too!** (937-0273), which rents mountain bikes, canoes, and kayaks. Canoe trips from their dock on the Big River estuary provide views of otter and blue heron, as well as isolated picnic spots along the river banks. (They also offer free use of bike racks, so you can drive their rental bikes to good trails a few miles away.)

Several sport-fishing and whale-watching charter boats are anchored in **Noyo Harbor,** just before Fort Bragg. Whale watching occurs between December and March; the best fishing is during the summer and fall when the salmon are running. Many of the boats go out twice a day, with rates as low as $10 per person; try **Anchor Charters** (964-3854).

Another way to see the coast is on horseback. **The Ricochet Ridge Ranch** (964-7669) at 24201 N. Hwy 1 (three miles north of Fort Bragg across from the MacKerricher State Park) takes group rides on the beach four times daily for two hours; private rides are also available. Rides start at $26/person.

A good foggy-day activity is a ride on the **Skunk Train** (964-6371), which pulls out of Fort Bragg from the California Western Railroad for a 40-mile scenic journey through towering redwood forests and over precarious gulches to Willits (where it might be sunny). The Skunk Train makes day-long runs ($16), as well as half-day trips.

Hot Tubs and Saunas

The vernacular for hot-tubbing on the North Coast is "soak." To enjoy a good soak in town, visit **Sweetwater Gardens** (937-4140) at 955 Ukiah Street (beneath a renovated water tower next door to Café Beaujolais). This hot tub and sauna spa offers massages for the hike-weary and private hot tubs for $9.50/hr per person. For end of the day bonding, there's one enormous group tub where, for $7.50 per person, you can spend as long as you want—bring your own towels to save an additional buck. Open M-Th 2pm-11pm; F-Su noon-11pm.

Restaurants

Picnic Fare

Cheese Shop: Little Lake & Lansing Sts., Mendocino, 937-0104. Gourmet picnic supplies. Daily 10am-6pm.

Corners of the Mouth: 45015 Ukiah Street (in the red church), Mendocino, 937-5345. Natural foods store for the healthy picnicker. M-Sa 9am-7pm; Su 11am-5pm.

Mendocino Market: 699 Ukiah St., Mendocino, 937-FISH. Locals' choice for deli supplies and sandwiches. Daily 10am-6:30pm.

Mendosa's Merchandise & Market: 10501 Lansing St., Mendocino, 937-5879. Groceries and just about anything else you might need. Daily 8am-9pm.

Tote Fête: 10450 Lansing St., Mendocino, 937-3383. Gourmet picnic fixings. M-Sa 10:30-7pm; Su 10:30am-4pm.

Budget

Brickery $: Located behind Café Beaujolais, Mendocino, 937-5614. An informal garden café serving wood-fired pizzas and a variety of sandwiches. Th-M 8am-9pm.

Mendo Burgers $: 10483 Lansing St., Mendocino, 937-1111. Serves every kind of burger under the sun, including veggie, beef, chicken, fish, and turkey. M-Sa 11am-7pm; Su noon-5pm.

Mendocino Bakery & Café $: 10485 Lansing St., Mendocino, 937-0836. The pastries here are every bit as fresh as the local gossip you're bound to catch a whiff of. Daily 8am-6pm.

Moderate

Bay View Café $$: 45040 Main St., Mendocino, 937-4197. Their second-story view of the Headlands can't be beat. Daily 8am-3pm, 5pm-9pm.

Mendocino Café $$: Albion and Lansing Sts., Mendocino, 937-2422. The owners of the café have successfully melded their globe-trotting experiences with California cuisine to produce some stellar dishes. The Thai burrito is a tasty example of one such creation. They boast a sunny deck, to boot. Breakfast, lunch, and dinner daily.

Expensive

Albion River Inn $$$$: 3790 Hwy 1, Albion, 937-1919. Excellent meals accompanied by panoramic views of the Pacific. Dinner nightly.

Café Beaujolais $$$$ (breakfast $$): 961 Ukiah St., Mendocino, 937-5614. A favorite of Julia Childs, this 1910 clapboard Victorian is well worth the visit. Breakfasts in the country-style dining room are savory and fit most budgets. Breakfast, lunch, and dinner Th-M; Reservations recommended for dinner.

Chocolate Moosse Café $$$: 390 Kasten St., Mendocino, 937-4323. Excellent food, lunches can be taken in the Adirondack chairs in the front yard, and the desserts are great. Lunch and dinner daily.

Heritage House $$$$: Hwy 1, Little River, 937-5885. A B&B with a formal dining room, mainly for guests, but open to the public. Dinner nightly.

Ledford House $$$: Hwy 1, Albion, 937-0282. Great views of the coast from Salmon Point. Dinner nightly.

Little River Inn $$$: 7750 Hwy 1, Little River, 937-5942. A place with a good reputation for its restaurant, and a long porch where you can sip a drink and watch the sunset with no obligation to dine later. Breakfast and dinners daily.

Little River Restaurant $$$$: 7750 N. Hwy 1 (on the west side of Hwy 1, attached to the market and Post Office), Little River, 937-4945. Among the best on the coast. Sumptuous meals in a cozy atmosphere. The dining room only seats about a dozen, so reservations are a must. Dinner nightly.

MacCallum House Restaurant / Grey Whale Bar & Café $$$$: 45020 Albion St., Mendocino, 937-5763. A B&B that serves memorable meals. Café: dinner nightly; Restaurant: dinner F-W.

Mendocino Hotel $$$$: 45080 Main St., Mendocino, 937-0511. The fancy, heavily ornamented barroom has tables with views of the water. You can settle in front of the fire in the sitting room and play backgammon—boards are available from the desk. The restaurant serves steak and chops. Breakfast, lunch, and dinner daily.

Restaurant 955 $$$$: 955 Ukiah St., Mendocino, 937-1955. Pricey, but worth it if you've always wondered what it would be like to eat in an artists' studio. Dinner W-Su.

Fort Bragg

D'Aurelio & Sons $$: 438 S. Franklin St., Ft. Bragg, 964-4227. Good Italian food at reasonable prices. Dinner Su-Th.

El Mexicano $$: 701 N. Harbor, Ft. Bragg, 967-7164. Traditional south-of-the-border fare for the compote- and infusion-weary. Lunch and dinner daily.

Katrina's $$: 546 South Main St., Fort Bragg, 964-7130. A charming trattoria offering good, inexpensive Italian fare. Dinner Tu-Su.

North Coast Brewing Co. $$$: 444 N. Main St., Ft. Bragg, 964-BREW. Serves meals in addition to excellent fresh-brewed ales, such as their renowned Red Seal Ale. Dinner Tu-Sa.

Entertainment

The **Caspar Inn** (964-5565), at 14961 Caspar Road in the town of Caspar, is noted far and wide as the local hot spot—there's dancing and live music nightly until 2am during the summer, and on weekends during the off-season. Next door is the **Caspar Café** (964-2233), the only restaurant around that's open past 10pm—they keep the same hours as the bar. **The North Coast Brewing Company** also has live music on Saturdays.

Places to Stay

Since condo developments don't exist in the Mendocino architectural canon, and hotel chains have been banished, bed-and-breakfasts and quaint inns have a monopoly on accommodations. **Mendocino Coast Reservations** (937-1913) handles bookings for about 20 B&Bs and several vacation homes in the area. For a comprehensive list of all lodging possibilities, contact the **Fort Bragg-Mendocino Coast Chamber of Commerce,** (800) 726-2780—they'll mail you brochures galore.

Camping

Most of the parks listed in the *Outdoors* Section allow camping, though policies vary between different state parks, and reservations are highly recommended. Call **Mistix** (800-444-7275), or the **Mendocino State Park Headquarters** (937-5804).

Budget

The real lodging bargain in the Mendocino area is the **Jug Handle Farm & Nature Center** (964-4630, 964-9912), a large red farmhouse about four miles north of Mendocino on Hwy 1. They provide simple accommodations in the farmhouse, as well as campsites and primitive cabins nearby, for $15 per person per night ($10 with a student ID). Bring bedding or sleeping bags, towels, and anything else you might need. Bathrooms and showers are provided, and there is a kitchen available for cooking. Everyone who spends the night is asked to perform an hour of work, which can mean chopping wood, sweeping, or gardening. Call ahead for reservations as groups tend to book the place.

Moderate

Blue Heron Inn: 390 Kasten St., Mendocino, 937-4323. Rooms are situated above the Chocolate Moosse Café. $64 (one room)-$90.

Inn at Schoolhouse Creek: 7051 Hwy 1, Little River, 937-5525. Located south of town on Hwy 1, with three rooms at $70 and two cottages which sleep four at $35/person (breakfast is extra). $35-$110.

McElroy's Inn: 998 Main St., Mendocino, 937-1734. A low-priced B&B located in town. $50-$75.

Ocean View Motel: 1141 North Main St., Fort Bragg, 964-1951. Good prices and average accommodations. $45-$110.

Sea Gull Inn: 44594 Albion St., Mendocino, 937-5204. A charming, centrally-located hostelry with inexpensive accommodations in downtown Mendocino. $35-$85.

Luxury

Agate Cove Inn: 11201 Lansing St., Mendocino, (800) 527-3111 or 937-0551. Magnificent views of the water. $80-$175.

Albion River Inn: 3790 Hwy 1, Albion, 937-1919. A spacious inn overlooking the Albion River. Twenty cottages on the river's edge offer deluxe accommodations, some with decks and Jacuzzis. $85-$225.

Brewery Gulch Inn: 9350 Hwy 1, off Brewery Gulch Ln., a mile south of Mendocino, 937-4752. Recognizable by the water tank on Hwy 1, this place is set amidst beautiful gardens. $85-$130.

Glendeven Inn: 8221 Hwy 1, Little River, (800) 822-4536 or 937-0083. A rustic country inn with well-kept grounds, hearty breakfasts, and an adjacent gallery with shows by local artists. $90-$200.

Headlands Inn: Corner of Howard & Albion Sts., Mendocino, 937-4431. A cozy place with ocean views. $103-$172.

Heritage House: Hwy 1, Little River, 937-5885. A renowned inn that requires both breakfast *and* dinner in their restaurant. Cottages $125-$335 (includes breakfast and dinner).

John Dougherty House: 571 Ukiah Street, Mendocino, 937-5266. A popular, standard-priced B&B in town. $85-$140.

Joshua Grindle Inn: 44800 Little Lake Road, Mendocino, 937-4143. A popular B&B overlooking the town. $90-$135.

MacCallum House Inn: 45020 Albion St., Mendocino, 937-0289. An oft-visited B&B, part of which occupies a restored barn. $75-$180.

Mendocino Farmhouse: Comptche-Ukiah Rd., Mendocino, 937-0241. This inland B&B offers privacy and a break from the fog. $80-$100.

Mendocino Hotel: 45080 Main St., Mendocino, (800) 548-0513 or 937-0511. A larger establishment with high-end offerings. $50-$225.

Stanford Inn by the Sea/Big River Lodge: Comptche-Ukiah Rd., (800) 331-8884, 937-5615. The best features of a B&B with the amenities of a larger hotel, including an indoor pool and hot tub, and resident llamas. Each room has a fireplace and TV. $140-$170.

Victorian Farmhouse: 7001 Hwy 1, Little River, (800) 264-4723 or 937-0697. Known for its hospitality, coziness, and proximity to an ocean path. $80-$120.

SONOMA & SOUTH MENDOCINO COASTS

The coastline from Marin County to South Mendocino is sparsely populated, but dotted with state parks, public beaches, and a good supply of offbeat restaurants and lodgings. The drive on Hwy 1 takes you through the bucolic farms and pastures that border the **Pt. Reyes National Seashore,** and up along **Bodega Bay,** the setting for Alfred Hitchcock's *The Birds.* **Bodega Head** is known for its good views of whales in the wintertime. Soon after Bodega Bay are the **Sonoma Coast State Beaches.** Different beaches appear every few miles and make good rest stops. For more information on Bodega Bay and the Sonoma Coast State Beaches, contact at the **Salmon Creek Ranger Station** (875-3483). Further north at 25050 Hwy 1 in Jenner, you'll find **Salt Point State Park** (847-3221), a primal landscape that is just beginning to recover from a recent fire. Within the park is the **Kruse Rhododendron State Preserve** (847-3221), with its 300+ acres of wild rhododendrons (especially spectacular in April and May). **The Sea Ranch** (800-842-3270 or 785-2371) is an award-winning planned community that rents vacation homes throughout the year. Close to the ocean, the **Sea Ranch Lodge** at 60 Sea Walk Drive also has rooms if you're not into group housing; prices run between $125 and $180.

A bit further north is **Gualala** (pronounced wah-la-la). Activities in the Gualala area include horseback riding, wine tasting, and sea kayaking. **The Roth Ranch** at 37100 Old Stage Road offers guided horseback rides through the Gualala River basin—$45 for the half-day ride. Call for directions: (707) 884-3124. **Gualala Kayak** (884-4705) at 39175 Hwy 1 (behind Don Berard Associates in the middle of Gualala), features river and ocean kayaking from $25/person, and offers mid-week and group discounts. Open daily 8:30am to 5:30pm. The **Annapolis Winery** (886-5460) is set back seven miles in the hills at 26055 Soda Springs Road, high above the wind and fog. It offers free tastings and picnic grounds with a sunny view of the coast. Open M-Th noon to 5pm.

Restaurants

Roadhouse Café $$: 6061 Hwy 1, Elk, 877-3285. Inexpensive, hearty food. M-Sa 8am-2pm; Su 8am-1pm.

St. Orres $$$$: 36601 South Hwy 1, Gualala, 884-3303. A Russian dome-topped inn with phenomenal French-meets-California cuisine, such as the mussels on black pasta. A prix-fixe dinner of $30 includes soup, salad, and an entree. Dinner M-Sa.

Places to Stay

Greenwood Pier Inn: 5928 Hwy 1, Elk, 877-9997. A group of cottages perched above a cut in the ocean cliffs. Gorgeous gardens and dazzling views complement the eclectically decorated cottages. $90-$195.

Harbor House: 5600 South Hwy 1, Elk, 877-3203. Sensational views and more traditional accommodations. $160-$240 (includes breakfast and dinner).

St. Orres: 36601 South Hwy 1, Gualala, 884-3303. The Russian restaurant also offers inexpensive rooms and rustic, secluded cabins. $60-$150.

This is it!: Off N. Hwy 1 on Mountain View Rd. between Pt. Arena and Manchester State Beach, 882-2320. Cottages in the redwoods, each with its own kitchenette, and one with a hot tub. Cottages are $75/night, $350/week, $900/month.

INLAND MENDOCINO

The other route to Mendocino involves more highway but is about an hour shorter (four hours versus five from Palo Alto). Stay on Hwy 101 until Cloverdale where you pick up Hwy 128. This road winds through vineyards, sere golden hills, and redwoods as it cuts across Anderson Valley to the coast. Once Hwy 128 hits the coast it's just another ten miles north on Hwy 1 to reach Mendocino. To reach Hopland, continue on Hwy 101 past Cloverdale for about 15 miles until you hit Hopland. To reach Mendocino, either retrace your steps to Cloverdale or continue north on Hwy 101 to Lakeport where you take Hwy 253 west until it meets Hwy 128 in Boonville.

Restaurants and Hotels

Anderson Valley Brewing Company $$: 14081 Hwy 128, Boonville, 895-2337. Some of the best microbrewed beer around. Daily 11am-10pm, closed W.

Boonville Hotel $$$$: 14050 Hwy 128, Boonville, 895-2210. Airy, open rooms in a Southwestern style. Their relaxing and informal restaurant, with gardens and a patio, serves an inventive menu that mixes the old and new West. W-Su 6pm-9pm.

Cheesecake Lady: Hwy 101, Hopland, (800) CAKE-LAD. Bay Area supplier of gourmet bakery treats of all flavors. Tours of the bakery are invited. M-W 7:30am-6pm; Th, F 7:30am-8pm; Sa, Su 9am-8pm.

Mendocino Brewing Company's Hopland Brewery $$: Hwy 101 in Hopland, 744-1361. Home to the ever-popular Red Tail Ale, Black Hawk Stout and Peregrine Pale Ale. Good bar food and live music on Saturday nights. Su-Th 11am-11pm; F 11am-midnight; Sa 11am-2am.

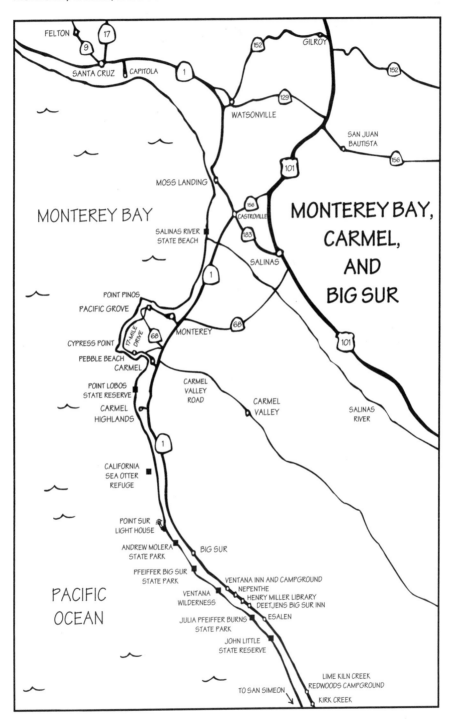

MONTEREY, CARMEL, & BIG SUR

MONTEREY & PACIFIC GROVE

Monterey is home to the famous Cannery Row and the Monterey Bay Aquarium, as well as the many special events it hosts every year—including golf tournaments and jazz, blues, Dixieland, and squid festivals. The town also celebrates the famous people who once chose to make the Monterey area home, including John Steinbeck and Robinson Jeffers.

Next to Monterey on the tip of the Monterey Peninsula sits the city of Pacific Grove. Founded by Methodists in 1875, Pacific Grove has the distinction of being the last dry town in California, with alcohol legal only since 1969. Pacific Grove is nicknamed "Butterfly City, USA" because thousands of migrating Monarch Butterflies winter here.

General Information

Area Code: 408

Monterey Peninsula Chamber of Commerce: 380 Alvarado St., 649-1770. 24-hour information hotline of events, lodging and dining information. Office open M-F 9am-5pm.

Tourist Information: 624-1711; (800) 847-8066 for room reservations.

Getting There

Depending on traffic it takes 1 to 1 1/2 hours to get to Monterey from San Jose; tack on another 15 minutes for Carmel and an additional half hour to reach the heart of Big Sur. There are two routes: the first is to take Hwy 17 south to Santa Cruz, then Hwy 1 south. This drive takes a little longer, but it is more scenic and there are other attractions along the way. A quicker alternative is to take Hwy 101 south to Hwy 156 south through Castroville, then Hwy 1 south.

Sights and Attractions

Once known as the sardine capital of the world, Cannery Row is the street immortalized in John Steinbeck's novel of the same name. In 1945, 19 operating canneries packed more than 235,000 tons of sardines. Transformed into a shopping bazaar, Cannery Row still stands, but now it's the tourists that are packed in like sardines. The main attraction is the state-of-the-art **Monterey Bay Aquarium** at 886 Cannery Row (648-4888; advance tickets 800-756-3737), which provides a comprehensive view of the bay, from the sloughs to the deep sea. To the left of the entrance is the famous **California Kelp Forest** exhibit; don't miss feeding time at this 335,000-gallon tank. Other attractions are the **Touch Pool** and the special rotating exhibit. Outside, take in the beauty of the bay itself and watch sea otters lounge on the rocks.

Nearby sights include an historic carousel and wax museum, and **Fisherman's Wharf,** just off Del Monte Avenue. Some of the many restaurants and shops there have been operated by the same families for generations. From December to early April, whale-watching tours depart from the wharf for close-up views of migrating whales.

153

Monterey State Historic Park (649-7118) manages a collection of historic buildings throughout Monterey. Stop by the headquarters at 20 Custom House Plaza behind Fisherman's Wharf for a free self-guided tour map and listing of each building's hours. Included on the tour are several fine old adobes, some with beautiful patios and gardens. A $5, two-day pass covers admission to four houses, while the walking tour ($2) leaves daily from Stanton Center on the Plaza at 10:30am, 12:30pm, and 2:30pm.

The **Allen Knight Maritime Museum** (373-2469) in Stanton Center displays artifacts from Monterey's whaling days. The **Monterey Peninsula Museum of Art** (372-5477) at 559 Pacific Street has an excellent collection of Western art, including several Charles M. Russell cowboy statues. **Colton Hall** (646-5640) at Pacific and Jefferson, where California's first constitution was crafted in 1849, is an architectural gem worth visiting.

Pacific Grove

On your way to Pacific Grove, check out Ocean View Boulevard, also known as **Three-Mile Drive** (begin at Cannery Row past the aquarium) for one of the best views of the region. Just beyond the aquarium at 125 Ocean View you'll find the **American Tin Cannery** (372-1442) with over 45 factory outlets. Further along the coast are **Shoreline Park**, **Marine Gardens Park**, and **Lover's Point Beach**, great spots to picnic. Follow the coast to **Point Piños Lighthouse and Museum** (375-4450 for private tours; 648-3116 for group tours), the oldest operating lighthouse on the West Coast. (Open to the public for tours Sa-Su 1pm-4pm.) **Doc's Great Tidepool**, a favored spot for microcosmic marine exploration, is at the base of the lighthouse. Check out more tide pools, as well as wind-sculpted cypress tress, at **Asilomar State Beach**.

You can get to the famous **17-Mile Drive** from Sunset Drive in Pacific Grove, Hwy 1 south of Monterey, or Ocean Avenue in Carmel. Admission is $6.50 per car. The famed scenery of this drive includes fancy houses, the golf courses in exclusive **Pebble Beach**, the famous lone cypress, and Crocker Grove, a 13-acre pine and cypress natural reserve.

You'll find the **Pacific Grove Museum of Natural History** (648-3116) at Forest and Central (turn on Forest from Lighthouse). One of the finest natural history museums in the country, it highlights local species including sea otters and over 400 species of birds; be sure to visit the Butterfly Tree.

Outdoor Activities

Monterey's scuba diving is ranked among the best in Northern California, and there are local dive shops ready to serve your needs. Kayaking is also very popular here, and there are several places that rent boats and offer tours.

Monterey Sport Fishing (372-2203) on 96 Fisherman's Wharf has various deep-sea fishing packages, and also offers a 45-minute sightseeing cruise of Monterey Bay ($7 per person) and whale-watching trips. **Randy's Fishing Trips** (372-7440), at 66 Fisherman's Wharf, also offers numerous packages.

For the land-bound, biking and mopeding are popular and convenient. **Monterey Moped Adventures** (373-2696) is at 1250 Del Monte, and has both bikes and mopeds for rent. **Joselyn's** (649-8520), at 638 Lighthouse, also rents bicycles. **Bay Bikes** (646-9090) on 640 Wave Street, rents mountain bikes and four-person pedal bikes called surreys. You can take off right behind the store on a bike path that follows the coast to Pacific Grove and 17-Mile Drive. **Monterey Bay Kayaks** (373-5357), at 693 Del Monte Avenue, rents kayaks and organizes overnight trips. See *Kayaking* section for more information.

Golf Courses

The Monterey Bay area is known world-wide as a golf mecca. There are several well-known golf courses in Pebble Beach where non-members are allowed to play. See *Golfing* section for more information.

Restaurants

Amarin Thai Cuisine $$: 807 Cannery Row, Monterey, 373-8811. Traditional Thai specialties like satay, pad thai, and curries, at decent prices in a casual atmosphere. Lunch and dinner daily.

Bagel Bakery $: 201 Lighthouse Ave., Monterey, 649-1714. Great bagels and sandwiches. Cash only. Daily 6:30am-6pm.

Cannery Restaurant $$$: 650 Cannery Row, Monterey, 372-8881. Excellent Italian food served up with a spectacular view. Lunch and dinner daily.

Clock Garden $$: 565 Abrego St., Monterey, 375-6100. A great place to eat breakfast outdoors. The food is imaginative, delicious, and reasonably priced. Lunch and dinner M-Sa; brunch and dinner Su.

The Fishwife at Asilomar Beach $$: 1996 1/2 Sunset Dr., Pacific Grove, 375-7107. Seafood with a Caribbean flair. Lunch and dinner W-M.

Gianni's Pizza $: 725 Lighthouse Ave., Monterey, 649-1500. The best pizza in Monterey—worth the wait you may have to endure. Lunch F-Su, dinner M-Su.

Jugem Japanese Restaurant & Sushi $$$: 409 Alvarado St., Monterey, 373-6463. For those who like their seafood raw. Lunch M-F, dinner M-Su.

Mark Thomas Outrigger $$$: 700 Cannery Row, Monterey, 372-8543. Fresh seafood and pasta. Perched on the bay, this is one of the last existing cannery buildings right on the water. Lunch and dinner daily.

Monterey Baking Company $: 406 Alvarado St., Monterey, 375-4511. Boasts a wide variety of homemade pastries and made-to-order sandwiches. Cash and local checks only. M-F 7am-5pm; Sa 8am-5pm.

O'Kane's Irish Pub $: 97 Prescott St., Monterey, 375-7564. Irish hospitality is in abundance here—food is half-price after 10pm with the purchase of a drink. Lunch and dinner daily.

Old Bath House Restaurant $$$$: 620 Ocean View Blvd., Pacific Grove, 375-5195. Pacific Grove's finest restaurant serves steak, chicken, seafood, and killer desserts in a charming Victorian overlooking the ocean. Dinner daily.

Pepper's Mexicali Café $$: 170 Forest Ave., Pacific Grove, 373-6892. Good, authentic Mexican fare. Lunch M, W-Sa, dinner W-M.

Rappa's End of the Wharf $$: Fisherman's Wharf, Monterey, 372-7562. Fresh seafood in a calm, comfortable retreat from the turmoil of the wharf. Lunch and dinner daily.

Red's Donuts $: 433 Alvarado St., Monterey, 372-9761. A good place for breakfast on the run. Cash only. M-Sa 6:30am-2:30pm, Su until 12:30pm.

Sardine Factory $$$: 701 Wave St., Monterey, 373-3775. Fine continental fare served in an elegant atmosphere. Dinner daily.

Taqueria del Mar $: 530 Lighthouse Ave., Pacific Grove, 372-7887. Awesome burritos and great, authentic Mexican dishes. Lunch M-Su, dinner M-Sa until 8pm.

The Tinnery $$: 631 Ocean View Blvd., Pacific Grove, 646-1040. A bar featuring live entertainment nightly, and plenty of seafood. Also offers complete breakfasts. Breakfast, lunch, and dinner daily. Happy hour 4pm-6pm and 11pm-1am.

Toastie's Café $: 702 Lighthouse Ave., Pacific Grove, 373-7543. A great place for breakfast. Breakfast and lunch daily, dinner Tu-Sa.

Warehouse Restaurant $$: 640 Wave St., Cannery Row, Monterey, 375-1921. A very good Italian restaurant. Lunch and dinner M-Su, brunch Su 10am-2:30pm.

Whaling Station Inn $$$: 763 Wave St., Monterey, 373-3778. Elegant setting for an excellent continental meal. Dinner daily.

Wharfside Restaurant $$: 60 Fisherman's Wharf #1, Monterey, 375-3956. More of that ubiquitous fresh seafood found on the wharf, and outdoor seating on the second floor. Lunch and dinner daily.

Places to Stay

Hotels in the area inevitably charge more for special events and weekends. For the budget-conscious, a midweek stay can be substantially cheaper.

Budget

Butterfly Grove Inn: 1073 Lighthouse Ave., Pacific Grove. 373-4921. An inexpensive option in butterfly country. $50-$120.

Californian Motel: 2042 N. Fremont St., Monterey, 372-5851. Some rooms have kitchens, and there's a pool and a whirlpool. $39-$109.

Comfort Inn-Carmel Hill: 1252 Munras Ave., Monterey, 372-2908. Heated pool. $58-$125.

Monterey Youth Hostel: Gymnasium, Monterey High School, Larkin St., Monterey (location may change annually). Open summers only, mid-June to mid-August. 649-0375 or 298-0670. 7:30am-9:30am; 6pm-11pm. $6-$9.

Pacific Grove Motel: Lighthouse Ave. and Grove Acres, Pacific Grove, 372-3218. Centrally located, with a hot tub. Refrigerators in each room. $59-$94.

Padre Oaks Motel: 1278 Munras Ave., Monterey. 373-3741. Pool. $65-$85.

Terrace Oaks Inn: 1095 Lighthouse Ave., Pacific Grove, 373-4382. Standard, reasonably priced lodging. $60-$82.

Westerner Motel: 2041 Fremont St., Monterey, 373-2911. $30-$120.

Moderate

Andril Fireplace Cottages: 569 Asilomar Blvd., Pacific Grove, 375-0994. Features separate cottages with fully equipped kitchens and fireplaces, set among the pines. $80-$110.

Asilomar Conference Center: 800 Asilomar Ave., Monterey, 372-8016. A historical landmark, right on the beach. Primarily for large groups; single rooms available. Reservations taken up to 30 days in advance. Breakfast included. $70-$90.

Beachcomber Inn: 1996 Sunset Dr., Pacific Grove, 373-4769. Heated pool; a few rooms have kitchen facilities. $60-$118.

Sand Dollar Inn: 755 Abrego St., Monterey, 372-7551. Offers a pool and spa, and includes continental breakfast. $64-$104.

Luxury

Best Western Lighthouse Lodge: 1249 Lighthouse Ave., Pacific Grove, 655-2111. A great view of the lighthouse; Jacuzzis, and in-room fireplaces. $79-$119, suites $185.

Best Western Victorian Inn: 487 Foam St., Monterey, 373-8000, (800) 424-6242. Don't forget to ask for available discounts—besides AAA and seniors, they sometimes have other specials. $99-$289.

Colton Inn: 707 Pacific St., Monterey, 649-6500. Rooms come with balconies, fireplaces, and Whirlpool tubs. $77-$189.

Hotel Pacific: 300 Pacific St., Monterey, 373-5700, (800) 424-6242. All rooms have a deck, wet bar, gas fireplace, and small refrigerator. $99-$269.

Jabberwock: 598 Laine St., Monterey, 372-4777. A 1911 post-Victorian decorated in an Alice in Wonderland theme. Complimentary hors d'oeuvres and wine are served in the evening, and milk and cookies await you at bedtime. $100-$150.

Martine Inn: 255 Ocean View Blvd., Pacific Grove, 373-3388. A grand Mediterranean mansion overlooking the crashing surf. Full breakfast and afternoon wine and hors d'oeuvres included. $125-$230.

Merritt House: 386 Pacific St., Monterey, 646-9686. A charming historic adobe with 25 adjoining new units. All rooms have fireplaces. Breakfast and parking included. $120-$200.

Monterey Bay Inn: 242 Cannery Row, Monterey, 373-6242, (800) 424-6242. A great location right on the bay, plus a rooftop hot tub with a panoramic view. $119-$319.

Spindrift Inn: 652 Cannery Row, Monterey, 646-8900, (800) 424-6242. Pamper yourself with goose down feather beds, fireplaces, and a rooftop garden. Complimentary continental breakfast and wine and cheese. $99-$189 for city views; $209-$289 for ocean views.

CARMEL

Carmel is located on Hwy 1 just south of Monterey, and is a traveler's paradise, known for its array of excellent restaurants, shops, and romantic inns and bed and breakfast. Accordingly, most restaurants and hotels cater to those travelers with big bank accounts. Parking is very limited in the downtown area. Local ordinances prohibit address numbers and parking meters, but you can still get a ticket from the vigilant police.

General Information

Area Code: 408

Sights and Attractions

Carmel's main street, **Ocean Avenue,** is a window-shopper's delight, with countless specialty shops, art galleries, and boutiques. An art colony gone berserk (and a bit sour), you can't walk down a street without seeing at least three galleries. Art lovers should investigate **Carmel Art Association Galleries** (624-6176) on Dolores Street between Fifth and Sixth, which tastefully displays the work of local artists and hosts major traveling exhibits.

At the end of Ocean Avenue, the town meets the sea, explaining the downtown area's official name, Carmel-by-the-Sea. You'll find a less populated beach south on Scenic Road. On the way, you'll pass by the house of poet Robinson Jeffers at 26304 Ocean View Avenue, known by locals as **Tor House** (624-1813). Jeffers built the home from rocks he carried up from the beach. Tours are given throughout the week and on Saturdays; reservations are suggested.

For a dose of California history, drop by the **Carmel Mission** (624-3600), west of Hwy 1 at 3080 Rio Road. The mission has a baroque stone church that was completed in 1797, three museums, and fabulous gardens. Across the street is **Mission Trail Park**, 35 acres ready and waiting for hikers and mountain bikers. For more activities in the area, check out the **Sunset Cultural Center** (624-3996), located on San Carlos Street between Eighth and Ninth, or pick up a copy of the *Monterey Peninsula Review*, a free weekly newspaper that includes listings of the week's events, a guide to recreational activities, and restaurant listings and reviews.

A few miles south of Carmel on Hwy 1 is **Point Lobos State Reserve** (624-4909), 1,250 acres of natural coastal and inland habitat. Hike along the reserve's numerous coastal and wilderness trails, check out the tide pools, or take a nature tour. Parking is very limited, so get there early; when the park is full you have to wait until a car exits before you can enter.

Restaurants

Clam Box $$/$$$: Mission between Fifth and Sixth, 624-8597. An original menu including various seafood casseroles. Lunch and dinner Tu-Su.

Flaherty's $$: Sixth Street between San Carlos and Dolores, 625-1500. Known as the best seafood place in town; expect to wait if you don't get there very early. Dinner daily; oyster bar from 11:30am.

Friar Tucks $: Fifth St. and Dolores, 624-4274. One of the best breakfast deals around. The food is delicious, and the pub-like atmosphere lends itself well to lunch, which consists largely of burgers, sandwiches, and salads. Breakfast, lunch, and dinner daily; call for winter hours.

Hog's Breath Inn $$: San Carlos St. between Fourth and Fifth, 625-1044. This Clint Eastwood-owned establishment is moody, low-lit, and wood-somber inside, but the outdoor patio is cheery and social, sporting fireplaces and a bar. Free hors d'oeuvres buffet 4pm-6pm. Lunch and dinner daily.

Le Bistro $: San Carlos between Ocean and 7th, 624-6545. Burgers, soup, and sandwiches in a colorful atmosphere that includes a small garden. Breakfast, lunch, and dinner daily.

Places to Stay

For budget accommodations, try the Monterey/Pacific Grove area.

Moderate

Carmel Valley Inn: Corner of Los Laureles Grade Rd. and Carmel Valley Rd., 659-3131; (800) 541-3113 for reservations. Tennis courts, swimming pool, and hot tub. $69-$149.

Coachman's Inn: On San Carlos St. at Seventh, (800) 336-6421. Close to the ocean with continental breakfast included. $75-$150.

Green Lantern: Seventh and Casanova, 624-4392. There's no superhero motif, as the name suggests, but it's funky all the same. Romantic rooms at a reasonable price. $75-$189.

Vagabond's House Inn: Dolores and 4th, 624-1880. The majority of rooms have fireplaces and kitchens; breakfast included. $79-$135.

Luxury

Carmel Mission Ranch: 26270 Dolores St., 624-6436. A rustic place replete with goats and grazing sheep, narrowly saved from condominium hell by none other than Clint Eastwood. Many cottages and rooms offer views of the ocean; continental breakfast included. $95-$225.

Lincoln Green Inn: Carmelo, between 15th and 16th, 624-1880. Excellent spot for couples and families. Cottages sleep four; almost all have fireplaces and full kitchens. $135 & up.

Pine Inn: Ocean Ave. between Lincoln and Monteverde, 624-3851. "Carmel-Victorian" decor. Some rooms have ocean views. $100-$205.

BIG SUR

Stretching along the mountains from Carmel south to San Simeon is the majestic coastline known as Big Sur. Seventy miles of cliff-hanging S-curves and switchbacks make up this span of the Pacific Coast Highway that runs perilously close to the ocean, with plenty of pull-offs to take in the views. The town of Big Sur is located about halfway down the stretch, but most use Big Sur as the collective term for the whole magnificent landscape.

There are several good camping areas, a few restaurants, and plenty of views and trails for hiking. It's possible to make a—very long—day's excursion to Big Sur from the Bay Area, with time for a short hike in one of the state parks and a drink at Nepenthe or Ventana. The views and the seclusion will cost you, though—Big Sur prices run high.

General Information

Area Code: 408

Big Sur Chamber of Commerce: P.O. Box 87, Big Sur 93920, 667-2100.

Big Sur Emergency Road Service: 667-2518.

Pfeiffer-Big Sur State Park: 667-2315. (For information about Andrew Molera State Park, Garrapata State Park, Julia Pfeiffer Burns State Park, and Point Sur Lighthouse State Park.)

United States National Forest Service-Big Sur Station: 667-2423. (For information about National Forests, Pfeiffer Beach, and Ventana Wilderness.)

Sights and Attractions

The state and national parks offer plenty of opportunities for the solitude that first drew the writer Henry Miller to Big Sur in the forties. Heading south from Carmel, you can easily spot **Garrapata State Park** by the dramatic Point Sur Lighthouse that marks its southern boundary. There's a beach and some high ground from which to watch whales in the winter, but there are few facilities and heavy winds. The **Point Sur Lighthouse State Park** (625-4419 or 625-2006), 19 miles south of Carmel on Hwy 1, is maintained by the Coast Guard. Tours last over two hours, and visits by small children and the unfit are discouraged. Arrive at the gate early since people are not permitted to enter or even wait outside the lighthouse if they miss the tour.

As you head south, the next park is the **Andrew Molera State Park**, with a two-mile beach, a coastal sanctuary for seabirds, and walk-in campsites a few hundred yards from the dirt parking lot. **Molera Trail Rides** (625-8664 or 659-0433) inside the campground has two-hour rides at daybreak, afternoon, and sunset for $40-$50. About a mile south on the east side of the highway is the **Pfeiffer-Big Sur State Park**; trails leading up into the mountain offer spectacular views of the Big Sur River gorge and the valley below, including the 60-foot Pfeiffer Falls.

Further inland is the **Ventana Wilderness**, the largest protected area in Big Sur. Visitors need a free permit to hike, build fires, or camp within the preserve. These can be obtained, along with maps, at the **Big Sur Station** (667-2423)—a multi-agency ranger station—located about a half-mile south of the Pfeiffer-Big Sur State Parks on Hwy 1.

Another half-mile south is the **National Forest's Pfeiffer Beach**, a good place to explore sea caves and watch divers.

About seven miles south of **Nepenthe**, Big Sur's most famous restaurant, is **Julia Pfeiffer Burns State Park,** which has the only California waterfall that drops directly into the sea. There are also walk-in campsites with limited facilities. Other parks further south include **John Little State Reserve** (667-2315), a small preserve just below the famed **Esalen Institute** and open only in the daytime, and the **Lime Kiln Beach Redwood Campground.** You can spend about an hour or two there hiking up to the ancient lime kilns, and then cool off in the waterfall.

The **Henry Miller Memorial Library** (667-2574) is on Hwy 1, a quarter mile south of Nepenthe. The unimposing wood structure houses Miller memorabilia—books, paintings, and photographs of Miller's friends and assorted wives. Also on Hwy 1 is the **Esalen Institute** (667-3000), formerly a symbol of 60s counterculture, but now a New Age Mecca that describes itself as a "center to encourage work in the humanities and sciences that promotes human values and potentials." The beautiful encampment and cliffside baths are open to the curious public between 1am and 3:30am, and reservations are required.

Restaurants and Entertainment

Big Sur Lodge $$: Hwy 1, Pfeiffer-Big Sur State Park, 667-2171. A rustic spot next to the Big Sur Campground. The food is much better than typical park concessionaires, particularly the fresh-baked pies. Breakfast, lunch, and dinner daily.

Café Kevah $: Hwy 1, next to Nepenthe, 667-2660. Much cheaper prices than its neighbor. The deck has amazing views. Breakfast and lunch daily.

Center Deli $: Hwy 1, next to the post office, 667-2225. A good place to pick up a sandwich and some fixings, but there is no seating on-site. Daily 8am-8:30pm.

Coast Gallery Café $: Hwy 1, 3 mi. south of Nepenthe, 667-2301. Hot and cold sandwiches and a great view. Daily 9am-5pm.

Deetjen's Big Sur Inn Restaurant $$$: Hwy 1, 667-2378. Wonderful brunches and dinners served in a country setting. Dinner reservations recommended. Breakfast and dinner daily.

Fernwood Burger Bar $$: Hwy 1, 26 mi. south of Carmel, 667-2422. A hopping place with occasional live music blasting through the redwoods. Daily 11:30am-11:30pm.

Nepenthe $$: Hwy 1, 30 mi. south of Carmel, 667-2345. Once the haunt of literary loafer Henry Miller and stars Liz Taylor and Richard Burton, today's famous eaters include the likes of Jane Fonda and Ted Turner. Exceptional views, of course. Once a month locals hold an astrology birthday party here and dance under the stars. Lunch and dinner daily.

Post Ranch Inn $$$$: Hwy 1, across from Ventana Inn, 667-2200. An expensive, near-ocean experience. Reservations only. Dinner daily, brunch Sa-Su noon-2pm.

River Inn $$: Pheneger Creek, 667-2700. Live music Saturday nights and Sunday afternoons. Daily 8am-9:30pm.

Rocky Point $$$: North of Point Sur Lighthouse (12 mi. south of Carmel), 624-2933. Located on top of the crashing breakers, but the price for eating in such a location is heady. Lunch and dinner daily; lounge open until 11:30pm.

Ventana Inn $$$$: Hwy 1, 28 mi. south of Carmel, 667-2331 or 624-4812. Breathtaking views and prices to match, but if you decide to splurge you won't be disappointed. Coffee or tea on the deck gives a great overlook of the ocean. Lunch and dinner daily.

Places to Stay

Camping

Big Sur Campground and Cabins: Hwy 1, after the River Inn, 667-2322. Campgrounds and cabins, some with kitchens, nestled among the redwoods. Campsites $22 for two, $3 for each additional person; tent cabins $40 for two, $10 each additional; cabins $88-$143.

Bottchers Gap Campground: North of the Point Sur Lighthouse, Palo Colorado Rd., 667-2423 (U.S. National Forest Service). Limited services and a first-come, first-served policy. $5.

Fernwood Motel & Campground: Hwy 1, 667-2422. Campsites $21 for 2, $4 each additional (add $2 for electrical hookup); rooms $55-$74.

Kirk Creek Campgrounds: Hwy 1, 15 mi. south of the Esalen Institute, 667-2423 (U.S. National Forest Service). Policy is first-come, first-served at these campsites set on an open bluff above the ocean. No phones or electricity. $10-$15.

Lime Kiln Beach Redwoods Campground: Situated in an old canyon and surrounded by good hiking trails. The campground recently changed owners; for updated information, call 667-2423 (U.S. National Forest Service).

Riverside Campground & Cabins: Hwy 1, located on the Big Sur river, 667-2414. No kitchens or fireplaces. Campsites $22 for two people, add $3 each additional person; cabins $50-$90.

Ventana Campground: Hwy 1, 667-2688. On the grounds of the Ventana Inn, so you're within reach of a meal or drink if those freeze-dried dinners aren't cutting it. $20 for 2. Reservations required, 10 days notice, and $20 deposit.

Budget and Moderate

Big Sur Lodge: located in Pfeiffer-Big Sur State Park, 667-3100, (800) 424-4787 for reservations. 61 cottage-style rooms with either a deck or a porch. Some with kitchens and fireplaces. $79-179.

Deetjen's Big Sur Inn: Hwy 1, 667-2377. It's hard to imagine a more picturesque inn with its garden, ever-stoked fire, and hearty, inventive breakfasts. Two months advance reservations recommended. Reservations received noon-4pm. $66-$121 and up.

Esalen Institute: Hwy 1, 667-3000. Private or shared bunk-bed rooms available; meals included. Pool and hot tub. Reservations taken only one week in advance. $70-$125.

Ripplewood Resort: Hwy 1, 667-2282. 16 well-kept cabins, nine of which are on the Big Sur River. Some cabins have kitchens, fireplaces, and decks. $45-$80.

River Inn: Pheneger Creek, 25 mi. south of Carmel's Rio Rd., 667-2700. The first business you'll encounter in the Big Sur Valley, with nice, clean, simple rooms. $88-$160.

Luxury

Post Ranch Inn: Hwy 1, 667-2200. The newest resort in Big Sur. Its luxurious rooms are filled with private fireplaces, Jacuzzis, and wet bars. $265-$525.

Ventana Inn: Hwy 1, 667-2331 or 624-4812. A woodsy retreat considered to be one of the finest in Northern California. Located high above the ocean, this sprawling, ranch-like compound is luxurious without being pretentious. Clothing-optional hot tubs and sunbathing areas are only a sampling of the amenities available. $195-$400.

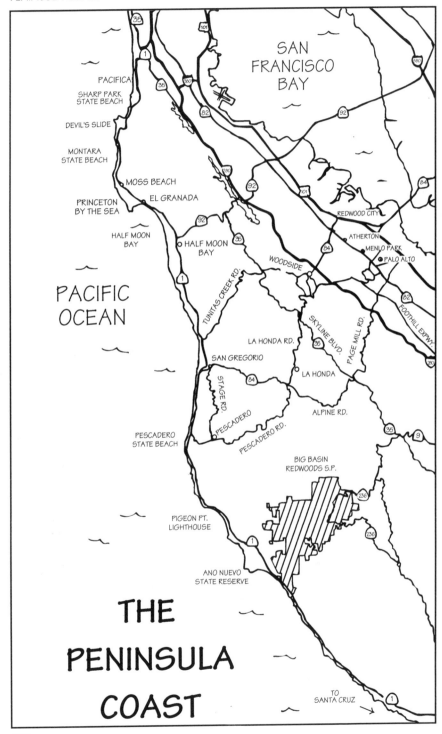

THE

PENINSULA

COAST

PENINSULA COAST

The wild and woolly Peninsula coast that begins just south of San Francisco is replete with rolling hills, fields of artichokes, and gorgeous rugged beaches. Towns like Pescadero, filled with ramshackle barns and Depression-era architecture, are more reminiscent of Tom Joad (Grapes of Wrath) than Steve Jobs (Apple Computers).

General Information

Area Code: 415

Half Moon Bay Chamber of Commerce: 520 Kelly Ave., 726-5202.

Getting There

To get to Pacifica, one of the first coastal towns south of San Francisco, take I-280 to Hwy 1 south into Pacifica. *Warning: Hwy 1 normally continues south to Moss Beach and Half Moon Bay, but heavy rains during the 1995 rainy season washed out the Devil's Slide portion of Hwy 1 between San Pedro Point and Montara Beach.* Until it is repaired, you must take I-280 to Hwy 92 west to Half Moon Bay to Hwy 1 north to reach Moss Beach and the surrounding area.

PACIFICA TO HALF MOON BAY

If you need a break from sunny, warm weather, visit fog-bound Pacifica. One of the first places you'll encounter is **Sharp Park State Beach**, with a sandy beach and a picnic and barbecue area. Further south on Hwy 1 is the smaller, semi-protected **Rockaway Beach**. The beach, which is framed between two outcroppings of rock, abuts a strip of hotels and restaurants. From Rockaway Beach, Hwy 1 winds up around **San Pedro Point**, a favorite with boogie-boarders and surfers. Just before you reach Montara Beach you will see **Gray Whale Cove**. This wonderful little spot is accessible only by a path down the cliffs, but the trip to this private, clothing-optional beach is well worth it. The next major stopping point is **Montara Beach**, a long, narrow beach just off the highway framed by rocks and low cliffs.

Hidden in **Moss Beach**, the next town down the coast, is the vast and fascinating **Fitzgerald Marine Reserve** (728-3584), one of the best places to tidepool on the coast, with up to 30 acres of exposed reef at low tide.

Restaurants and Entertainment

Barbara's Fishtrap $$$: 281 Capistrano Rd., Princeton-by-the-Sea, 728-7049. Offers the freshest seafood going in a casual ocean-side setting. Lunch and dinner daily.

Chart House $$$: 8150 Cabrillo Hwy., Montara, 728-7366. Popular with locals and tourists, this place offers simple, well-prepared seafood and a Mud Pie you could wallow in for days. Dinner daily; reservations suggested.

Moss Beach Distillery $$$/$$$$: Beach St. at Ocean St., Moss Beach, 728-5595. A great place for watching sunsets. Lays on the charm—wool blankets on the lower deck, lounge chairs, overhead heat lamps, and the ghost of a young woman murdered during the treacherous rum-running days of Prohibition. Dinner daily, brunch Su.

Playa de Acapulco $$: 145 Rockaway Beach, Pacifica, 359-3800. Serves cheap Mexican food. Lunch and dinner daily.

Shore Bird $$$: 390 Capistrano Rd., Princeton-by-the-Sea, 728-5541. This typical harbor-side establishment is a popular spot boasting excellent views of Pillar Point Harbor and the sunset. Seafood is the house specialty. Have your meal on their outdoor deck. Lunch and dinner daily, brunch and lunch Su.

Places to Stay

Point Montara Lighthouse Hostel: 16th St. and Hwy 1, Montara, 728-7177. Check-in 4:30pm-9:30pm, closed 9:30am-4:30pm. A very interesting, inexpensive option featuring an outdoor hot tub and a functioning lighthouse. Rooms are booked weeks, if not months, in advance. $8 for American Youth Hostel members, $10 for non-members.

HALF MOON BAY

Half Moon Bay is the only incorporated city between Pacifica and Santa Cruz. This commercial center of the Peninsula Coast is currently experiencing a bit of a boom and is growing at a fast clip. Take I-280 to Hwy 92 west. Hwy 92 cuts through the middle of town and ends at Hwy 1; beaches lie both north and south of that intersection.

Sights and Attractions

Originally known as Spanishtown, Half Moon Bay has a sleepy, historic Main Street lined with shops, restaurants, and inns. **The Spanishtown Historical Society/Half Moon Bay Jail** (726-7084) at 500 Johnston Street offers walking tours on weekend afternoons that start at the old jail—reservations are recommended. It's definitely worth stopping on Main Street to check out the interesting stores and galleries.

If you haven't brought a bike with you, stop by **The Bicyclery** (726-6000) at 432 Main Street. For $6 an hour, the friendly people at this bicycle store will supply you with mountain or road bikes, helmets, and locks. They're open M-F 9:30am to 6:30pm; Sa 10am to 5pm; Su 11am to 5pm.

Beaches span the entire length of Hwy 1. One of the largest is **Half Moon Bay State Park** (726-6238), just south of Hwy 92 at Kelly Avenue. This beach is also the only one in the area that allows overnight camping. There's a $4 charge for parking your car during the day or overnight, but this fee also entitles you to park at any of the state parks on the coast. If you plan to camp here you'll be on **Francis Beach**. There are 51 individual campsites located on the low bluff above the beach, all given out on a first-come first-served basis for $14 per campsite. You can make reservations through the park, or through **Mistix** (800-444-7275). There are many other beaches around the area, including **Elmar, Venice, Dunes, Naples, and Miramar,** each of which has a different personality and facilities, so check out a few sites before setting up for the day. You don't have to pay for parking at **Redondo Beach**, but you do have to maneuver through a long bumpy road and then scramble down the side of a cliff to reach the beach. However, the difficult access means that the beach is relatively uncrowded. Redondo Beach Road is a little south of Hwy 92.

If staying dry appeals to you, explore the Half Moon Bay coastline on horseback. Two local stables, **Sea Horse Ranch** and **Friendly Acres Ranch** (726-8550) at 1828 Cabrillo Highway offer horse rentals and guides that will set you up for a 90-minute walk through the surf for $30. The stables offer trail and beach rides for all levels of riding ability and are open daily from 8am to 6pm.

Another diversion in the area is the **Obester Winery** (726-9463) at 12341 San Mateo Road (Hwy 92). Obester makes a nice Sauvignon Blanc that you can taste on the spot or save for a picnic. They also produce their own mustard, olive oil, and herbal vinegars and are open 10am to 5pm daily.

Restaurants

California Girl's Café $: 80 North Cabrillo Hwy., Ste. S, Half Moon Bay, 726-4420. Tempting muffins and cinnamon rolls, weekend breakfast specials, and very imaginative sandwiches (try the marinated artichoke hearts, prosciutto, and basil on herbed focaccia bread). M-F 7am-5pm; Sa 9am-5pm.

Cunha's Country Store $: 448 Main St., Half Moon Bay, 726-4071. Huge, cheap sandwiches, and everything from Jello to wild mushroom pasta. M-Sa 8am-8pm; Su 8am-7pm.

Flying Fish Grill $$: 99 San Mateo Rd. (Corner of Hwy. 1 and Main St.), Half Moon Bay, 712-1125. Standard fried fish-and-chips and interesting grilled seafood. W-Su 11am-7pm.

Half Moon Bay Coffee Company $: 315 Main St., Half Moon Bay, 726-1994. The home of huge slices of amazing pie. M-F 6:30am-9pm; Sa-Su 7:30am-10pm.

LA DI DA $: 507A Purisima Rd., Half Moon Bay, 726-1663. Has a wacky approach to coffee, an offbeat selection of artwork, and live entertainment. M-W 6:30am-8pm; Th, F, Sa 6:30am-10pm; Su 8am-8pm; live music W, S, Su afternoons and F-Sa 8pm-10pm.

McCoffee $: 522 Main St., Half Moon Bay, 726-6241. A good local joint to nurse espresso. M-F 7am-6pm; Sa 8am-6pm; Su 9am-6pm.

Miramar Beach Inn $$$: 131 Mirada Rd., Miramar, 726-9053. A historic roadhouse dating back to Prohibition that keeps the roar of the 20s alive. Live music F-Sa nights. Lunch and dinner daily, brunch Su.

Pasta Moon $$$: 315 Main St., Half Moon Bay, 726-5125. Authentic, regional Italian food and great pasta made fresh daily. Lunch and dinner daily.

San Benito House $$$: 356 Main St., Half Moon Bay, 726-3425. A gourmet restaurant attached to a quaint inn with a good Sunday brunch and a deli that uses fresh bread to construct its huge sandwiches. Dinner Th-Su, Su brunch $$; Deli $ 11am-3pm.

3 Amigos Taqueria $: Kelly Ave. and Hwy. 1, Half Moon Bay, 726-6080. A fast-food atmosphere and great Mexican specialties. Daily 9:30am-midnight.

Places to Stay

Cypress Inn: 407 Mirada Rd., Half Moon Bay, 726-6002. A cozy Santa Fe-style hideaway. Each room is impressively equipped with a fireplace and French doors that open onto a private deck with a view of the ocean. $150-$275.

Mill Rose Inn: 615 Mill St., Half Moon Bay, 726-9794. A romantic inn with warm, caring service. Enjoy an inviting English Country garden setting. Private entrances, private Jacuzzis, fluffy feather beds, fireplaces, champagne breakfasts, VCRs, and phones complete this luxurious picture $180-$265.

Old Thyme Inn: 779 Main St., Half Moon Bay, 726-1616. This charming inn is cheerful and upbeat, with stuffed animals on every bed, and rooms named and decorated in an herbal theme. Weekdays $65-$110, weekends $150.

SAN GREGORIO TO AÑO NUEVO

San Gregorio Beach is located where Hwy 1 intersects Hwy 84, and is usually fairly crowded. Further down Hwy 1 is **Pomponio Beach**, a good place to fish or have a picnic. **Pescadero Beach**, which also has nature trails and exhibits, is next to the 587-acre

Pescadero Marsh Natural Preserve, where tidepools emerge along the rocky stretch at low tide. Other area beaches include **Pebble Beach** and rocky **Bean Hollow State Beach**.

If you're interested in a hike through the redwoods away from the coast, take Cloverdale Road from Pescadero to **Butano State Park** (879-0173). This stretch of forest was lightly logged in the 1880s, and it features a stand of old-growth redwoods. Follow the Doe Ridge Trail for a hike through virgin timber. The facilities include walk-in and trail campsites, often full in spring and summer—advance reservations are a must.

By far the most interesting coastal area south of Half Moon Bay, and perhaps on the entire Peninsula, is **Año Nuevo Reserve** (879-0227) on Hwy 1, 30 miles south of Half Moon Bay. This area is home to enormous elephant seals that range from about eight to 18 feet long and can weigh as much as two and a half tons. The female seals come on shore in December to give birth, and then mate again while the male seals battle to establish breeding rights. Stellar sea lions and harbor seals breed on the beaches here at other times of the year, so its always worth a visit. During the December to March breeding season, the reserve is only open to guided tours led by park rangers.

Just across from Año Nuevo is **Coastways U-Pick Ranch** (879-0414), where you can pick kiwis, olallieberries, and so forth, depending on the time of year. Enjoy your produce in their nice picnic area. Summer hours are daily 9am to 5pm; winter 10am to 4pm.

Farther south on Hwy 1 is the end of a trail that begins at Waddell Beach and runs through the **Big Basin Redwood State Park** (408-338-6132). The Skyline-to-the-Sea trail begins at the top of the Santa Cruz Mountains. From the mountain headquarters, there's easy access to Big Basin's many other trails, which run through miles of forest and along creeks and waterfalls. The park has some campgrounds, and the old logging roads make for some great mountain biking. The inland part of Big Basin can be reached by taking Hwy 85 to Hwy 9, and then following Hwy 236 into the park.

Restaurants and Entertainment

Apple Jacks $: Hwy 84, La Honda, 747-0331. A venerable saloon where all types meet to eat, drink, and be merry. M-F noon-2am; Sa-Su 10am-2pm.

Duarte's $$: 202 Stage Rd., Pescadero, 879-0464. Pescadero's most celebrated saloon. Great pie, garden-grown veggies, and local seafood give this 50s-style place its well-deserved reputation. Breakfast, lunch, and dinner daily.

McLuke's $$: 8865 La Honda Rd., La Honda, 747-0092. A country restaurant with a good collection of microbrews. Live music in the garden on summer weekends. Breakfast, lunch and dinner W-Su; dinner only M-Tu.

Norm's Market $: 287 Stage Rd., Pescadero, 879-0147. Great picnic fixings, fresh-baked bread, and an extensive wine cellar. M-Sa 10am-7pm; Su 10am-6pm.

Phipps Ranch $: 2700 Pescadero Rd., Pescadero, 879-0787. Seasonal produce, pick-your own berries, and a petting zoo. 10am-7pm daily (except Thanksgiving day and the week after Christmas).

San Gregorio General Store $: Hwy 84 and Stage Rd., San Gregorio, 726-0565. Everything you'll ever need—a bar, mercantile, bookstore, and music hall all in one. Bluegrass and Irish music starts at 2pm Sa-Su. 9am-6pm daily; Sa-Su often later than 6pm.

Places to Stay

Pigeon Point Lighthouse Hostel: Pigeon Point Rd. and Hwy 1, Pescadero, 879-0633. Four buildings next to the still-functioning lighthouse, this hostel can house up to 50 people overnight. Reservations are recommended since rooms are sometimes booked months in advance; check-in is from 4:30pm to 9:30pm; desk is closed from 9:30am to 4:30pm.

SAN FRANCISCO

NEIGHBORHOODS

The real sights and attractions of San Francisco are not the museums and monuments, but the neighborhoods themselves, each with its own character and identity. To glimpse the unique charm of each area, and to avoid parking nightmares, it's best to travel by foot (be ready to climb up the city's famous hills). Many San Francisco neighborhoods host fairs along major commercial streets during spring and summer weekends that usually typify the character of the community and provide excuses to spend a day in the city. Arm yourself with a good map and set out to discover the city.

Chinatown

You'll instantly know when you've entered Chinatown—an ornate gateway marks its entrance, and the streets suddenly take on the bustle, color, and richness of Asia. To get your bearings, stop by the **Chinese Cultural Center** on the third floor of the Holiday Inn (750 Kearny) for listings of sights and attractions. **Grant Avenue** is the main strip in Chinatown and, although now largely geared towards tourists, it maintains some outstanding Chinese architecture and all sorts of interesting shops. Some particularly good spots are the **Chinatown Kite Shop** (717 Grant), with a beautiful assortment of flying objects, and the **Wok Shop** (718 Grant), where you will find all the right tools for creating Chinese cuisine. Further up the street is **TenRen's** (949 Grant), a distinguished tea store with all sorts of soon-to-be steeped leaves, roots, and flowers. **The Li Po Lounge** (916 Grant) and **Buddha Lounge** (901 Grant) are just two of the local hangouts, both with friendly bartenders who will perhaps too gladly serve you mysterious brown liquor out of dusty old Chinese jugs (for the daring only). If making strange and beautiful noise is your calling, visit the **Clarion Music Center** (816 Sacramento), where you'll find exotic instruments from all corners of the earth. Then poke around **Stockton Avenue**, one block west of Grant, to find Chinatown locals. Here you can pick up all kinds of seafood and produce, and anything from live frogs and Chinese pornography to wheat gluten.

If the aroma of Chinese food makes you hungry, you're in luck—there are an enormous number of restaurants in the area. **Lucky Creation** (854 Washington), where you're often asked to share a table with the local clientele, serves delicious vegetarian meals. **The House of Nan King** (see review) is a very popular spot with quick service and unique, high-quality food. **The Far East Café** (631 Grant) serves slightly upscale Cantonese cuisine, and if you request it, will seat you in a secluded dining area.

To view a truly authentic centerpiece of Chinese culture, visit the **Tien Hou Temple** (125 Waverly), which is open to visitors, but should be respected as a place of worship. **The Golden Gate Fortune Cookie Factory** (56 Ross Alley) is a fun spot to explore the making of these crunchy treats. If you crave a comfy seat and unusual entertainment, visit one of the numerous local movie theaters, such as the **Great Star Theater** (636 Jackson), the **World Theater** (644 Broadway), or the **Pagoda** (1741 Powell), which feature the latest Hong Kong films (subtitled in English) throughout the day.

Union Square and the Civic Center

Union Square, framed by Geary, Powell, Post, and Stockton Streets is an enclave of palm trees, pigeons, park benches, and homeless people swarming with urgent, well-dressed shoppers. The best parking in the area is at the **Sutter Stockton Garage** (330 Sutter),

although the per-hour charge increases as your stay lengthens. The **Union Square Garage** at 333 Post has reasonable night rates, and there is also a garage beneath the **Civic Center**.

Among the famous department stores on the square are **Macy's, Neiman-Marcus, Saks Fifth Avenue, Gump's, Hermes, Tiffany's, and F.A.O. Schwartz**. The best way to experience this area is to start early (ensuring a space in the Sutter-Stockton parking garage) and walk the streets radiating from Union Square. For a large-scale shopping experience, try the stylish **San Francisco Centre** (Market and 5th Streets), which features anchor tenants **J. Crew, Ann Taylor, and Nordstrom**.

Along tiny **Maiden Lane** just off Stockton Street are chichi old world boutiques like **Chanel** and **Cartier**. Newcomers like **Metier**, which sells clothes and trendy jewelry by local designers, are also worth checking out. Don't miss the **Circle Gallery** building at 140 Maiden Lane, designed by Frank Lloyd Wright. Serious gallery-goers should pick up the *Gallery Guide*, a free-publication that lists exhibition schedules for the city's major galleries, some located around Union Square. Drop in at **49 Geary**, home of the world-class **Fraenkel Gallery** and the interesting **Stephen Wirtz Gallery**. If you're around Union Square on the first Thursday of each month, all participating galleries hold open houses from 5pm to 7pm.

Some of the hippest and most uniquely San Francisco spots are found around Union Square. San Francisco's own **Wilkes-Bashford** (375 Sutter) suits many of the city's business elite and celebrities. Check out **Emporio Armani** (1 Grant), located in a striking Roman-style building that once housed a bank. The store also features Armani-designed food at a chic café within the store. Speaking of chic cafés, **Café Claude** (see review) and **Café Bastille** (22 Belden Place) offer inexpensive bistro fare and free live jazz in authentic Parisian fashion. While you're in the vicinity, check out the lobby of the **Hotel Triton** (342 Grant), which has some of the funkiest hotel furnishings around.

The **theater district**, running along Geary Street, is the epitome of real urban culture in San Francisco. Make sure to see what's on the bill at San Francisco's renowned **American Conservatory Theater** (345 Mason Street). Check the pink section of the Sunday *San Francisco Examiner* for a comprehensive listing of shows and information on how to buy tickets. For low-priced tickets, try **TIX Bay Area** (Stockton Street at Union Square, 433-STBS), where half-price tickets are available the day of the show. Many theaters offer student discounts as well.

For your pre-show cocktail, visit any of the big hotels in Union Square—you'll find an abundance of piano bars and cocktail lounges where you can sip fine beverages in plush surroundings. The best of these are the **Equinox Bar** at the **Hyatt** (with its revolving bar and 360-degree view of the city) and the **Compass Rose at the St. Francis Hotel**. For cheap eats before the show, try **David's Delicatessen** (474 Geary), home of great Borscht, corned beef, and other New York deli treats.

The **Tenderloin** (the area between the Civic Center and Downtown) is best known as the red-light district; however, there are ultra-hip urban gems to be found in this seedy area. Make sure to visit **MAC** (812 Post), a super-trendy clothing boutique, and **Miss Pearl's Jam House** (see review) for great Caribbean food, exotic mixed drinks, and live music. The jazz and supper club **181 Eddy** (181 Eddy) is an oasis of beautiful people in the heart of the urban decay. The Tenderloin's growing Vietnamese community has opened a number of restaurants, **Tulan** (8 Sixth St.) being the best of these efforts.

The **Civic Center** area houses many city and state buildings. **City Hall**, at the center of the area, is crowned with a huge dome. **Louise M. Davies Symphony Hall** is an elegant addition to the architecture of the neighborhood, which includes the **San Francisco Public Library** (soon to move to a new building just a few blocks away), the **California State Building**, and the **United Nations Plaza. The War Memorial Veterans Building** houses **Herbst Theater**. The **War Memorial Opera House** is the setting for the performances of the city's opera and ballet companies, while the **Civic**

Auditorium is used for many modern music performances. **Brooks Exhibit Hall** is beneath the plaza.

Close to the **Civic Center**, **Max's Opera Café** (601 Van Ness) serves N.Y.-style deli sandwiches, dinners, and lusty desserts. **Stars** (see review) and **Stars Café** are fun for people-watching. For less-expensive fare, check out **Spuntino** (524 Van Ness), a speedy Italian caffè with salads, pasta, and foccacia.

Nob Hill and Russian Hill

Nob Hill and Russian Hill are two of the more prestigious residential areas of the city, featuring apartments and establishments with spectacular views and urban elegance. The top of **Nob Hill** is the site of the "Big Four" hotels: **Stanford Court, Mark Hopkins Inter-Continental, Fairmont,** and **Huntington**, named for the railroad barons whose mansions graced the hill until their demise in the 1906 earthquake. **The Pacific Union Club**, an elegant brownstone at the top of Nob Hill, is the only remnant of those elite structures, and is now a private club for old-money San Franciscans.

Of the many restaurants found within these hotels, **Fournou's Ovens** (in the Stanford Court Hotel) serves consistently pleasing and elegant fare. It boasts an open hearth where many of the game, meat, and vegetable dishes are prepared. And no visit to Nob Hill would be complete without a visit to one of these hotels' cocktail lounges or piano bars—try the **Top of the Mark** at the Mark Hopkins, or the **Crown Room** at the top of the Fairmont tower for a magnificent view of the city. If you're in for some campy fun, check out the Fairmount's **Tonga Room**, complete with a mechanical tropical storm and a floating band on a robotic "island."

Also at the top of Nob Hill is the striking **Grace Cathedral** (Taylor & California). Construction began in 1910, ended in 1964, and has been resumed this year with the erection of a grand staircase leading to the main entrance. Be sure to examine the doors; they're bronze casts of Ghiberti's original "Doors to Paradise" from the Florence Baptistery. The interior of the cathedral is as spectacular as the exterior, and includes a series of murals depicting San Francisco history. The nearby **Cable Car Barn** (1201 Mason) is a showcase for cable-car history and technology in the earlier years of this century. There is a room for viewing the cable system at work, and a museum of cable cars in the building. On the west side of the hill, stop by the **Tibet Shop** (1807 Polk) for jewelry, clothing, and antiques.

Russian Hill is a sophisticated residential area with diverse architecture, restaurants, and attractions. First on the list is a drive or walk down **Lombard Street** from the top of Russian Hill (at Hyde), a serpentine thoroughfare that descends precariously through immaculate flower gardens. (Lombard will be closed for repairs lasting roughly six months beginning February 1995.) Lesser known is the **San Francisco Art Institute** (800 Chestnut), which has a Spanish courtyard, a lovely rooftop café, and a lively collection of art, including a Diego Rivera mural. **Le Petit Café** (see review) is a terrific find that's open all day (breakfast is especially noteworthy). **Hyde Street Bistro** (see review) is a sure bet for an interesting meal with Austrian and Italian influences. Lively and inexpensive places to grab a bite include **The Real Food Deli**, featuring interesting neo-hippie fare (2164 Polk), **Oaxaca** (2141 Polk), a Mexican grill with excellent burritos, and **Za** (see review).

Night-time entertainment in this area varies from Euro-chic **Babylon** (2260 Van Ness Ave.) to post-fraternity/pre-yuppie hang outs like **Johnny Love's** (1500 Broadway) and **Shanghai Kelly's** (across the street).

North Beach/Telegraph Hill

North Beach is known as the Little Italy of San Francisco, reflecting the large Italian population which has lived here since the late 1800s. During the 1950s and 1960s North Beach was where much of the early Beatnik movement began, and was a haven of nightclubs famous for its flourishing jazz scene, drag shows, and comedy clubs (exhibiting such revolutionaries as Lenny Bruce). While the scene has changed, some landmarks remain intact—many near the intersection of Broadway and Columbus. **City Lights Bookstore** (261 Columbus) first published many of the early Beats, like Jack Kerouac and Allen Ginsberg. **Vesuvio Café** next door (255 Columbus) is one of many places where they drank.

Just across the street, **Tosca** (242 Columbus), a beautiful bar famous for its Irish Coffee, sports an antique jukebox filled with opera records. Visit early in the evening, since dance music comes through the floor from the Palladium nightclub next door and spoils the ambiance. Just outside of Tosca is a small alley leading to **Specs' Museum Café** (12 Adler), a bar decorated in W.W.II memorabilia and usually full of old-timers and other, more colorful residents of North Beach.

On Broadway among the strip clubs is a yuppie oasis, **Enricos Sidewalk Café** (504 Broadway). The food is good, they feature live music nightly (often good jazz), and the outdoor seating area is a great place to have a drink and take in the nightlife; the overhead heaters let you enjoy even the coldest San Francisco evenings. Around the corner **Tommaso's Restaurant** (see review), famed as Francis Ford Coppola's favorite Italian restaurant in the city, serves excellent wood-fired pizza in a dark, cozy hall.

Columbus Avenue is the main drag in North Beach, lined with countless cafés, pastry shops and Italian restaurants. **The Stinking Rose** (325 Columbus) is a very popular eatery, but is only for the true garlic lover or the truly antisocial. Further up on Columbus, **Il Pollaio** features grilled chickens at reasonable prices. Just across the street is **Mario's Bohemian Cigar Store Café**, a tiny bar and café well-known for its delicious foccacia sandwiches. Mario's overlooks **Washington Square Park**, a great place to absorb old-world charm—there are always aged Italian people gathering to chat, and Chinese people practicing Tai Chi. **Saints Peter and Paul Church** stands at the far end of the park. Founded in 1884, it was the first Italian parish established in the United States, and was the backdrop for Joe DiMaggio and Marilyn Monroe's wedding photos.

Grant Avenue is another main thoroughfare in North Beach, with plenty of blues bars, cafés, restaurants, and eclectic retail stores. **Caffè Trieste** (601 Vallejo) is a well-known Beat landmark with live Italian mandolin and opera music on weekends. The **Savoy Tivoli** (1434 Grant) is *the* place for the Euro set to see and be seen. **The Saloon** (1232 Grant) is a dingy little bar with live music nightly and all day Saturday. Up the street at the **Lost and Found** (1353 Grant) and **Grant and Green** (1371 Grant), you can dance to live blues with a long-neck in hand. **Quantity Postcards** (1441 Grant) has the best selection of postcards in the city, with subjects ranging from the historical to the perverse, as well as wacky funhouse props to play with.

Above North Beach is **Telegraph Hill**, a quiet residential area capped by **Coit Tower**, which is dedicated to volunteer firefighters. The inside houses WPA murals by students and associates of Diego Rivera, and the top (via elevator) has great views. You can drive to the top of the hill, but so can every other tourist, so parking is a problem and there are often long lines of cars waiting to get up the street.

On the east side of Telegraph Hill from Coit Tower are the **Filbert Steps**, a beautiful-ly landscaped walkway connecting the streets on the hill. The only part of North Beach that survived the 1906 quake and fire, this area has interesting cottages and beautiful gardens. Near the top of the steps, Humphrey Bogart fans should take note of the Art Deco building which was featured in the film *Dark Passage*.

Fisherman's Wharf

Fisherman's Wharf was at one time San Francisco's center for commercial fishing. Today, you can still spot fishing boats plying the harbor or unloading their catch of the day at the docks, but for the most part, the wharf, with its Wax Museum, Guinness Book of Records display, and innumerable T-shirt and souvenir shops, is primarily part of the local tourist industry. Throngs of people can always be found shopping or waiting in line for ferries to **Angel Island**, **Alcatraz**, and **Sausalito**, so if crowds aren't your scene, head for the hills.

Travel west along the waterfront on Jefferson Street into the heart of the tourist throng. Keep an eye on your wallet—pickpockets lurk everywhere. Stop at the boat marina and check out the sea lions that have taken over a number of docks and driven the remaining boat keepers crazy with their incessant barking. **Pier 39** is a modern (1978) shopping mall built on an old pier. It looks like a historic street and is a favorite spot to watch congregating seals and top-notch street performers. Across the street, **Boudin's Bakery** (156 Jefferson) continues to make sourdough bread as they have since 1849—a large window lets you view the process. A short distance west on Jefferson, you can pick up small samples of crab, squid, and other seafood from a group of retail fish peddlers—the remains of the active fish trade which gave the area its name.

Continue west on Jefferson and stop in at **Lou's Pier 47** (300 Jefferson), which features live blues seven nights a week and is open to all ages. Continue toward **The Cannery** (2801 Leavenworth), a former Del Monte peach canning plant converted into a shopping center. **The Fiddler's Green** (1333 Columbus), Van Morrison's preferred San Francisco hangout, features live music on weekends, and poached salmon and chips. Ask barman Myles O'Reilly for a slow-pour Guinness, the best pint in the city. Be sure to try their Irish Coffees, reputedly much better than the ones served at **Buena Vista** (2765 Hyde), the inventor of the libation. **Ghirardelli Square** is around the corner at 900 North Point. Originally a woolen mill during the Civil War, it later became the chocolate factory for which it is named. The current **Ghirardelli Chocolate Manufactory** is an old-fashioned ice cream parlor with long lines, great fudge, and examples of historic chocolate-making machines. Ghirardelli Square itself offers yet another shopping center, although this one's a bit more upscale than Pier 39.

Aquatic Park, on the shore just north of Ghirardelli Square, is a protected cove with a beach used primarily by the members of the Dolphin Club, a group of ocean swimmers who race from Alcatraz to Aquatic Park every New Year's. This is a great spot to catch the lively troupe of drummers and bongo players jamming and hanging out on the steps—if your feet are losing their spring, rest and recharge with the beat. For a good view of the city and a peek at the salty fishermen of the wharf, take a walk onto the pier several hundred yards west of Aquatic Park at the foot of Van Ness Avenue.

The Marina

The Marina has earned the dubious title of "The Neighborhood Most Damaged by the 1989 Earthquake." There are few visible scars remaining, but for posterity you might want to check out the empty lots on Fillmore Street, site of the great fire shown repeatedly on the TV networks.

Streets in the Marina tend to meander, and it's easy to get confused in the maze of 1920s luxury apartment buildings and Mediterranean-style stucco homes. A straight and definite route is to walk north on Fillmore until you hit the **Marina Green**, which is a popular kite-flying and in-line skating spot. Take a walk out on the peninsula behind the Yacht Club and look for **the wave organ**, a series of benches and ceramic tubes embedded in the rocks that magnify the sounds of the sea.

From the Marina Green you can walk east to **Fort Mason**. Originally used as Army barracks in the 1850s, Fort Mason is comprised of several long warehouse-type buildings that line the water's edge. **The S.S. Jeremiah O'Brien**, the last Liberty ship still afloat, is located here. Now part of the **Golden Gate Recreational Area**, which has headquarters next door, Fort Mason houses numerous small museums, workshops, theaters, and crafts stores, as well as the famous vegetarian restaurant **Greens** (see review). Fort Mason also includes a pleasant park good for picnicking and sunbathing, as well as an **AYH Youth Hostel** popular with budget tourists.

To the west, you can take an extended walk across **Crissy Field** to **Fort Point**, an old Army fort that affords a very close-up view of the Golden Gate Bridge. Watch daring surfers catch precarious waves under the bridge. You can take a handy audio tour of this historic site, the only Civil War fort on the West Coast. Although the trail directly up to the bridge is closed, you can follow the road up; this area has great spots to watch spectacular sunsets, particularly if you stay away from the highway.

The Palace of Fine Arts and the **Exploratorium** at Lyon Street and Marina Boulevard are well worth a visit. The Palace, designed by Bernard Maybeck, is the only remnant of the 1915 Panama-Pacific Exposition. An elaborate classical structure set next to a swan-filled pond, the Palace is a favorite spot for traditional Asian wedding photographs (on weekend afternoons you might see as many as ten bridal parties in full dress). The grounds also make a nice place for a picnic, if you don't mind the flocks of pigeons and ducks. **The Exploratorium** is a low-key, hands-on science and technology museum, engrossing for kids of all ages (see *Arts & Entertainment* section).

Chestnut Street, the main retail drag in the Marina, has a good selection of restaurants, boutiques, and cafés. **Bepple's Pies** (2142 Chestnut) serves huge slices of, you guessed it, homemade pies. Look for Chestnut Street outposts of both **Peet's Coffee** (2156 Chestnut) and **Noah's Bagels** (2075 Chestnut), or try **Java Bay** (2056 Chestnut), a home-grown alternative. **The Body Shop** (2106 Chestnut), the English purveyor of environmentally correct beauty products, has a friendly store here. Stock up for your next gourmet meal at **Lucca Delicatessen** (2120 Chestnut). When it's past shopping hours, check out the dark and smoky scene at **Blues** (2125 Lombard) and the tamer crowd at **The Horseshoe Tavern** (2024 Chestnut).

When the sun goes down, head toward the **"Triangle"**—so-named because singles enter and then vanish—at the intersection of Fillmore and Filbert Streets, where you'll find the **Balboa Café** (good and pricey food) and the **Golden Gate Bar and Grill**. For a wilder, sweatier crowd, the **Pierce Street Annex**, half a block up on Fillmore, is *the* place to see swinging singles at their finest.

Pacific Heights

Pacific Heights, a ritzy residential neighborhood perched atop one of San Francisco's hills, is a favorite place to see the Bay in panorama and view some of the city's most dazzling architecture. You can walk for hours on these quiet streets, gawking at the many well-preserved Victorians and sprawling mansions.

There are several hilltop parks for gazing at the views. **Alta Plaza Park** at Jackson and Steiner provides a cityscape view from the top and has public tennis courts and a playground. (Be sure to take a look at the quaint Victorians lining its south side.) On Sacramento and Laguna Streets is **Lafayette Park**, which has a terrific view of Russian Hill and the Bay Bridge—on a good day, you can see Mount Diablo in the distance to the east.

Fillmore and Union Streets are a boutique browser's paradise. On Fillmore between Sutter and Jackson, you'll find everything a well-heeled and well-purveyed yuppie could ever need. Some of the clothing stores are worth a visit, if only for inspiration. **Fillamento** (2185 Fillmore), a deluxe housewares store, is worth scoping for its many gourmet gadgets. No trip to Pacific Heights is complete without a visit to the **Spinelli Coffee Company** (2455 Fillmore) or the brand new **Royal Ground** (2060 Fillmore), the neighborhood java dispensers. **Browser Books** (2195 Fillmore) is open late and lives up to its name (it's easy to spend some time between its cozy shelves).

For a quick bite, pick up a fresh pastry or piece of excellent cheese at the **California Street Creamery** (2413 California). For a full meal, try **Jackson Fillmore** (2506 Fillmore), definitely one of the best meals around. A neighborhood favorite is **La Méditerranée** (2210 Fillmore), an inexpensive café serving Middle-Eastern dishes. For a yupscale beer and burger, visit **Harry's** (2020 Fillmore), or sit at the oak bar and enjoy the live jazz.

Walk north on Fillmore to view a breathtaking panorama of the Golden Gate Bridge. There are steps in the sidewalk to help make the going easier along one precariously steep stretch. Take a peek in the church on the corner of Green and Steiner, as the stained glass on a sunny day is spectacular. At the base of the hill is Union Street, one of the city's most famous shopping areas. For a pick-me-up, stop in at **Il Fornaio** (2298 Union) for a latté or **Tarr and Feathers** (2140 Union), where Jaegermeister is served on tap! Along the street, you'll find a plethora of gift stores offering a wide range of wares. Some notable shops include **Z Gallery** (2071 Union); **Kenneth Cole** (2078 Union); **Oggetti** (1846 Union), purveyor of fine Florentine papers; and **Body Time** (2072 Union), which sells all-natural bath and beauty products. Some of the renowned restaurants include **Pane e Vino** (see review), **Bontà** (see review), and **Yoshida-Ya** (1581 Webster).

Golden Gate Park

Who would have thought it possible in 1870 that a 1,017-acre plot of windswept sand dunes could be transformed into a lush green park? With the vision and guidance of William Hammond Hall, a young civil engineer, a whole new ecological system was born and has grown to become a verdant wonderland. Spanning three miles east to west and nine blocks north to south, Golden Gate Park is a city treasure, inviting enthusiasts of life to sample nature, sports, and culture. The park has more than 50 entryways, from the Great Highway at the west end of the park to the eastern boundary at Stanyan Street. The best way to start is with the *Map & Guide to Golden Gate Park*, found at most of the bike rental or sport shops on Haight or Stanyan Streets.

Two of Golden Gate Park's most famous attractions are the **California Academy of Sciences** and the **M.H. de Young Memorial Museum**. The Academy, recently renovated, is home to the **Steinhart Aquarium**—don't feed the crocodiles. The Academy also has a collection of Gary Larson cartoons. While you're there, take in the laser show at the **Morrison Planetarium**. The **de Young Museum**, also recently renovated, houses both the **Asian Art Museum** and a large collection of American and British art. Next door to the de Young is the famous **Japanese Tea Garden**, an incredibly beautiful setting where you can lose yourself in Zen contemplation and expensive tea.

As the park was originally created for strollers who wanted a respite from the frenetic pace of city life, there are hundreds of paths to explore. A walk through the varieties of plants and flowers in **Strybing Arboretum** can be particularly pleasant on a spring day. Vision-impaired visitors will enjoy the **Garden of Fragrance** in the Arboretum; its plants are specifically selected for scent and texture. Spring is also the best time to have a picnic in the **Rose Gardens**. The **Rhododendron Dell** contains a splendid abundance of the favorite flower of John McLaren, park planner. For a longer walk, or simply a peaceful place to sit, try the path around **Stow Lake**. Other scenic spots include the **Shakespeare Garden** (behind the Academy), which contains plants and flowers figuring in Shakespeare's works, and **Strawberry Hill**, which provides an impressive view of the San Francisco peninsula. For anyone especially interested in tropical plants and orchids, the **Conservatory of Flowers** is worth a visit.

To see some of the park's unique attractions, first visit the **Buffalo Paddock** at the west end of the park, a large section of land reserved for the descendants of the Park Commission's original set of buffalo. Following John F. Kennedy Drive east from the paddock, you reach the **Dutch Windmill** surrounded by a colorful tulip garden. If you continue on the drive and cross the highway, there's parking along the beach. Returning on JFK Drive, stop by **Spreckels Lake** to watch members of the Model Yacht Club sail their miniature boats. Then head over to the **Children's Playground** to climb, swing, and slide. Make sure to visit the carousel, a Herschel-Spillman restored to its original splendor, complete with horses, frogs and zebras.

If in-line skating or biking is your thing, a trip to the park on Sundays is a must. Traffic is blocked off so those on man-powered wheels can glide down the park streets in peace. The atmosphere at Golden Gate Park on Sundays is like a huge party—especially at the paved square near the Arboretum, where skaters perform elaborate dance sequences to disco music.

The Haight

The Haight's proximity to the University of San Francisco and its inexpensive communal-style homes made it a bastion of the hippie movement in the 1960s. The Haight's heyday was in 1967, when the Human Be-In and the Gathering of the Tribes were held at the Golden Gate Park Polo Grounds. Over 20,000 people gathered to listen to Timothy Leary, Jerry Rubin, Jefferson Airplane, and the Grateful Dead. The Haight has gradually matured since those days, but it hasn't lost its sixties feel. You'll find a mix of local residents: students; young, affluent professionals and homeowners; black-clad, pierced hipsters; and an enclave of sixties holdouts.

The Haight is divided into two sections—Upper and Lower. The Upper Haight runs down Haight Street from Golden Gate Park to Central Avenue, and contains the famous intersection of Haight and Ashbury. This area features most of the action and many of the curious shops. The Lower Haight, centered around the intersection of Haight and Fillmore, has a good cross section of skaters, ravers, rappers, and bohemians.

Start with brunch in the Lower Haight at **Kate's Kitchen** (471 Haight), where soul food meets the artistry of California cuisine. Look for Bobby McFerrin and ask for Eloise's recommendation. The 500 block of Haight contains an assortment of grungy cafés, bars and restaurants: try the **Squat and Gobble**, **Café International**, **Midtown**, **Spaghetti Western**, **Noc Noc**, and **Tornado**, all within a few doors of each other. **Mad Dog in the Fog** (530 Haight) is a little more mainstream, offering good pints and darts to a casual, post-college crowd. For an offbeat assortment of the latest in acid jazz, techno, and imports, descend into the cellar of **Tweekin Records** (593 Haight).

Now head to the upper Haight, making sure to notice the large and detailed Victorian homes along the way, many of which have been beautifully restored in luscious color schemes. The best house viewing is actually on the blocks north and south of Haight; cross-street Masonic Avenue is also a good spot.

Upper Haight Street is a kind of informal shopping mall of the offbeat. Since many shops are as unique inside as their storefronts suggest, wandering up and down the street until you expire from sensory overload seems to be the best strategy. To be a fashion plate in the Haight you need only to shop at **Daljeets** (1744 Haight), a punk-rock fashion haven that claims to have "The Largest Selection of Thi-Hi Boots." For a more eclectic selection, try the used clothing stores **Aardvark's Odd Ark** (1501 Haight), **Buffalo Exchange** (1555 Haight), and **Wasteland** (1660 Haight). The City's best selection of tights can be found in the cramped **Piedmont Boutique** (1452 Haight). **Behind the Post Office** (1504 Haight) may be short on space, but they're not short on style. Catering to the rave and rap scene, de rigeur oversized shirts, pants and street gear are their specialty.

Taking in a movie at the landmark **Red Vic** (1727 Haight) is an ideal way to experience the counter-culture. The communally-run theater features organic popcorn and movies which generally fall way outside the mainstream. **The Red Victorian Bed and Breakfast** just down the street bills itself as a "global village and networking center," and its casual café sells some great T-shirts. The interior is an absolute marvel, so be sure to ask to see some of the rooms upstairs. Right next door is **Café Paradiso**, which serves *the best* vegetarian chili and corn bread combo.

This area features the three Rs of record stores: **Reckless** (1401 Haight), **Recycled** (1377 Haight), and **Rough Trade** (1529 Haight). **Reckless** has the best cut-out and cassette selection, **Recycled** is the home of used vinyl, and **Rough Trade** has the best assortment of imports and reggae. For alternative-press reading material and any international or obscure periodical you might crave, head for **The Booksmith** (1644 Haight) at Haight and Cole, a well-known store with an excellent selection. **Great Expectations Bookstore** (1512 Haight) has a collection of T-shirts with political and social messages that reflect the neighborhood's history. Haight Street even boasts one of the best sneaker stores in the city—**Hoy's Sport** on Haight at Clayton, which specializes in running shoes.

Haight Street hosts as many eateries as it does shops. **Zona Rosa**, the modern Mexican eatery at Haight and Shrader, has become popular for its fast service and fresh ingredients. A burrito and beverage can be found for under $5 (perhaps another secret of popularity). Also try **Cha Cha Cha** (see review), a trendy and colorful Caribbean restaurant with consistently delectable dishes. If you're in a real hurry, stop by **Escape From New York Pizza** (1737 Haight) for a slice of authentic New York-style pizza. If you're in the mood to picnic, the best basket fillers are found at **The Real Food Company** on Stanyan and Carl. Try **The Real Foods Deli** on the corner for pastas, breads (try Metropolis potato and rosemary bread), imported cheeses, and wines.

The onset of evening adds an element of the bizarre to this already wacky neighborhood. The panhandling turns into comedy acts, the denizens appear in more fanciful trappings, and the streets seem to be crawling with people (some of them less than savory). Not surprisingly, there's a more than adequate supply of bars and clubs to explore. The **Thirsty Swede** (1821 Haight) has live alternative music and a colorful local crowd. **Club Deluxe** (1511 Haight) offers a mixture of live jazz and art deco sophistication. **The Achilles Heel** (1601 Haight) has comfortable couches and a mellow crowd. Drinking is a local sport in the Haight, and martini lovers will find a real challenge at **Persian Aub Zam Zam** (1633 Haight). Bruno, the proprietor, is a most discriminating bartender who sizes up potential patrons and either barks a welcome and motions you to take a seat at the bar or yelps "No more room at the bar, go to another bar down the street." You must order the prescribed libation, a martini, or Bruno won't serve you. Attitude aside, Persian Aub Zam Zam should definitely be put on top of every martini drinker's list as a necessary rite of passage.

South of Market

Like Dr. Jekyll and Mr. Hyde, the South of Market area of San Francisco leads a double life. By day, it's the hardworking, blue-collar backbone of the city's economy. The streets are lined with warehouses, auto-repair shops, building-supply wholesalers, and growing number of outlets. After dark, however, South of Market (SoMa, named after the trendy SoHo district in New York City) metamorphoses into the liveliest and most diverse night scene in San Francisco, complete with arty cafés, upscale restaurants, crowded bars, and swinging dance clubs.

While nighttime is definitely the time to visit SoMa, there are a few things to do during the day besides getting your car fixed. On weekdays, San Francisco's famous **Anchor Brewery** (1705 Mariposa) in nearby Potrero Hill offers free tours that include beer tasting in their tap room. The tours are popular and you *must* make a reservation in advance.

South of Market is also home to an increasing number of discount art, craft, and clothing stores. If you are willing to explore a little bit, some bargains can come your way. Many of the outlets sell maps to all the others—once you find the underground network, you've hit it big. **Gunne Sax** (634 2nd St.) has a discount outlet for formal clothes; if you prefer to make your own designs, they also carry fabrics. **Winterland Productions** makes most of the rock & roll T-shirts you see at concerts; they have an outlet called **Rock Express** (350 Spear). A bit more upscale is **T.J.'s Factory Store** (592 3rd St.), which sells more designer clothing. Outdoor types can find rugby shirts for less at the **ACA Joe outlet** (148 Townsend), while the indoor exercise types should buy cheap leggings and body suits at **City Lights** (333 9th St.). The famed **Esprit Outlet** (499 Illinois) has a selection that outlet shoppers only dream about, although the prices there don't really match the fantasy. And for one-stop outlet shopping, the **Six Sixty Factory Outlet Center** at, of course, 660 3rd Street, gives you a variety of outlet options.

Numerous cafés serve good food and great coffee. **Brain Wash** (Folsom at 7th St.) best captures the area's unique mixture of industry and social life with its self-service Laundromat, coffee shop, and grill. The record store upstairs has an eclectic mix of imports and musical weirdness. Nearby there's the European **Kaffee Kruetzburg** (289 9th St.), where "the coffee is really black," and the new **Ikon Bar and Grill** (297 9th St.), formerly the funky Limbo. On 11th Street is the artsy **Café Toma** (371 11th St.).

Before heading out to the clubs, hit one of the many restaurants in the area—some of the best food in the city can be found here. For a special dinner, your best bets are the **South Park Café** (see review), **Julie's Supper Club** (see review), and the **Up and Down Club** (1151 Folsom). (The latter two are also excellent places to hear straight-ahead jazz and its hiphop counterpart acid jazz.) Also good is **Ristorante Ecco** (see review), which serves Italian food, and **Manora Thai Cuisine** (1600 Folsom).

The 11th Street corridor at Folsom is the hub of SoMa night life. The **20 Tank Brewery** (316 11th St.), owned by the laid-back people responsible for Berkeley's Triple Rock, is a good place to fill up on beer before you move on to later night spots. For dancing, the top-40ish and single-ridden **Holy Cow** (1535 Folsom) has a straighter crowd than the more alternative, cutting-edge **DNA Lounge** (375 11th St.). **Slim's** (333 11th St.) is owned by Bay Area musician Boz Scaggs and features some of the best live roots, rock, and reggae, with regularly sold-out shows by Albert Collins, Taj Mahal, and the Judy Bats. **The Paradise Lounge** (1501 Folsom) is the best spot to see San Francisco's up-and-coming musicians; two or three bands usually play at the same time on different stages. Don't miss the veteran lounge lizard, The Fabulous Bud E. Love.

Although many never get beyond the concentration of bars and clubs at 11th and Folsom, this area represents just the tip of iceberg that is South of Market night life. If you head down Folsom in the direction of First Street, you'll encounter dozens of nightspots. Three places that should be visited are the **Covered Wagon Saloon** (915 Folsom) and **1015 Folsom** for dancing, and **The Hotel Utah** (500 4th St.) for live music most nights of the week. A bit further out towards Potrero Hill, you'll find **The Bottom of the Hill** (1233 17th St.), a dark, funky bar with a good musical venue, pool tables, and a patio. On Sundays they host a barbecue, where, for a measly $3 you can stuff yourself on typical picnic fare while listening to live music. Finally, if none of the above interests you, there is always **South Beach Billiards** (270 Brannan), a converted warehouse with 35 pool tables, a bocce ball court, and a full bar complete with home-brew.

The Mission

The Mission, a sunny neighborhood southwest of SOMA, is by far one of the most colorful neighborhoods in the city, rich in the sights, sounds, and flavors of Latin America, and abundant with the young, hip, and artistic. This eclectic mix provides a seemingly endless supply of things to observe, eat, and purchase.

To soak in the flavor of the Hispanic Mission, stroll east on 24th street where you'll encounter some of the freshest, cheapest produce in the city, interesting candle shops, tantalizing bakeries, and often, political protests against the injustices of South American governments. Incredible murals painted by locals lend greater voice to the political landscape of the Mission, depicting Hispanic culture and concerns in huge, vivid scenes. There's a concentration of excellent murals on 24th between Folsom and Potrero, with some of the best tucked away on Balmy Street, a small alley next to the **Mission Neighborhood Center** (3013 24th). Don't miss the gripping mural painted, perhaps ironically, on **St. Peter's Church** (corner of 24th and Florida).

To experience the local art scene on a smaller scale, visit **Galleria de la Raza** (24th and Bryant) and the **Mission Cultural Center** (2868 Mission), both of which show local and international Latino artwork. Galleria de la Raza's adjacent shop sells Mexican and South American folk art at very reasonable prices. The Mission Cultural Center is itself an object of art, covered with an enormous, vivid mural. This neighborhood center houses an active theater and a large gallery.

Twenty-fourth Street has a myriad of other ethnic treasures. **China Books** (2929 24th Street) publishes and distributes high-quality Chinese books and folk art. Their already reasonably priced books can be bought for almost nothing in their "slightly damaged" section.

The Saint Francis Creamery (2801 24th) hasn't changed much since the turn of the century, and still serves its delicious brand of old-fashioned homemade ice cream and candy.

When you've soaked in all the richness of 24th Street, explore Mission Street, which offers all the tacky, dirty, and somehow appealing elements of low-budget America. It's also a good place to experience the quintessence of the Mission: the burrito—they're big, delicious, and dirt cheap. Try **Taqueria El Faralito** (24th and Mission), **La Cumbre** (Valencia at 16th) and **Taqueria San Jose** (2830 Mission), all with good, cheap logs-O-food.

Yet another culinary gem is **Mitchell's Ice Cream Parlor** (688 San Jose), a bit out of the way, but well worth the journey. Standard homemade ice cream flavors like rocky road are scooped out with Mexican chocolate, mango, maize and cheese, or avocado. Maize and cheese excepted, everything's absolutely delicious.

To explore the cutting-edge scene in the Mission, go north on Valencia Street from 24th street to 16th—there's almost no end to the good restaurants and bars you'll encounter on the way. **Radio Valencia** (23rd and Valencia) serves great beer and has free live music on Friday nights, usually jazz or bluegrass. For a hip bar scene and game of pool, there's the **Latin America Club** (3286 22nd). **Elbo Room** (647 Valencia) is a happening, two-story bar with live music, poetry readings, and a dance floor. For great eats, try **Esperpento** for tapas or paella (see review), **Lucca's Italian Market** or **Rainbow Groceries** for delicious picnic fare (which can be enjoyed in Dolores Park at 18th and Dolores), and **La Rondalla** (901 Valencia) for Mexican food served in an unbelievable atmosphere. Be sure to browse in **Old Wives Tales** (1009 Valencia), a feminist bookstore with an excellent selection, and **Modern Times Bookstore** (888 Valencia), which has a particularly good selection of books dealing with political and social issues.

Once you make it to 16th Street, you'll be swimming in cafés, restaurants, bookstores, and bars. Good places include **Muddy Waters** (521 Valencia) for informed java sipping, **Café Istanbul** (525 Valencia) for chai served against a harem background, and the **New Dawn Café** (3174 16th) for dirt cheap breakfasts in a setting not unlike the Salvation Army. Check out a movie at the **Roxie** (3117 16th), a small funky theater with great, off-beat showings, followed by sweet or savory crepes across the street at **Ti Couz** (see review), home of the most dangerous desserts this side of Paris.

Finally, visit **Mission Dolores** (Dolores and 16th), the oldest building in San Francisco. The cemetery is particularly captivating, as is the small collection of artifacts on display.

Other City Neighborhoods

San Francisco's appeal is endless; almost every neighborhood is worthy of note. **Clement Street** in the **Richmond** has come to be known as "New Chinatown," and is also home to several fabulous used bookstores. **Japantown**, located off Geary, is centered around the prominent **Japan Center** building, which houses many shops selling Japanese goods. There are also a number of Japanese restaurants and grocery stores in the vicinity, as well as the popular **Kabuki Movie Theater** (1881 Post). **The Castro**, San Francisco's predominantly gay district, is a bustling shopping area and home to the **Castro Theater** (429 Castro), a wonderful old movie palace with great art, retro, and cult revivals. An organist plays while sinking into the floor as the curtains open, setting the mood for the avant-garde films shown here. **Noe Valley** is inhabited by bohemian yuppies who strive to maintain that contradiction by frequenting the many local cafés, record stores, and restaurants. Drop by the **Rat and Raven** (Noe and 24th Sts.) on Sunday nights to have a bargain beer while you watch *The Simpsons*. **San Francisco's coastline**, part of the Golden Gate National Recreation Area, offers a variety of leisure options for a visitor. Try cycling along the relatively new path created near the **Great Highway**. **China Beach**, tucked away in the shoreline west of **Baker Beach** is a good place to sunbathe and people-watch, and a perfect place from which to explore the **Presidio's** gorgeous grounds. If you want to take it all in, drive up to the top of **Twin Peaks** for a spectacular view of the city (on a clear day), or simply a romantic glimpse of the sunset.

SAN FRANCISCO RESTAURANTS

Ace Café $$ 1539 Folsom St., 621-4752. SoMa. This trendy post-industrial SoMa hangout makes a good stopping-off point for a sandwich or a round of appetizers. Try the prawn quesadillas, buckwheat noodles with spicy peanut sauce, or sea scallop ceviche before a night out on the town. Wear your best black duds. • Dinner daily.

Albona $$$$ 545 Francisco St., 441-1040. North Beach. Named after the owners' home town on the Istrian Peninsula (the point of land that sticks out below Trieste across the Adriatic from Venice), this eatery serves a unique menu that meshes cuisines from distinctive regions and cultures. The food is a blend of Yugoslav, Italian, and Venetian influences, served in an intimate dining room. Delicacies include homemade ravioli stuffed with nuts and cheeses, fried gnocchi in a savory sauce with bits of sirloin, and lamb in pomegranate sauce. Everything is memorable here, including the service, which is very friendly (you will leave thinking you were just served by your favorite uncle). All of the pastas and desserts are made on-premises. • Dinner Tu-Sa.

Alejandro's Sociedad Gastronomica $$$ 1840 Clement St., 668-1184. Richmond. A local's restaurant, with lots of plants, a dark, Mediterranean-looking interior, a friendly wait-staff, fantastic food, and an occasionally chaotic atmosphere. Enjoy a glass from the very affordable wine list as you peruse the menu, which is predominately Peruvian/Spanish fare, including special paellas. Try a selection from the extensive tapas menu, or make a meal out of these alone. • Dinner daily.

Appam $$ 1261 Folsom St., 626-2798. SoMa. Some of the best Indian food in the city is served at this elegant eatery South of Market. The dining room is dimly lit and romantic. Curries are prepared *dum phukt* style, cooked under a crust in a specially made clay pot, which allows them to gently steam. Sit out back under the gazebo on warm evenings. • Lunch M-F, dinner daily.

Aqua $$$$ 252 California St. (Battery St.), 956-9662. Financial District. This is one of the city's most glittery, stylish seafood restaurants. Enter the gleaming, mirrored dining room through an unmarked facade; you'll know you're in the right place by the fish-tail door handle and the glamorous patrons. Exquisitely prepared and beautifully presented fish is the order of the day—try the lobster, potato gnocchi, or the grilled swordfish. • Lunch M-F, dinner M-Sa.

Aux Delices $$ 1002 Potrero Ave. (22nd St.), 285-3196. Potrero Hill. • 2327 Polk St. (Green St.), 928-4977. Russian Hill. Reasonably priced Vietnamese/French food is served at these two sibling restaurants. The clean, airy interior is Spartan—pink tablecloths are the main decorative touch. Ask for a recommendation from the friendly waitstaff. You won't go wrong with the Vietnamese crepe or the chicken with ginger. • Potrero: Dinner daily • Polk: Lunch M-F, dinner M-Sa.

Bahia $$$ 41 Franklin St., 626-3306. Hayes Valley. Pay tribute to the World Cup victors here, and you'll come to realize that soccer's not all Brazilians are good at. The cheery, lilting music, and colorful, open interior with lots of plants and paintings give this spot a tropical feel. The menu is diverse and interesting—try the red snapper marinated in lime and cooked with coconut milk, tomatoes, and spices. The funky ice creams are especially memorable. Reservations are recommended. • Lunch, dinner daily.

Bistro Clovis $$$ 1596 Market St. (Franklin St.), 864-0231. Hayes Valley. A charming French eatery located on Market Street, with an emphasis on wine-tasting. Authentic French specialties are served at very reasonable prices, and the interior is spacious and airy, with an unmistakable Gallic feel (the owner, chef, and waitstaff are all French). A trio of different wines is available for tastings each night, some for a mere four or five dollars. All in all, trés raisonable. • Lunch M-F, dinner M-Sa.

Bontà $$ 2223 Union St., 929-0407. Pacific Heights. Excellent food, and friendly service make this cozy Italian restaurant, specializing in homemade pastas and Roman cuisine, a real find. Try the smoked buffalo mozzarella with mushrooms for an appetizer, or the three- cheese, deep-fried baby calzone. There is a tempting array of main courses to choose from, each ample enough for the moderately-hungry. Pastas, such as fettucine sapori or fettucini di mare, are excellent, and among the meat and seafood dishes the *saltimbocca alla romana* or *lombata di vitello* are outstanding. Be sure to save room for dessert, though— the fabulous tiramisu is huge. Bontà only seats about fifty people, so call ahead for reservations. • Dinner Tu-Su.

Café Claude $$ 7 Claude Lane (Bush and Grant), 392-3505. Union Square. The atmosphere in this café is airy and open, with French posters and original art on the walls, though it gets smoky at times. On nice days, tables are set out in the alley for that Parisian sidewalk-café feel. The espresso bar serves latte in a bowl, just like in the old country. For lunch or dinner, be sure to try the onion soup and huge Caesar salad, or such typical French standbys as croque monsieur or fresh baguette sandwiches. The desserts are worth trying, too. Don't miss glimpsing the antique zinc bar brought over from Paris. Tucked into a little alley off of Bush near the entrance to Chinatown, it's well hidden but worth the search. Live music most nights. • Breakfast, lunch, and dinner M-Sa.

Café Jacqueline $$ 1454 Grant Ave., 981-5565. North Beach. One of the city's more romantic eateries, with fresh flowers and candles on the tables. Jacqueline specializes in made-to-order soufflés. (The spinach tends to be a bit watery, go for the mushroom instead.) And don't skip dessert! The chocolate-raspberry soufflé is beyond decadent. • Dinner W-Su; open until 11pm.

Café Macondo $ 3159 16th St., 863-6517. Mission. This coffeehouse exudes atmosphere. The thrift-store furniture, quirky art (including a photo of Malcolm X with Martin Luther King), and chic clientele makes this a place to check out. The coffee is good and the food (which few seem to eat) is eccentric Mexican. Definitely a spot to feel equally comfortable doing physics homework or discussing Marxist politics. • M-F 9am-11pm, Sa-Su 11am-11pm.

Café Marimba $$ 2317 Chestnut St., 776-1506. Marina. A sizzling mix of inspired Mexican dishes and Chestnut Street nightlife, Cafe Marimba is the latest see and be seen spot in the Marina. The house drinks, like Habanero Martinis or Brazilian Batidas (alcoholic agua frescas), are potent but smooth and keep the crowd lively. Chips come with two kinds of homemade salsas, such as *rojo* and *el copil*. Main courses vary from light side dishes, such as squash blossom quesadillas, to one of several hearty chicken moles. The drunken bean, rice and plantain, and grilled corn side dishes are tasty and inexpensive. • Lunch Tu-Su, dinner daily.

Caffè delle Stella $$ • 330 Gough St. (Hayes St.), 252-1110. Hayes Valley. A newcomer to the ultracool Hayes Valley neighborhood, Caffè delle Stella serves rustic Tuscan cuisine at very reasonable prices. The modest interior feels like an authentic Italian trattoria, and the eclectic clientele ranges from stylish Euro types to doggedly determined foodies. Everything on the menu is a safe bet—try one of the unusual pasta dishes with a glass of rough country wine. • Lunch, dinner M-Sa.

Caffè Macaroni $$$ 59 Columbus Ave. (Jackson St.), 956-9737. North Beach. Southern nouvelle-rustic Italian food is served in this tiny, funky interior. Try to sit downstairs (the upstairs dining area has perilously low ceilings) where sponge-painted walls, lots of plants, and closely spaced tables make for an intimate atmosphere. Don't miss the antipasto plate, which includes red peppers and marinated dressings, or the excellent veal shank. Loud music, and friendly, helpful waiters. • Lunch M-F, dinner M-Sa.

Casa Aguila $$ 1240 Noriega St., 661-5593. Sunset. This Sunset District hole-in-the-wall has year-round Yuletide spirit (check out the dusty Christmas decorations) and serves up the tastiest authentic Mexican grub in San Francisco. The portions are enormous and the prices reasonable. Try the pork enchiladas, the chile rellenos, the tamales, the extra-fruity sangria—and anything else on the extensive menu, for that matter—it's all good. The service is efficient and friendly, although on weekends the line can be long (yes, this place has been discovered). Sign up for a table and hang out in the seedy bar (with pool table) next door while you wait. • Lunch M-F, dinner daily.

Cha Cha Cha $$ 1801 Haight St., 386-5758. Haight. You *will* have to wait for a table at this swinging Caribbean restaurant in the Haight, but it's a small inconvenience considering the quirky, palate-tingling food that comes out of the kitchen. Portions are tapas-size, so order a selection of dishes and share. Shrimp in creamy Cajun coconut sauce is sublime, as are fried plantains and just about everything else on the menu. The kooky, witch-doctorish decor adds to the experience. The yuppies are invading and prices are going up, but it's still one of the city's best meals. Cash only. • Lunch, dinner daily, brunch Sa-Su.

China Moon $$$ 639 Post St., 775-4789. Union Square. Exquisite renditions of classic and not-so-classic Chinese dishes are served at this tiny, elegant silver-diner-turned-gourmet-restaurant. The decor consists of glorious flower arrangements, moon-shaped hanging lamps, and the original diner booths and soda-fountain. Appetizers are a delight, especially the spring rolls and the unusual eggplant. Or try the China Moon chicken salad, a melange of chicken, black sesame seeds, shredded carrot, daikon radish, and Chinese parsley dressed in a Dijon vinaigrette. For dessert, homemade ginger ice cream is the only fitting conclusion. • Dinner daily.

Cypress Club $$$$ 500 Jackson St., 296-8555. Downtown. A visiting Bostonian described the interior of this supper club as "biological punk." Strange, anthropomorphic shapes dominate the interior; a copper door frame resembles a pair of balloon-shaped legs, and curvy purple velvet banquettes have a Jetsonesque appeal. The menu includes luxurious, well-prepared fare such as seared paillard of venison, grilled vegetable sandwiches, and fabulous braised sweetbreads. If you're not springing for dinner, have a drink at the bar and observe the scene. • Dinner daily.

Eliza's $$ 205 Oak St., 621-4819. Hayes Valley. • 1457 18th St. (at Connecticut), 648-9999. Potrero Hill. An unlikely name for a Chinese restaurant, but it doesn't fool those in search of the city's latest bargain in well-prepared Asian fare. Located in the Hayes Valley area, as well as on Potrero Hill, Eliza's delivers classic dishes with fresh ingredients and strong spices. Celery salad is a tasty and unusual appetizer. Main dishes include all the usuals plus lesser-known but successful dishes like minced chicken with deep fried basil. • Lunch and dinner daily.

Esperpento $$ 3295 22nd St., 282-8867. Mission. A boisterous crowd flocks to this festive, brightly painted tapas restaurant, so expect a wait if you go on a weekend night. (For the uninitiated, tapas are Spanish bar snacks.) Try the grilled squid, marinated pork, mussels in a red-pepper vinaigrette, or potatoes served with hot chile sauce—the perfect antidote to a foggy San Francisco evening. Cash only. • Lunch, dinner daily.

Flying Saucer $$$$ 1000 Guerrero St., 641-9955. Mission. Some of the most celestial food in San Francisco is served here. Choose from luxurious foie gras, homemade smoked oysters, or any of the other fabulous starters, and move on to a superb blackened catfish, ultra-sophisticated duck confit, or house-smoked pork loin. Culinary influences are Asian, and the platter-size dinner plates come decked out with a dizzying array of garnishes, all delightfully seasoned with mysterious flavors. Out-of-this-world desserts like three sorbets on a macadamia-nut shell arrive on huge plates dusted with sparkling blue sugar. The restaurant recently expanded into the beauty salon next door, so seating is not quite as tight as it used to be, though reservations are still essential and some of the original charm has been lost. Cash only. • Dinner Tu-Su.

Fog City Diner $$$$ 1300 Battery St., 982-2000. Downtown. The slick interior of this popular San Francisco institution only marginally resembles a diner, with its black leatherette banquettes, gleaming chrome fixtures, and polished wood accents. The eclectic menu is full of tantalizing choices—red-pepper-flecked cornsticks, grilled cheese-stuffed pasillo peppers, terrific chicken pot pie, and a diner chili dog. Portions are less than abundant, and it's hard to narrow your decisions, so order a selection and share. The clatter from the kitchen can be deafening, and the wait can be long. • Lunch and dinner daily; open until at least 11pm.

Fringale $$$ 570 Fourth St., 543-0573. SoMa. This sophisticated, sleek bistro located in the netherworld between Market Street and the Caltrain station is oh-so-French. The waiters speak in exaggerated accents, the menu features classic French fare such as bouillabaisse and cassoulets, and you begin to feel like an Ugly American. But the food is good, it's reasonably priced, and the scene is fun to observe. • Lunch M-F, dinner M-Sa.

Gira Polli $$$ 659 Union St., 434-GIRA. North Beach. The name says it all—"turning chicken." This is the place for lemon-and-rosemary-scented chicken roasted on a spit over an open fire. In the heart of North Beach, kitty-corner to Washington Square Park, this tiny, chic eatery has a huge fireplace and an equally warm owner, who is usually on hand to help pour the Chianti. The staff is friendly, and the chicken is incredible, as are the Palermo potatoes. Friday and Saturday nights are crowded; expect a wait. • Dinner daily.

Greens $$$ Fort Mason (Bldg. A), Buchanan St. at Marina Blvd., 771-6222. Marina. Sympathetic, soothing Greens has been catering to vegetarians for ten years from a light, airy dining room with a panoramic view of the marina and Golden Gate Bridge. The only creatures you'll find with spines in this place are the diners. Affiliated with the Zen Center, much of the produce served at the restaurant comes from the center's famous Green Gulch Farm. The menu changes periodically, but you might find delectable corn fritters, Southwestern corn tart, or any number of virtuous but delicious dishes. Excellent wine list. Reserve a table far in advance; Friday and Saturday nights there's a prix fixe menu. • Lunch Tu-Su, dinner M-Sa.

Hamburger Mary's $ 1582 Folsom St., 626-1985. SoMa. This SoMa institution is perfect for a quick meal before hitting the clubs. Not surprisingly, burgers (choose from beef or tofu) are the house specialty. You can also get breakfast all day long. The atmosphere is cluttered junk collector, the patrons are fascinating to watch (especially after nightfall), and the home fries are deliciously spicy. Decorated with garage-sale bargains (including a toilet seat hanging over the wait-station), Hamburger Mary's is famous for its offbeat atmosphere. This is the type of place where the waitstaff and patrons compete to see who has more tattoos. • Tu-Th, Su 11am-12am, F-Sa 11am-1am.

Helmand $$$ 430 Broadway, 362-0641. North Beach. Afghani food in North Beach? Strange but true. The Beats would surely have approved of the excellent, exotic food served at this elegant spot. Try the *kaddo borawni* (baby pumpkin served with yogurt and garlic sauce) to start, and move on to *chopan* (grilled lamb served on flat bread). A selection of vegetarian specialties will please non-meat eaters. • Lunch M-F, dinner daily.

House of Nanking $$ 919 Kearny St., 421-1429. Downtown. This quintessential Chinese restaurant in the heart of Chinatown always has a line snaking outside (there are only a few tables within). This is the kind of place where the waiter tries to order for you. The crowds flock here for the excellent preparations of updated Hunan specialties. • Lunch M-Sa, dinner daily.

Hyde Street Bistro $$$ 1521 Hyde St., 441-7778. Russian Hill. A comfortable, unpretentious neighborhood bistro serving some of the area's best food. The sponged pastel paint and lively local art on the walls don't quite make this place trendy: vestigial structural elements like an acoustic tile ceiling and fluorescent lighting fixtures are casually ignored relics of a more modest past. The elegant food blends Austrian and Northern Italian influences in wonderful combinations—try the pungently-spiced tomato soup, spaetzle with scallops in cream sauce, or duck with lingonberries. • Dinner daily.

Johnny Love's $$$ 1500 Broadway (at Polk St.), 931-8021. Russian Hill. Started by the eponymous Johnny "Love" Metheny, this establishment is well known for its nightlife and bar scene, but the food in the adjoining restaurant is worth a visit as well (and then you have a seat for the band). For openers, the fried calamari is lightly breaded and comes with a strong, house-made garlic aioli. Specials are strong on fish and seafood, usually with exotic sauces. The Sunday menu is all barbecue. • Dinner daily.

Julie's Supper Club $$$ 1123 Folsom St. (Seventh St.), 861-0707. SoMa. A pink vinyl-upholstered bar, 50s-style Holiday Inn lamps, and good, reasonably priced food make this swinging SoMa spot a worthy destination for kitsch lovers. The menu includes fun appetizers and side dishes—everything from french fries to eggplant to grilled chicken with corn soufflé, as well as a nineties version of wontons. Eat to the beat of Frank Sinatra and the Neville Brothers while you survey the scene. Save room for dessert. Expect prompt service and a hopping bar scene. • Dinner M-Sa.

Le Petit Café $$ 2164 Larkin St., 776-5356. Russian Hill. A Russian Hill favorite, this is a good place to spend a leisurely Sunday morning with the paper while breakfasting on fresh-baked muffins, various omelet combinations, or perhaps oatmeal. The country-style interior is warm and inviting without being overly adorable. The dinner menu is reasonably-priced and includes Italian-influenced specials such as pasta, polenta, and grilled chicken. Start off with the hot, spicy artichoke dip. • Breakfast and lunch daily, dinner Tu-Sa, brunch Sa-Su.

Le Soleil $$ 133 Clement St. (between Second and Third), 668-4848. Richmond. Found near the Eastern end of the Richmond, Le Soleil is among the best of the many ethnic eateries in the neighborhood. The decor is light and airy—not the usual antiseptic sterile or dingy grease-fest. Always full of all ages of Vietnamese and a smattering of other locals. The dishes, like five-spice chicken and lemon grass beef, are fresh and full of flavor. Start your meal off with shrimp wrapped in sugar cane or the Vietnamese crab. • Lunch and dinner daily.

Le Trou $$$ 1007 Guerrero St., (415) 550-8169. Mission. For a romantic night out in the city, Le Trou is a fine choice, especially when the fog rolls in and you're in a French existentialist mood. The cozy, dimly lit dining room is enchanting, and tables are set with mismatched silver and charming plates and glasses. The *prix fixe* menu is a great deal: For $20 you can order any appetizer, entrée, and dessert on the menu. The menu might include appetizers such as roasted red pepper soup or warm terrine of seafood and entrées like herb pasta with spring vegetables or roast loin of pork with spicy confit. • Dinner Tu–Sa.

LuLu $$$ 816 Folsom St., 495-5775. SoMa. The latest grand café to capture the fancy of San Francisco's discriminating epicureans, LuLu serves an intriguing menu of Mediterranean dishes. The airy, open dining room, done up in muted shades of blue and gray, encourages people-watching. The food deserves your full attention, though, especially side dishes like olive-oil mashed potatoes and grilled asparagus with shaved parmesan and lemon. Main dishes are equally alluring, especially the roasted mussels and anything off the grill. Prices are reasonable, but service can be uneven. • Lunch M-Sa, dinner daily.

LuLu Bis, LuLu Café $$$/$$ 816 Folsom St., 495-5775. SoMa. Adjoining either side of LuLu are its two recent siblings, LuLu Bis and LuLu Cafe. LuLu Bis is a long, thin space which creates a warmth missing from the chaotic scene next door. The country-style service and communal seating add to the cozy charm. The delicious fava bean and baby artichoke salad has been a staple first course, with Mediterranean fish, pasta, and meat completing the fixed menu. At the other end of the building is the Café, the most informal of the three eateries. Open all day, it serves breakfast fare, as well as light starters such as oven cooked pizzas, deep fried artichoke with aioli and a full raw bar. • LuLu Bis Dinner Tu-Sa • LuLu Café Breakfast and lunch M-Sa, dinner daily.

Mifune $ 1737 Post St., 922-0337. Japantown. For a quick, cheap noodle fix, head for Mifune in Japantown. Choose from udon or soba noodles served any which way: in broth, in broth topped with tempura, or served on a lacquer tray with dipping sauces and tempura. The Formica-heavy decor is nothing to write home about, but the noodles are worth the trip. • Lunch and dinner daily.

Miss Pearl's Jam House $$$ 601 Eddy St., 775-5267. Tenderloin. Popular with the young swanky set, Miss Pearl's serves Caribbean specialties like jerk chicken in a tropical, fun-filled ambience. Try the blackened fillet of beef served over black beans and roasted peppers. The bartenders make the best rum drinks around. At lunch there's outdoor dining around the aqua pool, Miami Beach style. Live music from Thursday to Saturday. • Dinner Tu-Su, brunch Su.

Mission Rock Resort $ 817 China Basin Blvd., 621-5538. China Basin. The food at this burger joint is nothing to crow about (although the sea gulls might disagree), but the views of the Bay and the funky biker ambiance make up for the kitchen's lapses. A good place to while away a Sunday afternoon on the upstairs outdoor deck with a watery, diner-style cup of coffee. Outdoor barbecues depend on the weather, as do the restaurant hours—keep in mind that rain may close the restaurant down. Live music Sa-Su. • Breakfast from 7am, lunch and light dinner daily, brunch Su.

Nippon Restaurant $$ 314 Church St. (at 15th St.), no phone. Mission. You'll have to work to find this place (the nondescript storefront is poorly marked), but it's a true discovery. Impeccably fresh, very inexpensive sushi is the specialty; the nine-piece nigiri combination is a steal. Sit at one of the eight tables or take a stool at the sushi bar, and if you'd like a Kirin to go with your meal, stop in at the corner deli—Nippon is strictly BYOB. • Lunch, dinner M-Sa.

North India $$$ 3131 Webster St., 931-1556. Marina. Only the best North Indian restaurant in the Bay Area. Run by an energetic owner who takes interest in every customer, this restaurant boasts mouth-watering tandoori delicacies. Nan, freshly baked from the oven with tandoori chicken and seekh kababs, is a hard combination to beat. Food is prepared from the freshest ingredients, presentation is imaginative, and service is excellent. Customers can see cooks working the tandoor (clay oven) through a glass window. • Lunch M-F, dinner daily.

One Market Restaurant $$$$ One Market St. (Steuart), 777-5577. Embarcadero. Bradley Ogden's large venture in One Market Plaza has a dining room that overlooks the bay but has a corporate feel, unlike Ogden's Lark Creek Inn. The menu changes daily and might include grilled Norwegian salmon with baby artichoke ragout, grilled barbecued pork loin, or oak-grilled chicken breast with crispy wild mushrooms. Desserts could include chilled apricot and plum compote with Champagne sabayon, rootbeer float granità, or chocolate brioche bread pudding. • Lunch M-F, dinner daily, brunch Su.

Pane e Vino $$$ 3011 Steiner St. (Union St.), 346-2111. Pacific Heights. This perfect neighborhood trattoria in Pacific Heights serves simple, classic Italian dishes like vitello tonnato, gnocchi, antipasto, and a great tiramisu. The interior is understated and rustic; a long wooden table divides the dining area and holds wildflower arrangements, hunks of parmesan, and bowls of antipasti. Service is friendly and professional. Reservations are essential. • Lunch M-Sa, dinner daily.

Pauline's Pizza Pie $$ 260 Valencia St. (14th St.), 552-2050. Mission. In a friendly, cheery setting, Pauline's has found the right mix of gourmet and traditional pizza making. The toppings don't overwhelm, but they do give the pizzas some new taste dimensions. Specials include combinations like tasso (smoked pork shoulder, chives), and gremolata (minced garlic, parsley, and lemon) or braised leeks, Kalamata, garlic, and tarragon. The salads are also fresh and inventive. • Dinner daily Tu-Sa..

The Ramp $ 855 China Basin Blvd., 621-2378. China Basin. The most popular of the several waterfront bars in the abandoned warehouse section of SoMa, the Ramp is San Francisco's premier post-fraternal party spot. On weeknights, this vast, outdoor concrete slab of a bar is regularly booked for informal, semiprivate, very drunken dance parties. The Ramp leads a double life—weekend mornings it's the perfect post-blowout brunch place, serving generous portions of fried hangover food. Bring sunglasses, and be prepared to wait half an hour for a table. Live music Thursday and Friday evenings, Saturday and Sunday afternoons. • Lunch M-F, light dinner F 5pm-7:30pm, brunch Sa-Su, BBQ Sa-Su 3:30pm-7:30pm.

Ristorante Ecco $$$ 101 South Park Ave., 495-3291. SoMa. A fine place to impress out-of-town visitors with your knowledge of out-of-the-way, trendy eateries. Located just off slightly grungy but pleasant South Park (near SoMa), the restaurant's interior is spacious and modern, with a view of the park from the front dining room. Moderately priced, well-prepared Tuscan specialties emerge from the kitchen; try the polenta pasticciata. • Lunch M-F, dinner M-Sa.

Saigon Saigon $$ 1132 Valencia St., (415) 206-9635. Mission. Excellent Vietnamese food is served at this modest but attractive Mission eatery. White tablecloths, flowers, and plants distinguish the dining room from the usual Formica-heavy Vietnamese eatery. Try the garlic or lemon grass prawns, the crispy rainbow trout, or the papaya beef salad. • Lunch M-F, dinner M-Sa.

San Francisco Brewing Company $ 155 Columbus Ave., 434-3344. North Beach. The rumor is that the Brewing Company has a menu somewhere, but the brewed-on-site beer is what people come for. The interior dates from 1907, with a long mahogany bar, dark wood tables, and a mix of scruffy locals and a few suits. If you can get hold of a menu, try the delicious onion rings or go all out and get a platter of fried calamari, onion rings, and clams. Live music ranging from traditional bluegrass to funky reggae on Monday, Wednesday, Thursday, and Saturday nights. • M-Sa 11:30am-9:30pm, Su 11:30am-7pm.

Slow Club $$ 2501 Mariposa St., 241-9390. Mission. Located in an urban no-man's-land, this chic, post-industrial café appeals to the artistic set that flocks here after hours to quaff

Red Hook on tap and indulge in Niman-Schell burgers and fries. The Mediterranean-style food is uniformly well done, imaginative, and generously proportioned. Media types from the *Bay Guardian* and KQED (both nearby) have made this their lunchtime canteen. • Breakfast, lunch, and dinner M-Sa.

South Park Café $$$ 108 South Park Ave., 495-7275. SoMa. For those contemplating film careers, we hear that Philip Kaufman (of *The Unbearable Lightness of Being* and *Henry and June* fame) frequents this classic French café. Pale yellow walls, morning sunlight, and European newspapers make this an attractive brunch spot. Or go during cocktail hour and sample the excellent tapas, which include golden fried potatoes with aioli sauce and anchovy toasts; for dinner, try the fabulous mussels. • Breakfast and lunch M-F, dinner M-Sa (tapas served M-F 5pm-7pm).

Stars $$$$ 555 Golden Gate Ave., 861-7827. Civic Center. San Francisco's much-loved grand café is as sizzling as ever. The glamorous dining room, decorated with framed French posters and a long, polished wooden bar, attracts a glittering crowd of sophisticates and a smattering of tourists along for the ride. The food can be overwrought, although some dishes are perfection, like the seared salmon served on a bed of lentils or the perfectly-cooked steak served with a cognac sauce. If the prices are out of your stratosphere, head around the corner to Stars Café, which serves excellent food in a less formal atmosphere. • Lunch M-F, dinner daily.

Suppenkueche $$$ 525 Laguna St., 252-9289. Hayes Valley. Suppenkueche brings new respect to German cooking. Opened by a wandering German design student, this fashionable beer hall serves food to take the chill off any summer night, as well as a range of unusual German brews on tap and by the bottle. Seating is family-style around long pine tables, so expect to make a few friends through the course of the meal. For starters, there is always a vegetarian soup, and the house salad is a large portion of slaw and cut vegetables. The main dishes come with delicious accompaniments such as spaetzle or pan fried potatoes. The entrees are authentic renditions of traditional dishes such as *sauerbraten* and *jager schnitzel*. But you'll keep coming back for the strudel. • Lunch Tu-Su, dinner Tu-Su.

Swan Oyster Depot $$ 1517 Polk St. (California & Sacramento St.), 673-1101. Nob Hill. This classic luncheonette serves great chowder and freshly-shucked oysters. Nothing but a counter and a few stools. • Lunch M-Sa until 5:30pm.

Thep Phanom $$ 400 Waller St. (at Fillmore), 431-2526. Lower Haight. Possessing one of the most pleasant and inviting interiors of any Thai restaurant in the Bay Area, Thep Phanom's menu stands out as well. A long list of tasty salad dishes provides more ways to get your vegetables than many Thai eateries, and the nightly specials board lists fresh, interesting entrees. One regular favorite is "The Weeping Lady," a delicious combination of minced chicken, garlic, chilis, and fresh basil served over broiled Japanese eggplant. • Dinner daily.

Ti Couz $ 3108 Sixteenth St., 252-7373. Mission. A charming Basque-style crêperie incongruously located on gritty Sixteenth Street in the Mission, Ti Couz serves an array of classic and delicious crêpes. With its white stucco walls crisscrossed with dark wood beams, French country tables and chairs, and photographs of peasants from the old country, Ti Couz is an enchanting spot to indulge your Gallic fantasies. Crêpe fillings range from ratatouille to Gruyère to salmon. The onion soup is excellent, as are the salads. Missing dessert here is a crime—they're absolutely amazing. Nutella, white chocolate, poached pears, fresh whipped cream—the possibilities are as endless as they are delicious. • Lunch and dinner daily.

Tommaso's $$ 1042 Kearny St., 398-9696. North Beach. Don't be deterred by the sleazy strip joints and peep shows as you hunt down this pizza joint, located in the midst of San Francisco's finest collection of smut houses. Down a flight of stairs and behind a heavy wooden door you'll find a dark, shadowy interior with Italian murals on the walls and plastic tablecloths. This is the place for thin-crusted, traditional Italian pizza, cooked in their famous wood-burning brick oven. Be sure to order one of the cold vegetable salads (asparagus, if it's in season). If you feel like dining with the locals, this is the place to go. • Dinner Tu-Su.

U-Lee Restaurant $ 1468 Hyde St., 771-9774. Russian Hill. This has got to be the best deal in San Francisco—where else can you feast on a Chinese banquet for less than $10? (Well, maybe there are cheaper places, but we doubt they're as good.) The tiny storefront space can only accommodate ten tables, so the atmosphere is cozy and convivial. The decor is of the basic Formica-tabletop school of design. Portions are huge—try any of the soups, chow meins, and the dinosaur-egg–sized pot stickers. Shrimp and asparagus with black-bean sauce is a delight. • Lunch and dinner Tu–Su.

Universal Cafe $$$ 2814 19th St. (at Florida), 821-4608. Mission. This sleek, stylish cafe started as a coffee roastery, but the zoning laws made it easier to become a full-service restaurant. Open all day, the Universal switches from a cafe in the day to a full-scale restaurant by night. The fresh-made soups and grilled sandwiches make a filling lunch; for dinner try one of the flatbread appetizers (either with caramelized onions or *branade* and tomatoes) and any of the grilled entrees for a main course. • Breakfast and lunch M-Sa, dinner Tu-Sa.

Val 21 $$ 995 Valencia St., (415) 821-6622. Mission. Design-studio hip, with Swiss track lighting, a corrugated metal awning over the bar, and tabletops stained grass-green. The menu reflects the cutting-edge attitude, with such plates as vegetarian pozole with pipian pesto, filet of wild salmon with Asian black bean sauce, and marinated tofu with vegetables and almond miso peanut sauce (your taste buds might experience culture shock, but don't worry, it's good for them). • Dinner daily, brunch Sa-Su.

Yuet Lee $$ 1300 Stockton St. (Broadway), 982-6020. Chinatown. This place has all the hallmarks of a dive—bright lights, green Formica tables, and brusque service—but the Cantonese seafood is unmatched for freshness and flavor. Try the clams in black bean sauce, the salt-and-pepper fried squid, and any other seafood items on the menu. Also good are the Peking spareribs and the clay pot, especially the oysters and scallions. Open very late. Don't get seated downstairs. • W-M 11am-3am.

Za $$ 1919 Hyde St., 771-3100. Russian Hill . Proprietors Buzz and Brian have performed a noble service by opening a tasteful and tasty gourmet pizza parlor amid the pricey bistros of Russian Hill. The neon sign out front reads "Pizza for Art," and they mean it—these guys not only serve some of the most palatable pizza in town, they also promote local artists by covering their walls with paintings. The menu usually features four specialty pizzas, including Pesto Picasso and our favorite, the MOMA, a modernistic mix of fresh onion, artichoke, basil, and oregano. Pizza by the slice and takeout. • Lunch F-Su, dinner daily.

Zuni Café and Grill $$$ 1658 Market St. (Gough St.), 552-2522. Lower Market. A die-hard temple of Southwestern/Mediterranean cuisine frequented by the artsy set, with a few advertising and business types mixed in. Very New Mexico, with a wood-fired adobe fireplace, a long copper bar, mismatched chairs, and lots of Mexican serapes thrown about. The best selection of oysters around, sold by the piece and served over shaved ice with seaweed garnish. Interesting preparations include house-cured anchovies with Parmesan and celery, or a divine whole roast chicken for two served with Tuscan bread salad. Service with attitude. • Breakfast, lunch, and dinner daily until at least 11pm.

SANTA CRUZ

Idyllic Santa Cruz is southwest of the urban sprawl of the Bay Area, in redwood-covered hills that roll down to the sandy shores of the Pacific. With both the mountains and the ocean, Santa Cruz has unparalleled beauty and unlimited potential for outdoor activities. Far more than just a beach town, Santa Cruz offers a refreshing and peaceful atmosphere for all, a blend of the best of Northern and Southern California.

General Information

Area Code: 408

Mistix Camping Reservations: (800) 444-7275.

State Parks District Office: 688-3241.

Vision Santa Cruz Tourist Office: 1543 Pacific Ave., 459-0900.

Getting There

The easiest way to get to Santa Cruz is by car. The most direct route is I-280 south to Hwy 17 west, which ends in Santa Cruz. For a more scenic drive, take I-280 north to Hwy 92 west to Hwy 1 south, a steep road that winds along the coast all the way to Santa Cruz.

The best method for getting to Santa Cruz sans car is to take the southbound train from the Palo Alto CalTrain station all the way to the San Jose stop. You should find a Metro stop by the station where you can board the Metro bus called the "Train Commuter." For $5 the Train Commuter will drop you off in downtown Santa Cruz, where you can then transfer to another bus depending on your final destination. On weekends between Memorial Day and Labor Day, the Metro Center also offers a free Beach Shuttle service that runs from the County Building at 701 Ocean Street, to River and Front Streets, and finally to the beach.

Sights and Attractions

Don't miss wandering around the redwood-shaded campus of **UC Santa Cruz** (Central operator 459-0111) on the hill above town. UCSC is one of the smaller UC schools, but it has a strong community of humanities scholars, and perhaps the most beautiful campus of all nine schools. Enjoy the beautiful views of Monterey Bay from the athletic field and the scent of both forest and ocean. The innovative **Shakespeare Santa Cruz** (459-4168) series of plays, held in a wooded grove on the campus from June to September, shouldn't be missed. These interpretations of Shakespeare's plays are non-traditional and humorous, filled with drag queens and gender bending. Bring a blanket, a jug of wine, and a picnic.

Downtown Santa Cruz offers a variety of intriguing bookstores, used record stores, and new-age crystal shops along the outdoor **Pacific Garden Mall** in the heart of downtown. Book lovers will enjoy **Bookshop Santa Cruz** (423-0900) at 1520 Pacific Ave., which has been in business for 27 years and has everything from bestsellers to a gay and lesbian bulletin board. They're open Su-Th 9am to 10pm, F-Sa 9am to 11pm. Later in the day, visit **Kiva Hot Tubs** at 702 Water Street (429-1142), which offers two outdoor tubs in a garden setting, as well as a dry redwood sauna. Two private tubs are also available. Clothing is optional; they're open Su-Th noon to 11pm, F-Sa noon to midnight. Sundays 9:30am-noon are reserved for women only.

Outdoor Activities

The sandy beaches of Santa Cruz draw crowds from far and wide, especially on the weekends. Sundays are so congested that the city provides shuttles from Ocean Street, where parking is available, to the **Santa Cruz Beach Boardwalk**, where it is not. The Boardwalk is a Coney Island-type amusement park with a hair-raising, old-fashioned wooden roller coaster (the Great Dipper), pinball machines, and lots of tourists. If crowds aren't your thing, skip the Boardwalk and head east toward Santa Cruz Harbor. **Sea Bright Beach** and **Twin Lakes State Beach** are two of the many pleasant places to enjoy the sand and sun. If you continue east along Portola Drive, you'll eventually come to **Capitola**, California's first seaside resort. Capitola is quaint, clean, and has great beachside shopping; however it can be just as crowded as Santa Cruz.

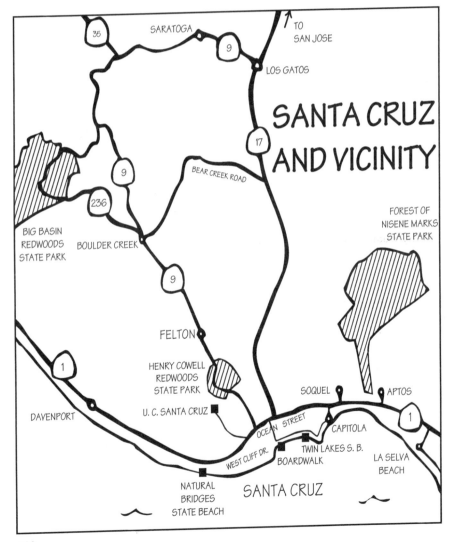

Heading west from the Boardwalk on West Cliff Drive, watch for the **Lighthouse Surfing Museum** (429-3429) at Lighthouse Point, marked by a statue of a young surfer dude. They're open M-F noon-4pm, Sa-Su noon-5pm. Lighthouse Point is a great place to watch the surfers below on **Steamer Lane,** or try the waves yourself. Just west of the Lighthouse, people gather daily at **It's Beach** to drum and dance at sunset. Continuing west from the point along West Cliff Drive you'll find beautiful natural rock formations at **Natural Bridges State Beach** (423-4609). Official parking is $6; street parking before the entrance is free.

A flat section of asphalt along West Cliff Drive between Natural Bridges and Capitola is perfect for rollerbladers, bikers, and joggers—no cars and lots of coastal scenery. Bring your bike, or rent one in Santa Cruz at **Dutchman Bicycles**, located at 3961 Portola Drive (476-9555), open M-Sa 9am to 6pm, Su 10am to 5pm. Rollerblades are also available for rent at **Go Skate Surf and Sport**, at 601 Beach Street (425-8578), open 10am to 7pm daily.

In addition to the beautiful beaches, the Santa Cruz area offers many excellent places for hiking and mountain biking in the redwood forests. East of Santa Cruz, **The Forest of Nisene Marks State Park**, off Hwy 1 on Aptos Creek Road in Aptos, has good hiking and mountain biking trails. About 30 minutes north of Santa Cruz on Hwy 236 lies **Big Basin Redwoods State Park** (338-6132), with hiking, camping, and the gorgeous **Berry Creek Falls.** Take a drive up Hwy 9 or Felton Empire Road to enjoy the redwoods and the small hippie towns along the way, such as **Felton**, **Ben Lomond** and **Boulder Creek**. Another attraction in the Santa Cruz mountains is the wacky **Mystery Spot**, at 1953 North Branciforte Drive (423-8897), a "natural phenomenon" where all laws of gravity are forgotten, balls roll uphill, and other bizarre events take place. Admission is $3 and includes a "Mystery Spot" bumper sticker; they're open 9:30am to 4:30pm daily.

Wineries

The Santa Cruz area has almost two dozen wineries. Many are only open during the week, but a few make great weekend trips.

Bargetto Winery: 3535-A N. Main St., Soquel, 475-2258. Known for its fruit wines, such as ollalieberry, raspberry, and apricot. Daily 10am-5:30pm; tours by appointment.

Bonny Doon: 10 Pine Flat Rd., Santa Cruz, 425-3625. Wins honors for its Italian wines. Sep. 15-Apr. 15: Th-M noon-5pm. Apr. 16-Sep. 14: daily noon-5pm.

David Bruce Winery: 21439 Bear Creek Rd., Los Gatos, 354-4214. Great winery for picnics. W-Su noon-5pm.

Devlin Wine Cellars: 3801 Park Ave., Soquel, 476-7288. Located on a 30-acre estate overlooking Monterey Bay. Try the champagne. Sa-Su noon-5pm.

Hallcrest Vineyards: 379 Felton Empire Rd., Felton, 335-4441. Specializes in organic wines. Daily 11am-5:30pm.

Storrs Winery: 303 Potrero St., Santa Cruz, 458-5030. Run by a husband-and-wife team who are both award-winning wine makers. Winter F-M noon-5pm; summer daily noon-5pm.

Restaurants and Entertainment

The Bagelry $: 320 Cedar St., Santa Cruz, 429-8049. Fresh, inexpensive bagels made on the premises. M-F 6:30am-5:30pm; Sa 7:30am-5:30pm; Su 7:30am-4pm.

Balzac Bistro $$: 112 Capitola Ave., Capitola, 476-5035. European cuisine served in a casual atmosphere. The prices are great, and so is the British beer on tap. Dinner daily, brunch Su.

The Blue Lagoon: 923 Pacific Ave., Santa Cruz, 423-7117. Small, hopping dance club playing the latest techno and rave for a mostly gay and bisexual crowd.

Benten $$: 1541 B Pacific Ave., Santa Cruz, 425-7079. A cozy, clean place serving great Japanese food and sushi. Lunch, dinner daily.

Broken Egg $: 7887 Soquel Dr., Aptos, 688-4322. Breakfast and light fare served all day. M-W 7am-3pm; Th-Su 7am-9:30pm.

Caffè Lido $: 110 Monterey Ave., Capitola, 475-6544. Rich desserts and strong espresso–the perfect place for unbridled decadence. Daily 11:30am-10pm.

Caffè Pergolesi $: 418 Cedar St., Santa Cruz, 426-1775. Bearing the name "Dr. Miller's," this is the artsy, UCSC slacker place for desserts, espresso, and Indian Chai. Daily 8am-midnight.

The Catalyst: 1011 Pacific Garden Mall, Santa Cruz, 423-1338. Good place to hear loud rock-n-roll/outlaw music. Cover charge $1 and up; 21 and over. Shows start around 9:30 pm.

Espresso Royale Café $: Pacific Ave., Santa Cruz, 429-9804. A great café with a peaceful garden courtyard to offset that coffee buzz. M-F 7am-11pm, Sa-Su 8am-11pm.

Hobee's $/$$: 740 Front St., Santa Cruz, 458-1212. A good place for simple and healthy meals—try the coffeecake. Breakfast and lunch daily, dinner W-Su.

India Joze $$: Art Center, 1001 Center St., Santa Cruz, 427-3554. An extremely original restaurant serving spicy Middle Eastern and Asian cuisine. For added fun, the decor changes weekly. Breakfast, lunch, and dinner daily, brunch Sa-Su.

Kuumbwa Jazz Center: 320-2 E. Cedar St., Santa Cruz, 427-2227. A jazz bar popular with older locals. Cover $5 and up. Call for showtimes and scheduling.

Little Shanghai $/$$: 1010 Cedar St., Santa Cruz, 458-2460. Good Chinese food served in a casual atmosphere. Lunch and dinner M-Sa.

Mr. Toots Coffeehouse $: 221 Esplanade, Capitola, 475-3679. A comfortable, earthy hang-out with live folk music nightly. Daily 8am-midnight.

Noah's Bagels $: 1411 Pacific Ave., Santa Cruz, 454-9555 • 1855 41st Ave., Capitola, 464-7667. This outlet of the popular East Bay chain serves New York-style bagels with fresh cream cheese and lox. Santa Cruz: M-F 7am-7pm, Sa 7:30am-7pm; Su 7:30am-5pm. Capitola: M-F 7am-9pm; Sa 7:30am-7pm; Su 7:30am-6pm.

Omei's $$: 2316 Mission St., Santa Cruz, 425-8458. A romantic setting for delicious Chinese food. Dinner daily.

The Poet and the Patriot Irish Pub: 320 E. Cedar St., Santa Cruz, 426-8620. A watering hole for the local and maturing. Daily noon-midnight; F-Sa til 2am.

The Red Room: 1003 Cedar St., Santa Cruz, 425-0591. It's actually two rooms, complete with dance floor, bar, live music, and hoards of student/slacker-types on weekends.

Royal Taj $$: 270 Soquel Ave., Santa Cruz, 427-2400. Reasonably priced Indian food served in peaceful and comfortable surroundings. Lunch, dinner daily.

Santa Cruz Brewing Company and Front Street Pub: 516 Front St., Santa Cruz, 429-8838. Great beer on tap, all brewed on the premises. Pub menu and live music Wed. and Sa. Daily 11:30am-midnight.

Seabright Brewery $$/$$$: 519 Seabright Ave., Santa Cruz, 426-2739. Good place for drinks and outdoor dining. Lunch and dinner daily.

Shadowbrook $$$: 1750 Wharf Rd., Capitola, 475-1511. An excellent place to test the aphrodisiac qualities of shellfish. Romantic seafood dinners by the sea. Dinner daily, lunch Sa-Su.

Tacos Moreno $: 1053 Water St., Santa Cruz, 429-6095. Inexpensive family-style Mexican food. Lunch and dinner daily.

Wharf House $$: 1400 Wharf Rd., Ste. B, Capitola, 476-3534. Built at the end of the 125-year old Capitola Wharf, this is a great place to catch outdoor jazz on weekends and enjoy the great view of the ocean. Breakfast, lunch, dinner daily.

The Whole Earth $$: Redwood Bldg., Hagar Dr., UC Santa Cruz, 426-8255. A good vegetarian restaurant next to the bookstore. M-F 7:30am-7:30pm; Sa-Su 9am-6pm; summer M-F 7:30am-4pm.

Yacht Harbor Café $: 535 7th Ave., Santa Cruz, 476-9973. A good breakfast standby serving variations on the theme of eggs and pancakes. Daily 7am-2pm.

Zackery's Restaurant $: 819 Pacific Ave., 427-0646. Popular place with great healthy breakfasts. You may have to wait as long as an hour on the weekend, but the curry-tofu scramble is well worth it. Tu-Su 7am-2:30pm.

Places to Stay

Camping

Big Basin Redwoods State Park: 338-6132. Take Hwy 9 north to Boulder Creek, Hwy 236 to the park entrance. One of the most heavily used parks in the state. Make reservations at least six weeks in advance during the summer. $14 per night, up to eight people per site; hikers and bikers $3 per person, maximum two-day stay.

New Brighton State Beach: 475-4850. From Santa Cruz, take Hwy 1 South to beach exit. This is a great wooded park with separate facilities for car and bike campers. Bicyclists $3/night; car campers $16/night; extra cars $6/night; dogs $1/night. Day use $6/day.

Hostels

Santa Cruz American Youth Hostel: 511 Broadway, Santa Cruz, 423-8304. Dubbed "the friendliest hostel in the West," this small, charming, post-Victorian house attracts foreign travelers and backpackers in the summer. The hostel is a ten-minute walk from the boardwalk and about 20 minutes from downtown, making parking problematic. $12.

Hotels, Motels, and B&Bs

Babbling Brook Bed and Breakfast Inn: 1025 Laurel St., Santa Cruz, 427-2437. A restored country inn with 12 rooms, all boasting private baths and French decor. Fireplaces, private decks, and a garden stream contribute to the romantic setting. Located near the beach, shops, and boardwalk. $75-$135.

Cliff Crest Bed and Breakfast Inn: 407 Cliff St., Santa Cruz, 427-2609. A Queen Anne-style house with five rooms, one with a fireplace. Full breakfast is served in the rooms or the solarium, and wine and cheese are offered in the evenings. $85-$135.

Inn Cal: 370 Ocean St., Santa Cruz, 458-9220. It's ten minutes from the boardwalk, and has all the comforts of home (color TV, air conditioning, and telephones), but is a bit noisy due to the location. $29.95 and up.

The Darling House: 314 West Cliff Dr., Santa Cruz, 458-1958. An eight-room oceanside mansion dating from 1910, with antique furnishings. Continental breakfast is served in the dining rooms, and most rooms have a shared bath. $60-$225.

Peter Pan Motel: 313 Riverside Ave., Santa Cruz, 423-1393. A low-cost option near the Beach Boardwalk. $48-98.

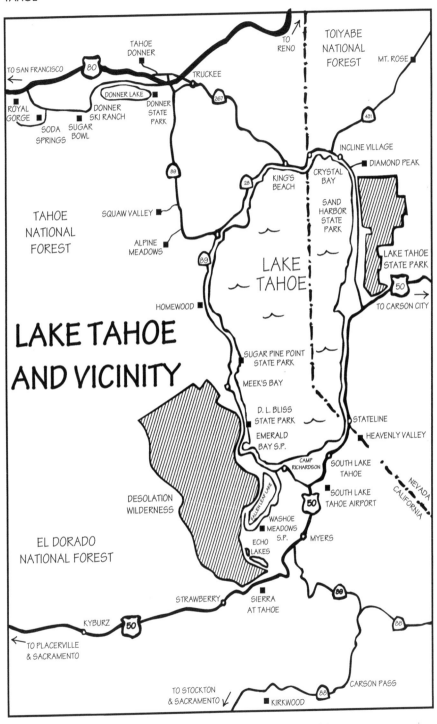

LAKE TAHOE
AND VICINITY

TAHOE

Lake Tahoe, the second deepest lake in the United States, is the center of the region known to many simply as "Tahoe." Rand MacNally has named the area America's Number One Resort Area, and justifiably so—there's skiing and snowboarding in the winter; hiking, camping, biking, water sports, and other outdoor activities in the summer; and gambling on the Nevada side year-round. Clearly boredom will not strike you here.

General Information

Area Code: 916

Road Conditions: (800) 427-7623.

South Tahoe Visitor's Bureau, Inc.: 1156 Ski Run, South Lake Tahoe, 544-5050. M-F 9am-5pm.

Tahoe North Visitors & Convention Bureau and Reservation Service: 950 North Lake Boulevard, Tahoe City, 583-3494, (800) 822-5959. Reservations M-F 7:30am-6pm; office M-F 9am-5pm.

Truckee-Donner Chamber of Commerce: 10065 Commercial Rd., Truckee, 587-2757. M, W-F 10am-4pm, Sa-Su 10am-3pm.

United States Forest Service Visitor Information, Lake Tahoe: 573-2674. Summer daily 8am-5:30pm; Winter closed.

Getting There

When driving, avoid leaving the Bay Area any time near 5pm on Friday. Take I-80 east to Sacramento; turn onto Hwy 50 to South Lake Tahoe or continue on I-80 toward Truckee and the North Shore. Reno is another 35 miles past Truckee. It can snow heavily without much warning at any time of the year; always carry chains.

Greyhound (800-231-2222 or 702-588-4645) runs a few buses to South Lake Tahoe, Truckee, and Reno from San Francisco daily. **Amtrak** (800-872-7245) runs from Oakland and San Jose to Truckee and Reno. Most trips involve a train to Sacramento and a bus to your destination, but one train goes all the way and offers spectacular views. **South Lake Tahoe Airport** (542-6180) is tiny, but has some service from the Bay Area, and is a short cab or shuttle-bus ride from South Lake Tahoe. There are more flights into **Reno Airport** (702-328-6400), but it's an hour from Lake Tahoe, so you may have to rent a car or take a shuttle; try the **Tahoe Casino Express** (800-446-6128).

Once in Tahoe, **TART**, Tahoe Area Regional Transit (581-6365), offers bus service through the North Lake area. **STAGE**, South Tahoe Area Ground Express (573-2080), serves the South Lake Tahoe area.

SKIING & SNOWBOARDING

Because the Sierra is the first mountain range in from the coast, storms bring heavy snows that are measured in feet, not inches. The season varies considerably from year to year, but it's reasonable to expect snow from December to May. The region offers a wide variety of skiing options, from huge resorts to tiny mom-and-pop hills. Most resorts now allow snowboarding—in fact, only **Alpine Meadows** forbids it. Most places offer half-pipes, but **Boreal**, **Homewood**, and **Donner Ski Ranch** have particularly satisfying ones.

Tahoe also has many good cross-country ski resorts. **Royal Gorge** claims to be the largest in the United States (it is the most expensive), while **Tahoe Donner's** cross-country trails surpass its downhill area. Downhill resorts such as **Northstar**, **Heavenly**, **Kirkwood**, and **Squaw** have trails, too. The Sierra Club's **Claire Tapaan Lodge** and **Alpine Skills Institute** (see *Lodging* section) also have trails. Many people prefer free "backwoods" skiing—you can often spot the trailhead by the cars parked on the side of the road. Stop in at any outdoors store for advice. **Castle Peak** is a good starting point, just across I-80 from Boreal Ski Area. In addition to ski-area shops, there are rental shops in Truckee, Tahoe City, and South Lake.

Alpine Meadows: Off Hwy 89 between Truckee and Tahoe City, 583-4232, 800-441-4423. The "other" large area in North Lake, but much smaller than Squaw. Offers ample variety, including steep chutes accessed by climbing. Well-sheltered in stormy weather. The last area to close in the spring. A local favorite, in part because of candid snow reports and retro feel (Mostly older chairs and **no snowboarding!**). 1,553' vert. $41 adult.

Boreal Ski Area: Just off I-80 at Boreal/Castle Peak exit, 426-3666. A little area that offers a good variety of runs for beginners and intermediates, and night skiing. Right off highway on top of Donner pass, so it's convenient and gets lots of snow. Popular with snowboarders. 600' vert. $31 adult.

Diamond Peak at Ski Incline: Off Hwy 28, Incline Village, Nevada, (702) 832-1126. 24-hour ski information: (702) 831-3211. Small area just across the state line. It's a bit harder to reach (which means smaller crowds), and can have good snow when other areas are lacking. Recently increased its skiable terrain, adding numerous expert runs at the top of the mountain. Cross-country area. 1,840' vert. $34 adult.

Donner Ski Ranch: Old Hwy 40 about six miles from I-80 Soda Springs/Norden exit, 426-3635. Mom-and-pop sized, but offers some good intermediate terrain, a homey atmosphere, and night skiing. 750' vert. $20 adult.

Heavenly Valley: Ski Run Blvd. from Hwy 50 in South Lake Tahoe, 541-1330, (702) 586-7000. Huge resort claiming the most skiable terrain of any resort in the United States. Experts prefer the Nevada side. It also offers great views and is just minutes from the casinos and accommodations in Stateline. Suffers from overcrowding. 3,600' vert. $42 adult.

Homewood: Hwy 89, 6 mi. south Tahoe City, 525-2992. Small area with mostly intermediate runs and classic postcard views of Lake Tahoe. It may be the best place to ski on the weekends, and is definitely an ideal place to learn to snowboard. 1,650' vert. $32 adult.

Kirkwood Ski and Summer Resort: Hwy 88 off Hwy 89, 1/2 hour south of South Lake Tahoe, (209) 258-6000. Medium-sized ski area with diverse terrain, including radical steeps and smaller crowds. High base elevation leads to claims of better snow. Cross country. 2,000' vert. $39 adult.

Mount Rose Ski Resort: Rt. 431 near Incline Village, Nevada, 800-SKI-ROSE. Another small area across the state line offering a surprising amount of challenging terrain. Good on powder days. 1,450' vert. $29 adult.

Northstar-at-Tahoe: Hwy 267 between Truckee and North Lake Tahoe, 562-1010. Large, planned resort with the motto, "Northstar has it all," including luxury condominiums, cross-country, and a golf course. Medium-sized ski area with many beginner and intermediate cruising runs (locals call it Flatstar); more advanced backside always seems to be closed. 2,200' vert. $42 adult.

Royal Gorge: Off Old Hwy 40 from I-80 Soda Springs/Norden exit, 426-3871. Huge cross-country ski area, with well-groomed tracks for kick-and-glide and skating. Serves all levels from beginners to competitive racers. Full-service lodge with rentals, lessons, etc. $18.50 adult.

Sierra at Tahoe: Off Hwy 50 between Echo Summit and South Lake Tahoe, 659-7453. Formerly named Sierra Ski Ranch. Provides bowl skiing for intermediates and a nurturing atmosphere for beginners. 2,212' vert. $37 adult.

Squaw Valley: Hwy 89 between Tahoe City and Truckee, 583-6985. Squaw Valley is huge, offering everything from serious cliff jumping to gentle bunny hills. But be prepared for long lift lines on weekends, steep ticket prices, and a glitzy scene. The upper lifts are often closed on windy days. There's even a mountain-top outdoor skating rink and bungee jumping. Squaw employees wear buttons that say "We Care," but everyone knows they don't. 2,850' vert. $43 adult.

Sugar Bowl Ski Resort: Old Hwy 40 about three miles from I-80 Soda Springs/Norden exit, 426-3651. Medium-sized area with varied terrain ranging from beginning to advanced, including chutes and trees. Ridge-top location draws good snow coverage. A recent expansion added road access to the Mr. Judah base area—good for those who don't like riding the old gondola to the base lodge—and new terrain. 1,500' vert. $37 adult.

Tahoe Donner: Northwoods Blvd., north of I-80 from first Truckee exit, 587-9444 or 587-9400. Tiny area associated with subdivision offering limited beginner and intermediate skiing. Family-oriented. Excellent cross-country area. $26 adult.

WARM-WEATHER ACTIVITIES

Parks and Beaches

Much of the area around Lake Tahoe is public land; either State Park, National Forest, or local park. **Donner Memorial State Park** (582-7893), off I-80 on Donner Pass Road near Truckee, lies on the edge of **Donner Lake**. It's a beautiful spot for a short visit or camping, and there's even a museum which tells the Donner Party's grisly story. The museum is open daily 10am to 5pm year-round. Off Hwy 89 along the west side of the lake, you'll find three state parks: **Sugar Pine Point** (525-7982), **D. L. Bliss** (525-7277), and **Emerald Bay** (541-3030), home to shoreline beaches, camping, and trails. While at Emerald Bay, visit the Scandinavian mansion Vikingsholm. In **Lake Tahoe Nevada State Park** (702-831-0494) on the northeastern side of Lake Tahoe, you'll find **Sand Harbor**, a beautiful beach with shallow water that warms up enough for swimming. During the summer, Sand Harbor often hosts theater or music performances on its outdoor stage.

Aquatic Sports

Because Lake Tahoe is so large, it is always very cold, but never freezes over. However, the brave still swim, ski, sail, and otherwise indulge in the lake. Donner Lake is also cold, but popular for skiing and fishing.

On Tahoe's north shore, **jet ski and boat rentals** are available at **Kings Beach** (546-7248) and at the **North Tahoe Marina** (546-8248). In Tahoe City, try **Lighthouse Watersports Center** (583-6000) and **Tahoe Water Adventures** (583-3225). In South Lake Tahoe, head for the **South Lake Tahoe Marina** (541-6626) or **Timber Cove Marina** (542-4472 for jet skis; 544-2942 for boats, parasailing, and canoes). For a more relaxed exploration of the lake, hop on the glass-bottomed **Tahoe Queen** (541-3364 or 800-23-TAHOE) at Hwy 50 and Ski Run Boulevard. They offer daily Emerald Bay cruises and sunset dinner-dance trips. The Emerald Bay trip costs about $14 for adults; the sunset cruise costs about $18 plus dinner. In winter, there's a ski shuttle to the North Shore.

Mountain Biking

There are a number of excellent rides throughout the hills. Most of the bike stores in the area can give you advice on their favorite rides, but there is an endless supply of fire roads from which to choose. Serious riders should ask about the Flume Trail. Most of the bigger ski areas listed above open their trails to bikes in summer and offer bike rentals and even lift service.

Rentals are available at bike stores in Tahoe City, Truckee, and South Lake for about $20-$25/day. Try the **Olympic Bicycle Shop** (581-2500) at 620 North Lake Boulevard in Tahoe City. Another good spot is **Porter's Ski & Sport** (583-2314) at 501 North Lake Boulevard, Tahoe City. In South Lake Tahoe, bike rentals of all sorts are available at **Anderson's** (541-0500), located at 645 Emerald Bay Road. **Sierra Cycleworks** (541-7505) at 3430 Hwy 50 rents bikes in South Lake Tahoe.

Gambling

Nevada's casinos conspicuously mark the border between that state and California. (Remember that you must be 21 to get in.) Tahoe's casinos can offer some great deals (Reno's are the best!), such as cheap entertainment in their lounges, and moderate room and meal prices. You might even find a medium-to-big star on stage. When hungry, look for all-you-can-eat buffet specials for $5 or less.

On the south shore, **Caesar's**, **Harrah's**, and the other big-name casinos are nice, but they cater to visitors with lots of cash—they raise the minimum betting limits throughout the night. If you're looking to test the waters with small bets, find a $2 or $3 blackjack table at **Harvey's**, **Bill's** or the **Horizon**, all friendly, low-key places. Most casinos on the north shore are in Crystal Bay, Nevada. **The Crystal Bay Club** is a laid-back alternative, and the **Tahoe Biltmore** recently went through a mega-renovation. The biggest club on the north shore, however, is the **Hyatt**, which is off by itself in Incline Village.

Bill's Lake Tahoe Casino: Hwy 50, Stateline, NV, (702) 588-2455.

Caesar's: 55 Hwy 50, Stateline, NV, (702) 588-3515; (800) 648-3353.

Crystal Bay: 14 Hwy 28, Crystal Bay, NV, (702) 831-0512.

Harrah's: Hwy 50, Stateline, NV, (702) 588-6611; (800) 648-3773; (800) AT-TAHOE ext. 412.

Harvey's: Hwy 50, Stateline, NV, (800) 648-3361; (800) AT-TAHOE Ext. 411.

Horizon Resort Hotel Casino: Hwy 50, Stateline, NV, (702) 588-6211.

Hyatt Regency Lake Tahoe Resort and Casino: 111 Country Club Dr. (at Lakeshore Dr.), Incline Village, NV, (702) 831-1111.

Tahoe Biltmore Lodge and Casino: Hwy. 28, Crystal Bay, NV, (702) 831-0660.

Restaurants and Entertainment

The Beacon $$: 1900 Jamieson Beach Rd., South Lake Tahoe, 541-0630. Standard California fare along with its signature Rum Runner cocktail. Lunch and dinner daily.

Bridge Tender $: 30 W. Lake Blvd., Tahoe City, 583-3342. Live trees grow through the roof, and outdoor seating overlooks Fanny Bridge. Burgers, fries, and other pub grub. 11am-11pm daily; bar open until 1:30am.

Cantina Los Tres Hombres $$: 765 Emerald Bay Rd., South Lake Tahoe, 544-1233. Margaritas and Mexican food. Lunch and dinner daily; bar open later.

Chart House $$$/$$$$: 392 Kingsberry Grade, Stateline, NV, (702) 588-6276. Well-done surf-and-turf with great views of the lake. Dinner daily.

Donner Lake Kitchen $: 13710 Donner Pass Rd., Truckee (behind Donner Pines Store along Donner Lake), 587-3119. Popular local diner for home-style and Mexican breakfasts and lunches. Love the velvet paintings. Cash only. Breakfast and lunch daily.

Fire Sign Café $/$$: 1785 W. Lake Blvd., Tahoe Park, 583-0871. A great spot for breakfast or a healthy lunch. Outdoor patio. Breakfast and lunch daily.

Frank's Restaurant $: 1207 Hwy 50, South Lake Tahoe, 544-3434. An amazing place for home-cooked breakfast in South Lake. Breakfast and lunch daily.

La Hacienda del Lago $: Boatworks Mall, 760 N. Lake Blvd., Tahoe City, 583-0358. Tasty Mexican food and free-flowing margaritas at this festive local hangout. Happening night life. Lunch and dinner daily.

Heidi's $: 3485 Hwy 50, South Lake Tahoe, 544-8113. They claim to serve "the best breakfast you'll ever have." Great, hearty lunches, too. Breakfast and lunch daily.

Izzy's Burger Spa $: 2591 Hwy 50, South Lake Tahoe, 544-5030. "Spa" is a bit of a mystery descriptive, as the place is more of a fast food burger joint. Lunch and dinner daily.

Jake's on the Lake $$/$$$: Boatworks Mall, 780 W. Lake Blvd., Tahoe City, 583-0188. A swinging night spot ("snakes on the make"), with surprisingly good American food, especially seafood and pasta. Breakfast, lunch and dinner daily.

Lake Tahoe Pizza Co. $: 1168 Hwy 50, just south of the Y, South Lake Tahoe, 544-1919. Fantastic pizza place. Dinner daily.

Lakehouse Pizza $: 120 Grove St., Tahoe City, 583-2222. Popular hangout serving good pizza with gobs of toppings. Great views. Lunch and dinner daily.

O.B.'s Pub and Restaurant $$/$$$: 10046 Commercial Row, Truckee, 587-4164. A favorite among locals. Large, dark saloon serving a range of hearty American food from burgers to pasta to grilled salmon. Lunch and dinner daily, brunch Su.

The Passage $$$: Truckee Hotel, Commercial & Bridge Sts., Truckee, 587-7619. Creatively prepared and presented California cuisine in a historic, candlelit dining room. Game specials can be superb. Lunch and dinner daily, brunch Sa-Su.

River Ranch Lodging and Dining $$/$$$: Hwy 89 at Alpine Meadows Rd., Tahoe City, 583-4264. Dark and cozy restaurant near Alpine Meadows with good basic food and great views of the Truckee River. If you don't want a serious meal, get a burger by the fireplace in the bar. Lunch and dinner daily.

Rosie's Café $$/$$$: 571 North Lake Blvd., Tahoe City, 583-8504. Eclectic, healthy menu in cozy country setting. Particularly good breakfasts. Breakfast, lunch, and dinner daily.

Squeeze Inn $: Commercial Row, Truckee, 587-9814. Very popular local spot for great omelets (limitless variety of options), as well as other breakfast and lunch dishes. Breakfast and lunch daily.

Steamers Bar and Grill $$: 2236 Lake Tahoe Blvd., South Lake Tahoe, 541-8818. Decent pizza, and a good place for large groups to party. Lunch and dinner daily.

Sunnyside Resort $$/$$$: 1850 West Lake Boulevard, Tahoe City, 583-7200. Sports a large deck on the lake and standard sandwich and burger fare. Especially pleasant for summer brunch. Lunch and dinner daily; brunch Su.

Truckee Trattoría $$/$$$: Gateway Shopping Center, Hwy 89 at Old Hwy 40, Truckee, 582-1266. Surprising find in a Safeway strip mall. Bright and clean setting for light California and Italian cuisine. Special entrees shine more than pastas. Liberal BYOB policy for good wines. Lunch and dinner W-Su.

Wolfdale's $$$$: 640 N. Lake Blvd., Tahoe City, 583-5700. Highly-regarded Asian-California vegetarian cuisine. Dinner W-M; nightly during summer.

Places to Stay

Try the North and South Tahoe Visitors Bureaus listed under *General Information* for places to stay; they handle rentals, hotels, or inns. Just describe what you want and they'll find it. Also, casinos frequently offer good deals on weekend packages, figuring what you don't cough up in lodging you'll spend on gambling. The best casino deals are in Reno. Renting houses for a week or weekend is a good option for groups. Many people rent a house for the entire ski season. Central Reservations' numbers should be able to handle short-term rentals. Local realty companies have listings of available properties for short-term or seasonal rentals, and you can usually find ads in the classified section of Bay Area newspapers.

Camping

Camping is available on most of the public lands around Tahoe, including the parks listed above. There are also several state campgrounds as you go south on Highway 89 past Squaw Valley and Alpine Meadows. **Sugar Pine Point** and **Grover Hot Springs State Park** are both available for year-round camping. If you intend to camp in organized campgrounds between May and September, make reservations in advance. All State Park reservations go through Mistix (800-444-7275). **Fallen Leaf Lake** is the most popular national forest campground; use a different Mistix number (800-283-2267) for reservations.

Camp Richardson: Hwy 89 2 mi. north of Hwy 50, South Lake Tahoe, 541-1801. Private development with an 83-acre campground on the south shore that boasts 112 campsites with hot showers, a beach, a marina, and Nordic skiing in the winter. Lodging includes cabins as well. $17/campsite, $64-84/lodging.

Budget

Alpine Skills Institute Lodge: Old Hwy 40 off I-80 at Norden/Soda Springs exit, 426-9108. A mountaineering school that offers reasonably-priced bunk-and-breakfast accommodations. $22 bunk bed; $70 double-occupancy room.

Clair Tappaan Lodge: Old Hwy 40 off I-80 at Norden/Soda Springs exit, 426-3632. Run by the Sierra Club, this huge old building has dormitory-style rooms; price includes a family-style meal. $30/Sierra Club members, $36/non-members.

Motel 6: 2375 Lake Tahoe Blvd., South Lake Tahoe, 542-1400. Tom Bodette will leave the light on. $40-$47.

Trade Winds Motel: 944 Friday Ave., Stateline, NV, (800) 628-1829. Two blocks from the casinos. In-room coffee makers, and a year-round spa and pool are included. $38-$68.

Moderate

Best Western Truckee Tahoe: 11331 Hwy 267, 1 mi. south of Truckee, 587-4525. Basic, clean, and comfortable, with pool. $68-$80.

Donner Country Inn: 10070 Gregory Place (Donner Lake Rd. at Donner Pass Rd.), Truckee, 587-5574. Tiny, unassuming motel has comfortable rooms—some with fireplaces. Minimum 2 night stay. $95.

Loch Leven Lodge: 13855 Donner Pass Rd., along Donner Lake, Truckee, 587-3773. Lakeside lodge with a big deck and hot tubs. Some rooms have fireplaces or kitchenettes. Cash or checks only. $66-$86.

Super 8 Lodge: 11506 Deerfield Dr., Truckee, 587-8888. Not charming, but convenient and reasonable. $56-$88.

Tahoe City Travelodge: 455 N. Lake Blvd., Tahoe City, 583-3766, 800-255-3050. Basic, clean, and comfortable, with pool. In town. $73-$93.

Truckee Hotel: 10007 Bridge St. (at Commercial Row), Truckee, 587-4444, 800-659-6921. A country-quaint historic building with reasonable prices. Breakfast included, $75-$105.

Luxury

Squaw Valley Central Reservations: (800) 545-4350. Handles reservations for Squaw Valley and beyond. **Resort at Squaw Creek** is newest, most deluxe property. Also handles condos and houses. Also see *Casino* Section.

WINE COUNTRY

Almost as famous as the vineyards of France, the Napa and Sonoma valleys are renowned as much for their scenery as for their award-winning wines. One trip will convince you that their popularity is well deserved. As a tourist destination, California wine country consists primarily of the Napa and Sonoma Valleys north of San Francisco, though there are wine-growing areas throughout the state. In the Napa Valley, vineyards are scattered along a 35-mile stretch of land between the towns of Napa to the south and Calistoga (home of the hot springs and the bottled water) to the north. In between are Yountville, Rutherford, Oakville, and St. Helena; all quaint communities. The Sonoma Valley is less traveled than its neighbor, but is home to many quality wineries and other points of interest in Sonoma, Kenwood, and the Russian River Valley. For lovers of the drink, this area is heaven: top-notch wineries are all within driving distance of each other and offer regularly scheduled tours and tastings for visitors. Besides the beautiful vistas, there are museums, galleries, and state parks to see. Couples favor the numerous bed-and-breakfasts and intimate restaurants, which make for romantic (though pricey) weekend retreats.

NAPA

The Napa Valley was once populated by the Nappa Indian tribe, until Spanish explorers arrived in 1823. American farmers began settling the region in the 1830s, and in 1833, George Calvert Yount (Yountville's namesake) planted the first vineyard in the valley. It was Charles Krug, however, who brought Riesling grapes to the region in 1861, launching the wine business in earnest. Since then, wine-making in the Napa Valley has steadily expanded and improved, making the region one of the major wine producers in the country.

General Information

Area Code: 707

Calistoga Chamber of Commerce: 1458 Lincoln Ave. #4, Calistoga, 942-6333. Daily 10am-5pm.

Napa Chamber of Commerce: 1556 First St., Napa, 226-7455. M-F 9am-5pm.

Napa City Bus: 1151 Pearl St., Napa, 255-7631. Office M-F 8am-noon, 1pm-5pm; Sa 10am-3pm. Buses run M-F 6:45am-6:30pm; Sa 7:45am-5:30pm.

St. Helena Chamber of Commerce: 1080 Main St., St. Helena, 963-4456. M-F 10am-noon, 1pm-4pm.

Yountville Chamber of Commerce: 6515 Washington St., Yountville, 944-0904. M-Sa 10am-3pm; some Sundays noon-3pm.

Getting There

By car, take Hwy 101 or I-280 through San Francisco over the Golden Gate Bridge. From Hwy 101 take Hwy 37 to Hwy 121 to Hwy 29 which runs the length of the valley from Napa to Calistoga. For a less crowded route, travel along the Silverado Trail, which runs parallel to Hwy 29 (turnoffs are clearly marked on Hwy 29). Along this road you'll find a host of smaller wineries tucked into the wooded hillside that forms Napa's eastern border. These wineries may be hard to find if you're not paying attention to the blue road signs, but if you tear yourself away from the quiet beauty of the valley, you'll find them—many of them—without any trouble.

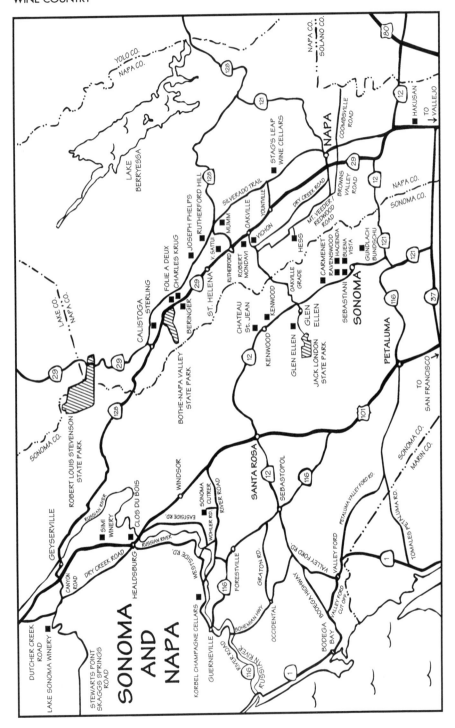

Napa Valley Wineries

Many wineries offer tours and tastings, some free of charge and others for a nominal fee.

Beringer Vineyards: 2000 Main St. (Hwy 29), St. Helena, 963-7115 or 963-4812. Daily guided tours of the winery's caves, and a Germanic mansion where tasting and purchasing take place. Tasting is complimentary. Summer hours may vary; call ahead for information. Group tours by reservation. Tours daily 9:30am-5pm. Tasting 10am-4:30pm.

Charles Krug Winery: 2800 Main St. (Hwy 29), St. Helena, 963-5057. The valley's first winery, and a must-visit. Daily tours are $1. No reservations required. Group tours by appointment. M-F 10am-5pm; weekends 10am-6pm. Last tour at 3:30pm, weekends 4:30pm.

Domaine Chandon: 1 California Dr., Yountville, 944-2280. The place to visit if you get a kick from champagne—this vineyard is owned and operated by the French vintners Moet and Chandon, makers of Dom Perignon. Group tours by reservation. Daily tours May-Oct. 11am-6pm; Nov.-April W-Su 11am-6pm.

Folie à Deux Winery: 3070 N. St. Helena Hwy., St. Helena, 963-1160. Some of the best Chardonnay and dry Chenin Blanc around, along with tours and free, laid-back tasting sessions. Daily 11am-5pm for tastings, groups by arrangement.

Hakusan Sake Gardens: One Executive Wy., Napa, 258-6160. For a change of genre, visit this place for sake served in a beautiful Japanese garden. Daily 9am-6pm for tours and tasting.

Hess Collection Winery: 4411 Redwood Rd., Napa, 255-1144. Immaculate premises, an amazing modern art collection, and a renovated historic building form the backdrop of this winery. Tasting is charged by the glass. Daily 10am-4pm for tours and tasting.

Joseph Phelps Vineyard: 200 Taplin Rd., St. Helena, 963-2745 or (800) 707-5789. Informative tours, ample tastings, and one of the best-designed vineyards in the valley. Tours and tastings by appointment only. Daily 10am-4pm.

Mumm Napa Valley: 8445 Silverado Trail, Rutherford, 942-3359; Visitor Center 942-3434. The new kids on the champagne-makers' block, this vineyard offers informative tours. Tours every hour 11am-3pm; tastings daily 10:30am-6pm.

Robert Mondavi Winery: 7801 St. Helena Hwy., Oakville, 259-9463. A good place for first-time visitors. A tour is required prior to tasting, and you may have to wait quite a while since they fill up quickly. Tasting is charged by the glass. Concerts and events are often held here during the summer. Reservations suggested. Daily 9am-5:30pm; tours summer 10am-4pm, winter 9:30am-4:30pm. Concert and event information: 963-9617 ext. 4384.

Rutherford Hill Winery: 200 Rutherford Hill Rd. (off the Silverado Trail), Rutherford, 963-7194. Good tours and excellent Merlot. Tasting costs $3 and includes crackers and a glass. Tours last 30 minutes. Tasting and sales M-F 10am-4:30pm; Sa-Su 10am-5pm. Tours M-F 11:30am, 1:30pm, and 3:30pm, and Sa-Su 12:30pm and 2:30pm.

V. Sattui Winery: Hwy 29 at White Ln., St. Helena, 963-7774. A small place with good wine. If you like what you taste, buy it, because you won't find it anywhere else. Tours by appointment only. Daily summer 9am-6pm, winter 9am-5pm.

Stag's Leap Wine Cellars: 5766 Silverado Trail, Napa, 944-2020. A small, unassuming place with great Cabernets and Chardonnays. Tastings are held throughout the day for $3 and include a glass. Free non-alcoholic drinks for the driver. Daily 10am-4pm; tours by appointment only.

Sterling Vineyards: 1111 Dunaweal Ln., Calistoga, 942-3300. Accessible to visitors by tram; the views and scenery are amazing. Tasting, tour, and tram ride included in the $6 visitor fee. Self-guided tours. Persons over 16 years only; under 21 admitted free. Daily 10:30am-4:30pm.

Vichon Winery: 1595 Oakville Grade,Oakville,944-2811. Shady picnic grounds over-looking the valley make this a nice place to stop for lunch, but they ask that you buy a bottle of their vino in exchange for the setting. Daily 10am-4:30pm.

Other Attractions

While wine is the main attraction in Napa, you might consider some of the many options for exploring the region from the ground, air, and water.

Take to the skies in a hot air balloon for a panoramic view of the valley. Though not-for the frugal or the acrophobic, ballooning has become a popular and romantic tourist activity. Balloons typically depart at dawn, so most companies provide a champagne brunch afterward. Try **Above the West Ballooning** (944-8638 or 800-NAPA-SKY) in Yountville, or **Bonaventura Balloon Company** (944-2822 or 800-FLY-NAPA) in Napa at 133 Wall Road. Flights start at $160.

Or try flying in a different kind of machine: **Calistoga Gliderport** (942-5000), at 1546 Lincoln Avenue, will fly you and a friend around seven miles of the Napa Valley in a glider plane. Rides last either 20 or 30 minutes and offer some spectacular views. Reservations are recommended on the weekend. Hours are daily 9am-6pm. Flights for 2 people are $110 for 20 minutes, $150 for 30 minutes.

Landlubbers take heart—you can also see the countryside on horseback with a guided trail ride at **Wild Horse Valley Ranch** (224-0727), located at the end of Coombsville Road in Napa. The two-hour rides wind through the ranch's 4,000 acres of meadows and hills and are suitable for all levels of rider. Even the drive to the ranch affords spectacular views of the valley. They're open W-M, with guided rides at 9am, 11:30am, and 2pm. Reserve one day in advance for groups of 4 or fewer; one week in advance for larger groups—the cost is $35 per person. If you prefer swimming, head for the shores of **Lake Berryessa**. The 167-mile shoreline provides ample opportunities for swimming, boating, and fishing, as well as camping, hiking, and picnicking.

Athletic types may want to bring bikes and cycle through the flat valley. If you lack a bike or a way to transport yours, you can rent wheels at **St.Helena Cyclery** (963-7736), at 1156 Main Street. Located in the heart of Napa Valley, it rents hybrids (a combination of a mountain and a road bike) for $7 per hour, $25 per business day. Rental includes a lock, helmet, saddlebag, and water-bottle rack. Hours are M-Sa 9:30am-5:30pm; Su 10am-5pm.

Bryan's Napa Valley Cyclery (255-3377), at 4080 Byway East, rents road bikes and hybrids for $4-6 per hour, or for $15-20 for an entire day. All-day guided bike tours along the Silverado Trail are also available for groups of two to ten for $85 per person. Tours include bike and helmet rentals, and visits to three or four wineries with tastings and lunch. Make reservations at least four days in advance. Hours are M-Sa 9am-6pm; Su 10am-4pm.

If you'd rather use your feet to get around, **Bothe-Napa Valley State Park** (942-4575), at Hwy 29 between St. Helena and Calistoga, offers 1,800 acres of hiking amid red-woods, oaks, and wildflowers, as well as camping, picnicking, and a swimming pool. **Robert Louis Stevenson State Park** (Hwy 29, 5 miles north of Calistoga) features an abandoned silver mine and the bunkhouse where the writer spent his honeymoon in 1880 and collected material for his novel *Silverado Springs*. There are no facilities in the park (not even water and restrooms), but climb to the summit of **Mt. Helena** (rumored to have been Stevenson's inspiration for Spyglass Hill in *Treasure Island*) for the breathtaking view of the Bay Area and the Sierra Nevada. True Stevenson aficionados can also visit the **Silverado Museum** (963-3757), which is filled with manuscript notes and other memorabilia. The museum is conveniently located in the St. Helena library where you can bone up on the author's works. Hours are Tu-Su noon to 4pm.

Don't leave Napa Valley without a visit to one of the many Calistoga spas and mineral baths. Indulgences range from basic mud and mineral baths to extra treatments like herbal facials, acupressure, and manicures. The staff at **Calistoga Village Inn and Spa** (942-0991), at 1880 Lincoln Ave., will pamper you at reasonable prices. There are also hotel accommodations here, but you don't have to be a guest to use the spa facilities, though you do need a reservation (call from 8am-9pm daily). The spa is open M-Th 10am-8:30pm; F-Su 8am-9pm. On your way to the healing baths of Calistoga, take a detour from Hwy 29 to Tubbs Lane to watch a different kind of steam bath, the **Old Faithful Geyser** of California (942-6463). This natural wonder spews a 60-foot stream of boiling water into the air every 40 minutes. It's open daily from 9am to 5pm. Admission for adults is $5.00, seniors $4, children 6-12 $2, and children under 6 free.

If you long to exercise your purchasing power, stop by the **Village Outlets of Napa Valley** (963-7282), two miles south of St. Helena on Hwy 29. This nice, shaded factory outlet center offers big bargains on such famous-name merchandise as Donna Karan, Brooks Brothers, and Joan & David.

Restaurants

Catahoula $$$: 1457 Lincoln Ave., St. Helena 942-2275. A truly inspired Southern menu that can be enjoyed in the dining room or by the pool. Definitely order dessert. Lunch and dinner W-M; brunch Sa-Su.

Foothill Café $$/$$$: 2766 Old Sonoma Rd., Napa, 252-6178. This place is an enigma—it's located in a strip-mall, and it's an amazing restaurant. Great barbecued ribs, fresh fish, and a good wine list. Dinner W-Su.

The Grill $$$: Meadowood Resort, 900 Meadowood Ln., St. Helena, 963-3646 or (800) 458-8080. Steep prices, sylvan surroundings, and savory sandwiches. Breakfast and lunch daily, dinner F-Sa. Call for winery hours.

Guigni's Grocery Good $: 1227 Main St., St. Helena, 963-3421. A good place for sandwiches, which can be eaten in the back room. Daily 9am-5pm.

Mustard's Grill $$$: 7399 St. Helena Hwy, Napa, 944-2424. Upscale, popular, and interesting. Lunch and dinner daily.

Nation's Giant Hamburgers $: 1441 3rd St., Napa, 252-8500. Inexpensive, huge, delicious burgers served in a non-aesthetic setting. Daily 6am-midnight; F-Sa 6am-2am.

Oakville Grocery Co. $: 7856 St. Helena Hwy, Oakville, 944-8802. The gourmet's choice for picnic fixings. Daily 10am-6pm.

Piatti $$$: 6480 Washington Street, Yountville, 944-2070. A fun trattoria with innovative, reasonably priced food. Lunch and dinner daily.

The Restaurant $$$$: Meadowood Resort, 900 Meadowood Ln., St. Helena, 963-3646 or (800) 458-8080. A place to avoid if you become a bit free with the cash after a few glasses of wine. The food is a gourmet whirlwind adventure. Reservations recommended. Dinner daily, brunch Su.

Terra $$$/$$$$: 1345 Railroad Ave., St. Helena, 963-8931. An elegant, expensive, sophisticated eatery. Dinner W-M.

Tra Vigne $$$: 1050 Charter Oak, Hwy 29, St. Helena, 963-4444. Delicious Italian/French meals in a sharp, trendy setting. Lunch and dinner daily.

Wappo Bar Bistro $$: 1226-B Washington St., Calistoga, 942-4712. Eclectic California cuisine served on a beautiful backyard garden patio. Lunch W-M, dinner Th-M.

Places to Stay

Spending the night in Napa isn't cheap. Traveling off-season (November–April) and during the week may save you money. For more information and reservations, call **Napa Valley Reservations Unlimited** (252-1985), at 1819 Tanen Street in Napa, open M-F 9am-5pm. If you want to stay on a summer weekend, you may need to make reservations as far as two months in advance for some of the more upscale accommodations. Some places require a two-night stay on weekends.

Budget and Moderate

Bothe-Napa Valley State Park: 3601 St. Helena Hwy N., St. Helena, 942-4575. Reservations: (800) 444-7275. Facilities include hot water, restrooms, and showers. $14 per campsite, $5 per extra vehicle.

Calistoga Ranch Campground: 580 Lommel Rd., Calistoga, 942-6565. A cheap stay, with showers available. Tent site with elevated barbecue and picnic table $19 for 4 people, $2 for each additional person. 28-day maximum stay.

Calistoga Spa and Hot Springs: 1006 Washington St., Calistoga, 942-6269. Frequent discounts are offered—inquire when making reservations. Appointments must be made for the spa, which offers mud and mineral baths, massages, mineral water baths, and steam blanket wraps. With bath, kitchenette $70-$105.

Calistoga Village Inn and Spa: 1880 Lincoln Ave., Calistoga, 942-0991 or (800) 543-1049. Sunken tubs, geothermal baths, whirlpools, and a swimming pool are included in the reasonable rate. With private bath $75-$150. No minimum stay.

Napa Town & Country Fairgrounds: 575 3rd St., Napa, 253-4900. Water and electricity included. Campsites $15.

Triple S Ranch: 4600 Mtn. Home Ranch Rd., Calistoga, 942-6730. Eight wooden cabins located near the Old Faithful Geyser of California and numerous hiking trails—a true bargain for a double room. $49.

Luxury

Auberge du Soleil: 180 Rutherford Hill Rd., Rutherford, 963-1211. The place to go for very special occasions. Located in a secluded olive grove, rooms come with the works—fireplaces, terraces, sofas, king-size beds, and resplendent bathrooms. Some rooms available in the main house. Double rooms with private bath $200-$950.

Pink Mansion: 1415 Foothill Blvd, Calistoga, 942-0558. An elegant, restored mansion with in-house wine tasting and an indoor pool filled with local waters. Full breakfast included. $85-$165.

Shady Oaks Country Inn: 399 Zinfandel Ln., St. Helena, 963-1190. A quiet, romantic setting. Gourmet champagne breakfasts and wine and hors d'oeuvres every night add to the charm. $135-$155; mid-week rates are available.

SONOMA

When George Yount and Charles Krug were establishing Napa Valley as a wine-growing region, Sonoma County was undergoing a time of chaos. The Russian, Mexican, and the American governments were engaged in fierce territorial skirmishes over the region until the United States finally took possession of Sonoma and its riches. The area has quieted considerably since then; the peaceful vineyards and scenic landscapes give little indication of the region's tumultuous past. Wineries in Sonoma County are centered in the Sonoma

Valley, which is in the southern part of the county, and in northern Sonoma County around the town of Healdsburg and the Russian River Valley. Exploration of Sonoma requires an investigator's eye—the treasures abound, but you'll have to look a bit harder to find them.

General Information

Area Code: 707

The Petaluma Chamber of Commerce: 314 Western Ave., Petaluma, 762-2785. M-F 9am-5pm (phone hours 9am-4pm).

Sonoma County Visitors Bureau: 5000 Roberts Lake Rd., Rohnert Park, 935-0758. Maps, brochures, and information on the wineries, including a tasting guide. M-F 8am-5pm; Sa-Su 10am-4pm.

Sonoma Valley Visitors Bureau: 453 First St. E., Sonoma, 996-1090. Maps of Sonoma County. Daily 9am-5pm, 9am-7pm summer.

Getting There

The most direct route to the Sonoma Valley is via Hwy 101 across the Golden Gate Bridge. Continue on Hwy 101 to visit Healdsburg, Santa Rosa, and Sebastopol. If you want to head straight for the town of Sonoma, Hwy 37 to Hwy 121 to Hwy 12 is the quickest route to take.

Sonoma Wineries

Napa may have made the California wine country famous, but Sonoma is where it all began. Stories about the true origins of the wine business here vary, but it seems to have begun in 1823 at the vineyards of the Sonoma Mission. Wine making spread with arrival of the Hungarian immigrant Agoston Haraszthy, who brought thousands of vines back from Europe in 1861. The vineyards of Sonoma Valley and Northern Sonoma County still have a lot to offer both the wine connoisseur and the dilettante, and unlike Napa, most vineyards offer free tasting. When traveling through Sonoma, bear in mind that most of the wineries are not directly on the highway; keep your eyes open for the turnoffs, and dare to venture off into the countryside—you never know what delights you might discover.

Buena Vista Winery: 18000 Old Winery Rd., Sonoma, 938-1266. Self-guided tours through the historic stone winery, picnic spots, and a wine museum and gallery are some of the attractions beyond the internationally-acclaimed wines. Daily 10:30am-5pm (summer); 10:30am-4pm (winter).

Carmenet Vineyard: 1700 Moon Mountain Dr., Sonoma, 996-5870. Tours and tasting are by appointment only, and well worth the call. The scenery of the Mayacamas Mountains, underground aging caves, and the Sauvignon Blanc and Cabernet are all outstanding reasons for a visit. Tu-Sa 10am-4pm; tours by appointment only.

Chateau St. Jean: 8555 Sonoma Hwy, P.O. Box 293, Kenwood, 833-4134. The 20s-inspired tasting room and small fee for tastings make this an attractive option. A toll-free hotline for wine buffs is also sponsored by the vineyard, and offers serving suggestions and important wine news updates. Tastings daily 10am-4:30pm. "Wineline" vineyard and winery reports (800) 332-WINE.

Clos Du Bois: 5 Fitch St., Healdsburg, 433-8268. A friendly staff serves up award-winning wines. (Try the Pinot Noir and the Gewurztraminer.) Daily 10am-4:30pm.

Glen Ellen Winery: 1883 London Ranch Rd., Glen Ellen, 935-3000. This ranch was once owned by General Vallejo. Free tasting, a self-guided tour, and picnic spots among the redwoods make this an inviting destination. Self-guided tour. Tastings daily 10am-4:30pm.

Gundlach-Bundschu Winery: 2000 Denmark St., Sonoma, 938-5277. A small, family-run winery known for its Merlot and dessert wines. Self-guided tours. Daily 11am-4:30pm.

Kenwood Vineyards: 9592 Sonoma Hwy, Kenwood, 833-5891. Some of the wines made here are the product of grapes still grown on Jack London's estate in Glen Ellen. Tours are by appointment only. Daily 10am-4:30pm.

Korbel Champagne Cellars: 13250 River Rd., Guerneville, 887-2294. To get your fill of bubbles, brandy, and wine, visit this 100 year-old winery. The picturesque place resembles a castle tucked away in the redwoods, and has a nice picnic area. Summer hours: 10am-3:45 daily. Call for winery hours.

Lake Sonoma Winery: 9990 Dry Creek Rd., Geyserville, 431-1550. Its proximity to Warm Springs Dam and the Lake Sonoma Recreation Area make it worthwhile to stop here. An in-house deli offers picnic fixings to accompany the family-produced vino. Daily 10am-5pm; tours by appointment only.

Ravenswood Winery: 18701 Gehricke Rd., Sonoma, 938-1960. Noted for its red wines, traditional production techniques, and summer weekend barbecues, this is a good place for a taste and a snack. Daily for tours, tasting, and sales 10am-4:30pm.

Sebastiani Vineyards: 389 4th St. E., Sonoma, 938-5532. One of the better-known wineries, boasting the country's largest collection of hand-carved wine casks. Tours and tasting 10:30am-4pm daily (every 30 minutes).

Simi Winery, Inc.: 16275 Healdsburg Ave., Healdsburg, 433-6981. Two Italian immigrants began making wine here in 1876 and built the beautiful stone building in 1890. Now owned by the French company Moet-Hennessey, the winery offers three excellent guided tours per day, and tasting and picnicking on the grounds. Daily 10am-4:30pm for tasting and sales; tours at 11am, 1pm, 3pm.

Other Attractions

Sonoma County's rich history has been well preserved, and you are sure to find plenty to keep you busy after your fill of wine. Like the wineries, points of interest in Sonoma are spread out, so plan your trip carefully in order to take in as much as possible.

A good place to start is in the town of Sonoma, where many of the battles for control of the region took place. Sonoma Plaza was laid out in 1834 by General Mariano Guadalupe Vallejo, the Mexican commander sent to keep the territory out of the hands of the Russians; several historical landmarks, open daily 10am-5pm, are sprinkled among the shops and restaurants that now line the square. (At the first monument you visit you will have to buy a ticket (adults $2, children $1), which will get you into all the others.) Among them are: General Vallejo's first home, **La Casa Grande** (938-1519); the **Sonoma Mission** (938-1578), the last of the great California missions; the **Sonoma Barracks** (938-1519) where Vallejo's troops were housed; and **Lachryma Montis** (938-1578), the General's second, even more stately home. Sonoma Plaza also houses the **Sonoma Cheese Factory** (938-5225), which has been making Sonoma Jack from the same recipe since 1931, and lets you view the process daily from 9am-6pm.

West of Sonoma is the town of Petaluma, famous for its beautiful old buildings, featured in the films *Peggy Sue Got Married* and *American Graffiti*. **The Petaluma Chamber of Commerce** provides free maps for walking tours of the downtown area and the historic district of Victorian homes. Just east of Petaluma at 3325 Adobe Road is the **Petaluma Adobe State Historic Park** (762-4871), the ranch built by General Vallejo in 1836. Take a self-guided tour of the grounds (watch your step—goats and chickens roam freely) and visit the small museum, which is open daily 10am-5pm.

Moving north from Sonoma, be sure to visit **Jack London State Historic Park** (938-5216) on Jack London Ranch Road in Glen Ellen, the writer's former ranch. Hiking and horse trails (horse rentals available) crisscross the ranch and lead you past old barns, pigpens, and the charred remains of **Wolf House**, which was to be London's home but was destroyed by fire shortly before he could move in. **The House of Happy Walls** was built by London's widow, Charmian, and now houses many of his manuscripts, notes, and personal effects. The ranch is open from 8am to sunset.

Lest you think that Sonoma County is too much like school, be assured that there are plenty of other recreational activities to entertain you, especially in the northern portions of the county. Recapture part of your childhood by visiting **Snoopy's Gallery and Gift Shop** (546-3385) at 1665 W. Steele Lane in Santa Rosa, owned and operated by the clever beagle's creator, Charles Schultz. This Santa Rosa gallery boasts the world's largest collection of *Peanuts* memorabilia and is open daily from 10am to 6pm.

If you want to cycle your way through the area, **Rincon Cyclery** (538-0868) rents mountain bikes for $7 per hour (2-hour minimum), and $25 per day, and is not too far from Jack London State Park's bike trails. The shop is located at 4927 Sonoma Hwy (at Hwy 12 and Middle Rincon) and is open daily 10am-6pm. You can also rent bikes at the **Spoke Folk Cyclery** (433-7171) at 249 Center Street in Healdsburg—$15 for 4 hours, $20 for the entire day. They're open Tu-F 10am-6pm; Sat 10am-5pm.

Sonoma has its share of hot air balloon companies eager to take you up for a champagne breakfast flight. **Once in a Lifetime Balloon Co.** (578-0580) picks you up at the Doubletree Inn in Santa Rosa, then takes you to a vineyard for an hour-long flight (the exact route depends on the weather). Afterward, you are returned to the hotel for a gourmet brunch. Prices vary by tour, so call in advance.

Farther north in Healdsburg, **Trowbridge Recreation** (433-7247) organizes canoe, kayak, and camping trips along the Russian River for groups. You can also rent canoes and kayaks: a one-day canoe rental is $32 and must be reserved by noon. You can also rent two-person canoes for $27 at **Burke's Canoe Trips** (887-1222) at 8600 River Road in Forestville and paddle the ten miles to Guerneville. Once you get to Guerneville, a shuttle will take you back to your car in Forestville. Hours are daily 9am-6pm.

Restaurants

Caffé Portofino $$: 535 Fourth St., Santa Rosa, 523-1171. Known for its delicious stuffed artichokes. Reservations recommended. Lunch and dinner M-Sa.

East Side Oyster Bar $$$: 133 E. Napa St., 939-1266. Happening spot for trendy California cuisine. Lunch and dinner daily; brunch Su.

John Ash & Co. $$$$: 4330 Barnes Rd., Santa Rosa, 527-7687. One of the culinary giants of wine country, with a great melange of cuisines. Reservations recommended. Lunch Tu-Sa; dinner Tu-Su; brunch Su.

La Casa $$: 121 E. Spain St., Sonoma, 996-3406. Serves good Mexican food in an authentic setting. Reservations recommended. Lunch and dinner daily.

Lisa Hemenway's $$$: 714 Village Ct., Santa Rosa, 526-5111. Special-occasion dining in a European setting. Lunch and dinner daily; brunch Su.

Madrona Manor $$$/$$$$: 1001 Westside Rd., Healdsburg, (800) 258-4003. Very upscale, with dishes like local quail and pheasant. A prix fixe menu of hors d'oeuvres, goat-cheese wonton soup, grilled rack of lamb, tiramisu, and coffee is a mere $50 per person. Reservations recommended. Dinner nightly; brunch Su.

Ristorante Piatti $$$: 405 1st St. West, Sonoma, 996-2351. A breezy, modern Italian restaurant, twin to the Napa original. Try the risotto. Lunch and dinner daily.

Samba Java $$/$$$: 109A Plaza St., Healdsburg, 433-5282. A lively, stylish place with a Caribbean/California influenced design and California-influenced menu. Breakfast Sa-Su; lunch daily; dinner Th-Sa.

Tre Scalini $$$: 241 Healdsburg Ave., Healdsburg, 433-1772. Excellent, upscale Italian cuisine, with entrees like pan-fried baby frog legs and seafood lasagna. Reservations recommended. Dinner M-Su.

World Famous Hamburger Ranch and Pasta Farm $/$$: 31995 N. Redwood Hwy (Hwy 101), Cloverdale, 894-5616. Nothing but good food, with something for every palate. Breakfast, lunch, and dinner daily. No credit cards.

Places to Stay

Camping

Lake Sonoma/Warm Springs Dam: 3333 Skaggs Springs Rd., Healdsburg 433-9483. Drive-in sites $8 per night per vehicle; primitive sites free. All sites first-come, first-served.

Spring Lake Park: Santa Rosa, between Howarth Park and Annadel State Park, 539-8092. Sites $14; 10 sites need 2-week advance reservation, 20 sites first-come, first-served.

Sugarloaf Ridge State Park: 2605 Adobe Canyon Rd., Kenwood, 833-5712. For reservations call Mistix (800) 444-7275. Campsites $14.

Budget

Econo Lodge: 1800 Santa Rosa Ave., Santa Rosa, 523-3480. Standard clean and spartan chain offering. $35-$59.

Moderate

Best Western Garden Inn: 1500 Santa Rosa Ave., Santa Rosa, 546-4031. Landscaped grounds with two swimming pools. $58-$71.

Best Western Hillside Inn: 2901 Fourth St., Santa Rosa, 546-9353 or (800) 528-1234. Rooms with kitchens and two-bedroom family units. $50.

Glenelly Inn: 5131 Warm Springs Rd., Glen Ellen, 996-6720. Eight rooms with private baths and entrances, a garden, and an outdoor Jacuzzi. $95-$130.

Grape Leaf Inn: 539 Johnson St., Healdsburg, 433-8140. Seven rooms with private baths, whirlpool tubs for two, breakfast in the morning, and wine and cheese at night. $80-$125.

Luxury

Madrona Manor: 1001 Westside Rd., Healdsburg, 433-4231. 21 rooms all with private baths, and some with fireplaces. Enjoy the pool and gourmet restaurant. $135-$225.

Raford House: 10630 Wohler Rd., Healdsburg, (707) 887-9573. An authentic victorian farmhouse, complete with period furnishings, set on a hill among the vinyards. The seven guest rooms are cozy and private, and views from the deck are spectacular. $85-$130.

Sonoma Mission Inn & Spa: 18140 Sonoma Hwy. (Hwy 12), Boyes Hot Springs, (707) 938-9000, (800) 862-4945. This sprawling landmark offers all the amenities and pampering you'd expect in a big luxury hotel. The rooms are rather small, but expect to spend most of your time by the pool, in the spa, or on a golf or tennis course. $140-$290.

YOSEMITE

Famous throughout the world, Yosemite National Park has stupendous scenery, challenging hikes, and, unfortunately, hordes of tourists—three and a half million a year. Yosemite Valley, the park's best-known attraction, inspired photographers Ansel Adams and Galen Rowell, the 19th-century painter Albert Bierstadt, and the naturalist and Sierra Club founder John Muir. Sheer granite cliffs rise 3,000 feet above this scenic valley. Cascading down these cliffs are waterfalls that rank among the world's highest, most spectacular, and most visited—it isn't unheard of to be caught in traffic on a busy summer weekend. Try to see the valley in the spring (April or May) when the waterfalls are raging, the flowers are blooming, and free parking spots aren't as elusive as deer. In the summer, Tuolumne Meadows in the northern area of the park is an outstanding and less crowded place for walking, hiking, or climbing. In the fall, you can explore the Mist Trail without being trampled. The backcountry skiing in Yosemite is among the best in the Sierra, and there's both a touring center and a downhill area at Badger Pass, in the southern area of the park.

General Information

Area Code: 209

Yosemite National Park: P. O. Box 577, Yosemite, CA 95389; Operator: 372-0200; Recorded Announcements: 372-0264; Public Information: 372-0265; Road and Weather Conditions: 372-0209; Wilderness Office: 372-0285; Wilderness conditions: 372-0307; Permit Information: 372-0310. M-F 8am-5pm.

Backcountry Stations: Yosemite Valley: 372-0308. Tuolumne 372-0309. Su-F 7:30am-7:30pm; Sa 6:30am-7:30pm.

Horse Rentals: Valley Stables; located at the far east end of Yosemite valley near Mirror Lake, 372-1248. Reservations by mail or in person only.

Tuolumne Visitors Center: Tuolumne Meadows, 372-0263. 9am-7pm daily.

Yosemite Concession Services: 372-1000.

Yosemite Valley Visitors Center: 372-0299. Daily 8am-8pm summer, 8am-5pm winter.

Getting There

By car, plan on it taking three and one-half hours to Yosemite Valley. Take I-580 east toward Livermore, then I-205 east toward Stockton. I-205 runs into Hwy 120 East, which you follow all the way to Yosemite. Pay attention to the signs or you'll lose it; there's a tricky stretch where Hwys 108 and 120 split; you'll have to take a right turn to stay on Hwy 120, which heads toward Chinese Camp, Groveland, Buck Meadows, and Yosemite.

Other mountain byways that enter the park from the west and south give you driving and scenic options through alternate park entrances. Hwy 140 enters through the town of El Portal and Hwy 41 enters through the towns of Fish Camp and Mariposa. If you are lucky enough to enter on 41 at sunset, the view from the Wawona Tunnel is breathtaking.

If you're using public transportation, you'll have to be patient. **California Yosemite Tours** (800) 640-6306, and **Via Yosemite**, 722-0366, both run buses from Merced to Yosemite. Via Yosemite is slightly cheaper and more frequent ($26 round-trip; four times daily), but California Yosemite tours will provide you with a tour as well ($45 round-trip; once daily). You can get to Merced from the Bay Area by **Greyhound** bus (800-231-2222) or **Amtrak** (800-872-7245).

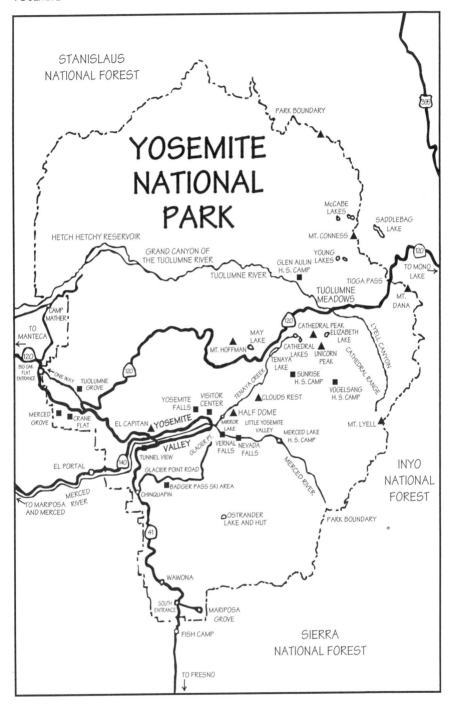

YOSEMITE VALLEY

All road signs and the park map (available at the entrance stations) lead you to the day-use parking lot in **Curry Village**. When exploring Yosemite Valley, park your car there and take the free and frequent shuttle bus to the Visitor Center and all other valley destinations.

You might start by dropping by the **Visitors Center** in Yosemite Village. Pick up the park newspaper here (if you didn't receive one at the park entrance) for a listing of events and schedules. Guided nature walks leave from the Visitors Center. The **Ansel Adams Gallery** (372-4413), a tribute to the photographer who made the park so famous, is open from 8:30am to 6:30pm in the summer, and 9am to 5pm in the winter. **The Ahwahnee Hotel**, a national historic landmark with lavish rooms and high rates, is well worth a look-in, if only for a walk through the grand common rooms. Built from native stones and logs, the hotel has an impressive fireplace, a huge dining hall with exposed log beams, and big windows to take in the sweeping vistas.

Yosemite Concession Services offers a **guided bus tour**. Obtain more information at any of the information desks located at Yosemite Lodge, Curry Village, the Ahwahnee Hotel, and beside the Village Store. Advance reservations are required. On the nights of a full moon and for two nights before, night tours through the valley floor are offered.

If you'd prefer to see the valley on your own, but don't have the time for a tour on foot, investigate **bike rentals**. **Curry Village** (372-1000) rents bikes seasonally. **The Yosemite Lodge** offers year-round rentals, as does **Lodge Bike Rentals**, across from parking lot for Yosemite Falls. They're open from 8am to 7pm daily, with the last rental out at 5:30pm; call 372-1208 for details. Ride the eight miles of bike trails in the valley or venture onto the main road out of the valley. A popular destination is Mirror Lake and Meadow, where you can gaze straight up at the massive, sheer cliff of Half Dome's north side. You're required to walk the last quarter of a mile to what remains of the lake (a fair amount during the spring run-off, very little in the late fall), a bit of an uphill.

If you'd prefer to see the valley from a different perspective, drive or hike from the valley to Glacier Point, where you'll have a bird's-eye view of the valley and Half Dome. On the way back, be sure to stop at Tunnel View (a turn-out at the eastern end of the Wawona Tunnel) and gaze at the valley, its cliffs and waterfalls, and the Sierras in the distance.

If you give yourself at least a half day, why not saddle up? The Curry Company runs horse trips around the valley. This is a fantastic option for folks who want a little adventure on horseback but are intimidated by the length or altitude gain in the trails. However, the trails and hikes in and around the valley are best appreciated on foot.

Hikes

There are also a number of good hikes that you can complete in a half day. You can take a hike of any length by heading up the trail to **Vernal Falls**. The trail follows a sparkling river up a scenic valley, so you don't have to get to any peak destination to make it worth your while. Vernal Falls is a three-mile round trip, perfect for a half day. Though the trail is very popular, and its construction is reminiscent of a railroad track, it's well worth the effort. This trail is also known as the Mist Trail because the spray from the falls frequently soaks the trail and its travelers, making the ground slick. The trail starts from Curry Village, but you can take a shuttle bus all the way to Happy Isles. If you have the better part of a day, the Mist Trail continues past Vernal Falls to Nevada Falls, a seven-mile round-trip. The extra climb gives you views of a second, bigger waterfall and the valley.

An even shorter hike is to the bottom of **Yosemite Falls** (about half a mile, round-trip). It doesn't sound like much, but it's impressive to stand at the base of the pounding water as it surges and sprays. During a full moon, when the falls are raging, one can even see "moonbows" at the base of the falls, a lunar rainbow of sorts. On a busy summer day it's not uncommon to see 20 tour buses parked at this trailhead across from the Yosemite Lodge, but don't be daunted—it's the only place for buses to park in the valley.

If you're feeling very ambitious, hike up to **Glacier Point** for breathtaking views. The trailhead is on the southern road in the valley, west of the Chapel. You can also take the shuttle bus up to Glacier Point, and hike back to the valley. Another enjoyable hike is to the top of Yosemite Falls, 6.6 miles round-trip. A nice extension to Yosemite Point puts you on the rim above the valley across from Glacier Point. Both trails are steep—about 3,000 vertical feet—and give a good workout, so bring adequate food, water, and clothing.

If you're truly hard-core, climb **Half Dome** by the cables route—not an undertaking for the fainthearted. It's 16 miles round-trip with a vertical gain of over 5,000 feet. The last half-mile is so steep that the Park Service has installed cables and steps. (Lightning storms are not uncommon; avoid being up there in a storm.) Start very early and bring warm, windproof clothing, lots of water, and rain gear.

The advantage of going on a multi-day hike is that once you leave the valley, the crowds thin rapidly. The number of routes is virtually limitless, so buy a good topographic map and have some fun planning. Remember, all overnight trips in the park require a permit. Permits are available at the backcountry stations around the park. Always hang your food in a tree or rent a bear box , lest the bears hold a midnight feast with your breakfast.

An enjoyable two or three-day outing is a trek up the **Mist Trail** to Little Yosemite Valley. From camp you can do a day trip up Half Dome and return home, or, for an even longer trip, continue over Clouds Rest for one of the best views in the park. In the summer, a hiker's shuttle runs once a day from the valley to Tuolumne and back. It leaves the valley hotels around 8am, arrives in Tuolumne about two hours later, and continues all the way to Lee Vining on the East Side. It returns in the afternoon, stops in Tuolumne at 4pm and returns to the valley by 6pm. See the Wilderness Office or the Visitors Center for times and reservations.

Climbing

Yosemite is one of the most challenging and scenic places to rock climb in the world. **The Yosemite Mountaineering School** offers excellent classes for first-time climbers—call 372-1244 for schedules and rates. There are numerous books describing the many challenging routes in Yosemite. If you're a hard-core climber, scale El Capitan by the Nose Route, giving yourself five days. Don't forget to leave your fear behind.

TUOLUMNE MEADOWS

Unlike the valley, where temperatures can soar into the 90s (and the crowds seemingly into the millions), Tuolumne's altitude (8,000 feet) keeps the temperature bearable in the summer, and there are fewer people milling about. There are no "attractions," but walking the trails around the heart of Tuolumne Meadows, watching birds of prey, enjoying the flora and fauna, and peering at the brightly-clad climbers can be tremendously rewarding. A new shuttle bus even allows you to park at the main lot and spend the day unencumbered by your automobile.

Hiking & Climbing

You should get the USGS Tuolumne Meadows map of trails. Remember, you need a permit (available at the Tuolumne Wilderness Office near the Tuolumne Meadows lodge) for all overnight trips. Also, bring enough cord and stuff sacks to hang your food at night or rent a bear box from the park—it's bulkier but it requires less strategic planning. **Young's Lakes** is a good day or overnight hike. It's a bit crowded, but offers great views of the lakes, **Ragged Peak**, and **Mt. Conness**. Equine packers frequent the lakes, so pick another destination if you don't like horses. From Young's Lakes there's a Class 2 scramble leading up Mt. Conness. There's also a harder route (Class 2 to 3) from the other side, starting from Saddlebag Lake.

Mt. Hoffman offers one of the best views in Tuolumne. There's a moderately challenging trail from May Lake. **Elizabeth Lake** is popular, and offers great views of the Clark Range and the Sierra. **Cathedral Peak** is a Class 4 climb, but it's quite reasonable for experienced rock climbers and provides great views. **Unicorn Peak** is a Class 3 scramble. **The Grand Canyon of the Tuolumne River** is spectacular in the spring and early summer when the water is high. You can reach it from Glen Aulin High Sierra Camp.

To get to **Mt. Dana**, a half-day climb, follow a footpath that runs from Tioga Pass (on Hwy 120 toward the East Side, Mono Lake, and the town of Lee Vining). Ice climbers may want to try a scenic, if not too challenging, 40-degree ice route on the northeast side. **Mt. Lyell**, the highest peak in the park, is a nice two-day, Class 3 climb. An ice ax, crampons, and a rope are advisable. To get to the base camp, hike up the beautiful Lyell Canyon, a worthwhile trip in itself.

OTHER AREAS

Yosemite is also home to three **Sequoia Groves**. Sequoia trees, cousins of the taller but less massive redwood trees, are the largest living things on earth. **Tuolumne and Merced Groves** are near the Big Oak Flat entrance, on Hwy 120, and include the famous drive-through tree. The other grove is **Mariposa Grove**, in the Wawona Basin (the south part of the park on Hwy 41). A tour bus will take you the final distance from the Mariposa Grove parking lot to the giant sequoias. This is an amazing place for a long walk and a picnic. **Wawona** is a much quieter area than the valley; you can also hike into Wawona Point and Chilnualna Falls.

Seasonal Activities

In the early spring when the waters are high, the Merced River, which runs down Yosemite Valley, offers exciting rafting. There are innumerable lakes and rivers in Yosemite, all open for fishing. New environmental rules only allow sport fishing in the Merced. The Mountain Shop in Curry Village and the camping store next to the supermarket sell fishing licenses and gear.

In the winter, there's downhill skiing at Badger Pass. The terrain is limited, but the views are priceless. The cross-country skiing, however, is excellent. Beginners enjoy the road out to Glacier Point, which is closed to cars in the winter and groomed daily. The trip all the way to Glacier Point is challenging; a long but reasonable day for experienced skiers. Side trails off this road that lead to **Ostrander Hut** (a possible overnight—call the Yosemite Association at 379-2646 for reservations), **Dewey Point**, and the back of the ski area offer more challenging skiing. For real outback skiing, try a multi-day trip into Tuolumne Meadows. From the Bay Area, the quickest access is via the **Snow Creek Trail** that starts in the valley (Tioga Pass Road is closed in the winter).

Restaurants & Entertainment

While there are several options for eating in and around the park, you may want to consider bringing your own food, a particularly good plan if you're heading for the back country and want no part of the valley scene. High prices and crowds are often more ominous than your appetite. But if you really need that hot meal and the camp stove isn't lighting, a foray into the eateries in the park will reward you with a hot meal.

Ahwahnee Dining Room $$$: Ahwahnee Hotel, 372-1488. This is a one of the priciest meals in the area, and one of the best. Daily 7am-10:30am, 11:30am-4pm, 5:30pm-9pm.

Degnan's Deli $: Yosemite Village, 372-1454. Daily 7am-10:30pm (Summer), 7am-7pm (Winter). Good snacks and pizzas, and the grill upstairs is the best deal in town.

Yosemite Lodge: $ 372-1265. Cafeteria offerings at an okay price. Daily 6:30am-10pm, 11:30am-2:45pm, 4:30pm-8pm. Also within the lodge: **Four Seasons $$** 372-1269. Pretty good food at moderate prices. Daily 7am-11am, 5pm-9pm. **Mountain Room Broiler $$$/$$$$** 372-1281. Quality food at sequoia-sized prices. Daily 5pm-9pm.

Places to Stay

Camping

For overnights on the trail, contact the **Wilderness Office** for free wilderness backpacking permits. For car camping, there are two types of campgrounds in the park: walk-ins (first come, first served), and those that require a reservation. The walk-ins tend to be filled to capacity in the peak season, so it's quite a gamble. The best way to get one is to be at the campground in the early morning on a weekday and grab a site just as someone is vacating it. The walk-in sites are **Hetch Hetchy, Tenaya** (on a lake close to Tuolumne Meadows), and **Sunnyside** (a climbers' hangout right next to the valley's gasoline station). From June 1 to September 15, there's a seven-day limit for Valley sites, and a 14-day limit outside the valley. At all other times of the year, there's a 30-day limit.

Reservation campgrounds are handled through a special **Mistix** office, which can be rather difficult to deal with. Reservations can be made no sooner than eight weeks beforehand, a task best done early in the morning. The campgrounds in the valley are **Upper Pines, North Pines, Lower Pines, Upper River, and Lower River.** They're all roughly the same. Three more options in the park are **Crane Flat** (on the Big Oak Flat Road), **Bridalveil Creek** (on the road to Glacier point), and **Wawona**. In order of preference and distance from Tuolumne Meadows, the best campgrounds are **Tuolumne, Porcupine Flat, Yosemite Creek, White Wolf, Tamarack Creek, and Hodgdon Meadow.**

Mistix (campground reservations): (800) 365-CAMP (2267).

Yosemite Association: 5020 El Portal Rd., El Portal, 379-2646. Mailing address: P.O. Box 230, El Portal, CA 95318

Lodging

Ahwahnee Hotel: Yosemite Park, 372-1406. Rugged luxury, spectacular views, and conveniently located right in the Valley. $208 rooms, $400-$600 suites.

Buck Meadows Lodge: Hwy 120, Buck Meadows, 962-6366. Located 30 miles from the park. Summer $50-$80; Winter $35-$65.

Cedar Lodge Resort (14 m): Hwy 140, El Portal, 379-2612. Just outside park. $85-$115.

Mariposa Lodge: Hwy 140, Mariposa, 966-3607. Located 43 miles from the park in downtown Mariposa, this six-room historic inn features a rear garden verandah and elegant design. Summer F-Sa $70, Su-Th $65; Winter $55-$60.

Marriott Resort: 2 miles from the south entrance of the park, 683-6555. Good restaurants, a convenient location, and clean, simple lodging. Summer $200-$215; Winter $159-$179.

The Redwoods: Wawona, 375-6666. Books private homes for vacation rentals, with one- to six-room rentals available. Summer $78-$335; Winter $72-$315.

Shilo Inn at Oakurst: 15 miles south of southern entrance of Yosemite, 683-3555. Summer weekdays $88-$110, weekends $98-$110, Winter weekdays $68-$96, weekends $79-$96.

Yosemite Concession Services: Reservations 252-4848. Handles reservations for all park lodging except camping. Includes Ahwahnee Hotel, Yosemite Lodge, Wawona Hotel, White Wolf Lodge, and the wood cabins and tent cabins in Curry Village.

Yosemite West (20 m): 454-2033. Rents condos to skiers. Nov.-Mar. $88-$158.